Palgrave Studies in Accounting and Finance Practice

The Palgrave Studies in Accounting and Finance Practice series focuses on unexplored areas in accounting and finance (professions, day-to-day practices), and bridges the gap between very technical and abstract philosophical accounting research. Produced by both academics and practitioners, it illustrates how accounting and finance professionals operate and make decisions intermingled with modern technologies and emerging practices.

Raffi G. Chammassian

Costs, Value, and the Entrepreneurial Venture Journey

Developing Value-Driven Ventures

palgrave
macmillan

Raffi G. Chammassian
Geneva, Switzerland

ISSN 2524-8251 ISSN 2524-826X (electronic)
Palgrave Studies in Accounting and Finance Practice
ISBN 978-3-031-86215-1 ISBN 978-3-031-86216-8 (eBook)
https://doi.org/10.1007/978-3-031-86216-8

This Palgrave Macmillan imprint is published by the registered company Springer Nature Switzerland AG
The registered company address is: Gewerbestrasse 11, 6330 Cham, Switzerland

Introduction

Entrepreneurial startups (ESUs) are value-driven ventures that aim to develop untested ideas into scalable, replicable, and growth-oriented businesses. They go through different entrepreneurial lifecycle stages, often requiring substantial amounts of external financing. There are no certainties of success or advancement for these high-risk endeavors. What is certain, however, are costs, whereas profitability is not. Costs are inevitable at every stage of the entrepreneurial lifecycle, whether as actual costs or opportunity costs. Yet, costs are often either misunderstood or addressed with a broad brush by ESU founders—and for good reasons. An ESU is created to achieve scalability, monetization, and high valuation potential. However, the vast majority of ESUs ultimately fail due to running out of cash or their inability to secure financing. This suggests that founders either lacked a compelling narrative to attract investors, did not plan effectively, or failed to realistically account for their costs, cash needs, and investments.

ESUs operate in environments of ambiguity, uncertainty, and complexity. They require extended periods of incubation and development, supported by substantial incremental investments from external sources. Initially, financing often comes from the founders, public organizations, and entrepreneurial ecosystem players (e.g., government, nonprofits, incubators, accelerators, foundations, and platforms), either in-kind or in cash. As ESUs progress, they secure funding from high net-worth individuals (e.g., business angels), venture capital (VC), and corporate venture capital (CVC). While founders cover past expenses, external investors fund future development and growth with the aim of earning a return on their investment.

To achieve a return on investment (ROI), ESUs are designed to create, capture, and extract value through new venture development (NVD) with the goal of exiting via a high-value liquidation event, such as a trade sale, merger and acquisition (M&A), or initial public offering (IPO). They progress through prescribed lifecycle stages: beginning with development and startup in the early stages; followed by survival and early growth in the mid-stages; and culminating in high growth and an exit to a larger firm or IPO in the later stages. As a result, ESUs act as vital drivers of innovation for both industry and the broader economy.

With the rise of the Knowledge Economy and the Fourth Industrial Revolution, most investments in ESUs focus on intangible assets, particularly intellectual capital, which includes human, organizational, social, and relational capital. These investments have a multi-year value capture horizon, rather than relying on traditional annualized profitability models. The ultimate goal is to extract value for shareholders through an exit scenario to achieve ROI. ESUs accomplish this by developing three-dimensional (3D) business models that are high-tech or problem-driven, market/demand-driven, and exit-driven, working in unison as the ventures progress through each lifecycle stage.

Costs and investments are two sides of the same coin. ESU founders invest in costs to develop their projects and seek external financing through compelling pitches as part of their narrative. However, many founders overlook that potential investors are key stakeholders who should be treated as unique customers interested in *buying into their ESU's story*. To attract these "financing customers," founders must demonstrate that their ESU can grow into a formidable business with high ROI potential through an exit event, such as a trade sale, M&A, or IPO.

Thus, ESUs must build three-dimensional (3D) business models with strong value propositions tailored to three types of key customers simultaneously: paying customers for monetization, financing customers for investment, and trade sale customers for eventual exit scenarios. Understanding and addressing these complexities when launching an entrepreneurial venture is challenging, yet essential to developing a strong ESU with a higher chance of success.

The genesis of this book lies in my doctoral dissertation and subsequent experiences applying my research in real-world contexts. Having navigated both the entrepreneurial and corporate finance worlds, I developed a deep curiosity about why tech-oriented startups with little or no revenue or profitability can still achieve high valuations upon exit. How do ESU founders plan, execute, and attract financing? Why are investors willing to fund such ventures, and why do large corporations acquire small startups for seemingly exorbitant prices?

These questions led me on a journey of research and development, collaborating with startup founders across Switzerland (EPFL Innovation Park), the USA (Silicon Valley), and France. Some of these startups succeeded in scaling and exiting their ventures, others were still refining their value propositions, while a few failed despite having secured significant funding. The results of my work indicated certain *patterns of development* that were consistent with all ESU types. These patterns are well known within a very small circle of experienced investors and serial entrepreneurs, but not by many aspiring and novice entrepreneurs and entrepreneurial ecosystem players.

One size does not fit all, and this book is no exception. However, it aims to provide a blueprint for understanding how value is created and captured through strategic investments in costs that enable, mediate, and moderate value extraction through an eventual exit. The goal is to introduce a new dimension for developing ESUs into formidable businesses, helping them avoid premature or unnecessary failure.

The purpose of this book is to share the knowledge and experiences I've gained over the years as an entrepreneur, corporate finance professional, researcher, professor, startup coach, mentor, advisor, and investor. The target audience includes educational institutions, students of innovation and entrepreneurship, entrepreneurial ecosystem players, and both aspiring and seasoned entrepreneurs. The book is organized into five independent, but interconnected chapters as follows.

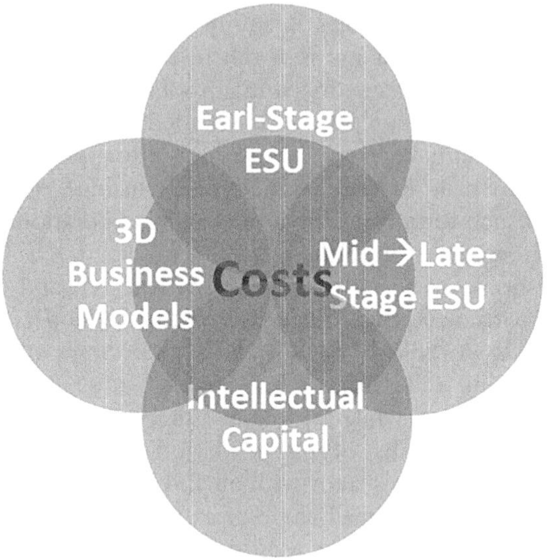

Chapter one, *The Meaning of Costs—Insights from Tech Startup Founders*, focuses on the meaning of costs viewed from the perspective of ESU founders and the three customers (paying, financing, and trade sales) versus modern management accounting principles. The chapter first highlights *the problem* with understanding and *defining what a cost is* by reviewing precedence and development of our modern accounting practices. Majority of these accounting practices have been developed through the lens of larger, industrialized firms and new product development (NPD) aimed at driving affordability, improved predictability, and profitability.

This chapter begins by exploring existing principles and definitions of costs, then shifts to examining costs from the ESU perspective, operating in unpredictable and ambiguous environments. It emphasizes that ESU business models are value driven rather than product-driven, introducing a new value coefficient in how costs are perceived and managed across different stages of the entrepreneurial lifecycle.

Subjectivity plays a significant role in the perception of costs: just as value is in the eye of the beholder, so are costs. ESU founders, along with their three main customer types—paying, financing, and trade sales—each view costs differently. In the early stages, costs are seen as enablers of value creation, akin to *sunk cost benefits*. In the mid-stages, they are treated as investments or mediators of value capture. In later stages, costs serve as both mediators of value capture and extraction, as well as moderators of profitability during monetization.

The chapter concludes by defining what a cost is, distinguishing between cost and cash, and discussing how to develop *good cost habits* while avoiding bad ones.

Chapter Two, *Costs and Entrepreneurial Startup Lifecycles—Early Stages*, dives into the early development and startup stages where ESUs need research and development (R&D), effectual experimentation, and deep analysis of the problem they are solving. It distinguishes between two types of ESUs. The first type is high-tech-driven, requiring substantial upfront investments to research technological challenges and develop core technologies, such as deeptech, pharmaceuticals, and medical tech. The second type is non-high-tech-driven, focusing on addressing societal, environmental, or economic problems—or a mix of these—by developing problem-solution fits using enabling and general-purpose technologies to enhance efficiency, effectiveness, and positive impact.

This chapter explores the characteristics, approaches, activities, expectations, cost considerations, and risk factors involved in understanding how costs function in the ESU business landscape. Many early-stage ESU founders I mentor and advise often struggle with the basics of understanding, forecasting, and planning for costs—and sometimes even deny their importance. Given that costs are omnipresent throughout all stages, this chapter emphasizes how different entrepreneurial ecosystem players perceive the same costs, helping ESU founders align their pitch narratives accordingly. For example, what constitutes revenue for an ESU is effectively a cost to its paying customers. Therefore, it is crucial to develop pricing strategies that support sustainable revenue models and to establish sound revenue recognition practices from the outset.

Chapter Three, *Costs and Entrepreneurial Startup Lifecycles—Mid-to-Late Stages*, characterizes the survival stage as pivotal and transformational in every sense of the words. At the mid-stage of the ESU lifecycle, founders must develop sustainable, scalable, and replicable business models with prioritized, incremental investment milestones. The focus is on refining value propositions, establishing go-to-market strategies, and achieving proof of concept with sales revenue and profitability. Additionally, founders must build the ESU's intellectual capital—intangible assets such as human, organizational, social, and relational capital.

In the later stages, the focus shifts to value capture from replicable, profitable growth, culminating in value extraction through exit events like trade sales, M&A, or IPO. At this point, attention returns to the three customer types, each with its own cost perspective. Paying customers must see that the price they pay (i.e., their costs) provides greater value in terms of efficiency and effectiveness than it reduces their margins. For financing customers, the cost of capital must be much lower than their internal rate of return (IRR) and ROI expectations in a future exit. For trade sales customers, the acquisition price must carry strategic value for future development.

Lastly, ESUs must be positioned as *desirable products* for future M&A markets. For founders, this means reshaping and transitioning into strategic leadership roles and bringing in professional managers to scale, grow, and run their business.

Chapter Four, *Cost and Intellectual Capital Development*, explores how investments in intellectual capital (IC) are made in the context of the Knowledge Economy and the Fourth Industrial Revolution. IC consists of human, organizational, relational, and social capital, with an additional component—technological capital—relevant for high-tech ESUs. Since IC represents the knowledge-based equity held by ESUs, this chapter contrasts the traditional industrial model with the unique lifecycle of *ESUs as products* in the knowledge economy.

The components of intellectual capital (IC) are analyzed in detail, focusing on their iterative input, development processes, and output approaches. In all cases, human capital—with its dynamic capabilities—is the most critical asset, receiving the majority of investments. In fact, in the early and mid stages, people and technology are effectively synonymous with ESUs. Additionally, since most M&As are strategic, many larger companies engage in *acqui-hiring*, that is acquiring ESUs primarily for their talent.

Intangibles, especially intellectual capital (IC), have internal and external spillover effects that are difficult to quantify or measure. However, ESU investments in IC development cannot be recorded as intangible assets on the balance sheet; instead, they are expensed on the income statement. Thus, there is a need for extra-financial reporting, voluntarily tracked through management control systems and disclosed using the Integrated Reporting (<IR>) framework.

Chapter Five, ***Costs and Three-Dimensional (3D) Business Models***, explores how experienced and serial entrepreneurs achieve key stakeholder value alignment through distinct three-dimensional (3D) business models. These models are high-tech or problem-driven, market/demand-driven, and exit-driven, designed to function simultaneously. Each business model follows its own iterative process of inputs, development, and outputs. Within these frameworks, costs play enabling, mediating, and moderating roles.

The chapter begins by defining what a business model is—and what it is not. It then delves into how business models should be designed like an ESU's own ecosystem platform to accommodate and integrate various stakeholder value propositions. This approach requires a different mindset, incorporating design thinking, prioritization, and incrementalization. The chapter provides step-by-step guidance for developing 3D business models, emphasizing the importance of understanding *what's in it for ESU shareholders* and the three key customer groups. It concludes by arguing that ESU's "luck" is largely a result of a strategic business model design for preparedness, rather than being driven by unforeseen external events.

The main contributions of this book are as follows:

- Defining costs in environments of ambiguity, uncertainty, and complexity in which entrepreneurial startups (ESUs) operate, with scalability to larger corporate settings.
- Providing a holistic view of entrepreneurial venture development across lifecycle stages in a complex, interconnected, and unpredictable environments.
- Strategically qualifying costs as enablers, mediators, and moderators in a venture's value creation, capture, and extraction processes across different lifecycle stages.
- Introducing and emphasizing the pivotal, transformative mid-lifecycle stage of ESUs.
- Developing the ESU itself as the main product for eventual sale in M&A markets.
- Viewing costs from the perspectives of three key ESU customer types: paying customers (revenue generation), financing customers (investment attraction), and trade sale acquirers (wealth generation).

- Demonstrating how intangibles, particularly intellectual capital, create, capture, and extract more value for ESUs than traditional revenue and profitability models.
- ESU business models in the knowledge economy are value driven, not product driven, with a focus on holistic value propositions rather than merely on products and services.
- Introducing three-dimensional business models that are high-tech or problem-driven, market/demand-driven, and exit-driven.
- Designing business models as platforms of unique value propositions that encompass users, customers, and stakeholder values in action.

Contents

1 The Meaning of Costs—Insights from Tech Startup Founders 1

1.1 Introduction—The Definitional Problem *of Costs* 1

1.2 A Modern Management Accounting History of Costs 6

1.3 The Strategic Component of Costs 9

1.4 Costs and the Entrepreneurial Narrative 12

1.5 Costs, Value and ESU's Triple Bottom Line Narrative 16

1.6 Subjectivity in the Perception of Costs 21

1.7 Experienced Entrepreneurs' Perception of Costs 24

1.8 Costs and the Role of Learning and Experience 28

1.9 Time Value of Cost Habits 35

1.10 Defining Costs 38

1.10.1 Cost as a Perceived Value 39

1.10.2 Cost as an Assigned Value 41

1.10.3 Cost of Tangible and Intangible Assets 41

1.10.4 Cost and Experiences 43

1.11 Costs vs. Cash 44

Bibliography 46

2 Costs and Entrepreneurial Startup Lifecycles—Early Stages 55

2.1 Introduction—The Entrepreneurial Startup Lifecycles 55

2.1.1 Early Stages 57

2.1.2 Mid Stages 58

2.1.3 *Late Stages* 59
2.1.4 *ESU Lifecycle Stages in Agricultural Terms* 59
2.2 *Early Stages—Developmental Journey* 61
2.2.1 *Characteristics of Developmental Stage* 62
2.2.2 *Approaches* 67
2.2.3 *Activities and Expectations* 71
2.2.4 *Cost Considerations and Risk Factors* 76
2.2.5 *Costs and Financial Statements* 78
2.3 *Early Stages—The Startup Stage Is a Serious Endeavor* 86
2.3.1 *Characteristics of the Startup Stage* 87
2.3.2 *Approaches, Activities, and Expectations at the Startup Stage* 91
2.3.3 *Cost Considerations and Risk Factors* 99
Bibliography 111

3 Costs and Entrepreneurial Startup Lifecycles—Mid-to-Late Stages 119
3.1 *Introduction—The Entrepreneurial Startup Survival Stage* 119
3.2 *Value Creation, Capture, and Extraction* 121
3.3 *Early Mid Stage—Survival of the Fittest* 126
3.3.1 *Early Survival Stage Financing Options* 129
3.3.2 *Financing Opportunity Costs and Trust Factors* 132
3.3.3 *Do's and Don'ts of Financing at Early Mid-Survival Stage* 134
3.4 *Mid-Stage—Surviving the Scale and Early Growth* 140
3.4.1 *Developing a Scalable Business* 142
3.4.2 *Financing a Scalable Growth Business* 149
3.5 *Late Mid Stage—Preparing for a Growth Business and Organization* 167
3.6 *Late Stage—Fast Growth with Multiplication Effect* 173
3.7 *Late Stage—Maturity and Harvesting* 178
3.7.1 *Mergers & Acquisitions (M&A)* 178
3.7.2 *Initial Public Offering (IPO)* 180
3.7.3 *ESU Maturity* 181
Bibliography 183

4 **Costs and Intellectual Capital Development** 191
4.1 *Introduction—The Transformative Knowledge Economy* 191
4.2 *Knowledge Economy* Product *LifeCycles* 199
4.3 *Intangible Assets and Costs* 203
4.3.1 *Costs, Intangibles, and International Accounting Standards* 203
4.3.2 *Spillovers of Intangible Cost Investments* 205
4.3.3 *Intangible Capital Costs Versus Value* 206
4.3.4 *Intangibles and ESUs* 207
4.4 *Developing Intellectual Capital (IC)* 209
4.4.1 *Dynamic Capabilities of Human Capital* 211
4.4.2 *Internal and External Capital of IC* 213
4.4.3 *IC and Financial Reporting Standards* 214
4.4.4 *IC Inputs, Process, and Outputs* 216
4.5 *The Role of Human Capital* 219
4.5.1 *General and Specific Human Capital* 223
4.5.2 *Human Capital Development: Inputs, Process, and Outputs* 224
4.5.3 *Human Capital Characteristics and Associated Costs in Different Stages* 227
4.6 *All-in-One Organizational Capital* 230
4.6.1 *Costs of Organizational Capital Development* 233
4.6.2 *ESU Lifecycles and Organizational Capital Costs* 235
4.6.3 *Management Control Systems (MCS)* 235
4.7 *Social Capital and Purpose* 238
4.7.1 *Social Capital and Technology* 240
4.7.2 *Moderators and Mediators of Social Capital* 241
4.7.3 *Investing in Social Capital Development* 242
4.7.4 *Social Capital Development and Founders' Experience* 244
4.8 *Uniqueness of Relational Capital* 246
4.8.1 *Building Relationships with Suppliers* 246
4.8.2 *Characteristics and Development Costs of Relational Capital* 249

4.8.3 *Transforming Challenges into Relational Capital* 251
4.8.4 *Proprietary Relational Capital* 252
4.9 *Conclusion* 255
Bibliography 256

5 Costs and Three-Dimensional (3D) Business Models 273
5.1 *An Introduction to Three-Dimensional Business Models* 273
5.2 *Cost Investments in the Knowledge Economy* 275
5.3 *Entrepreneurial Startups (ESU)* 277
5.3.1 *The Two Categories of ESUs* 278
5.3.2 *ESUs' Value Development Financial Requirements* 280
5.3.3 *ESUs as Value Proposition Platforms* 281
5.4 *Business Models* 282
5.4.1 *The Main Drivers of ESU Business Models* 283
5.4.2 *Business Models as a Platform vs. Platform Business Models* 285
5.4.3 *The Business Model as an ESU Ecosystem Platform* 286
5.5 *ESU Lifecycles and Business Model Development* 290
5.6 *Intellectual Capital and Business Model Design* 297
5.7 *Three-Dimensional (3D) Business Models* 300
5.7.1 *Technology- or Problem-Driven Business Model Inputs* 302
5.7.2 *Demand- and Markets-Driven Business Models* 307
5.7.3 *Exit-Driven Business Models* 314
5.8 *3D BMs Combined and Simplified: How Does It Work?* 330
5.9 *Conclusion: ESU Luck is a Residue of Business Model Design* 332
Bibliography 334

Index 345

List of Figures

Fig. 1.1	The value proposition narrative—How do we get there?	14
Fig. 1.2	Costs vs. cash	45
Fig. 2.1	Entrepreneurial startup lifecycle	57
Fig. 2.2	Entrepreneurial ecosystem facilitators	67
Fig. 2.3	Cash inflow and outflow	79
Fig. 2.4	Accounting and accountability basics	81
Fig. 2.5	Entrepreneurial ecosystem investors	84
Fig. 2.6	Early stages financing and cost investments	100
Fig. 3.1	Mid-stage financing customers	129
Fig. 3.2	Entrepreneurial lifecycle investment and financing early mid stages	142
Fig. 3.3	Entrepreneurial startup customer relationship	151
Fig. 3.4	Entrepreneurial startup lifecycle and customers	152
Fig. 3.5	Inputs to Discounted Cash Flow (DCF) valuation	155
Fig. 3.6	Entrepreneurial lifecycle investment and financing mid-late stages	174
Fig. 4.1	Fundamental marketplace changes with the knowledge economy	195
Fig. 4.2	Transformation of innovation examples with the knowledge economy	195
Fig. 4.3	Standard industrial model of value creation, capture, and extraction	200
Fig. 4.4	Knowledge economy model of value creation, capture, and extraction	202
Fig. 4.5	Interrelationship of intellectual capital	213

Fig. 4.6	Intellectual capital strategic development	216
Fig. 4.7	Human capital development process	225
Fig. 4.8	Organizational capital development process	232
Fig. 4.9	Social capital development process	240
Fig. 4.10	Social capital development variables	243
Fig. 4.11	Relational capital development process	247
Fig. 5.1	Entrepreneurial startup lifecycles	290
Fig. 5.2	ESU lifecycle and business model development	296
Fig. 5.3	ESU intellectual capital characteristics	298
Fig. 5.4	Drivers of the three-dimensional business models	301
Fig. 5.5	Technology/problem-driven business model components	305
Fig. 5.6	Technology/problem-driven business model development questions	307
Fig. 5.7	Market/Demand-driven business model components	307
Fig. 5.8	Market/demand-driven business model development questions	310
Fig. 5.9	Exit-driven business model components	319
Fig. 5.10	Exit-driven business model development questions	327
Fig. 5.11	3D business model iterative process	331

List of Tables

Table 1.1	The role of predictability, affordability, and perception of costs	3
Table 2.1	Characteristics of the Developmental Stage	63
Table 2.2	Characteristics of the startup stage	88
Table 2.3	Limited liability company and share corporations	89
Table 3.1	Value creation, capture, and extraction	123
Table 3.2	Tangible resources and cost considerations using 80–20 rule	143
Table 3.3	Intangible resources and cost considerations using 80–20 rule	147
Table 4.1	ESU human capital characteristics and associated costs	228
Table 4.2	Organizational capital cost types	235
Table 4.3	Organizational capital characteristics and associated costs per ESU stage	236
Table 4.4	Social capital characteristics and associated costs per ESU stage	244
Table 4.5	Relational capital characteristics and associated costs per ESU stage	250
Table 5.1	ESU lifecycle and business model development characteristics	292
Table 5.2	Exit-driven business model outputs: *What's in it for …?*	322

CHAPTER 1

The Meaning of Costs—Insights from Tech Startup Founders

1.1 Introduction—The *Definitional Problem* of Costs

Costs have diverse meanings to different people in a dizzying array of circumstances. The word *cost* is often used liberally to describe many activities, usually with negative or pessimistic connotations. People mix costs with cash and expenses, interchangeably use it to denote a value (i.e., "This marketing campaign cost us $200 K") or to counter an opportunity (i.e., "It cost me a lot of time and effort to deal with client X"). The word *cost* can be an adjective, a verb, a subject or an object in a sentence. In business, it is about ***managing, optimizing, saving, and controlling*** costs—to name a few adjectives used to add meaning to the word *cost*. However, what is really a *cost*? How and when does it happen? Such questions open the pandora's box of additional inquiries, such as "what do we mean by costs?" "What costs?" "Depends on which context or circumstances we are referring to." When we get *technical* about *costs* (i.e., accounting-wise), we then try to categorize them in some shape or form that eventually maps to the three financial statements—whether it is capitalized or expensed, such as:

R. G. Chammassian, *Costs, Value, and the Entrepreneurial Venture Journey*, Palgrave Studies in Accounting and Finance Practice, https://doi.org/10.1007/978-3-031-86216-8_1

- A purchase of a *capital asset* is recorded on a *cost basis* as a fixed, long-term asset in the balance sheet, and depreciated over its economic life.
- Inventory is recorded as a current asset on the balance sheet. It is made up of its manufacturing cost, which includes labor, material, and overhead costs.
- A sold product is recorded as a *cost of goods sold* (COGS) based on the value of the inventory average value, first-in-first-out, or last-in-last-out company policy. COGS is then considered a *variable cost.*
- A *fixed* or *mixed operating expense,* such as a marketing expense or IT department employee costs, is an *incurred cost.*

The list goes on. There are many lexicons on the types of costs one could refer to, such as Datar and Rajan (2021). It may seem a little simplistic or naïve to ask the above questions. However, we live in a world with much more value placed on intangibles than tangibles (Haskel & Westlake, 2018) and innovative business models are value driven and not product driven (Amit & Zott, 2021). With the onset of artificial intelligence (AI) and rapid technological advancements, these questions are even more important in defining how value is created, captured, and extracted whether physical goods are exchanged or not. The meaning of costs has changed with the knowledge economy (OECD, 1996), automation drive, and *the reduction in reliance on the human function to perform certain tasks* (Petkov, 2020) even though its accounting treatment has not. Costs have an intangible value, such as opportunity cost, reputation, trust, and sustainability as much as a tangible value, such as financial or recurring revenue.

The word cost can be an adjective, a verb, a subject, or an object in a sentence

Management accounting scholars, instructors, and professionals refer to the notion of costs without really providing a clear definition of what is really meant by it, and how to define it in a way that resonates in today's realities, especially when it comes to strategy. In larger industrialized companies, costs are neatly fit in financial statements, defined and managed based on historical precedence as *run rates* in order to identify gaps and opportunities to improve and to predict the future with financial forecasts. Hence, improved *predictability* of costs is a major goal with larger industrialized firms that strive to forecast accurately, thrive in stable environments, and are rewarded with stock price increases when they exceed their profitability targets due to lower costs, higher margins, and profitability.

However, in entrepreneurial startups (ESUs), where they operate in uncertain, unpredictable, and ambiguous environments (Weick, 2015), costs have different meanings and importance than with industrialized companies. Metaphorically, although one Euro is financially accounted as one Euro for both large and small organizations (i.e., a Euro is a Euro!), the perceptive strategic weight, importance, and value are much different (in fact, higher) with ESUs than with industrialized companies. Whereas the latter may *afford to lose* a few thousand Euros and recover from it unscathed in most cases; the former, cannot *afford* to as it could lead to a life-and-death situation. Hence, Table 1.1 lists the different roles *predictability, perception,* and *affordability* play when defining costs between large industrialized firms and ESUs.

Table 1.1 The role of predictability, affordability, and perception of costs

Costs	*Large, industrialized firms*	*Entrepreneurial startups*
Predictability	Strive to forecast future costs as predictably as possible based on run rates (inventory costs, COGS, operating expenses); and capital expenditures. It is expected to meet or beat its targeted cost forecasts	Operating in highly unpredictable, uncertain, and ambiguous environments, forecasts are based on assumptions on development opportunities depending on the ESU lifecycle stages (early, mid, or late stage)
Perception	Costs are to be managed, controlled, saved, and lowered; treated as a *value moderator* or a *moderator of profitability* and margin, measured as a percentage of revenue	Costs enable and mediate value creation, capture, and extraction in early—and mid-stages. At mid—to later-stages, costs act as a mediator of firm value and moderator of profitability
Affordability	Can afford to lose (and sometimes waste) costs within the larger financial picture	Cannot afford to lose or waste costs due to very limited availability and high importance on where to spend in order to create real value and attract investments and survive

With the emergence of the *Knowledge Economy* (Drucker, 1969; OECD, 1996),[1] new ventures with innovative, (human) knowledge-driven, technology-oriented, intangible-intensive startups with a major focus on value creation through intellectual capital, majority of the industrialized firms and new product development (NPD) notions of costs no longer apply as the norm. This is especially true for ESUs with untested ideas that usually require long periods of incubation and development, with scalable business models, high-growth potential, and large incremental investment requirements. These investments are in costs to develop mainly intangible assets (i.e., intellectual capital) in new venture development (NVD) that often have the potential for higher returns on investment (ROI) than traditional NPD margin and profitability-focused business models. Factors determining value include qualitative changes to product design leading to rapid decline in legacy product lifecycles, cost of change instead of cost of production, and (discounted) rates of return on costs of innovation (OECD, 1996).

With ESUs, investments are in costs to develop intangible assets in new ventures rather than new products

In this chapter, we will first review the meaning of costs within business and management accounting, beginning with a brief historical examination and a theoretical foundation of costs from a modern management accounting perspective and its evolution to current times. Then we will analyze costs from ESUs' perspective where costs begin from their onset and evolve through their different lifecycles, from developmental to survival, growth, and harvest. The focus will be on how successful[2]

[1] *Knowledge Economy* was first coined by Peter Drucker in 1969 in his book titled *The Age of Discontinuity*. Organization for Economic Cooperation and Development (OECD) further defined it as the bulwark of development and growth in advanced *knowledge-based economies* where they increasingly rely on the knowledge, information, and high-skilled labor as upgraded human capital.

[2] *Successful* is defined as survived more than three years, raising large sums of money to finance and invest into the startup development (which is mainly in people), to acquire customers, and to achieve a large firm valuation.

entrepreneurial[3] startup founders[4] perceive costs by relentlessly focusing on strategic value creation through effectual experimentation. It then focuses on how costs in strategic value creation supersedes any other type of strategy with innovative ESUs within different entrepreneurial lifecycles. How costs treated as an input and an investment to create value from early stages have influence on the ESUs survival and growth processes to capture value, and eventual value extraction output through exits. The chapter elaborates on findings and develops a revised definition of costs with different categorization and perceived returns, setting the precedent for the rest of the book chapters.

Takeaways:

- The word costs has diverse meaning to different people in varying circumstances
  - It can be an adjective, a verb, a subject, or an object in a sentence
  - There is no clear definition of what a cost is
- The same cost as a value has different weight with large vs. small organizations, such as entrepreneurial startups (ESUs)
  - Predictability, perception, and affordability are vastly different
- The traditional notions of costs no longer apply to the knowledge economy with its intangible-intensive innovative ESUs with intellectual capital development and expenditures
- With ESUs, investments are in costs to develop intangible assets in new ventures rather than new products

[3] I resort to the definition of *entrepreneurial firms* by Leach and Melicher's (2021), which are performance- and growth-oriented, reflected in the startups' value creation, capture, and extraction over time. This contrasts with *lifestyle* and *salary-replacement firms*. This chapter's (and book's) focus is on *entrepreneurial firms*.

[4] These founders can be classified in three categories: (1) First-time novice and inexperienced entrepreneurs who survived three years or more, learned a great deal, and gained enormous experience; (2) entrepreneurs who had failed and relaunched new startups; and (3) Serial entrepreneurs who have founded and exited multiple startups.

1.2 A Modern Management Accounting History of Costs

In modern management accounting, the strategic importance of costs has been mainly addressed within mature industrialized firms and new product development (NPD) for strategic differentiation, margin, profitability, market positioning, and contingencies, such as to control and to optimize. Its significance was highlighted by Anthony (1952, 1965), who is considered to be one of the forefathers of modern management accounting. He added a new human component, a behavioral dimension, and the imperativeness to include *any cost* for decision-making purposes. Previously, such topics were covered in cost accounting as an output of activities to understand *full costing* within manufacturing. Management accounting addressed a much broader sense of costs, such as to influence human behavior.

Since Anthony, almost all references to cost within management accounting, has been based in the manufacturing or production environment or the industrialized stage of a firm (Banker et al., 2014); in NPD (Cooper, 2002; Gopalakrishnan et al., 2015; Mihm, 2010) where direct and indirect cost allocations have been used to determine selling price and profitability (Cooper & Kaplan, 1988, 1991); product lifecycle cost management (Cooper & Slagmulder, 2004; Shields & Young, 1994); and in controlling and contingency planning (Anthony, 1965, 1988; Chenhall, 2003; R. Simons, 1987, 1991).

The notion of costs has expanded to include different meanings, purposes, specific cost definitions, and uses. According to managerial accounting, they can be input oriented to record the purchase of a capital asset on the balance sheet on a *cost basis*. Costs can be "caused by resources, including both activity resources and physical capital" (Banker et al, 2014, p. 840). Costs can be process oriented, such as *activity-based costing* (Cooper & Kaplan, 1988). They can also be operational to determine breakeven, gross profit and margin, and operating profits through *cost-volume-profit (CVP)* analysis (Jaedicke & Robichek, 1964) in order to justify a firm's *cost structure* to market entry and long-term sustainability in the face of competition (Bromwich, 1990).

Strategic relevance of costs in new venture development (NVD) is missing

However, there are limited debates in management accounting literature on the strategic relevance of costs within new venture development (NVD) which functions within highly unpredictable, ambiguous, and uncertain environments (Weick, 2015), such as nanotechnology startups (Santos & Eisenhardt, 2009). Within these ESU settings usually there is no historical precedence or information (whether financial or operational), except for perhaps research and development (R&D) cost models. There are some studies that address the value-relevance of costs in the financial reporting of entrepreneurial firms (such as Brinckmann et al., 2010; Hand, 2005; Sievers et al., 2013; Smith & Cordina, 2014). Others address costs from a management controls perspective. For instance, a study by Rockness and Shields (1994) states that within innovative firms input controls, such as financial plans and budgets, are more important than output controls. Chenhall and Moers (2015) conclude that management controls research should also expand from product innovation into the innovation process itself. As innovation is dynamic, it affects organizational processes, direction, investment requirements, and outcomes in unpredictable ways.

The notion of cost by itself has been ill-defined in general

Apart from conventional classifications, there is no one definition of the word *cost* in literature but we have a variety of costs defined by an *adjective as a qualifier* that accompanies it. Thus, *fixed costs* can mean an expense that does not change over time in relation to revenue increases or decreases or to activity levels, while *variable costs* change with volume or unit. Datar and Rajan's (2021) glossary includes varying listings of costs with different meanings (see pp. 986–996). Most scholars don't attempt to address it as a word by itself and possibly take it for granted. The attempt at defining *costs* is probably most visible in textbooks, dictionaries, and online educational sites. Follows some examples:

- AccountingTools.com (3 January 2024) defines costs as an "expenditure required to create and sell products and services, or to acquire assets. When sold or consumed, a cost is charged to expense. In the case of an asset, the charge to expense could be significantly deferred. The cost concept underlies the transition of assets from the balance sheet to expenses in the income statement."

- Reviso.com (n.d.) describes "in business and accounting, cost is the monetary value that has been spent by a company in order to produce something."
- My Accounting Course—an Online Learning Institute (n.d.) simplifies the meaning of cost as "an expenditure required to produce or sell a product or get an asset ready for normal use. In other words, it's the amount paid to manufacture a product, purchase inventory, sell merchandise, or get equipment ready to use in a business process."
- Finance Strategists (n.d.) define cost as "the sacrifice made that is usually measured by the resources given up to achieve a particular purpose. It is a sacrifice made in order to obtain some goods or services. Costs are not always expenses. Some costs are assets, others are expenses. Expenses are expired (used up) costs. Eventually, costs will become expenses."

There appears to be an overarching negative, *sacrificing* view that leads to a *pessimistic* assessment of costs. This may be generally attributed to the sense and practice of giving up something, or for its *deductibility* from a financial statement, or a sunken unrecoverable notion of an expenditure foregone. A purchase leads to an expenditure, which results in cash reduction. When we incur an operational expense, we deduct it from revenue, which leads to a reduction in profits in the income statement and a reduction in cash in the bank and balance sheet. This appears to be bad news. Yet, whether it is a purchase of an asset or a service, the general term of reference used is *cost*.

Takeaways

- Costs are either ill-defined or there are multiple definitions for the word.
- Most references to costs are based on manufacturing, new product development (NPD), direct and indirect allocation, product lifecycle, controlling and contingency planning.
- They can be input oriented (cost basis), process oriented (activity-based costing), or output oriented (income statement).
- Strategic relevance of costs in new venture development (NVD) is missing.

- NVD has unpredictable outcomes. Input controls are more important than output controls.
- Costs are viewed pessimistically in management accounting as sacrificing, deductible, sunken, unrecoverable, a reduction, or bad news.

1.3 The Strategic Component of Costs

The definitions of costs in academic and business literature are as diverse as its meaning with qualifying adjectives attached to the word. However, a more focused meaning of costs is when costs are addressed strategically within a business model of an enterprise, whether implicitly or explicitly. Since the 1980s, academics have attempted to address this strategic component of costs within a business model. Almost all the debates, however, focused within the context of existing large and mature industrialized firms with a focus predominantly on New Product Development (NPD). These debates are continuing within the context of Strategic Management Accounting (SMA),[5] Strategic Cost Management (SCM), and in the evaluation of investments strategically,[6] and similar strategic approaches to cost management,[7] which largely view costs and investment with strategic importance and meaning.

The concept of *cost leadership* was defined by Porter (1980), who proposed it as a model of competitive advantage, mainly through strategic planning and incurring lower costs to differentiate from competitors. In simple terms, cost leadership meant offering standardized products at a lower cost than competitors. This may work for highly competitive, possibly commoditized, and mature industries, but not with innovative value-driven ESUs with differentiating strategies.

Historically cost leadership meant offering standardized products at a lower cost than competitors

[5] See Bromwich 1990, Brouthers and Roozen (1999), Cadez and Guilding (2008), Lee and Cobia (2013), Lord (1996), Roslender and Hart (2003), and Simmonds (1982).

[6] See Anderson and Dekker (2009a, 2009b), Cooper and Slagmulder (2004), Cugini et al. (2007), Fayard et al. (2012), Kumar and Kumar (2011), Shank (1989, 1996), Shank and Govindarajan (1989, 1992a) or 1992b, 1993, and Grundy (1993, 1996).

[7] See Cooper and Kaplan (1988, 1991), and Kaplan and Norton (2001, 2004, 2007).

Later, Porter (1985) introduced the *value-chain model* and stated that a business is a set of *value-creating activities*, and hence, all activities related to it are a chain of events associated with value creation. A product or service lifecycle value chain starts as early as the organization's ability to identify and acquire all the necessary components for production purposes, and it ends with the final beneficiary of the product or service. Porter's model was used and overlapped with the birth of SMA and SCM in accounting literature during the same period and was debated over the following decades. Since Porter's introduction of cost leadership, accounting literature has branched out from classical cost accounting to managerial cost analysis.

A product/service lifecycle value-chain model
is a set of value-creating activities over time

However, SMA and SCM research have traditionally focused on large established businesses with historical accounting records and information. This research had mainly assumed that market demand exists, and revenue is generated through product sales. In other words, a firm has a pre-existing structure and systems and has certain levels of stability with historical accounting transactions.

In retrospect, several authors have contended that no substantial inroads of far-reaching adoption of the SMA and SCM frameworks have been made in practice even within large mature industrialized companies (Lord, 1996; Roslender & Hart, 2003). Some authors have found that pure and systematic accounting at the strategic level has been lacking (Taipaleenmäki, 2014). There also appear to be misapprehensions of how to track and who should measure the impact of SCM. At times, such tracking approaches and processes have led to analysis by paralysis or *death by detail* (Aluko et al., 2010). Whereas, others believed that the value-chain approach taken by SCM not only should be confined to costs but also should be organized across all resources within the value chain, linking strategic costing to operational improvement (Cooper & Slagmulder, 2004); incorporate cost, customer value, and revenue considerations (Kumar & Kumar, 2011); be specifically within dual payment systems, in which cost-revenue-enhancing is coupled with cost-reduction strategies to improve a firm's profitability (Hsu & Qu, 2012); and be across the supply chain through structural and executional cost management (Anderson & Dekker, 2009a, 2009b). Other explanations might be found in the tendency of actors to strategize (Jørgensen & Messner, 2010) rather than rely on formal control devices. Jørgensen and Messner (2010) have provided a case in which they explored the relationship between accounting and strategy in the context of NPD.

None of this literature really addresses how an ESU, usually launched by first-time inexperienced founders, should address costs in a way that makes sense and doesn't require a university degree or a certification in accounting. This chapter (and this book), however, will not focus on reopening an academic debate on costs. It will address costs by its perception, meaning, and usage throughout the ESU lifecycle from its earliest stages through development of an innovative and valuable new venture.

To define these lifecycles, I use an adaptation of Leach and Melicher's (2021) definition of *entrepreneurial ventures* from their inception as entrepreneurial startups (ESU) as a form of NVD, through its different lifecycle stages, with the ultimate purpose of high-value extraction through exits. These ESUs' performance is reflected in value creation, capture, and extraction with scalability and growth over time. In most cases, they require a staged, sometimes substantial amount of external financing to invest in their development and growth strategy. This contrasts with lifestyle[8] and salary-replacement[9] firms.

Takeaways

- Strategic importance and meaning of costs have been addressed but within larger industrial companies, such as Strategic Management Accounting (SMA) and Strategic Cost Management (SCM) to name a couple.
- Historically cost leadership meant offering standardized products at a lower cost than competitors.
- A product/service lifecycle value-chain model is a set of value-creating activities over time.

[8] *Lifestyle firms* are established by people who would like to pursue specific hobbies and lifestyles as a business while being paid for it. Examples of this would be a ski enthusiast who becomes a ski instructor, or a surfer who decides to quit her corporate job and open a surf training and rental shop on the coast.

[9] *Salary-replacement firms* are those that provide the founders an income level that is equivalent to what they could have been earning in a larger firm. Examples include a chef of a restaurant chain who decides to open his own pizza parlor, or a corporate lawyer who starts his own law firm specialized in an area that he is passionate about.

- An ESU is strategic by design and goes through several value lifecycle stages to develop scalable business models and to attract external financing.

1.4 Costs and the Entrepreneurial Narrative

ESUs by default and design are solving PESTEL problems (Political, Economic, Social, Technological, Environmental, Legal) by offering solutions through value propositions to improve efficiency and effectiveness, usually with the use of advanced *core* or *enabling* technologies, such as artificial intelligence (AI), blockchain, or cloud computing. Their solutions are primed to be scalable and growth oriented, attracting different types of investors at their various stages, with the promise of higher returns on investments due to higher risk taking than with traditional investments, such as in the stock market or in real estate. At each lifecycle stage, costs are omnipresent. Yet they play different roles that can be enabling, mediating, or moderating value creation, capture, and extraction.

Risk taking and investing go hand in hand in the value creation, capture, and extraction processes. Even though the essence of costs may not be explicit within the TSU entrepreneurs' narratives, it is implicit as a value enabling and mediating investment involving rational thought and decision-making within an effectual logic. In the earlier stages, the unpredictability and associated risk are higher due to many unknowns even though the enabling costs are relatively lower than in later stages. In the pivotal mid-stages, repetitive and replicable processes are put in place to leverage and gain from economies of scale. In later stages, predictability improves due to replication, learnt experiences, and historical precedence.[10]

The entrepreneurial narrative plays a key role in defining the investment rationale. From the early stages, the narrative must match the early results and justification to advance their entrepreneurial project further and develop their business models. In fact, ESU business models become narratives conveying how the ESU creates, captures, and extracts value

[10] For more details on how ESU processes and associated risks evolve, see chapters two and three on ESU early and late-stage ESU lifecycle.

(Amit & Zott, 2012, 2021). These narratives usually begin with an idea or a hypothesis that is tested and re-tested until the narrative test aligns with the financial test (Magretta, 2002). If the early-stage narrative is convincing with a good believable prospective future, then early-stage investors such as incubators, accelerators, and business angels will follow the project by investing in it. This narrative is presented through *a pitch* which becomes *the window to the soul of the startup*. As a minimum, the pitch includes:

- An introductory definition to the problem the ESU is solving (with hard and specific data), including the cost *impact* (value) of the problem (i.e., social, environmental, and economic).
- The proposed solution through its unique value proposition (UVP) or *the problem–solution fit* which has a positive cost-impact value.
- The technological median through which the value is proposed, captured, and extracted, for instance, through a multi-sided platform, products, services, networks, blogs, and similar.
    - For high-tech ESU, that will be its core technology and enabling technologies (Bailetti, 2012; Van Meeteren et al., 2022).
    - For non-high-tech ESUs, that will be through *enabling technologies* and *application domains* (or *general-purpose* technologies) (Van Meeteren et al., 2022; Waßenhoven et al., 2023).
- Its business model followed by its revenue model.
- The addressed markets and the ESU traction to-date and forecasts.
- Competition analysis.
- A financial dashboard, including up-to-date revenue, expenditures, and future investment plans (i.e., which costs to invest into over the coming months) with scenarios.
- Overview of the founding team composition.
- Depending on the audience (i.e., directed at investors, a customers, accelerators, etc.).
    - Highlights and challenges it is facing, including some financials.
    - The "ask" from the audience, depending on the purpose of the pitch.

A pitch is the window to the soul of the startup

Figure 1.1 illustrates how the process of value proposition narrative begins with defining the key problem that needs to be solved, followed by the solution definition, and its fit to the problem as well as analysis of the market demand and competitive landscape, and how enabling technologies mediate the solutions' efficiency and effectiveness. Finally, and importantly, what is the triple bottom line impact of the problem, problem–solution fit and the enabling technologies. However, the most important aspect of an early-stage ESU is to really understand and define the *problem* it is trying to solve.

The majority of early-stage ESUs I have encountered and mentored, whether in ideation, incubation, or acceleration, and even in their mid-stage, have either not defined the problem properly or don't really understand the problem they are solving. They appear to have fallen into the trap of "their solution" being the "best in the marketplace," having the "highest quality" and "lowest price" without really having real market/demand data from reputable sources to prove their assertion, especially from customers who are willing to pay for such services. Their narrative leads to a discussion of product or service positioning, revenue, and profits, falling into the trap of being another product in a crowded marketplace where product lifecycles are shorter than value

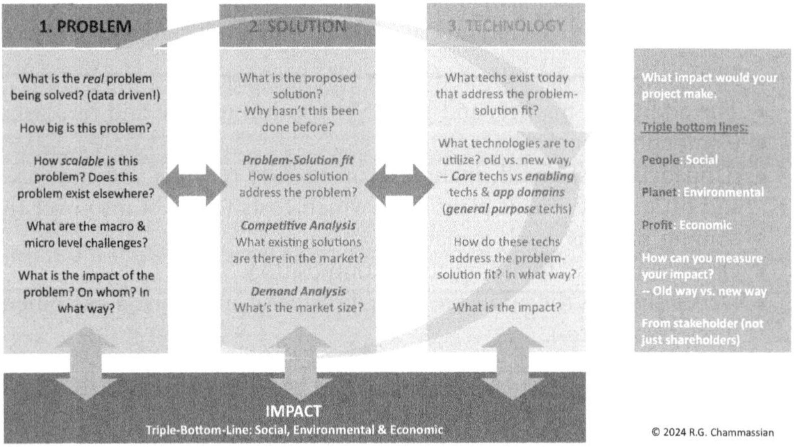

Fig. 1.1 The value proposition narrative—How do we get there?

lifecycles due to constant technological advancements. This is why business models ought to be value driven, not product driven (Amit & Zott, 2021). At times, the narratives sound like *a solution in search of a problem*. This does not lead to real value creation and capture for investors. Such a start usually leads to the early demise of the ESU, especially when novice founders double-down on their assertions based on self-beliefs without any real proof and contrary to the questioning and negative signaling they are receiving from their support ecosystem (i.e., mentors, potential investors, incubators, and similar).

Business models ought to be value driven, not product driven. Value lifecycles are longer than product lifecycles.

With high-tech ESUs, sometimes it is a technological discovery in search of a market. They may have a very promising discovery, but they have not been able to identify how and where it can be applied (i.e., a market for it). This has been a big challenge with AI/ML-oriented startups, for instance. However. Some high-tech ESUs may have an exception. That is, their value proposition may be a technological discovery, such as a patented enzyme, process, or device that can be licensed, utilized, or incorporated into other products, processes, or industries. In this case, the ESU's strategic investment in costs would be a mediator of firm value where the ESU is developed as *the product* from the start for eventual sale or a merger with a larger company instead of a revenue-generating company. For these ESUs, the real value lies in their intellectual capital, which is mainly made of their human capital and their dynamic capabilities (Teece, 2009, 2010, 2012).

What is important to note is the fact that early-stage investors mostly bet on the founder(s) and the founders' human capital *to make it happen* rather than the project. Also, the preference is to bet on ESUs with two or more founders with diverse and complementary backgrounds and experiences, such as industry, entrepreneurial, marketing, business, and financial literacy (Eisenmann, 2020). Diversity matters, and includes a mix of gender, nationality, knowledge, experience, education, and networks. This diversity brings different perspectives together and improves dynamic capabilities of its human capital. Multi-founder teams also have a positive impact on attracting investors, successful fundraising, and exits (Shetty & Sundaram, 2020).

"No matter how brilliant your mind or strategy, if you're playing a solo game, you'll always lose out to a team." Reid Hoffman, LinkedIn co-founder[11]

Takeaways

- By default and design, ESUs are risky endeavors that are created to solve PESTEL problems (Political, Economic, Social, Technological, Environmental, Legal).
- Risk taking and investing go hand in hand in the value creation, capture, and extraction processes.
- The entrepreneurial narrative plays a key role conveying how the ESU intends to create, capture, and extract value. This narrative is most often communicated through entrepreneurial pitches by founders.
- An entrepreneurial pitch is the window to the soul of an ESU.
- A pitch must first address the problem the ESU is solving, followed by the problem–solution fit, with technology as the mediator of efficiency and effectiveness, and how this narrative is making a real social, environmental, or economic impact.
- This narrative is captured through the ESU's business model.
- Business models are value driven, not product driven.
- Value lifecycles are longer than product lifecycles.
- Narratives are presented by ESU founders.
- Investors, especially in early stages, invest in the founders and prefer multi-founder teams with diverse backgrounds.

1.5 Costs, Value and ESU's Triple Bottom Line Narrative

What is the real problem the ESU is addressing requires real data that can lead to a convincing argument if the problem is big enough, and has negative social, environmental, and/or economic impact on stakeholders, users, and customers. The size of the problem, its impact, and the multidimensionality will determine the scalability, growth, and investability potential of the problem–solution fit.

[11] https://www.nationalbusinesscapital.com/blog/quotes-from-top-business-leaders/.

"Data beats emotions."—Sean Rad, Tinder founder[12]

Since we live in a networked, circular, and knowledge economy (OECD, 1996), problem analysis needs to consider the issue from different angles and dimensions. Besides defining the real problem, data has to also address the impact on people, the environment, and, most importantly, the impact on associated opportunity costs. The identified problem should address at least one, if not two, or all of the social, environmental, and economic aspects, referred to as the triple bottom line (Elkington, 1994, 1997) impact from a sustainability perspective.

Triple bottom line (3BL) was first coined by John Elkington in 1994 as a writer and founder of SustainAbility—a consultancy—and later popularized through a book in 1997. 3BL was termed to assess large corporate evaluation of their corporate social responsibility (CSR) metrics. Instead of simply improving their economic bottom line, Elkington suggested including social metrics, such as corporate contribution to social welfare and equity; and an environmental one, such as their ecological impact and footprint. Social impact is perhaps the toughest to assess due to a lack of *clear, reliable, and accessible social performance referents*. However, those ESUs that do integrate a *social value creation strategy* will develop a competitive advantage within their narratives (Robb et al., 2024).

There are many ways to measure 3BL. Unless an ESU has a real sustainability mission-driven business model, in most early stage problem definition, ESU can utilize wider, simpler, but specific (not generic) definition of social, environmental, and economic impact with data. Examples of this include current costs associated with health and safety issues (i.e., chemical use, confined space entry), environmental impact on communities and ecology (i.e., usage of plastics, disposable vs. recyclable), and economic impact (i.e., on underrepresented communities, job creation or loss). ESUs can use their own discretion on what and how to measure and report as long as they are using reputable data and not simply *greenwashing*. For guidance to identify approaches to analyzing and assessing 3BL, ESUs can revert to reputable organization, such as the International Association of Impact Assessment,[13] European Commission's guidelines

[12] https://www.nationalbusinesscapital.com/blog/quotes-from-top-business-leaders/.

[13] https://www.iaia.org/.

on impact assessment,[14] OECD's Evaluation Criteria,[15] and U.S. Agency for International Development *Collecting and Using Data for Impact Assessment*.

Problem analytics and problem definition are key to developing value-driven solutions with unique technologies applied to improve efficiency and effectiveness, and usually with triple bottom line impact. So, by default, most ESUs are solving a problem that addresses a social, environmental, and/or economic problem either directly or indirectly. However, many ESU narratives do not consider or include such data directly, indirectly, or discreetly. In retrospect, almost all customers, investors, and larger M&A companies are specifically looking for ESUs with 3BL impact values put in practice. With a little realignment and reconfiguration, ESUs can and should include 3BL impact measurable values within their narratives.

When addressing the problem and its analysis, ESUs need to consider both internal and external (to the ESU's) 3BL impact. Successful ESU founders tend to:

- Be laser focused on their understanding of the PESTEL problem they are trying to solve. In fact, they have an in-depth intimate knowledge of various aspects of the PESTEL problem through their analysis.
- View the problem from multiple angles and triple bottom line impact perspectives, such as social, environmental, and/or economic impact of the problem they are solving.
- Focus is externally oriented, that encompasses:
  - Stakeholder approach
  - Demand and customer needs analysis
  - Competition analysis
- Analyze it from an opportunity cost (impact) and real cost of the problem they are addressing from a marketplace, stakeholder, customer, and user perspective.
- Question:

[14] https://commission.europa.eu/law/law-making-process/planning-and-proposing-law/impact-assessments_en.

[15] https://www.oecd.org/dac/evaluation/daccriteriaforevaluatingdevelopmentassista nce.htm.

- What is the *real* problem all about (with data support)?
- How big, widespread, and scalable is the problem?
- Does the problem exist elsewhere?
- What is the opportunity cost impact of the problem they are trying to solve, on whom, and in what way? Usually, these involve efficiency and effectiveness issues.
- What are the current or existing solutions addressing the problem (i.e., competitive landscape)? How do they address the problem and where are the gaps?

Fall in love with the problem they are trying to solve, and not with their solution is what should be the ESU entrepreneurs' motto. The belief behind this comprehension is that problems are multidimensional and never linear or simple especially in a networked, circular, and multidimensional world we live in where intangible values play a bigger role than tangible ones. Once the complexity and interconnectivity of the problem is understood, drawn out, highlighted, narrated, and prioritized, solutions should naturally fit the problem narrative with multidimensional offerings with positive experiences and impact that could be tangible and intangible.

"Fall in love with the problem you are solving and not your solution"

ESU founders tend to find multidimensional solutions grounded on the various aspects of the problem they are solving through innovative business models that identify unique value propositions (UVP). What is *unique* about the problem–solution fit?

1. How *value* is created and proposed, to whom, and in what way with the offered solutions
2. How *value* is captured by the stakeholders, customers, and/or users, measured through the efficiency and effectiveness impact metrics.
3. How *value* is extracted from the stakeholders, customers, and/ or users in terms of revenue, satisfaction, trust, experiences, and feedback.

The problem–solution fit is to be developed and proposed multidimensionally by developing intellectual capital capacities and capabilities. They include:

- Human Capital: Team composition and diversity of knowledge, know-how, experiences, education, passion, and drive (Eisenmann, 2020), and the team's dynamic capabilities to develop the firm's resources that are rare, valuable, not easily imitable, and well-organized (Teece, 2009, 2012)
- Organizational Capital: innovative business model, innovation capabilities, unique processes and organizational capabilities, R&D, technologies[16] and Intellectual Property (IP—if any),[17] big data, company culture, and sustainability orientation.
- Social Capital: Expansive social networks, the social trust and legitimacy, reputation, authenticity, safety, security, and impact orientation (with values in action) built over time that give the startup its uniqueness and value.

"Your reputation is more important than your paycheck, and your integrity is worth more than your career." (Ryan Freitas, co-founder of About.me)[18]

- Relational Capital: strategic partnerships, proprietary manufacturing and/or marketing, external R&D centers, universities, external financial sources and partnerships, and sponsorships (i.e., corporate, government)

[16] I define *technologies* in a broader sense adopting various comprehensive definitions (such as Bailetti's, 2012; Carroll's, 2017; and Coad and Reid's, 2012 notions), for example, "to capture not only the equipment, software or instruments used to produce a good or service but also the (tacit) knowledge, techniques, organizational methods, etc. used to design, develop and market the products and services by businesses (and the public and not for profit sector), in cooperation with other actors in the innovation system" (Coad & Reid, 2012, p. 1).

[17] With pure R&D-oriented and high-tech-driven startups, such as deeptech, nanotech, and pharmatech university spinoffs, Technological Capital can be separated from organizational capital. The latter's focus would be to build an organization, including processes and procedures, in support of the unique technologies.

[18] https://www.nationalbusinesscapital.com/blog/quotes-from-top-business-leaders/.

Takeaways

- Real problems to solve usually have a negative social, environmental, and/or economic impact on customers, users, and stakeholders.
- They require the use of reputable data to measure the impact.
- Value-driven problem–solution technology fit improves efficiency and effectiveness, usually with triple bottom line impact.
- ESUs must actively and systematically address this value impact since customers, investors, and M&A corporations are actively looking for it.
- Value is created, captured, and extracted through the ESU's intellectual capital capabilities, consisting of its human capital (most important), followed by organizational capital, social capital, and relational capital.

1.6 Subjectivity in the Perception of Costs

Costs are omnipresent in the value creation, capture, and extraction process through innovative business models with ESUs.[19] As *value is in the eye of the value beholder*, perception of costs associated with this process plays a key role in strategic decision-making, beginning with ESU founders, and later with investors, customers, users, and other stakeholders. Founders' Perception includes a major *subjective* component (Felin et al., 2017) where time-calibrated decisions are made through the ESU founders' own narratives (Wood et al., 2021).

Perception towards costs is subjective to the founders' perceptive capacity, which is grounded in experiences, financial literacy, learning, and adaptation capabilities

By default, earlier stage ESUs operate in highly unpredictable environments and uncertain futures, which are usually external to the firm. Yet, founders have to make decisions based on uncertainties that will influence the future of their firms. These decisions on uncertainties are *subjective* to the founders' perceptive capacity (Bylund & Packard, 2022), which comes with the founder's experience and background or the lack

[19] See Chapter 5, Costs and 3D Business Models for more details.

thereof, especially when it comes to financial literacy (Eisemann, 2020; Graña-Alvarez et al., 2024), learning, and adaptations (Sarasvathy, 2001, 2004) no matter how *objective* the founders' goals are. One of the biggest reasons why ESUs fail is financial, either running out of cash, lack of financing or attracting investors, or pricing and cost issues (CB Insights, 2022).[20]

These subjective decisions are based on the entrepreneur's continuous work with given assumptions, technologies, concepts, and approaches to identify new or potential applications, commercial uses, and markets through an exploratory process. Sarasvathy (2001) defines this as the *effectuation* process: "to take a set of means as given and focus on selecting between possible effects that can be created with that set of means" (p. 245). Effectuation is further reinforced and made real by the fact that the majority of ESUs operate in a world of great uncertainty, with *non-predictive controls* when they are in the process of establishing ESUs and evolving ideas into new, marketable products (Sarasvathy, 2008). The founders' strong or acceptable financial literacy mitigates the effects between financial and non-financial MCS that are non-predictive (Graña-Alvarez et al., 2024).

Value is in the eye of the value stakeholder

Value is effectuated during the ESUs' journey through the perceptions of ESU founders. Within this effectuation process, costs are an important common denominator—a critical link in the value chain of early-stage ESUs—from conceptualization of the business model, determining competitive advantage in a strategy, to its investment in intellectual capital (i.e., human, organizational, technological, social and relational)[21] to create, capture, and extract value.

The only financial certainty with ESUs
is costs! In fact, costs are guaranteed!

On the surface, costs do not appear to be an explicit dimension of a TSU entrepreneur's strategy where their general narratives are concerned. This is predictively due to a greater focus on the development of the

[20] https://www.skynova.com/blog/top-reasons-startups-fail.

[21] See Chapter 4, Cost Planning and Intellectual Capital Development for more details.

business model and strategy at a higher level, and eventually how to generate revenue and become profitable. However, once *the surface is scratched*, either with a specific question on costs, such as asking for an ESU's *cash burn rate*,[22] or through the entrepreneurs' narratives' implicit sensemaking,[23] costs are strategically and practically omnipresent throughout the narrative evolution of developing value proposition solutions into multiple marketable products and services. In fact, the only financial certainty with ESUs is costs. In fact, costs are guaranteed with ESUs. Yet, costs are hardly the center of any narrative. That is for good reason: founders do not launch ESUs because of costs. They do so to explore and exploit unmet market needs and opportunities and become a valuable company. To do so, however, ESU founders must take big risks, which include investments that are predominantly made in the costs of developing its value proposition.

Takeaways

- Costs are omnipresent throughout ESU lifecycles. It is a common denominator and a critical link in the value chain of the ESU's development from early stages.
- Founders' perception towards costs includes a major subjective component.
- This subjective perceptive capacity is based on the founders' experiences and financial literacy (or the lack thereof), learning, and adaptation capabilities.
- One of the biggest reasons why ESUs fail is financial illiteracy, including financial planning, non-financial MCS, and a thorough understanding of costs.
- The only financial certainty with ESUs is costs! In fact, costs are guaranteed.
- Founders do not launch ESUs because of costs, but despite it to explore and exploit market opportunities, and invest heavily in costs to develop their value propositions.

[22] Cash burn rate denotes how much costs an ESU is incurring monthly. Incurred costs = cash outflow or *cash burn*.

[23] From their evolving stories and unfolding narratives (Boje, 2001), to deconstructing their stories to *unmask narratives* (Martin, 1990) and to interpret what is said and done, not said, but done, and said, but not done (Boje, 2001) that captures meaning and experiences (Charmaz, 2011).

1.7 Experienced Entrepreneurs' Perception of Costs

In the early stages, experienced and serial ESU founders perceive costs (whether opportunity or financial/cash) as a means and *enabler* to create value instead of a burden, a cause of value reduction or destruction, or a reason for lower profitability or loss as in an accounting and financial reporting perspective (Chammassian, 2016). These costs are early investments into the project that are predominantly made of time, effort (i.e., in-kind), and cash. The purpose of this early investment is to research the market (i.e., demand and competitor analysis), prototype, experiment, test products and services in the marketplace for proof of concept, and determine the prices potential customers would be willing to pay (i.e., eventual ESU revenue). These early developmental stage costs are sometimes referred to as *sunk costs* or *sunk benefit* in management accounting (Datar & Rajan, 2021; Duxbury, 2012).

For definitional purposes, a *sunk cost* is deemed to be foregone and unrecoverable in the future. They cannot be used for valuation purposes or credited back by future investors. As Leach and Melicher (2021) note, *entrepreneurs pay for the past and investors pay for the future*. In no circumstances should founders ask future investors *to pay them back for the initial investment that they've made into their startups*. The latter will certainly lead to investors pulling out of any deal. This rule also applies to any public/private grants or personal loans[24] that founders have taken for their project.

Entrepreneurs pay for the past. Investors pay for the future

Management accounting scholars also refer to a *sunk cost effect*, where founders make irrational decisions through their subjective bias to commit more funds to recover previous sunk costs, to avoid the wasted time and money, to self-justify, and to stake their own reputation on the line. In simple words, founders pour money into a project that is not producing any results, but they insist (based on their *subjective bias*) and pitch to others that their idea would work with a little more time and money.

[24] Except for foundation-supported, public–private or government supplied booster grants whether to be paid back or not, it is almost impossible to get a bank loan in early stages as it is too risky and there is hardly any collateral.

This usually occurs when founders have not done the proper research and problem analytics, and insist that "their solution is the best in the marketplace and will work." This follows the cliché definition of insanity: doing the same thing repeatedly (in this case, pouring more money into the same processes), and expecting different results.

Whereas a *sunk benefit* is when there are positive results in the early experimentation or prototyping, leading to further incremental investment in time and money to expand on initial benefits or successes (Duxbury, 2012). The key word here is *incrementality*, which includes making small but measurable steps and improvements:

- *Developing a unique value proposition* (UVP) through an innovative business model that is value driven and not product driven.
- *Product/service development* and multiple offerings with the right problem–solution fit, that is holistic and staged over time, incrementally.
- *Proof of concept* market testing through pilot programs, partnerships, and experimentation that provide realistic user feedback and data.
- *Market definition*, segmentation through channels, and prioritization on which channels to focus first, followed by potential growth and scalability.
- *Customer acquisition* approaches seek the lowest costs, commonly known as *customer acquisition costs (CAC)*, and quickest wins to develop market awareness, generate revenue, and learn and recalibrate from the experience.
- *Different Monetization strategies* for revenue generation and scalability by developing the startup as a multidimensional platform company with varying value propositions to paying customers, to user experiences, and for stakeholder impact.
- *Company development* through the development of intellectual capital, including building the team, optimized processes, social and business networks, and relationships.

"So often people are working hard at the wrong thing. Working on the right thing is probably more important than working hard." (Caterina Fake, co-founder of Flickr)[25]

The ESU's journey is more important than the destination because we can learn from it, recalibrate and improve. Incrementality involves adaptability, flexibility, learning, openness, controlled experimentation, and healthy levels of questioning and self-doubt. It also requires small but important milestone achievements realistically set and measured to qualify for the next stage. Each of these milestones is like a roundabout at the crossroads where decisions must be made as to which direction to take for the best next results and milestone.

These small measurable steps that facilitate improvements and recalibrations collectively will lead to significant progress, value, and interest over time both internally and externally. Internally, incrementality will ground the ESU's team to realistic goals and expectations. While externally, it will create better visibility, interest, trust, and reputation with stakeholders, especially with future investors.[26] I am amazed, amused, and distraught by how often I see startup pitches where the founders believe they will be the next Google by planning to capture 10% of a $50 billion market from zero. It takes 30–60 seconds for an investor to tune out when she or he hears this fiction narrative.

The ESU's staged journeys are more important than its destination

The incremental investment into (and development strategy of) the ESU starts from the earliest stages and continues throughout the later stages. The relentless focus is on value creation. In the early stages, costs are treated as an input and an enabler and should be viewed as a sunk benefit. Usually, in the early stages, these *enabling costs* are (and ought to be) the lowest or the least expensive due to being a stage of frugality, which is crucial in extending minimal resources efficiently and effectively. Frugality, however, has its limitations. There would come a time when decisions are to be made about where to focus on, bet, and invest in, for the next incremental development phase, such as a broader market testing

[25] https://www.nationalbusinesscapital.com/blog/quotes-from-top-business-leaders/.

[26] In the next chapter, I will also discuss how investors look for incremental development growth, rather than the holy grail of the promise land.

or value proposition development.[27] In fact, these focused cost investments are mainly in new venture development to mediate value capture through revenue, scaling and growth, and eventual extraction through profitability and liquidation event (i.e., an exit).

> *"Some entrepreneurs focus so much on costs that they forget to focus on the opportunities. If you're always penny-pinching, you may miss the big idea that could change everything."*
> (Richard Branson, founder of the Virgin Group)[28]

The early-stage investments as enabling costs are made by the founder's own time, resources, and funds, except in cases of high tech (i.e., deeptech or pharmatech) where larger sums of investments in R&D are needed from the get-go.[29] Sometimes, early-stage adopters and supporters of the ESU, such as friends, family, and fools (FFF), crowd funding platforms, and business angels, provide some of the initial enabling funds.

In almost all cases, these enabling costs lead to recalibration, re-focus, and fine-tuning of the ESU's initial strategy in order to avoid *sunk cost effects*. It is an iterative process that reflects back and grounds the ESU founders to the real problem that they are trying to solve. In due time, it also leads to the "go"/ "no-go" decision of the project to its next stage, whether to abandon or expand the project, to invest further, to incorporate into a legal company, and/or to seek further external financing. If the decision is made to "go" to the next stage, it requires a different mindset and approaches that depart from the frugal incubation to company development even though incrementality continues to be in play.

With incrementality, time and timing play key roles within the dynamics between strategy and investment in costs throughout the ESU journey. They play an important role in opportunity cost of time. The longer it takes to achieve an incremental milestone, the more it will cost the ESU. However, *taking the time* to produce the right results and value for customers is important in managing expectations, especially

[27] I will discuss this more in detail in the next two chapters on *costs and the entrepreneurial venture lifecycles*.

[28] Branson (2017).

[29] These costs are predominantly related to people and their salaries which need to be compatible to market rates for high-cost engineers, scientists, programmers, researchers, lab technicians, and similar.

in the early stages where costs are usually lower. Realistically, it usually takes much longer to develop a problem-solving fit idea or a technology into value propositions through marketable products and services, even though the founders' experience or inexperience may or may not lead to faster development. Most of the time ESU founders underestimate the time variable.

Takeaways

- Entrepreneurs pay for the past. Investors pay for the future.
- In the earlier stages, founders incur sunk costs that are unrecoverable with the goal of achieving a benefit, a sunk (cost) benefit.
- Beware of the sunk cost *effect* due to subjective biases as the cliché definition of insanity.
- Incrementality and incremental development are the keys to making small progress with measurable steps.
- The ESU's staged journeys are more important than its destination.
- Incrementality will ground the ESU's team to realistic goals and expectations, and attract better interest externally from customers and investors alike.
- Investments are also made incrementally.
- Taking the time to produce the right results in the early stages because it costs much less.

1.8 Costs and the Role of Learning and Experience

This chapter (and book) has been conceived from narratives of entrepreneurs with different backgrounds, expertise, and experiences, such as scientific, academic, startup, industry, business, and entrepreneurial. In all cases, expertise and experiences, whether technology-based, startup, or industry, drive "experimentation, a subdimension of effectuation, [which] is positively correlated with uncertainty" (Chandler et al., 2011, p. 375). The key to understanding these behaviors leading to perceptions towards and experiences with costs is to deconstruct the narratives and stories and read between the lines of what is said and what is not said or implied. Boje (2001) has found that "reading the silence between the lines is a way to deconstruct the forces that oppose" (p. 29). What is relevant here is the fact that to understand how costs are perceived and treated by ESUs, it is important to deconstruct both the narratives and the antenarratives of the TSU entrepreneur.

In early-stage ESUs, there is a great deal of subjectivity in the narrative because factual evidence is limited or missing, technologies are untested, market demand is unknown, and objective information is unavailable. Instead, early-stage entrepreneurs use an *impression management approach*, in which they use various techniques to *seduce* investors (for instance) with positive language and the promotion of innovativeness (Parhankangas & Ehrlich, 2014). By default, entrepreneurs are optimists rather than just opportunists who are only on self-serving missions (Dushnitsky, 2010). This optimism may be a result of entrepreneurial passion, which is defined as an *intense positive feeling* (Cardon et al., 2009). Entrepreneurial passion must be sincere, however, in order to be appreciated, especially by investors (Chen et al., 2009). Boje (2001) concludes that "no narrative or story is ideologically neutral," (p. 18), so there is a risk of exaggeration, overoptimism, or overestimation (Cassar, 2009). However, experience with startups plays a role in tempering this overoptimism with entrepreneurs (Ucbasaran et al., 2010). Overconfidence through subjective perception and cultural propensity to over-believe in one's abilities (Koellinger et al., 2007) may contribute to overoptimism, which, at times (in extreme cases), is referred to as *optimistic overconfidence* (M. Simon & Shrader, 2012). Overly optimistic entrepreneurial emotions could lead to erroneous evaluation of opportunities and entrepreneurial exploitation (Welpe et al., 2012).

The realities of costs in ESU value creation eventually surface when investors assess their involvement and eventual investment into ESU costs. This may be a controlling correlation between the ESU entrepreneurs' passion, experiences, and perception towards costs. This can only be assessed by deconstructing what is said and what is not said in the antenarratives and the narratives of founders. In order to comprehend how the value of cost is perceived, it is important to recognize the background and experiences of ESU founders. Learning comes from previous experiences, where education, ideas, and concepts are put into practice. Experienced entrepreneurs know what it takes to launch an ESU, how to learn from mistakes and from the marketplace, and how/when to pivot, scale, or grow. Novice entrepreneurs are learning for the first time about entrepreneurship and how to launch a successful ESU. Learning from the beginning plays a key role in surviving (or failing), to pivot for scalability and growth-oriented businesses.

Learning comes from previous experiences, where education, ideas, and concepts are put into practice

We can categorize three sets of founders: novice entrepreneurs, repeat entrepreneurs, and serial entrepreneurs. Novices are first-time entrepreneurs with no entrepreneurial experience. Repeat entrepreneurs have at least one entrepreneurial experience (whether successful or not). Whereas serial entrepreneurs are the most experienced in launching and exiting ESUs (Dabić et al., 2023).

In all scenarios, the experienced and inexperienced entrepreneurs' views towards costs appear to converge at the mid-to-late lifecycle stages of their narratives, especially when it comes to costs related to people. In almost all cases, founders view costs as investments to create, capture, and extract value from the new venture development rather than simple product development (Chammassian, 2016; Chammassian & Sabatier, 2020). The vast majority of the costs are invested in people. Learned from experience, founders put a lot of importance on the choice of the people and especially at the beginning for the development of the product (Chammassian, 2016), which is actually the company they are building. In fact, for them, costs and investments are the flip side of the same coin for ESUs. This is a very interesting phenomenon and mindset that experienced ESU founders understand and live by.

Costs and investments are the flip side of the same coin

As a case in point, when I ask a simple question to my students, founders and people in general, "when I say the word *cost* what is the first thing that comes to your mind?" The answer is usually, "what do you mean by a cost?" Or, "it depends on the circumstances," and more than often, a value reducer as in cash out, a burden. In other words, the consensus is that of a *pessimistic* notion of cost, that it is a value reducer or destroyer, and a cash outflow.

When I ask the following question to the same people immediately afterward, "when I say the word *investment*, what is the first thing that comes to your mind." The responses are more positive or hopeful that one invests and expects to receive something in return, such as a higher value, experience, time savings, a profit or a *return on investment*. The answer, in other words, is usually more *optimistic*.

When I asked the same question to experienced entrepreneurs during my research, the predominant answer was that the majority of costs are an investment, specifically in people, where they expect to create, capture, and extract a major return in value, such as from the company development. The *choice of people*, and the diversity of their human capital, will make or break an ESU. One experienced ESU founder said, "cost to me, that means money out, which means either you can waste it or you can invest it. To us, cost, which reflects wasting on actually marketing: if we invested or spent the money for marketing, to us, was more a cost without any guarantee that we would have any income…When we invested, we wanted to make sure that we get something back. So that was primarily [in] employees or employing more people. It means that we could develop our products, better products, more secure. And one of the biggest cost centers we had was the database center…The biggest assessment, as I said, was investing in people… We were very careful with not investing too much on infrastructure [so] like we rented offices" (Chammassian, 2016, pp. 108–109).

This is where frugality does not work and goes on the wayside. Many younger and novice entrepreneurs don't understand this and don't know how and when to transition. For them, *Lean startup* (Ries, 2011) means free work to be extracted from co-founders or friends for as long and as much as possible. They expect people and advisors to provide free services, which usually only works in the short term. However, in my experience, anything that is given or received for free (such as *free* advice) has very little value… I have mentored hundreds of novice ESU founders and found that when I bring up the topic of somehow *paying* for advice, the vast majority disappear, ghost me, never to be heard from again. One of the key suggestions I have for all novice entrepreneurs is to have an advisory board from the start and to compensate them (initially) in-kind with *advisory shares*; and later, pay them a reasonable quarterly stipend in addition to shares. Advisors, whether generalist or specialist, provide invaluable feedback as a sounding board with their experiences, business acumen, financial literacy, and contacts. Advisory boards are generally not an issue with experienced entrepreneurs because they know and understand that in order to build a great ESU, one needs to attract knowledgeable people instead of saving money, cutting costs, or discounting salaries, where frugality simply does not work. A study found that startups who received formal advice helped them improve their people management approaches by "instituting regular meetings, setting goals consistently, and providing frequent feedback to employees… [these startups then] grew 28% larger and were 10 percentage points less likely to fail than those who got advice from peers with an informal approach to managing people" (Chatterji et al., 2019).

Research has repeatedly confirmed that experienced entrepreneurs—those who have launched and exited firms—have a higher potential to start and exit another ESU successfully than novice or inexperienced entrepreneurs. They are more optimistic about perceiving costs as an investment in value creation, capture, and extraction of their project than novices. They see costs as an enabler of value creation and a mediator of value capture and extraction. "Money, cost, investment, funding, budget, maybe have different shades but can also probably be interchanged. That's the point of an [early-stage technology] startup, because there is no revenue. Whatever goes in goes into a cost…which is an investment" (Chammassian, 2016, p. 103). They also see costs from the flip side: how paying customers perceive costs and how ESU offerings through their platform of products and services can improve their businesses by making them more efficient and effective. In other words, how their ESUs are saving their customers time and money, while improving their KPIs. In general, let's remember that revenue for the ESU is a cost to its customers. One needs to take this into consideration when designing their *revenue models* which should follow the same value logic as their business model. Your customers per their needs are always looking at their costs as a value driver. Such costs will be the first to be cut as discretionary spending when economic conditions shift downwards. More on this in the following chapters.

Always consider that revenue for the ESU is a cost to its customers

Learning plays a pivotal role in the survival, lifecycle success and growth (i.e., moving from one lifecycle to the next appropriately), especially how costs are to be perceived and utilized at different lifecycle stages. At earlier stages, usually costs are the lowest and the ESU is at its least "costly" or "expensive" period. At these stages, learning is a key driver to survival and pivoting, with the lowest costs. Defining the real problem they are solving; analyzing customer needs, market demand and the competitive landscape; prototyping and experimenting; testing go-to-market strategies; and discussing with stakeholders, users, and customers will bring a lot of knowledge and learning opportunities. It is up to the ESU founders to decipher, recalibrate, and act upon.

> *"Wonder what your customer really wants? Ask. Don't tell."* (Lisa Stone, CEO and c-founder of BlogHer[30])

What happens in reality though, most novice ESU founders either embrace and gauge early external signals as a sign of approval of their initial idea or ignore them without learning and applying. At times when users and potential customers show interest and buy into their products or services, novice founders believe in these signals as absolute proof that their business model is the right one. In other words, they develop an *optimistic overconfidence* in their ideas' value proposition very early in their development process without further market testing or customer need validation. Although such early-stage wins and generated revenue are positive signals as *proof of concept* for potential replication, the development and objective learning must continue as recalibration usually continues.

The issue arises when founders put aside their learning and believe they're ready to replicate, scale, or grow. They start pitching to investors as if they are ready for growth. When investors ask rhetorical or direct questions about their business model, many of the answers come across as generic or brushed off to the unanticipated questions. That means the founders have either not considered them or they looked at the problem they are solving from their own angle or perception, or they are simply ignorant that their problem–solution fit may not be well-aligned. If founders ignore such questions, they are usually setting themselves up for failure. If they embrace them in good faith and attempt to answer or accept that they haven't considered different scenarios, this may be an opportunity to learn from and find reasonable, data-driven answers.

Such questions and answers are learning opportunities for both the founders and investors, to see if there is a fit to form a relationship. Let's remember that investor-founder relationships are very personal and private ones (Leach & Melicher, 2021). Founders must know that these exchanges are opportunities for investors to screen them and their projects for *investability* with the following order:

[30] https://www.nationalbusinesscapital.com/blog/quotes-from-top-business-leaders/.

A. **The People**: Do the founders understand their line of business well? Are the founders good learners? Are the founders coachable? Can they learn actively or through coaching, act, and recalibrate their businesses? (Johnson et al., 2021; Kuratko et al., 2021; Marvel et al., 2020)
B. **The Project**: How would their investments be used, in what ways, and what type of costs? Would these cost investments make sense with the project? After all, investments and costs are the flip side of the same coin: we invest in costs!
C. **The Profitable Returns**: Do the founders have the grit to scale and grow the ESU and make it a high-valued company? Would the project have the potential for value capture and eventual value extraction through an exit scenario, such as trade sale M&A?

During my research, experienced ESU founders defined the perception of value is in the eye of their paying customers, investors, and eventually a trade sale. These values are defined and created at different levels of ESU lifecycles as an input to its mission and strategic decisions, as a process of ESU development, and as an output measured via Key Performance Indicators (KPI) and eventual exit.

Takeaways

- As entrepreneurs are passionate and optimistic by default, they need to avoid the risk of exaggeration, overoptimism, or optimistic overconfidence.
- Overly optimistic entrepreneurial emotions could lead to erroneous evaluation of opportunities and entrepreneurial exploitation.
- Learning comes from previous experiences, where education, ideas, and concepts are put into practice.
- Experienced entrepreneurs have the mindset that costs and investments are the flip side of the same coin.
- They also view costs from a paying customer's perspective: how the ESUs value proposition should benefit the customer's bottom line by savings time and money with efficient and effective value propositions.
- They know that revenue for the ESU is a cost to its paying customers.

- In the early stages, learning is a key driver to survival and pivoting, with the lowest costs. Novice entrepreneurs need to ensure that early win signals are a means and not an end of learning.
- Investors look at the founder's learning ability and coachability as a key qualification for investability.

1.9 Time Value of Cost Habits

We know money has a time value: a Euro today is not worth a Euro in a year's time. It should be worth more since a discount is applied to determine the opportunity cost of capital: whether to invest in a risky startup or a safer financial instrument (i.e., stock market, certificate of deposit, or real estate). Each type of investment has its risks and rewards. Investing in real estate, for instance, has a safer and longer-term prospect. A physical building is a tangible asset with collateral and potential for value appreciation as well as rental income opportunity making it secure. On the other hand, cash is tied up in the long term and it may not be easy to divest when extra cash is needed. Plus, the real estate market may change in an economic downturn. Renting and getting a good rental value may no longer be possible.

Whereas investing in an ESU is a riskier bet since the vast majority of ESUs fail within three to five years of their launch. However, risks and rewards go hand in hand: expected return on investment from an ESU would be much higher than from investing in real estate, especially if the intangible and intellectual capital value is considered much higher than the traditional discounted cash flow (DCF) model used during the valuation of the company on its future cash flow potential.

As money and investments have a time value, so do ESU Costs since we invest in costs. This depends on the type of costs applied in what ESU stage, whether high-tech or non-high-tech ESU and the investor. The same time-value logic is applied for costs:

- As an enabler, costs have a short-term time value usually as a sunk (cost) benefit.
- As a mediator, costs have a long-term value usually as an investment with ROI.

- As a moderator, costs have a short-term time value as they moderate margin and profitability which are tracked and measured on an annual basis.

How costs are allocated (as inputs) in a highly uncertain, unpredictable, and ambiguous environment is key to its perceived benefits (as outputs). An incremental cost investment mindset over time makes all the difference, as clarity with shorter and longer time-valued choices becomes more relevant.

This incremental time-valued approach needs to be made a habit—a *cost habit*. Using a reference from James Clear's (2018) acclaimed book *Atomic Habits*, *tiny changes* [in habits lead to] *remarkable results*. This applies to cost habits also. Time will compound or magnify the results and returns, whether positively or negatively. The key is to differentiate good cost habits from bad cost habits.

Good cost habits include:

- *Cost literacy* by having good financial literacy of what and how to account for costs and be accountable through monitoring and managing cash flows and burn rates, including reporting and comprehending financial statements (i.e., the startup scoreboard).
- *Incrementality mindset* and approaches in all ESU lifecycle stages.
- Viewing costs as *enabling sunk benefits* in earlier stages; and as a *mediating investment* in value creation, capture, and extraction as well as a *moderator of margin and profitability* thereafter.
- Understanding when to be frugal and bootstrap, versus when to bet higher, prioritize, and invest in key choices that give the best ROI with costs.
- *Learning* from experiences and *listening* to experts and advisors who are somehow compensated for their support, initially in-kind through advisory shares and products; and later, with cash or both.
- *Cost scenario* planning with different perceived outcomes and consequences (i.e., optimistic, realistic, and pessimistic), including a hedge for the unexpected.
- Consistently aligning the ESU's *pitch narrative* to its *financial KPIs*, especially to cost allocations for investment.

Bad cost habits include:

- Not understanding and/or being ignorant about how costs are *accounted* for strategically and operationally.
- Not having a general understanding of reporting differentiates between financial, statutory, and management accounting, cash burn rate or sunk cost vs. sunk benefit.
- Not taking costs seriously. Having *optimistic overconfidence* from early positive signals and betting the farm on early proof of concept instead of taking a more cautious incremental approach.
- Repeat spending on unproven costs leading to *sunk cost effects*, and then soliciting funding to cover these incurred costs.
- Remaining too frugal and bootstrapping throughout different ESU lifecycles when bigger investment bets are needed. Not knowing when to bet and when not to spend on the unnecessary at different lifecycle stages.
- Not learning from negative signals or not listening to good advice or from customers per their needs.
- Soliciting free work and advice without having some form of compensation, whether in-kind or in cash.

Cost Accounting *for ESU founders is more about*
cost accountability *than* cost transactioning

These cost habits can and must be learned from the early onset of an ESU. I hear many founders who defer their *cost accountability* to their bookkeeper, tax accountant, or accounting software without realizing that such professionals and software don't own the ESU business. They are intermediaries (or software tools) that simply transact business activities with invoices and payments based on how they see fit within accounting rules based on the explanation or reasoning given to them by the founders. *How costs are accounted for* in a business is the responsibility of the ESU founding team. *Cost Accounting* for ESU founders is more about *cost accountability* than *cost transactioning* done by bookkeepers, tax accountants, or accounting software.

Takeaways

- As money has a time value; so do costs.
- Cost risks and rewards (ROI costs) go hand in hand.

- Costs' time value depends on the perceived type of costs: an enabler (short term), a mediator (long term), and a moderator (short term).
- How costs are allocated as inputs have an impact on its perceived benefits (or outputs).
- Incremental cost investment mindset and cost habits are crucial to have.
- There are good cost habits and bad cost habits.

1.10 Defining Costs

The majority of novice ESU founders come from non-business and non-financial backgrounds. They are also younger and inexperienced. It is not difficult to see why strategic accounting and accountability for costs are neither known nor appreciated and simply ignored. The ESU founders' focus is usually to transform their idea into a profitable company. Even founders with business or corporate experience do not distinguish the difference between regular business or corporate costs and ESU costs. Only experienced and serial ESU entrepreneurs have a good comprehension of what costs are. In this section, I will cover the key elements of how ESU costs should be understood, planned, and accounted for using commonly known financial statements and their relevance in different ESU lifecycles. But first, let's attempt to define what a cost is.

Based on my research, experiences, observations, and interview narratives of ESU founders, I have come across different variations of the same notion of ESU costs. First and foremost, it is important to understand that ESUs are strategic by nature. Therefore, most of the costs should be treated as investments to form part of the ESU's strategic positioning. Hence, a *strategic cost valuation process* occurs in which ESU entrepreneurs assess where to allocate costs to drive the highest value and investment returns.

The strategic importance and impact of costs as a value creator within early-stage ESUs are not present in the academic literature on entrepreneurship, strategic management, and innovation disciplines. However, opportunity cost has been the bedrock of economics and later adopted into accounting, consumer behavior, and supply chain, and also found its place in conventional definitions in online dictionaries.

Economists have been using the term opportunity cost and incremental costs since the 1960s. Samuelson (1967) defined it as "foregone opportunities that have been sacrificed" (p. 443), and Leininger (1977) termed "Opportunity Cost (Cost Situation) [as] the difference between the cost incurred and the cost that would have been incurred if the correct policy had been adopted" (p. 249). There are plenty of popular definitions of opportunity cost, including that an opportunity cost occurs when a "cost of using a resource arises from the value of what it could be used for instead" (Henderson, 2008, p. 1). Opportunity cost is also defined as "the potential benefits that an individual, investor, or business misses out on when choosing one alternative over another" (Investopedia.com, n.d.). Or "the potential gain lost by the choice to take a different course of action when considering multiple investments or avenues of business (Sage, 2021). Or "the potential benefits that are lost when an individual, business or investor chooses a substitute over another. As the opportunity cost definition defines it to be hidden, the costs could go unnoticed very easily" (The Economic Times, n.d.). In other words, they include costs that are seen and known and costs that are not seen or known.

Based on this background, my research, interviews, and narratives of ESU founders, I have developed an over-encompassing definition of costs.

> *"A cost is a value we assign or the amount we (are willing to) pay to acquire, produce, or maintain an asset (whether tangible or intangible), to experience, or to purchase a product or service, in order to receive a benefit in return"*[31]

1.10.1 Cost as a Perceived Value

Deconstructing this definition, first and foremost, *cost is a value*. This value is either perceived or assigned. *A perceived value* of cost is what we believe something is worth, whether pursuing it or not worth pursuing to receive a perceived benefit in return; whether it is tangible or intangible, high or low worth return, regardless of its market or book value.

For instance, during an early stage, an ESU founder can choose to pay nothing or pay an above-average stipend for an intern to set up an ESU marketing plan. In the former case, the founder simply claims that the ESU does not have the funds to pay for an intern but could promise a

[31] Chammassian (2016), and Chammassian and Sabatier (2020).

good reference or a future position within the ESU. The founder accepts the consequences (i.e., the opportunity cost) that the intern may leave if there is a better (and paid) opportunity elsewhere. The founder in this case, puts little financial value on the intern's work, tries to get the most out of the work, and should expect a high risk of discontinuity with the intern's abrupt departure. The unpaid internship value is in fact pro bono work. The intern may accept to work for free in return for the experience, a work reference, and the potential for a future position within the ESU. However, this has a short-term motivational effect, especially when the unpaid intern's workload becomes demanding and reality sets in where the intern needs to cover their own costs.

On the other hand, the founder decides it is important to pay for an intern due to the role's importance, intern's retention, and the motivation to attract a bright individual. In this case, the founder assigns a higher perceived value on the internship. The ESU may or may not have the funds, but the founder searches and solicits alternative funding mechanisms, such as through an innovation fund, a grant, or a local government initiative to pay for the internship creating a win–win situation to various stakeholders. Hence, this value is perceived to be high for the ESU founder and the intern since it is paid; and for the entrepreneurial funding agency, since it creates new learning opportunities for the intern and a valuable short-term resource for the ESU.

For technology-driven ESUs, such as deep tech, for instance, founders and investors *assign* a much higher value for the costs invested in people to develop intellectual capital. The value of human capital in deep tech is much higher, and human capital is their biggest investment throughout the startup's lifecycle. In the words, for high-tech founders: "team is core." "This wasn't going to be solved by a few students. So, we had an average age of 45 in the engineering team." "Technology and people are one and the same at the start of the tech startup." "Having the right people in the team is key, and you can't compromise on this." "People is [sic] investment" and "retention plans is [sic] clearly an investment for us." "You need to build a really ambitious product. You need to solve really hard problems. You need to hire the best people and very often, a lot of them, and therefore, you need to incur really high-fix costs." (Chammassian, 2016)

1.10.2 *Cost as an* Assigned Value

An *assigned value* is a labeled value (i.e., a price tag) of an asset, a person, a product, or a service to acquire: a market rate for an engineer; a market price for a product or a manufacturer's suggested price; a calculated value, such as the cost of producing a product or service. An assigned value is closest to the *accounted value*, a *book value* recorded on a *cost basis* on the balance sheet or the income statement.[32] This does not mean that we are always willing to pay the assigned value amount. It simply means that if we decide to pursue a certain strategy, investment, time or direction, hire a certain engineer, or purchase an equipment, there is a known market-assigned value (a cost) associated with it we have to be willing to pay, along with an opportunity cost of not willing to pay. These assigned, perceived, or calculated values are used to build assumptions for operational forecasting, financial and scenario planning, cash budgeting, and valuation purposes.

1.10.3 Cost of Tangible and Intangible Assets

Tangible assets are usually[33] long-term assets in physical form that can be touched, seen, and easily valued, such as buildings and equipment. Costs invested in tangible assets are directly recorded on the balance sheet of a firm on a *cost basis*. This means they are recorded in the amount that has been transacted or paid for. Tangible assets are depreciated over their economic life. However, with the advancement of the knowledge economy, powered by technological innovation, most investments in firms (i.e., over 90% of S&P 500 companies[34] and especially in ESUs) are made in intangible assets (Haskel & Westlake, 2018; OECD, 1996).

Intangible assets are non-physical by nature. They represent a current economic value and a potentially much higher future economic benefit or value, which are difficult to assess and determine with conventional valuation methods. They may require specialized valuation methods.

[32] Chapter 2 covers how ESU costs are accounted for and reported in the financial statement at different ESU lifecycles.

[33] Inventory is also tangible, except majority is classified as a current or short-term asset. There are exceptions to this, such as high-valued inventory (i.e., over $1000 value) that can be reworkable/circular economy (i.e., high valued spare parts for aircraft or cash machines).

[34] Source: Ocean Tomo in Haskel and Westlake (2018).

For instance, hiring and retaining experienced and qualified engineers for R&D purposes as human capital to internally-generate organizational capital is very difficult to evaluate and value. From a modern accounting perspective, people's costs—whether a high-salaried engineer who develops unique algorithms or an admin assistant—are expensed in the income statement, and rarely captured in the balance sheet as an intangible asset.[35] Other examples of intangible assets include intellectual property (i.e., patents, trademarks, and copyrights)[36]; specialized software; big data; social networks;and customer lists, whether internally generated or externally-acquired. Intangible capital valuation depends on its rareness, utility, and inimitability (Newbert, 2008). Those intangible assets that are recorded on the balance sheet, such as when acquired externally, are ***amortized*** over their economic life, which is difficult to determine.

Cost as a value could be in terms of allocating time and resources to build key relationships with unique partners, such as proprietary manufacturing or marketing (i.e., relational capital) or acquiring customers (i.e., customer acquisition costs). All in all, there is always a perceived opportunity cost benefit in return on the invested costs, whether we receive that benefit as originally perceived or not.

Both tangible and intangible assets are considered long-term (noncurrent) assets, sometimes referred to as *capital*. Long-term value is defined as having an economic life that is more than a year, usually two or more years, depending on the type of asset. For instance, a building has a much longer economic life than a laptop computer. A pharmaceutical patent may have an economic life of up to 20 years. Whereas a developed agri-tech software may have a three-year economic life. Intangible assets that have a perceived multi-year future value are usually initially recorded as an incurred cost—an expense—in the income statement which has

[35] There are rare exceptions to this, such as if a new discovery by an R&D team that can be patented.

[36] IP valuations are complex and require special approaches. Some common valuation methods include income method (i.e., future cash flow or economic income generation potential), market value (i.e., assigned by market or paid for similar patents previously), and cost method (i.e., replacement value). Source: https://www.wipo.int/sme/en/ip-valuation.html.

a 12-month or less horizon. However, when an ESU is acquired with a trade sale M&A event, the value of the acquisition is recorded on a *cost basis* as a non-current asset on the balance sheet of the acquiring company (i.e., investment, intangible assets and goodwill).

1.10.4 Cost and Experiences

Costs associated with *experiences* are a phenomenon that is grounded on the notion of the *experience economy* first coined by Joseph Pine Ii and James Gilmore (1998). Our economies have evolved from extracting commodities to industrialization, to making products and then delivering services, to enhancing experiences. "As goods and services become commoditized, the customer experiences that companies create will matter most" (Pine Ii & Gilmore, 1998, p.1). Experiences are transformative by nature. They create memorable events for customers. Experience offerings include customer participation and involvement. Experience value propositions are about improving the efficiency of time (as "the currency of experiences") and the effectiveness of business (offerings). Sometimes simple experiences that we take for granted or don't consider could have a significant buying-decision impact. It adds value to how customers spend time and how ESUs design, develop, promote, and fulfill customer experiences around customer needs.

In a commoditized world, where multiple offerings of similar products and services exist, offering unique experiences could differentiate, create a competitive advantage, and capture intangible value. People pay a premium for experiences that are perceived to be positive, authentic, unique, and unusual. Costs associated with developing simple, effective, holistic comprehensive experiences, from the first sales to repeat sales, to warranties and customer satisfaction guarantees, to after-sale services (i.e., maintenance for products and subscription to services that keep providing customer-needed features), will lead to customer satisfaction, trust, and positive reputation, all part of social capital value. These will lead to referrals, monetization, and increased revenue channels. Experiences (whether positive or negative) have a mediating effect on satisfaction, loyalty, and consumption.

Takeaways

- Costs are ill-defined in the literature. There does not appear to be an overarching one.
- There are good inferences to opportunity cost which usually denote a "sacrifice" made, "foregone opportunity" for the benefit of "alternatives."
- An over-encompassing definition: "A cost is a value we assign or the amount we (are willing to) pay to acquire, produce, or maintain an asset (whether tangible or intangible), to experience, or to purchase a product or service, in order to receive a benefit in return."
- Costs can have a perceived and/or assigned value.
- Costs vary for tangible assets (i.e., easier to assign) vs. intangible assets (i.e., more perceived, difficult to determine).
- People and companies will pay a premium and remain loyal for positive experiences improving efficiency and effectiveness (i.e., time and money).

1.11 Costs vs. Cash

Costs and cash are intermittently used to explain expenditure's nature, purpose (operating, investing, or financing), timing of when costs incur, and their impact. Costs have a more overarching meaning and application that can be strategic (i.e., long term or more than one year) or operational (i.e., short term or within 12 months). It can be used as a long-term investment, enabler, and mediator of value creation, capture, and extraction (i.e., as a future return on investment). It can also be used for the purpose of generating revenue (i.e., direct cost of goods sold as a *moderator of margin*) and as an expense (or an *incurred cost*) to support revenue generation indirectly and as a *moderator of profitability*.

Cash has a more existential implication as actual (liquid) money available to an ESU to cover or pay for costs at any given stage. One either has cash or doesn't have cash. *Liquid* means cash available in the bank that can be easily, immediately, or within a short reasonable time used to pay for costs. Cash includes currencies in bank accounts or similar highly liquid assets, such as certificates of deposit or short-term marketable securities that can be quickly and easily converted into cash. There is *cash inflow* from varying sources, such as founders' own funds, grants, prizes, donations, investments into the ESU, and revenue generated from ESUs

Fig. 1.2 Costs vs. cash

operating activities. There is *cash outflow*, which denotes payment towards expenditures and investments. Costs are the moderator between cash inflows and outflows as denoted in Fig. 1.2.

Cash inflow and outflow derive from three types of business activities, that are operating, investing, and financing. *Operating cash* is sourced from (i.e., inflow) and used for (i.e., outflow) core business activities of an ESU, such as revenue receipts (i.e., sources) and operating expenses (i.e., uses). *Investing cash* flows are related to the purchase and disposal of long-term assets, tangible and intangible, such as equipment, buildings, cars, patents, and copyrights. *Financing cash* flows include how an ESU is financed or funded, either through issuing of ESU shares (i.e., common or preferred stock) or through loans (i.e., convertibles, bridge, or bank); and how financing is paid back (i.e., through dividends, buyback of ESU shares or payback of a loan principle).

When cash outflows exceed cash inflows, this is referred to as *cash burn*. Investors often ask ESU founders "what is your cash burn rate?" The answer usually should be answered either monthly average, quarterly, or annual cash burn. When cash inflows exceed cash outflows, it is referred to as *cash build*. In majority of the time, early to mid-stage startups are in a survival stage. They operate in a net cash burn state, either purely incurring costs to enable and mediate value creation and capture (such as high-tech ESUs), or operating at a loss where operating costs exceed earned revenue and margin. The latter usually occurs during survival and early growth stages. In both situations, ESUs operate at a loss and usually need external financing to cover costs and to survive.

Since one of the top reasons why startups fail is financial, usually *running out of cash*, this is where incrementality and prioritization play a key role in survival and development. Doing too much or going in different directions at the same time without prioritization can easily lead to both cash and founder burnout. Prioritizing what to spend on, and when, what to extract from cost outlays, and how to define incremental milestones are key to survival. For instance, if an early-stage ESU is testing a solution in the marketplace, time and money are better spent on identifying customers, getting their feedback, identifying revenue price points, defining customer acquisition costs, and recalibrating, instead of spending valuable time, resources, and money on expensive equipment, complex web design, multi-directional marketing, or an integrated financial system. Whereas larger companies may survive with such expenditures due to cash reserves, ESUs will not survive due to lack of it. They will run out of cash very quickly. It is also essential to be initially frugal, to prioritize the most effective processes and their costs, and determine when it is time to shift from hands-on frugal mode into betting on the next phase which may require higher investment (and external financing) after having educated confidence.

Takeaways

- Costs and cash are sometimes intermittently used, but they have different roles, purposes, and meanings.
- Costs have a more overarching meaning. They could be strategic, expenses incurred (from the past), or forecasted in financial planning.
- Cash has more existential implications: one either has it or doesn't have it.
- Cash inflow and outflow occur from operating, investing, and financing activities.
- Net cash burns occur when cash outflows exceed cash inflows.
- Net cash build occurs when cash inflows exceed cash outflows.
- The top financial reasons why ESU's fail is due to running out of cash and underestimating its costs of development.

Chapters Two and Three (*Costs and Entrepreneurial Startup Lifecycles—early* and *late stages* respectively) cover how ESU costs are made up and differ from each other in their corresponding lifecycles, from ideation and early stages to mid—and late stages in more detail.

Bibliography

Aluko, S., Mayhall, J., Wauquiez, M., & Vercio, A. (2010). Strategic cost management. *Financial Management,* 34–35.

Amit, R., & Zott, C. (2012). Creating value through business model innovation. *MIT Sloan Management Review, 53*(3), 40–50.

Amit, R., & Zott, C. (2021). *Business model innovation strategy*. John Wiley & Sons.

Anderson, S. W., & Dekker, H. C. (2009a). Strategic cost management in supply chains, part 1: Structural cost management. *Accounting Horizons, 23*(2), 201–220. https://doi.org/10.2308/acch.2009.23.2.201

Anderson, S. W., & Dekker, H. C. (2009b). Strategic cost management in supply chains, part 2: Executional cost management. *Accounting Horizons, 23*(3), 289–305. https://doi.org/10.2308/acch.2009.23.3.289

Anthony, R. N. (1952). *Management controls in industrial research organizations*. Harvard University Press.

Anthony, R. N. (1965). *Planning and control systems: A framework for analysis*. Harvard Business School Publishing.

Anthony, R. N. (1988). *The management control function*. Harvard Business School Publishing.

Aparicio, G., Iturralde, T., & Rodríguez, A. V. (2023). Developments in the knowledge-based economy research field: A bibliometric literature review. *Management Review Quarterly*, 73, 317–352 (2023). https://doi.org/10.1007/s11301-021-00241-w

Bailetti, T. (2012). Technology entrepreneurship: Overview, definition, and distinctive aspects. *Technology Innovation Management Review*, February 2012: 5–12.

Banker, R., Byzalov, D., & Plehn-Dujowich, J. (2014). Demand uncertainty and cost behavior. *The Accounting Review, 89*(3), 839–865.

Boje, D. (2001). *Narrative methods for organizational and communication research*. Sage.

Branson, R. (2017). *Screw business as usual*. Penguin Random House.

Brinckmann, J., Grichnik, D., & Kapsa, D. (2010). Should entrepreneurs plan or just storm the castle? A meta-analysis on contextual factors impacting the business planning–performance relationship in small firms. *Journal of Business Venturing, 25*(1), 24–40.

Bromwich, M. (1990). The case for strategic management accounting: The role of accounting information for strategy in competitive markets. *Accounting, Organizations & Society, 15*(1–2), 27–46.

Brouthers, K. D., & Roozen, F. A. (1999). Is it time to start thinking about strategic accounting? *Long Range Planning, 32*(3), 311–322.

Bylund, P. L., & Packard, M. D. (2022). Subjective value in entrepreneurship. *Small Business Economics, 58*(3), 1243–1260. https://doi.org/10.1007/s11187-021-00451-2

Cadez, S., & Guilding, C. (2008). An exploratory investigation of an integrated contingency model of strategic management accounting. *Accounting, Organizations and Society, 33*(7–8), 836–863. https://doi.org/10.1016/j.aos.2008.01.003

Cardon, M. S., Wincent, J., Singh, J., & Drnovsek, M. (2009). The nature and experience of entrepreneurial passion. *Academy of Management Review, 34*(3), 511–532.

Carroll, L. (2017). A Comprehensive definition of technology from an Ethological perspective. *Social Sciences, 6*(4), 126. https://doi.org/10.3390/socsci6040126

Cassar, G. (2009). Financial statement and projection preparation in start-up ventures. *The Accounting Review, 84*(1), 27–51.

CB Insights. (2022, December 1). *The top 12 reasons Startups fail.* CB Insights Research. https://www.cbinsights.com/research/report/startup-failure-reasons-top/

Chammassian, R. G. (2016). *Towards a new cost paradigm for technology startup entrepreneurs* (Doctoral Dissertation). Grenoble Ecole de Management.

Chammassian, R. G., & Sabatier, V. (2020). The role of costs in business model design for early-stage technology startups. *Technological Forecasting and Social Change, 157*, 120090. https://doi.org/10.1016/j.techfore.2020.120090

Chandler, G. N., DeTienne, D. R., McKelvie, A., & Mumford, T. V. (2011). Causation and effectuation processes: A validation study. *Journal of Business Venturing*, 26(3), 375–390. Retrieved from http://doi.org/10.1016/j.jbusvent.2009.10.006

Charmaz, K. (2011). *Constructing grounded theory: A practical guide through qualitative research.* Sage.

Chatterji, A., Delecourt, S., Hasan, S., & Koning, R. (2019). When does advice impact startup performance? *Strategic Management Journal, 40*(3), 331–356. https://doi.org/10.1002/smj.2987

Chen, X.-P., Yao, X., & Kotha, S. (2009). Entrepreneur passion and preparedness in business plan presentations: A persuasion analysis of venture capitalists' funding decisions. *Academy of Management Journal, 52*(1), 199–214.

Chenhall, R. H. (2003). Management control systems design within its organizational context: Findings from contingency-based research and directions for the future. *Accounting, Organizations and Society, 28*(2–3), 127–168.

Chenhall, R. H., & Moers, F. (2015). The role of innovation in the evolution of management accounting and its integration into management control. *Accounting, Organizations & Society, 47*(1), 1–13.

Clear, J. (2018). *Atomic habits: Tiny changes, remarkable results.* New York, New York, Avery, an imprint of Penguin Random House.

Coad, A., & Reid, A. (2012). *The role of technology and technology-based firms in economic development: Rethinking innovation and enterprise policy in Scotland.* Technopolis Group.

Cooper, R. (2002). Target costing for new product development. *Journal of Cost Management, 16*(3), 5–12.

Cooper, R., & Kaplan, R. (1988). Measure costs right: Make the right decision. *Harvard Business Review, 66*(5), 96–103.

Cooper, R., & Kaplan, R. (1991). Profit priorities from activity-based costing. *Harvard Business Review, 69*(3), 130–135.

Cooper, R., & Slagmulder, R. (2004). Interorganizational cost management and relational context. *Accounting, Organizations and Society, 29*(1), 1–26.

Cost Definition. (2024 January 3). In AccountingTools *what is a cost?* https://www.accountingtools.com/articles/cost

Cost: Definition. (n.d.). In Finance Strategists. https://www.financestrategists.com/accounting/cost-accounting/cost-and-its-types/

Cugini, A., Carù, A., & Zerbini, F. (2007). The cost of customer satisfaction: A framework for strategic cost management in service industries. *European Accounting Review, 16*(3), 499–530. https://doi.org/10.1080/09638180701507130

Dabić, M., Vlačić, B., Kiessling, T., Caputo, A., & Pellegrini, M. (2023). Serial entrepreneurs: A review of literature and guidance for future research. *Journal of Small Business Management, 61*(3), 1107–1142. https://doi.org/10.1080/00472778.2021.1969657

Datar, S. M., & Rajan, M. V. (2021). *Horngren's cost accounting: A managerial emphasis* (17th ed., Global edition). Pearson

Drucker, P. (1969). *The age of discontinuity: Guidelines to our changing society.* Harper and Row.

Dushnitsky, G. (2010). Entrepreneurial optimism in the market for technological inventions. *Organization Science, 21*(1), 150–167. https://doi.org/10.1287/orsc.1090.0454

Duxbury, D. (2012). Sunk costs and sunk benefits: A re-examination of re-investment decisions. *The British Accounting Review, 44*(3), 144–156. https://doi.org/10.1016/j.bar.2012.07.004

Eisenmann, T. R. (2020). Determinants of Early-Stage Startup Performance: Survey Results. *Harvard Business School.* 21–057, 1–63. https://doi.org/10.2139/ssrn.3725023. Entrepreneurial Management Working paper.

Elkington, J. (1994). Towards the sustainable corporation: Win-win-win business strategies for sustainable development. *California Management Review, 36*(2), 90–100.

Elkington, J. (1997). *Cannibals with forks: The triple bottom line of 21st century business.* Capstone Publishing.

Fayard, D., Lee, L. S., Leitch, R. A., & Kettinger, W. J. (2012). Effect of internal cost management, information systems integration, and absorptive capacity on inter-organizational cost management in supply chains. *Accounting, Organizations and Society, 37*(3), 168–187. https://doi.org/10.1016/j.aos.2012.02.001

Felin, T., Koenderink, J., & Krueger, J. I. (2017). Rationality, perception, and the all-seeing eye. *Psychonomic Bulletin & Review, 24*(4), 1040–1059.
Gopalakrishnan, M., Libby, T., Samuels, J. A., & Swenson, D. (2015). The effect of cost goal specificity and new product development process on cost reduction performance. *Accounting, Organizations & Society, 42*(1), 1–11.
Graña-Alvarez, R., Gomez-Conde, J., Lopez-Valeiras, E., & González-Loureiro, M. (2024). Management control systems, business financial literacy and financial leverage in business-incubated start-ups. *The British Accounting Review*, 101427. https://doi.org/10.1016/j.bar.2024.101427
Grundy, T. (1993). Putting value on a strategy. *Long Range Planning, 26*(6), 151–151.
Grundy, T. (1996). Valuing business change. *Strategic Change, 5*(5), 287–298.
Hand, J. R. (2005). The value relevance of financial statements in the venture capital market. *The Accounting Review, 80*(2), 613–648.
Haskel, J., & Westlake, S. (2018). *Capitalism without capital: The rise of the intangible economy*. Princeton University Press.
Henderson, D. R. (2008). Opportunity Cost. In D. R. Henderson (Ed.), *The concise encyclopedia of economics*. Library of Economics and Liberty. http://www.econlib.org/library/Enc/OpportunityCost.html
Hsu, S. H., & Qu, S. Q. (2012). Strategic Cost Management and Institutional Changes in Hospitals. *European Accounting Review*, 21(3), 499–531.
Jaedicke, R., & Robichek, A. A. (1964). Cost-volume-profit analysis under conditions of uncertainty. *The Accounting Review, 39*(4), 917–926.
Johnson, M. J., Kim, K. H., Colarelli, S. M., & Boyajian, M. (2021). Coachability and the development of the coachability scale. *Journal of Management Development, 40*(7/8), 585–610. https://doi.org/10.1108/JMD-06-2020-0174
Jørgensen, B., & Messner, M. (2010). Accounting and strategising: A case study from new product development. *Accounting, Organizations & Society, 35*(2), 184–204.
Kaplan, R. S., & Norton, D. P. (2001). Transforming the balanced scorecard from performance measurement to strategic management: Part I. *Accounting Horizons, 15*(1), 87–104.
Kaplan, R. S., & Norton, D. P. (2004). How strategy maps frame an organization's objectives. *Financial Executive, 20*(2), 40–45.
Kaplan, R. S., & Norton, D. P. (2007). Using the balanced scorecard as a strategic management system. *Harvard Business Review, 85*(7/8), 150–161.
Koellinger, P., Minniti, M., & Schade, C. (2007). "I think I can, I think I can": Overconfidence and entrepreneurial behavior. *Journal of Economic Psychology, 28*(4), 502–527. https://doi.org/10.1016/j.joep.2006.11.002

Kumar, A., & Kumar, S. (2011). Strategic cost management–suggested framework for 21st Century. *Journal of Business and Retail Management Research, 5*(2), 118–130.

Kuratko, D. F., Neubert, E., & Marvel, M. R. (2021). Insights on the mentorship and coachability of entrepreneurs. *Business Horizons, 64*(2), 199–209. https://doi.org/10.1016/j.bushor.2020.11.001

Leach, C., & Melicher, R. (2021). *Entrepreneurial Finance* (7th ed.). Cengage.

Lee, M., & Cobia, S. R. (2013). Management accounting systems support startup business growth. *Management Accounting Quarterly, 14*(3), 1–17.

Leininger, W. (1977). Opportunity costs: Some definitions and examples. *Accounting Review, 52*(1), 248–251.

Lord, B. R. (1996). Strategic management accounting: The emperor's new clothes? *Management Accounting Research, 7*(3), 347–366.

Magretta, J. (2002). Why business models matter. *Harvard Business Review*, 80(5), 86–92.

Martin, J. (1990). Deconstructing organizational taboos: The suppression of gender conflict in organizations. *Organization Science, 1*(4), 339–359.

Marvel, M. R., Wolfe, M. T., & Kuratko, D. F. (2020). Escaping the knowledge corridor: How founder human capital and founder coachability impacts product innovation in new ventures. *Journal of Business Venturing, 35*(6), 106060. https://doi.org/10.1016/j.jbusvent.2020.106060

Mihm, J. (2010). Incentives in new product development projects and the role of target costing. *Management Science, 56*(8), 1324–1344.

Newbert, S. L. (2008). Value, rareness, competitive advantage, and performance: A conceptual-level empirical investigation of the resource-based view of the firm. *Strategic Management Journal, 29*(7), 745–768. https://doi.org/10.1002/smj.686

OECD. (1996). *The knowledge-based economy*. OECD.

Opportunity Cost. (n.d.). In Investopedia's online dictionary. Retrieved September 23, 2024 from https://www.investopedia.com/terms/o/opportunitycost.asp

Parhankangas, A., & Ehrlich, M. (2014). How entrepreneurs seduce business angels: An impression management approach. *Journal of Business Venturing, 29*(4), 543–564. https://doi.org/10.1016/j.jbusvent.2013.08.001

Ries, E. (2011). *The lean startup: How today's entrepreneurs use continuous innovation to create radically successful businesses*. Crown Publishing.

Petkov, R. (2020). Artificial Intelligence (AI) and the accounting function—a revisit and a new perspective for developing framework. *Journal of Emerging Technologies in Accounting, 17*(1), 99–105. https://doi.org/10.2308/jeta-52648

Pine li, B. J., & Gilmore, J. H. (1998). *The experience economy*. Harvard Business Press.

Porter, M. E. (1980). *Competitive strategy: Techniques for analyzing industries and competitors*. Free Press.
Porter, M. E. (1985). *The competitive advantage: Creating and sustaining superior performance*. Free Press.
Rockness, H. O., & Shields, M. D. (1994). Organizational control systems in research and development. *Accounting, Organizations and Society, 9*(2), 165–177.
Robb, C. C., Brownell, K. M., Brännback, M., & Rumi, S. (2024). Applying resource-based theory to social value creation: A conceptual model of contributive advantage. *Journal of Small Business Management,* 1–23. https://doi.org/10.1080/00472778.2024.2309498
Roslender, R., & Hart, S. J. (2003). In search of strategic management accounting: Theoretical and field study perspectives. *Management Accounting Research, 14*(3), 255–279.
Sage. (2021, October 7). *What is opportunity cost?—Sage advice Australia*. Sage Advice Australia. https://www.sage.com/en-au/blog/glossary/what-is-opportunity-cost/
Samuelson, P. (1967). *Economics: An introductory analysis* (7th ed.). McGraw-Hill.
Santos, F. M., & Eisenhardt, K. M. (2009). Constructing markets and shaping boundaries: Entrepreneurial power in nascent fields. *Academy of Management Journal, 52*(4), 643–671.
Sarasvathy, S. D. (2001). Causation and effectuation: Toward a theoretical shift from economic inevitability to entrepreneurial contingency. *Academy of Management Review*, 26(2), 243–263.
Sarasvathy, S. D. (2004). Making it happen: Beyond theories of the firm to theories of firm design. *Entrepreneurship Theory and Practice*, 28(6), 519–531.
Sarasvathy, S. D. (2008). *Effectuation: Elements of entrepreneurial expertise*. Northampton, MA: Edward Elgar.
Shank, J. K. (1989). Strategic cost management: New wine, or just new bottles? *Management Accounting Research, 1*(1), 47–65.
Shank, J. K. (1996). Analysing technology investments—from NPV to strategic cost management (SCM). *Management Accounting Research, 7*(2), 185–197.
Shank, J. K., & Govindarajan, V. (1989). *Strategic cost analysis*. Irwin.
Shank, J. K., & Govindarajan, V. (1992a). Strategic cost analysis of technological investments. *Sloan Management Review, 34*(1), 39–51.
Shank, J. K., & Govindarajan, V. (1992b). Strategic cost management: The value chain perspective. *Journal of Management Accounting Research, 4*(2), 179–197.
Shank, J. K., & Govindarajan, V. (1993). *Strategic cost management*. The Free Press.

Shetty, S., & Sundaram, R. (2020). Two heads are better than one: Multi-founder firms and quality signals to investors and acquirers. *International Journal on Emerging Technologies, 11*(3), 574–578.

Shields, M. D., & Young, S. M. (1994). Managing innovation costs: A study of cost consciousness behavior by R&D professionals. *Journal of Management Accounting Research, 6*(2), 175.

Sievers, S., Mokwa, C. F., & Keienburg, G. (2013). The Relevance of financial versus Non-financial information for the valuation of venture capital-backed firms. *European Accounting Review, 22*(3), 467–511.

Simmonds, K. (1982). Strategic management accounting for pricing: A case example. *Accounting and Business Research, 12*(47), 206–214.

Simon, M., & Shrader, R. C. (2012). Entrepreneurial actions and optimistic overconfidence: The role of motivated reasoning in new product introductions. *Journal of Business Venturing, 27*(3), 291–309. https://doi.org/10.1016/j.jbusvent.2011.04.003

Smith, J. A., & Cordina, R. (2014). The role of accounting in high-technology investments. *The British Accounting Review, 46*(3), 309–322.

Simons, R. (1987). Accounting control systems and business strategy: An empirical analysis. *Accounting, Organizations and Society, 12*(4), 357–374. https://doi.org/10.1016/0361-3682(87)90024-9

Simons, R. (1991). Strategic orientation and top management attention to control systems. *Strategic Management Journal, 12*(1), 49–62.

Taipaleenmäki, J. (2014). Absence and variant modes of presence of management accounting in new product development—theoretical refinement and some empirical evidence. *23*(2), 291–334.

Teece, D. J. (2009). *Dynamic capabilities and strategic management: Organizing for innovation and growth*. Oxford University Press.

Teece, D. J. (2010). Business models, business strategy and innovation. *Long Range Planning, 43*(2–3), 172–194.

Teece, D. J. (2012). Dynamic capabilities: Routines versus entrepreneurial action. *Journal of Management Studies, 49*(8), 1395–1401. https://doi.org/10.1111/j.1467-6486.2012.01080.x

Teece, D. J. (2014). The foundations of enterprise performance: Dynamic and ordinary capabilities in an (economic) theory of firms. *Academy of Management Perspectives, 28*(4), 328–352. https://doi.org/10.5465/amp.2013.0116

Ucbasaran, D., Westhead, P., Wright, M., & Flores, M. (2010). The nature of entrepreneurial experience, business failure and comparative optimism. *Journal of Business Venturing, 25*(6), 541–555. https://doi.org/10.1016/j.jbusvent.2009.04.001

Van Meeteren, M., Trincado-Munoz, F., Rubin, T. H., & Vorley, T. (2022). Rethinking the digital transformation in knowledge-intensive services: A technology space analysis. *Technological Forecasting and Social Change, 179*, 121631. https://doi.org/10.1016/j.techfore.2022.121631

Waßenhoven, A., Rennings, M., Laibach, N., & Bröring, S. (2023). What constitutes a "Key Enabling Technology" for transition processes: Insights from the bioeconomy's technological landscape. *Technological Forecasting and Social Change, 197*, 122873. https://doi.org/10.1016/j.techfore.2023.122873

Weick, K. (2015). Ambiguity as grasp: The reworking of sense. *Journal of Contingencies and Crisis Management, 23*(2), 117–123.

Welpe, I. M., Spörrle, M., Grichnik, D., Michl, T., & Audretsch, D. B. (2012). Emotions and opportunities: The interplay of opportunity evaluation, fear, joy, and anger as antecedent of entrepreneurial exploitation. *Entrepreneurship Theory and Practice, 36*(1), 69–96. https://doi.org/10.1111/j.1540-6520.2011.00481.x

What is a cost? (2024 January 3). In accounting tools' cost definition. https://www.accountingtools.com/articles/cost

What is cost? (n.d.). In Reviso accounting terms. https://www.reviso.com/cost/

What is Opportunity Cost? Definition of Opportunity Cost, Opportunity Cost Meaning—The Economic Times. (n.d.). The Economic Times. https://economictimes.indiatimes.com/definition/opportunity-cost

What does cost mean? (n.d.). In my accounting course definition of a cost. https://www.myaccountingcourse.com/accounting-dictionary/cost

Wood, M. S., Bakker, R. M., & Fisher, G. (2021). Back to the future: A time-calibrated theory of entrepreneurial action. *Academy of Management Review, 46*(1), 147–171. https://doi.org/10.5465/amr.2018.0060

CHAPTER 2

Costs and Entrepreneurial Startup Lifecycles—Early Stages

2.1 Introduction—The Entrepreneurial Startup Lifecycles

An entrepreneurial startup (ESU) by design means a startup company that develops a value proposition that is scalable, replicable, and growth oriented. This process is sometimes referred to as the *entrepreneurial journey* (McMullen & Dimov, 2013; Zaheer et al., 2022). Its characteristics are usually developing and executing innovative value propositions with a positive impact on tackling a business, social, environmental, technological, or legal/financial problem. Its ultimate mission is to be disruptive to existing markets or to create new ones, where it offers unique values to its stakeholders, customers, and users. With ESUs, founders' human capital is key to ESU's success. However, their focus has moved from founder-centric ideation to customer needs-centric, where they treat stakeholders as peers *providing resources and driving benefits* (Karami & Read, 2021; Van Le & Suh, 2019).

ESU's success is 100% dependent on its founding team's human capital, including its:

- Dynamic capabilities (Teece, 2009, 2012).
- Team's composition and diversity.

R. G. Chammassian, *Costs, Value, and the Entrepreneurial Venture Journey*, Palgrave Studies in Accounting and Finance Practice,
https://doi.org/10.1007/978-3-031-86216-8_2

- Functional capacities like technological and marketing skills, and financial literacy (Banal-Estañol et al., 2023; Eisenmann, 2020).
- Capabilities to develop relationships.
- Strategic thinking and abilities to grow the organization (Jiang & Murmann, 2023).
- Eventual decision-making structure depends on the lifecycle stage of the ESU (Tzabbar & Margolis, 2017).

Financing ESUs follows the same lifecycle stage logic with staged approaches. In earlier stages non-high-tech ESUs initially require lower external financing through friends, family, and fools (FFF), business angels, and from public and social sources (i.e., government grants and crowdfunding respectively). High-tech ESUs require much higher investment into costs in the early stages which is mostly related to human capital to develop the ESUs' value proposition. In mid to later stages, both types of ESUs need higher external financing, usually through private equity, commonly known as venture capital (VC), who invest in highly risky and unpredictable ESU projects in stages with the goal of an exit scenario for return on their investment (Lukas et al., 2016).

The ESU lifecycles begin with ideation in its development stage, followed by the Startup, survival, growth, and maturity (see Fig. 2.1 for an illustration).[1] These stages are like a video game where once one stage is successfully concluded, ESUs enter a new stage (in the game) with mostly different, bigger, and costlier challenges. Each of these stages has its unique characteristics, approaches, and cost challenges. The latter starts with assumptions that lead to operational planning, financial forecasting, and cash budgeting, determining investment milestones and financing requirements—all in that order. There are no certainties or guarantees of success or going from one stage to another. What is certain and guaranteed, however, is costs in all stages. At each stage, cost requirements and characteristics change to dramatically higher value (and associated risks) when ventures pivot, scale, and grow.

The only financial element that is guaranteed with entrepreneurial startups is costs!

[1] The ESU stages terminology is adopted from Leach and Melicher (2021) textbook, *Entrepreneurial Finance*.

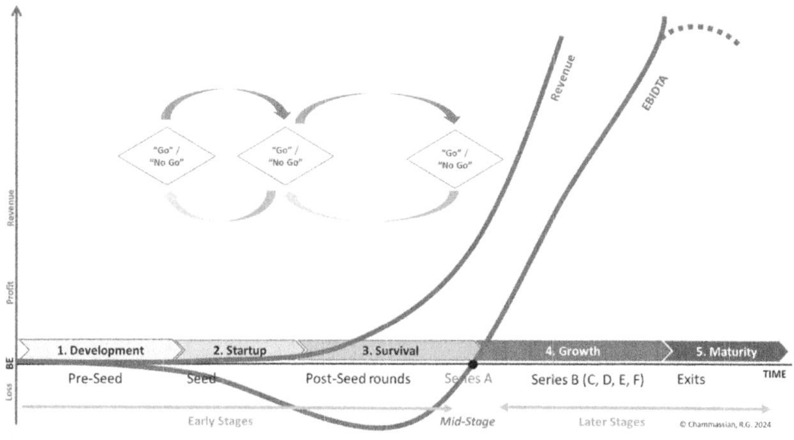

Fig. 2.1 Entrepreneurial startup lifecycle

One size does not fit all. There are no limits to time and timing as to when an ESU moves from one stage to the other. It all depends on the type of problem the ESU is solving, and the duration of development and execution. For instance, developing a value proposition with delivery of farm-to-table agricultural products will require less time and costs, than a technology-driven ESU specialized in hydrogen-powered fuel cell batteries. It also all depends on how well the ESU develops its value proposition through experimentation, learning, recalibration, pivoting, and executing. Moving from one stage to the other depends on the readiness, feedback from peers, advisors, and investors, and positive (or negative) signals from potential customers and the marketplace.

2.1.1 *Early Stages*

Development, Startup, and early Survival Stages are considered Early Stages with various seed rounds for financing. Early stages have the highest risk of failure, the least predictability, and higher reward or ROI expectations for investors. They are usually *net cash burn* stages. The strategic focus is on problem and impact definition, problem-solution fit through proof of concept and early customer acquisition (costs) to pilot. Costs play an enabling role (development to startup stages) and a mediating role (startup through survival stages) in new venture development. In early-stages, ESU entrepreneurs' relentless focus is on value creation through effectual logic (Read & Sarasvathy, 2005; Sarasvathy, 2001, 2004), experimentation, affordable loss, and flexibility, in pursuit of innovation (Deligianni et al., 2022) and intellectual capital development, consisting of human capital, organizational capital, social capital, and relational capital. "People and technology are one of the same in early-stage ventures, and people are the single-most important capital to invest in for ESUs" (Chammassian, 2016). That is why investors, such as business angels and venture capital firms, first and foremost invest in the people, the management team, and their dynamic capabilities, rather than the project, the product, or the technology (Gompers et al., 2020). Costs, specifically the cost of human capital, are perceived as an investment to create value and play a major strategic role in ESU's evolution, even though financial accounting-wise we expense people costs in the income statement as salary expense.

2.1.2 Mid Stages

Survival to the early Growth Stage is considered a mid-stage, referred to by its financing term as Series A, including some *pre-* or *post-Series A* periods. Survival is not simply having enough cash to cover costs. Survival very much depends on how the ESU is developing its growth path and attracting investors to finance this growth. In fact, *growth paths influence the survival* of ESUs (Coad et al., 2013). This mid-stage has a completely different set of requirements, which include developing replicable operations and revenue models while conducting continuous *simultaneous experimentation* (Andries et al., 2013), automated processes, and adopting 80–20 rules for sustainable growth. They are usually still in the net cash burn stages (i.e., sunk cost benefit), with higher cost to develop, invest in, and externally finance. Costs play a mediating role in value creation, capture, and future extraction through exits. The Time to take between stages depends on how well the venture has established a sustainable business model that is scalable, staged, replicable, and growth oriented. This depends on the type of business. For instance, biotech ventures take a much longer incubation period than an agrifood web-based platform business.

2.1.3 Late Stages

High Growth and Maturity Stages are considered as Late Stages with different and usually much higher financing requirements and rounds (i.e., referred to as *alphabet Series B, C, D, E* ...) to invest in growth-oriented costs, such as international expansion, new market and channel development, and scaling[2] into different industries. The leap from mid to later stages has vastly different cost assumptions and operational planning requirements, which entail completely different entrepreneurial mindsets and strategies to develop and execute. Most of the investments are in fixed costs in establishing new but replicable operations in different locations. While costs continue to play a mediating role in value creation in new venture development (NVD), they also play a moderating role in gross margin and operating profitability (i.e., EBIDTA) from gained economies of scale. Late stages carry different risks, although they are considered less risky than earlier stages with improved predictability due to replicable processes, better-understood cost run rates, established pricing mechanisms, and historical data. Later stages are closer to industrialized company approaches to cost assumptions, even though they still must remain highly innovative, disruptive, and competitive in the marketplace. ESU's ultimate goal is value extraction through an exit, either trade sales, merger, or initial public offering (IPO).

2.1.4 ESU Lifecycle Stages in Agricultural Terms

In entrepreneurship and entrepreneurial finance, we use a great deal of agricultural terminology when we describe entrepreneurial lifecycle stages. The developmental stage is sometimes referred to as the (pre- or post-) *seed stage*. Seeds (in this case, ideas) can be planted in a small pot incubated to grow into a seedling (i.e., ESU incubation), and then into a bigger plant pot with more soil to grow into a small tree (i.e., a startup to mid-/survival stage). Once the general conditions are favorable (i.e., soil, weather, and season), we then re-plant from the pot into a garden or orchard (i.e., mid-stage) so that it can grow into a bigger tree that will hopefully bear a great deal of fruit (i.e., Growth stage). In this growth stage, we expect to harvest and sell its fruits annually (i.e., revenue and profitability), and eventually find a buyer who would buy the orchard for

[2] For robust explanations and definition of scaling, see Coviello et al.'s (2024) work.

its productive trees and land for a high price (i.e., exit).[3] In this analogy, an ESU *farms* an entrepreneurial idea that can be:

- Transformed into a unique value proposition (UVP) through an innovative business model, creating and capturing value for its stakeholders, customers, and users.
- Scalable, replicable, and growth oriented.
- Investible to finance its development and growth with a good potential for return on investment (ROI).
- Profitable.
- Sellable to a larger company (i.e., exit through a trade sale, merger, or IPO), extracting real value through ROI for its investors, founders, and employees (i.e., wealth creation).

If the seed is not curated and planted properly, the seedling will not develop into a plant or a tree and will wilt away in a short time. This seed curation process is commonly known as ***an idea incubation*** where the founders are vigorously defining the real problem that the ESU is trying to solve, understanding its characteristics, its triple bottom line impact that is social, environmental, and economical (Elkington, 1994, 1997), the demand in the marketplace and customer needs, and the competitive landscape. Even if the small tree is re-planted into the garden, there is no guarantee that it will grow or bear fruit.

Through each of these lifecycle stages, we will cover the different characteristics, challenges and opportunities, development patterns, and cost considerations, such as monetary costs, opportunity costs, personal costs, sustainability, and triple bottom-line impact. This chapter focuses on the ESU's early lifecycle stages that have vastly different characteristics, approaches, activities and expectations, cost requirements and considerations, and risk factors.

[3] Refer to Fig. 2.1 for an illustration.

Takeaways

- Entrepreneurial startups (ESU) are scalable, replicable, and growth oriented by design.
- They go through various lifecycle stages during their entrepreneurial journey to develop and execute innovative value propositions with positive impact on their customers, users, and stakeholders.
- The founders' human capital and their dynamic capabilities are key to success.
- The ESU lifecycles begin with ideation in its development stage, followed by startup, survival, growth, and maturity stages.
- One size does not fit all, and there are no particular time and timing going from one stage to the other
    - Early stages include development, startup, and early survival.
    - The mid stage includes survival and early growth.
    - Late stages include fast growth and maturity.
- Costs play an enabling role in development to startup stages, mediating role in startup through survival stages, and mediating and moderating role in later stages.
- The terminology used to describe ESU lifecycle stages is similar to agricultural stages, from planting and incubating a seed (i.e., early-stage idea incubation), then into a bigger pot (i.e., mid stage) and eventually into the soil to reap its fruits (i.e., growth and harvest)

2.2 Early Stages—Developmental Journey

The Development stage is a pre-company startup stage where an idea is being screened through in-depth analysis, discovery, and iteration. The vast majority of ideas remain in the developmental stage of the ESU and do not (or should not) advance to the startup stage without critical analysis that is fundamental to the launch of an ESU, such as a comprehensive definition of the problem it is solving and prototyping. The funnel of choices and options is wide at the start, but it gets narrower over time as most options need to be crossed off and prioritized in order to develop an innovative business model. This is where ideas that do not pan out to be formidable in the marketplace would be shelved. The old Silicon Valley notion of "if you are to fail, fail early" very much applies here. It underlines that it is better to conclude on the shortcomings of the idea early in the ESU developmental process, rather than later in ESU lifecycle stages when more time, resources, and costs are required. Due to the highly experimental, exploratory, and iterative nature, this stage also has one of the longest lists of choices and decisions to make.

There are several characteristics, approaches, activities and expectations, financial and cost considerations, and risk factors. Table 2.1 summarizes these notions:

2.2.1 Characteristics of Developmental Stage

First and foremost, early-stage ESUs are very *founder based*. An ESU could have a single founder or a multi-founder team. There are pros and cons for each category. The pros of a single founder are individually driven, depending on the founder's vision, background, passion, drive, and entrepreneurial resilience. In theory, single founders should get things done quicker and have full control over decision-making on their own without having to discuss every action with anyone and build consensus with others. There is an early but limited opportunity to get things done. However, this eventually becomes a challenge as single founders (especially novices) usually lack specific skills, knowledge, and experiences to get everything done on their own. They would need support on topics that are not within their expertise. This becomes even more relevant when the single founders manage to move to another lifecycle stage and when the ESU needs financing. Workload and responsibilities become a major challenge. Investors usually prefer to work with a founding team rather than a single founder due to those cons.

Multi-founding teams are preferred, especially by investors (Shetty & Sundaram, 2020), since they espouse a diversity of complementary skills, expertise, experience, and knowledge. Cultural and gender diversity add another dimension of value since they complement to the diversity of thinking, planning, and work ethics. Ideally, decisions are made in consensus from brainstorming and feedback loops (Hmieleski & Ensley, 2007; Klotz et al., 2014). The workload is also divided amongst different founders with shared support dynamics. When one member is busy or not available (i.e., due to illness) or decides to leave the team to pursue another opportunity, another founding member can cover the work. The cons could be disagreements and *paralysis by analysis* leading to dysfunction and deadlock. Also, equity is usually divided amongst the founders and diluted. At times disputes arise on compensation and equity splits if

Table 2.1 Characteristics of the Developmental Stage

Characteristics	• Very founder-oriented (single or multi-founder) with no teams • Limited resources: financial, human, physical, technological • Flexible, agile, iterative and change oriented • Frugal with bootstrapping, usually with no revenue or income • Highly unpredictable and experimental
Approaches	• Lean startup with building, measuring, learning, and validation with incremental development • In depth problem and impact definition with metrics • Market demand and customer needs analysis • Competition analysis • Problem-solution fit options, including tech requirements • Seeking support through mentorship and advise
Activities and Expectations	• Developing unique and innovative business model • Testing markets with value proposition (products, services) • Proof of concept through attempted sales, customer acquisition, engagement, and feedback loop • Resource planning for the next stage: team, assumptions, operational and financial planning, cash and financing needs • Networking and building relationships • Fundraising options and type of investors to attract • Pitching to different audiences: incubators, accelerators, investors, customers, and other stakeholders for feedback
Cost considerations	• Lean, low financial costs with spending prioritization • Low/no fixed costs • Opportunity cost analysis of development, failure, Low personal opportunity cost of failure • Startup, human, technological, material assumptions • Cash management and burn rate, with sunk cost-benefit analysis
Risk factors	• High risk, high return expectations • Reputational • High failure due to no traction • Insufficient research, development, and planning: market/demand/customer analysis, capital/financial/cash, competitor analysis, team issues, legal/regulatory/statutory, underdeveloped BM, poor marketing/BD/customer acquisition, failure to pivot, poor prioritization/planning/execution • Inability to read positive vs. negative signals

one founder is perceived not to be committed to the work that is assigned. Finally, at times ESU multi-founders may have the same background, such as engineering or business only, leading to the lack of skills diversity and sometimes to *groupthink* (Klotz et al., 2014; West & Meyer, 1998). Ideally, multi-founder teams should have complementary skills, such as engineering, business development, and IT.

Although in the early stages, an ESU does not need to have a chief financial officer (CFO) or someone with a strong finance background, it is imperative that founders have the financial literacy (Eisenmann, 2020; Graña-Alvarez et al., 2024), and especially cost literacy, for a good understanding on how to:

1. Prioritize assumptions and make incremental development plans with scenarios.
2. Operationalize and calendarize those assumptions.
3. Determine the costs associated with those assumptions, and re-prioritize and incrementalize.
4. Develop financial plans (calendarized) with milestones to see when and how much cash is needed for operations, investment, and financing needs (usually external).
5. Monitor, control, and report those costs (and cash burn rates) through financial statements with actuals versus original forecasts.

I have seen time and again many talented and capable ESU founders ignoring the above or leaving the financials to the "bookkeepers" or "accountants" to manage them. Accountants and bookkeepers are professionals who only *process* financial transactions based on business activities. In other words, they do not manage strategies, inputs, plans, or budgets. The ultimate *accountability to own* the financial plans from input to actual output is the founders'. In fact, one of the biggest reasons why ESUs fail is due to financial mismanagement, whether running out of cash or being overoptimistic with their forecasts, or simply ignoring the entire process altogether as unimportant and leaving it to chance.

The founders have the ultimate accountability to financial plan ownership

Another major characteristic of early-stage ESUs is *limited resources*. It usually starts with limited financial resources, such as cash, revenue from sales, and early-stage investment. At early stages, the founder's own funds and possibly early-stage supporters, followers, and enthusiasts, such as family, friends, and fools (FFF), or through crowdfunding means, cover the needed *enabling cost*. At rare times, there may be a little revenue income when founders decide to sell a few units or to do side work (i.e., consulting) to generate cash, although the latter can be a distraction also.

In the early stages, ESUs have limited human resources to support them in their venture's development. Hence, they resort to *pro bono* sources for such services, such as mentoring in strategy, business modeling, legal and financial. Clayton (2024) has found that mentored ESUs perform better financially than non-mentored ones, even though there is no guarantee for ESU survival. However, such pro bono work has its limitations as they are short term and reduced to one-off support.

Limited resources also include physical resources, such as office space, warehouse, lab, or a workshop. To overcome these limitations, many early-stage ESUs resort to support organizations to overcome those limitations, such as incubators, startup hubs, university workshops, or innovation centers. There are many off-the-shelf common software that can be used, such as Microsoft Office Professional that can cover many of the desired tasks. On the technological side, there is no major need to buy or subscribe to expensive software or programmers. Universities and incubators may be good sources for certain software that founders can initially utilize.

Flexibility, agility, and iterative planning are also key characteristics of early-stage ESUs. This is due to the highly unpredictable and experimental state of being. It is essential to test, learn, and recalibrate as much as possible. As an old saying goes, ESU development never goes according to plan. At many intervals, there is also the *24–48-hour crisis*. This is when an event or a discovery can lead the founder to believe that the initial premises were completely wrong and off the mark, and it is pretty much over for the ESU. In most cases, within a short period (i.e., 24–48-hours) the *crisis* inevitably leads to finding alternatives and recalibrations that resolve the issue for the time being. It may also lead to pivoting to a different direction, business model design, and strategy (Dhir et al., 2024; Sala et al., 2022).

Financially, these stages with little or no income make founders to be more frugal with bootstrapping (Ries, 2011), by finding alternative ways to overcome the financial shortcomings. Key characteristics of being frugal at the developmental stage include:

- Define what is the core focus and spend on core activities that will give the ESU the most value for its proposition. Try to postpone or source non-core activities elsewhere.
- Get into the habit of building assumptions → calendarize operations → financial planning and cash budgeting → ID investment requirements → financing needs.
- Work with *ecosystem facilitators*, such as universities, incubators, and accelerators for support, networks, grants, mentoring, advising, and resources (i.e., legal, HR, R&D space).
- Leverage from open-source tools, free available services, and general business software such as MS Office and cloud services (i.e., AWS for early-stage startups).
- Barter services and negotiate with suppliers and service providers where you can. Ask for samples, discounts, and favorable payment terms. Find alternative solutions by bartering your specialized services with needed external services.
- Where needed, hire interns for specific functions (i.e., digital marketing, web design, supply chain) but try to compensate them somehow (not just with sweat equity). If you can't afford it, find a sponsor who would pay for the internship.
- Test markets, price points, and customer needs on a shoestring through social media, blogging, and simple partnerships, such as industry associations, university communities, incubators, and accelerator networks.
- Financially, avoid or minimize fixed costs, such as rent, office space, warehouse, hiring people, leasing cars, and maintain a 6–9-month rolling working capital when possible.
- Purchase very little inventory even if bulk purchases are more attractive. Initially developing value-driven products may be expensive. Even so, focus on high inventory turnover to prevent unnecessary cash outflow and inventory carrying costs to preserve working capital (Tatikonda et al., 2013).
- Always treat and prioritize costs as an enabler to create value or as a (sunk cost) benefit.
- Regularly/daily review and track costs, and compare them to the cash budget and cash flows (inflow vs. outflow)

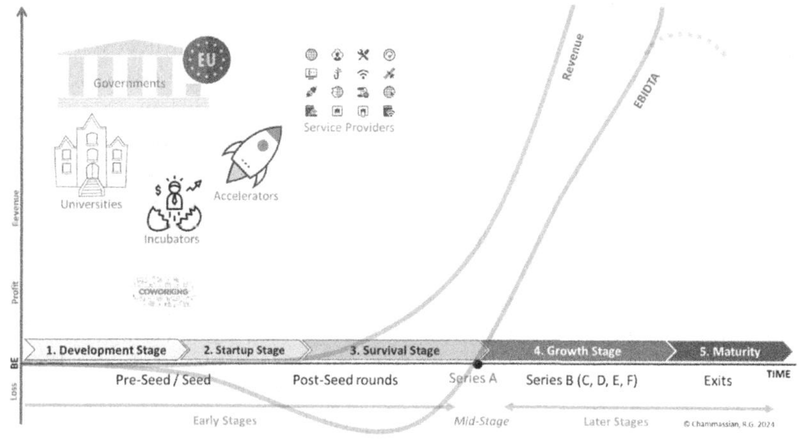

Fig. 2.2 Entrepreneurial ecosystem facilitators

As indicated above, there are many *facilitators* within the innovation and entrepreneurial ecosystem[4] for early-stage ESUs that provide technical and subsidized (sometimes free) support to founders willing to put together a project based on their ideas (Marcon & Ribeiro, 2021). There are also low-cost co-working spaces where founders can work from. As Fig. 2.2 highlights, these facilitators include the government with innovation programs, universities and their ecosystems, incubators, and accelerators (public and private), and some subsidized service providers, such as legal, accounting, marketing, and HR.

2.2.2 *Approaches*

At early stages, *lean* is the key word. Using lean methodologies to build, measure, learn, and validate with incremental development leads to *optimal pivoting* and *strong seed equity valuation growth* (Eisenmann, 2020; Ries, 2011). The goal is to eventually identify value propositions that are core to the ESU's business model grounded on the main problem the ESU is trying to solve. Experimentation, getting feedback,

[4] There is increasing focus on mapping entrepreneurial ecosystems, their performance and impact, such as the Startup Cartography Project https://www.startupcartography.com/ (Andrews et al., 2022).

and listening to signals (positive or negative) from advisors and potential customers, sometimes pivoting partially or 180 degrees, if necessary, help ESU founders to pitch their business models convincingly (Bojovic et al., 2018; Burnell et al., 2023; Hunt et al., 2024). Agility is key.

Sometimes founders get positive feedback from their closest peers, such as friends, family, and colleagues, who want to be supportive and encouraging. Although it is nice to hear these positive messages reinforcing what the founders also believe, they could be false-positive signals to watch out for. People may say they will buy what the ESU is selling just to be nice sometimes. This doesn't mean there is a real market for the ESU's value propositions when it comes to scaling. To avoid falling into this trap, there are many notable methods to discover, plan and design ESU's value proposition (Mansoori & Lackéus, 2020). Below are steps ESUs can follow to have a much better chance of advancing to the next stages.

1. **Problem Analytics**:
    - Have an intricate knowledge of the problem the ESU is solving and determine its impact on target customers, users, and stakeholders.
    - Literally draw a picture of the problem they are solving using *design thinking* (Brown, 2008; Liedtka, 2018).
    - Identify where the real issues or need-based customer pain points are with actual data to prove it.
    - Determine how the problem is addressed today and who are the players in the marketplace (i.e., competition analysis). How big is this problem and why it has not been addressed?
    - Who is impacted by this problem and what's in it for them if the problem is addressed or not? This leads to market, demand, and customer needs analysis.
    - Always review a problem multidimensionally. Our world has moved from a linear economy to a highly networked interconnected circular, sharing knowledge economy (Haskel & Westlake, 2018; OECD, 1996).
    - Reviewing the negative impact of the problem will lead the ESU to identify the social, environmental, and economic cost impact associated with it.
    - An example of this would be getting into hazardous locations or confined spaces to inspect cracks, leakages, or other damage.

This requires people to wear hazmat suits to get in and inspect such spaces:

- This is costly: it requires trained people and equipment, which is hazardous to health.
- It is inefficient: a person can only inspect with own vision so many hours at a location.
- It is ineffective: a person may not identify all issues that could be hidden, leading to missed problems.
- The social impact is the health and safety of workers.
- The environmental impact is missed problems leading to hazardous conditions in the future including environmental damage, leakages, and clean-up.
- The economic impact is the people's costs, the opportunity costs of failures and future mishaps, the technology is outdated and it's very people driven leading to human errors.

2. **Problem-Solution Fit:**

- Potential solutions should follow the narrative emerging from the problem analytics.
- For each identified problematic, there needs to be alternative solutions to address.
- Prioritization is key. What is the primary problem to focus on and how to address it with what solution(s)? How does this solution have a positive impact on the problem? What are the cost implications for the customer using this solution?
- What would be the incremental steps to solve the multi-layered problem? Incremental solutions are like targets with a bullseye: the center is the main priority or target, and the circles around the bullseye are the incremental solutions that are complementary.
- This leads to a multidimensional value proposition addressing the problem.
- Partnering with an early adopter to test the solutions, and seeking support from mentors, advisors, experts, and specialists are all part of the problem-solution development.
- To solve the problem, multidimensional solutions must be cost efficient and effective to both the customer and the ESU.

- With the above example, what ways can a company solve the issue of confined space entry and inspection that is efficient and effective with little direct human intervention?

3. **Technology:**

 Technology and digitalization are the highlights of the Industry 4.0 (Schwab, 2016) ESU business models, whether it is technology driven to solve a tech problem or technology mediated to solve a societal, environmental, or economic problem (Marcon et al., 2022).

Technology-driven ESUs are usually known as high-tech ESUs solving core *technological* problems through mainly R&D (Bailetti, 2012; Burmaoglu et al., 2019; Giones & Brem, 2017; Van Meeteren et al., 2022).

Technology-mediated ESUs are non-tech problem-driven where the problem-solution fit is mediated by technology and digitalization for improved efficiency and effectiveness. They use ***digital enabling technologies*** and ***application domains*** (or *general-purpose technologies*) as a means and mediator to solve non-tech problems more efficiently and effectively (Ancillai et al., 2023; Carroll, 2017; Coad & Reid, 2012; Van meeteren et al, 2022; Waßenhoven et al., 2023). These technologies either exist, are adopted, or adapted to the problem-solution fit. Examples include AI, social media, cloud computing, block chain, white-label online platforms, and hybrids.

Below are key characteristics of the role technology:

- Technology follows the same problem-solution logic to make the *fit* more time and cost efficient and effective for customers, users, and stakeholders.
- It could be newly developed, specialized technology, such as patentable innovation as the core tool solution to address the problem.
- It could also be existing (and multiple) technologies adopted for the purpose of solving the problem, where combined makes it unique in its value.
- Technology must be ***interactive***, ***communicative***, and ***adaptable***. This means that it needs to interface with other existing or new/latest

systems, interact with people, and communicate with various users and stakeholders.

- The *experience* of using the technology should espouse confidence and adoption by its customers, users, and stakeholders. This could be through web- and app-based platforms that are user-friendly.
- *Multidimensionality* is important, but *prioritization* and *incrementality* are what would make it investable and cost efficient.
- Following the example above, the problem-solution fit would be mediated by an encased secured drone imbedded with high-precision laser technology that can operate unhindered in confined spaces covering 360 degrees autonomously, while an operator in a safe and remote location watches over and monitors the results. Data is captured into analytic software that produces and distributes online reports to various affected parties via a web- and app-based platform
  - The social impact is dramatically improved health and safety for the operators.
  - Screening is much more accurate in identifying problems in advance where the human eye may not capture. This also leads to avoidance of future mishaps and positive environmental impact.
  - The economic impact is that the benefits outweigh its costs. The problem-solution-technology fit improves the efficiency of time use and problem detection and makes it a much more effective solution than the alternative.

2.2.3 Activities and Expectations

No one says being an entrepreneur is easy. When many novice founders start incubating their ideas, they realize that it is way more complex than they ever thought it would be. The *honeymoon period* of initial euphoria of *becoming an entrepreneur* disappears as founders grasp the realities that there is much more than the idea. The notion of being *totally independent* disappears as novice founders realize that they are both lonely and interdependent on others at the same time. They realize that there are activities that they need to follow and expectations of parties (i.e., stakeholders) that they never knew existed before. Experience and knowledge can be gained, and entrepreneurship can be learned (Neck et al., 2021). It takes openness, learning, humility, and appreciation to really understand what problem they are solving in the marketplace.

In my experience, the biggest reasons for failure at the developmental stage are:

- Inexperience of the founder(s) leading to stubbornness with limited exploration, openness to experimentation, and learning.
- The idea is *a solution in search of a problem* to be the next big concept, or the next Google or another "me too" product in an already overcrowded product marketplace with little or no competitive advantage.
- Improperly defined or undefined problem, market demand, and competitor analysis.
- Running out of cash due to mistiming, mis-planning, or overspending.

Following the approaches prescribed in the previous section, the *problem-solution-technology-impact* model would eventually lead to developing unique value propositions through innovative business models. It is imperative that the value propositions are viewed from the customers' perspective: *what's in it for them*? This perspective has become increasingly a key trend and will continue to do so, coupled with safety, security, and trust legitimacy (Van Le & Suh, 2019).

- What is unique about value proposition?
- How is the value measured from the customers' perspective (and not the ESUs) in terms of efficiency and effectiveness for the customers' key performance indicators (KPI)?
- How is that value proposed and in what ways?
  - What are the included products, services, and expected experiences for the customer?
  - What is the number one solution component that they would first propose and execute?
- What could follow as future developments to complement the initial value proposal from learned experiences? This is the multidimensional approach with prioritized incremental execution.

- How is the value propositions priced? What is the cost to the customer?

Reminder: revenue for the ESU is a cost to its customers

This would require testing markets with pilot projects with early adopting customers with value proposition with combined products, services, a median of delivery, installation, training and development, and ongoing services (i.e., warranties, maintenance, upgrades, remote diagnostics, and similar). The pilot projects allow direct customer engagement and feedback loop. They provide fine-tuning opportunities, fixing the bugs, addressing efficiencies, important customer KPI components, and time and timing issues, while identifying unique selling propositions (USP) for customer acquisition and associated costs.

These costs are both internal and external to the ESU. Internal ones are associated with customer acquisition costs (CAC), and resources needed to research, develop, test, and execute growth plans. They are very much assumptions driven, which are projections on what it will cost to do X versus Y. What benefits do these experimental sunk costs deliver? Which *sunk cost-benefit* will lead to a better understanding of the problem and how various solutions fit? Once these assumptions are put in place, they need to be operationalized through a calendarized plan:

- The estimated time it would take to get the jobs done.
- The estimated costs associated with those jobs.
- The estimated timing of when the costs will incur to determine the cash budget.
- What are investment milestones?
- Where would the cash (funds) come from to finance those investments? It is better to self-finance at this stage instead of soliciting from external sources. However, many founding teams do not have the necessary financial resources to finance these costs. Hence, they resort to external sources for financing, especially high-tech-driven ESUs.

Assumptions are estimations at this stage since there is no real historical data to develop and/or improve upon past run rates. In the later stage, assumptions become easier since there would be experiences, and historical run rates to learn from and forecast.

Resource planning is mainly associated with human capital or labor. Even experienced and talented founders need specialized support, such as web design, digital marketing, supply chain, and financial planning. Almost everything ESU founders plan to do, they need to take into consideration the impact of emerging technologies on their strategies, such as digital marketing whether B2B or B2C (Rizvanović et al., 2023). People-related questions that come up are: would we hire someone full-time or part-time? Would we bring in another co-founder for a critical function in exchange for sweat equity? Should we outsource this task? In all cases, early-stage ESU founders should refrain from having fixed labor costs until they are certain to on-board such people. A good option would be to hire qualified, talented, and motivated interns from universities, either from undergraduate or graduate programs depending on the complexity and nature of the task at hand. Interns are a great resource. They bring alternative perspectives, approaches, and experiences to the ESU. They are also inexpensive. I always suggest paying interns at least a minimum wage to cover their living expenses and to keep them motivated. Otherwise, they can leave quickly if they find paid work somewhere else. A good intern could also become a future employee or even a co-founder of the ESU.

Another critical internal cost consideration is customer acquisition costs (CAC). This is a holistic and super critical metric to develop for early-stage ESUs (Ang & Buttle, 2006). CACs cover all costs associated with the acquisition of a customer, whether direct, indirect, or opportunity costs (Min et al., 2016). They include:

- Calculated selling costs, such as direct cost of sales (i.e., cost of goods/services sold) for margin determination, and indirect cost of labor, marketing, advertising, overhead, and out-of-pocket expenses (i.e., travel and accommodation if any).
- Calculated timeframe to acquire a customer (i.e., days and months).
- Number of new customers acquired with X number of resources and Y costs.
- Profitability margin compared to revenue generated per customer.
  - Early-stage ESU costs usually have a higher CAC due to experimentation.

  - How would economies of scale improve this margin?
  - This is a critical factor that potential investors question and scrutinize to determine the efficiency, scalability, and growth of the ESU's business model.

- Comparison to industry benchmarks critical to which industry and competition the CAC is compared to short- versus long-term.
- Markets, channels, customer segments, and target personas to determine.
  - Where to focus on and who to target?
  - What customer segments give the best proof of concept results?
  - What are the best channels to use or needed to reach the targeted customers, and how to optimize these channels to get the lowest CAC? Channels include social media, network referrals, email campaigns, and industry events to name a few.
  - Who is the buyer or the decision maker for direct targeting?
  - What are the current market conditions and forecasts, such as the competition, current and future economic projections, and technological developments?
- Customer acquisition and retention rates. For instance:
  - What is the percentage of customers that visit the website to purchase products?
  - How many new customers become long-term customers?
  - How do we retain customers for our services, short- vs. long-term, either as a repeat buyer or moving from a one-time service revenue to a recurring revenue model?
- Tools and metrics that track and measure performance for continuous improvement as well as the customer lifetime value (CLV) to predict how much revenue would a customer generate during its relationship with the ESU (Dandis et al., 2022).

CAC calculations very much depend on the type of industry, customer the ESU is addressing, its market position, and competitive landscape (Min et al., 2016; Voss & Voss, 2008). They include industry purchasing frequency, product/service lifespan, and length of sales cycle as examples. A manufacturing company, a technology company, and a consumer goods company have vastly different customer acquisition sales cycles and lifespans. For instance, an online shop for grocery delivery is vastly different than selling industrial drones. There are many CAC online tracking tools and software available to use. Some of them are free with limited features; others are subscription based. In either case, in the early stages, to stay frugal, using an Excel spreadsheet or a freemium online tool should suffice. A simple formula for CAC calculation is (per above definition):

$$\frac{\text{Direct costs of product/services sales} + \text{Indirect costs of sales and marketing}}{\text{Newly acquired customers}}$$

During customer acquisition, product/service prototyping, working with suppliers, and resource planning, ESUs build and maintain networks and relationships with potential customers, suppliers, investors, industry insiders, experts, and organizations (i.e., universities, research institutes, incubators, and accelerators), stakeholders and users, sometimes referred to *social networks*. These networks are essential for ESU survival (Song et al., 2021). They not only provide a way to test, learn, and improve upon the ESUs value proposition but also to build strong networks that can eventually be converted into social capital and relational capital (as stated earlier and covered more in detail in Chapter 4). Such networks are critical in developing intangible firm value during the new venture development and will extract higher acquisition valuation during an exit scenario.

ESU founders also spend a tremendous amount of time attending conferences, pitching to different audiences, and fundraising. This opportunity time spent takes a tremendous toll on the founders' availability to focus on their business. As *time is money*, many founders do not realize and appreciate how long it takes to go out and build networks by pitching, networking, and talking to people for feedback and leads. If founders are trying to fundraise at the developmental stage with no real proof of concept, customers, or any revenue, they must be laser-sharp on building their narratives to be convincing.

2.2.4 *Cost Considerations and Risk Factors*

Each of these stages have its unique considerations, approaches and cost challenges that start with assumptions, then lead to operational planning, financial forecasting and cash budgeting, investment milestones, and financing requirements—all in that order. The developmental stage for non-high-tech ESUs is the leanest cost stage where it has the lowest financial costs with a very high spending prioritization. Bootstrapping is key to keeping costs low, including using any open-source and free or low-cost tools, products, and services, working from home, or using a co-working space. In other words, it is a stage that should have very low (if no) fixed costs and inventory levels to avoid unnecessary cash burn or sunk costs with little benefit, or cash tied up on unnecessary inventory.

The developmental stage may have a lower personal opportunity cost of failure. That means, if the founders fail to advance their ESU from this stage, they can recover from this failure easier than at later stages since they won't have a large, incurred costs (except for sunk costs using their personal savings), major liabilities, or debt to others (i.e., investors and suppliers), and don't have to lay off employees. They don't have to liquidate a company, which takes further time and money. However, they do have a very high opportunity cost if they do not conduct the proper analytics and identify the right calculated trajectory when moving to the next stage.

The personal reputational risk of failure depends on the national culture the founders are working in. For instance, in the US failure is tolerated much more (and at times celebrated) because it denotes entrepreneurial learning and experiences. Whereas in Europe, failure may not be an option or tolerated as much: once failed, people may not take you seriously the next time, although there is a slow shift in mindset towards more tolerance in this regard. Taking risks is important. *If one does not take risks, one does not grow*. An entrepreneurial venture is a risk-taking endeavor, where high risks and high rewards go hand in hand.

High risk of failure usually occurs due to insufficient research, development, financial planning, and business modeling. Many studies have identified different reasons why startups fail. A much-quoted study conducted by CBinsights[5] (2022) suggests the top two reasons why startups fail[6] are lack of financing/investors (47%) and running out of cash (44%). Although this takes into account startups in all stages, financial issues remain the top reason of the three main clusters why startups fail. Most financial issues relate to underestimated and over-exposed cost

[5] https://www.skynova.com/blog/top-reasons-startups-fail.

[6] Excluding the one-time Covid-19 pandemic reason failures.

models, whether it is optimistic forecasting, overspending on or unnecessary fixed costs, underestimating time, and timing of business launch. In the developmental stages, although running out of cash could be a reason for failure, it has also to do with problem-solution fit, lack of market or demand, unrecognized competition oversight, or bad timing. Another intangible reason is related to people or team issues, such as not having the right team or limited talent, and the inability to read positive vs. negative signals. However, in all cases, underestimated and overspent costs with no financial backing or investment planning play a pivotal role in early-stage startup failure.

2.2.5 *Costs and Financial Statements*

Many early-stage ESU founders I encounter, mentor, and advise really struggle with forecasting and planning for financials. They are sometimes in denial. They believe that it is not important, or the responsibility lies with their bookkeeper or tax accountant to take care of reporting and forecasting. They do not take it seriously. That is, until they realize that they are running out of cash or need external financing in some shape or form to develop and go to market. Lack of financial (especially cost) literacy, basics to understanding financial KPIs, and planning are part of the top reasons why startups fail in addition to no market need for their solutions.

A business and especially an ESU is like a sport. To play any sport, one needs to understand what the rules are, be or get in shape, and know how scoring works. To play the game of business, besides the basic rules of business (i.e., understanding customer needs), one needs to understand how scoring works in business. That scoring in business and with startups is usually conveyed and measured through the three financial statements as a scoreboard, which is about *accountability than financial accounting*. Understanding how cost mechanics work in relations to cash, forecasting, and management reporting is key to financial literacy, a highly desired and required functional skill set (Eisenmann, 2020; Graña-Alvarez et al., 2024).[7]

[7] I strongly recommend that ESU founders spend some time understanding the basics of management accounting and finance for non-finance business professionals. This would include a clear understanding of how the three financial statements work. How financial

Costs are omnipresent throughout the ESU stages, even though they have different meanings. In the early stages, they are enablers and sometimes mediators to value creation and should be treated as a *benefit* to sunk costs. At mid stage, costs are mediators of ESU value creation and capture. Whereas in later stages, costs play a moderating role in profitability and a mediating role of firm-value capture and extraction. However, they are not *reported* as such (i.e., *enabler, mediator, and moderator of value*) in internationally accepted standard financial reports.

To start with, financial statements and reporting are outputs of business activities transacted (or processed) through financial accounting. In other words, financial transactions are a by-product of business transactions that are divided into three main activities: operating, investing, and financing. Their financial *output depends* upon business transaction *inputs*. If the inputs are not understood or controlled well, outputs will follow the input logic. It is the *garbage-in, garbage-out* scenario.

Fig. 2.3 Cash inflow and outflow

As Fig. 2.3 suggests, cash *inflows* with revenue and financing are required to plan for cost planning and eventually incurring costs which result in cash *outflows*. Cash requirements are directly linked to cost requirements. The earlier ESU founders comprehend this basic notion, the better it is to control, plan, measure, and improve upon in the future. In other words, when it comes to costs, they need to be constantly reviewed and assessed in parallel to the building, measuring, learning, validation, recalibration, prioritization with incremental development of the business.

Cash in-flows with revenue and financing
(the project), and out-flows with costs.

Cash requirements are directly linked to costs.

transactions are a by-product of business transactions that are divided into three main activities that are operating, investing and financing.

The biggest strategic objective of ESUs is to create, capture, and extract firm value.

- To create value, ESUs have to develop the problem-solution-technology-impact narrative into a value proposition that satisfies customer needs and is scalable and replicable. Costs are enablers and mediators of value creation.
- To capture value, ESU founders must generate revenue with good margins and low fixed costs to be profitable. They must understand that revenue for their ESU is a cost to their customers. Therefore, the best way to calibrate revenue (i.e., pricing) is to clearly understand how much efficiency, productivity improvement, savings, and positive impact their value proposition is creating for their customers. So, value capture must be customer centric than ESU centric. Costs play a mediating role for the customer and ESU firm value capture and a moderating role for profitability for both.
- To extract value is to plan and get a high return on investment (ROI) or net worth for the future during an exit event, such as a trade sale or acquisition, merger, or IPO. It is a common knowledge and acceptable principle within the entrepreneurial and venture capital world that the vast majority of wealth for an ESU is created at exit—at times over 90%. Hence, exit determination, exit-driven business models, and exit mindset must begin at the early stages (see Chapter 5 for more details on the three-dimensional business models). Costs as a long-term investment have a mediating effect on value extraction at exit.

In the early stages, financial forecasting and tracking is usually handled in a spreadsheet even though the official *general ledger* may be maintained by an external bookkeeper for statutory reporting purposes. These spreadsheet-based forecasts act as cash statements in earlier stages, especially when value propositions lead to product development is involved in a highly competitive environment. More formalized financial projections are needed for sales forecasts when cost investments are in R&D and intangible for tech-driven ESUs, especially when ESUs require competitive analysis scaling and external financing (Cassar, 2009).

All financial transactions incurred are recorded in a source database (i.e., the general ledger). From this database, different reports and financial statements are generated for different target audiences: one set for management and other financial stakeholders, and another set for statutory/tax reporting purposes. The data source is the same. The report formatting is different. ESU founders need to understand the difference between the two and should be mainly concerned about the management-reported statements in the form of the balance sheet,[8] the income statement,[9] and the statement of cash flows.[10] Figure 2.4 illustrates the differences between financial accounting (associated with the past), managerial accounting (associated with the future), and the role of ESU accountability.

As the development stage is the earliest, most frugal, lowest cost, and least transaction-oriented stage of the ESU's lifecycle, it is very limited as to what is reported and where. However, there are still basics to consider and to start planning from the start. Since at this stage usually, there is no legal entity established (except for some high-tech ESUs), technically

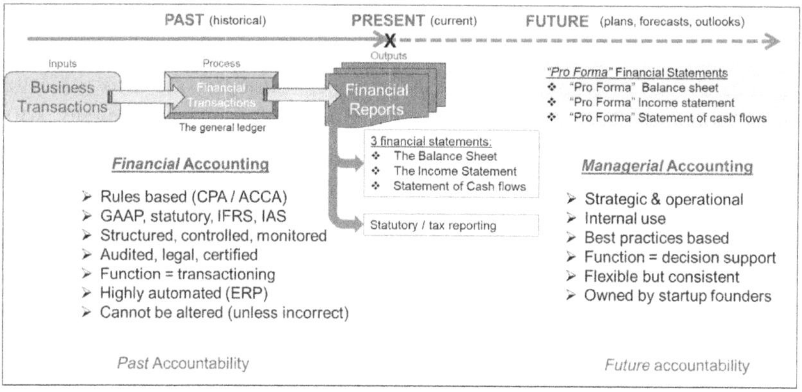

Fig. 2.4 Accounting and accountability basics

[8] Referred to as *statement of ownership*: what is owned by the ESU and what is owed to whom (i.e., suppliers, customers, employees, lenders and shareholders).

[9] Sometimes referred to as *profit and loss (P&L) statement* or the *statement of earnings* where revenue and expenses are recorded.

[10] Inflows and outflows from operating, investing, and financing activities.

there are no financial transactions to record and report. However, sunk costs incur at the founders' own expense (i.e., out of pocket) which are not recoverable. Founders need to start planning as to what to include in their forecast if/when their problem-solution-technology-impact analysis leads them to conclude to move to the next stage of the ESU's venture, which is the startup stage. This is also a good time to learn about how the financial statements work. Below is a short list of what to learn, understand, plan, and forecast for the next (startup) stage:

1. The Balance Sheet: technically there should be very little to forecast in the balance sheet except for the following:
   a. *Working Capital* is the difference between *current* or *operating assets* and *current* or *operating liabilities*. In simple terms, the liquid funds (i.e., cash and equivalent) that are needed and should be available to the startup to run day-to-day operations and to cover any short-term expenses. On a *net working capital* basis (operating assets minus operating liabilities), this must be a positive number. Based on the operating financial plans, founders must determine how much net cash they need to have and maintain for the next 6–9 months on a rolling basis to survive.
   b. *Owner's Equity* is the initial amount founders put into the legal business to start the company. Each country has a legally stipulated minimum amount for the type of company established. It also includes a supporting document called *capitalization* or *cap tables* on how the ESU's shares or *shareholdings* are divided amongst the founders and other shareholders as ownership percentages.
   c. *Non-Current Assets and Liabilities* are usually non-existent for majority of early-stage ESUs, except for high-tech startups which may include intellectual property (IP) and possible external investments or *convertible loans* from the start.
2. The Income Statement is the most actively used statement by founders. It determines ESU's profitability (i.e., revenue, margin, and operating income). To forecast for the startup stage, it usually includes assumptions that are calendarized to determine operating expenses, and eventually when the first revenue will be earned along with its associated cost of sales.

a. *Revenue* should be forecasted on a *net basis*, which is *gross sales* minus projected returns and allowances. This line is sometimes referred to as *net sales* or *net revenue*. VAT should be excluded from revenue reporting. Revenue should be forecasted based on *the price x quantity* of a particular type of sales product or services, calendarized over 12 months. It is imperative that *pricing* corresponds to customer expectations, and considers additional charges related to potential credit card fees, commissions, discounts, and included transportation costs, for instance.

b. *Cost of Revenue* is the direct costs associated with revenue. If there is no sales or revenue, there is no cost of sales. Each product and service has its own unique cost of sales.

   i. *Cost of goods sold* includes all direct costs associated to acquiring the product or manufacturing it. If the product is purchased as an inventory, then it would include the purchase costs and freight-in (shipping and handling costs incurred to ship the product into the company warehouse). If the ESU manufactures the product, then it would include direct material and labor costs, manufacturing overhead (i.e., utilities, maintenance, and repairs), freight-in and storage costs related to raw materials, and work-in-progress goods.

   ii. *Cost of services* would include all direct labor, materials and supplies, and travel expenses to deliver a particular service.

c. *Selling, General, and Administrative Expenses (SG&A)* are usually the main line considered as operating expenses. However, eventually, ESU founders must break this line down into detail levels (i.e., itemized by department) as to how the total is made up.

3. Statement of Cash Flows is a by-product of the balance sheet and the income statement whose figures are divided into three activities: operating, investing, and financing. However, *cash budgeting* is more important in the early stages than the statement of cash flows, which is used more in the late stages by investors and for trade sales valuations. *Cash budgeting* is dependent on the calendarized and line-itemized revenue and expenses. The timing of cash inflows and outflows are the most important aspects of cash budgeting. For instance, a company can recognize revenue in month 1, but receive cash payment in month 3. On the other hand, they could

have prepayment on a project in month 1, whereas the revenue is recognized in month 6 when the total services are delivered.

High-tech ESUs may require larger sums for investment in their projects during the startup stage. These costs are mainly associated with R&D, which is mostly people driven. For non-high-tech ESUs, most of the time the founders cover the initial capital to develop their projects. Even though funding requirements may be low for non-high-tech ESUs, there are still opportunities to get some funding support through FFFs, government programs (i.e., national or federal, European Innovation Fund), foundations with grants (i.e., private or public), incubators and accelerators (i.e., private, corporate, and public/university), funding platforms of various types (i.e., crowdfunding, crowdlending, business angel), business angels, and some early-stage venture funds. Figure 2.5 illustrates the different entrepreneurial ecosystem investors.

Eventually, a decision must be made to "go" or "no-go" with the venture to the next phase. This is dependent on several aspects, including:

- If the project is deemed to have a good problem-solution-technology-impact narrative which could lead to a unique value

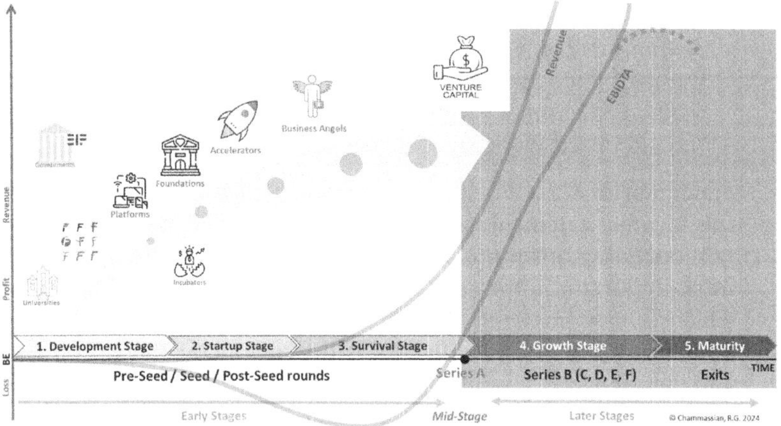

Fig. 2.5 Entrepreneurial ecosystem investors

proposition with an innovative business model; that could be scalable, replicable, and growth oriented even though this would be tested over again in the next stages.

- The financial forecasts make sense, directly relate to and tie to the narrative.
- There is sufficient cash to cover the ESUs costs in the coming 6–9 months on a rolling basis, including the startup costs and monthly running expenses. This initial cash to start with usually comes from the founders' own funds.

Takeaways

- Developmental stage is pre-company setup stage where many choices are screened, the real problem is defined with demand/customer needs and competition analysis.
- It is (and ought to be) the least costly stage to invest in or fail.
- Multi-founder teams and their diversity in complementary skills, expertise, experience, knowledge, culture and gender will make a positive difference.
- Financial (and especially cost) literacy is a must to have by at least one founder.
- The founders have the ultimate accountability to (besides ownership of) the ESU's financial plans.
- ESUs have very limited resources, including financial and physical. They must be frugal with a lean startup mindset and utilize subsided ecosystem facilitators.
- Flexibility, agility, and iterative planning are key requirements and characteristics as "nothing goes according to plan..."
- Steps to take to develop the idea: define the problem (with analytics), identify the problem-solution fit, and mediating technologies leading to a positive triple bottom-line impact.
- Once the above is defined, then a business model emerges with unique value propositions that are customer centric: what's in it for them.
- Business is like a team sport. To play a team sport, one needs to understand how scoring works (besides knowing the rules of the game, being in shape, and being a team player). To play the game of business, one needs to understand how scoring works in business, which is mainly conveyed through financial statements as its scoreboard.

- At this stage, the most important financial statement items are working capital on the balance sheet (6–9 months' worth of net cash); net revenue, cost of revenue and selling, general and administrative expenses (SG&A) as operating expenses on the income statement; and cash budgets based on the previous two statements.
- The founders cover most of the costs at this stage. There are, however, different investors who may support it, such as public investors (i.e., universities, government programs, incubators, accelerators, and some foundations) and private investors (i.e., incubators, accelerators, foundations, platforms, business angels, and early-stage VCs).

2.3 Early Stages—The Startup Stage Is a Serious Endeavor

The Startup Stage has its own characteristics. First and foremost, it denotes that the founder(s) made the decision *to go ahead* with the idea validated in the Developmental Stage and incorporate it into a startup legal company. Excluding high-tech startups, it is highly advisable to go through the developmental stage suggestions before incorporating them into a company. If not, then founders are still bound to do the required preliminary work under a company name with a higher recurring fixed cost environment leading to pressure to move faster due to cash flow constraints. Starting a company costs time and money, and requires having a physical address with overhead costs, required tax, social and health insurance implications, and other *costly surprises*.

High-techs startups operate under different circumstances and need to incorporate into a company at their Developmental Stage for several reasons. First, their incubation period is generally much longer than non-high-tech ESUs since they are heavily R&D-driven rather than purely social, environmental, or business problem-driven. Second, they require larger sums of investment from the get-go to conduct further R&D, with the need to hire high-salaried engineers and scientists. Hence, they need major external financing sources. Third, IP is best protected under a legal entity. For instance, a university-developed technology transfer through an IP can only be transferred into a legal entity or a company and not to a person. Universities have a short period to transfer or spinoff the IP, usually within two years.

At the Startup Stage, there are several characteristics, approaches, activities and expectations, financial and cost considerations, and risk factors. Table 2.2 summarizes these notions:

All the assumptions made in the Developmental Stage are brought into the legal company at the Startup Stage, tested in the marketplace under a company and brand name, re-defining the value proposition and its business model based on feedback received from the marketplace.

2.3.1 Characteristics of the Startup Stage

The Startup Stage is a *formalization of the Developmental Stage* in the format of a legal entity company. It means that the initial market demand research and value proposition development has been somewhat achieved successfully, and the founders have reasonably educated confidence that the idea could work, and now it should be transformed into a formal project.

What denotes the beginning of this stage is the formation of a legal entity (i.e., a company). First, it adds a positive perception in the marketplace as being a serious business. Second, incorporating the ESU as a legal entity provides protection to the idea, business, and its value proposition, the innovation (especially IP, such as patents, copyrights, and brands), and shareholders' rights. Finally, it is necessary for scalable and high-growth ESUs that require external financing from business angels and VCs with the goal to exit through trade sales or M&A (Cotei & Farhat, 2018). Once the company is incorporated, the real cost ticker starts with initial setup and then monthly recurring costs of maintaining a company.

Generally, there are two commonly used legal entity formats throughout the world for an ESU to incorporate such as a Limited Liability Company (LLC) and a share corporation. They have different names and acronyms in different countries, but their principal meaning is the same (see Table 2.3). Which legal entity to select depends on its developmental state, readiness to test-launch value propositions or still in need of further R&D, financial plans, external financing requirements and the type of investors the ESU seeks, and the timing of financing needs.

Before deciding which form to utilize and incorporate as a company, it is important to consider several legal, strategic, and financial aspects. ESU founders should consult with professionals (i.e., accelerators, legal and tax

Table 2.2 Characteristics of the startup stage

Characteristics	• A newly incorporated legal company • Founder-owner focused (single or multi-founders) • Limited resources: financial, human, physical, technological • Flexible, agile, iterative, and pivoting • Frugal with some bootstrapping, with no or little revenue • Somewhat unpredictable and untested
Approaches	• Lean startup continues with new company development • Building, measuring, learning, and validation with incremental development of core business value proposition • Further market demand and customer needs analysis • Developing and prioritizing marketing channels • Developing problem-solution fit, including tech requirements • Seeking further expertise
Activities and Expectations	• A legal company with a name and possibly a brand • A public presence through a website and social media • Testing marketing with value proposition (products, services) • Proof of concept development through some sales/ customer acquisition, engagement, and feedback loop • Business model development, validation, and re-design • Resource acquisition: team, equipment, office space • Social/business networking and building relationships • Seed fundraising (FFF, accelerators, business angels, some VCs) • Pitching to different audiences: incubators, accelerators, investors, customers, and other stakeholders

(continued)

Table 2.2 (continued)

Cost considerations	• Startup costs: company setup, office rental, and initial equipment • Lean operations, minimal recurring cash fixed costs • Cost assumptions on human, technological, and material • Forecasting and spending prioritization • Cash management and burn rate, with sunk cost-benefit analysis • Costs as an enabler and mediator of value creation
Risk factors	• High risk, high return • Reputational • High failure rate due to insufficient testing, validation of market fit, and running out of cash

Table 2.3 Limited liability company and share corporations

Country	*Limited liability company*	*Share corporation*
United States	LLC	C Corp or S Corp
UK	Ltd	PLC
Australia	Pty Ltd	Ltd
Germany	GmbH	AG
France	SARL	SA
Italy	SRL	SpA
Spain	SL	SA
Norway	AS	ASA
Sweden	AB	AB
Switzerland	SarL/GmbH	SA/AG
Netherlands	BV	NV
Singapore	Pte Ltd	Ltd
Japan	GK	KK

advisors) to determine which legal format is best suited. It is also important to comprehend state or country-specific guidelines to determine which jurisdiction to choose from.

LLC Pros: they are easier to set up and require less paperwork, fewer startup and ongoing formalities, compliance requirements, record keeping, and mandatory shareholder meetings. It requires less initial capital to start an LLC. They are very owner focused. That means, it is made up of one to three owners whose names are part of the company registry. It has a flexible management structure, which can be owner-managed or run by professional managers who may not necessarily be owners. Taxation can be either pass-through to individual owner's personal tax returns or taxed as a company depending on the setup and national jurisdiction.

LLC Cons: It offers a limited number of ownerships. It is not flexible when it comes to ownership changes. Every time a new shareholder comes, the process can lead to going through the *company's registry* of the local jurisdiction with the necessary use of a notary. That means, it is not investor and share-sales friendly.

Corporation Pros: It is multi-shareholder oriented, and shares can be bought and sold on a *Shareholder Register* that does not have to go through the *company's registry* or other formalized state administrative procedures. That means corporations are investor and share-sales friendly, preferred by business angels and venture capitalists. It is easier to issue various classes of stock, notably *common shares* or *preferred shares*, and the potential for partial or full IPOs.

Corporation Cons: It is more cumbersome to set up and maintain with stricter regulatory requirements and compliance with mandatory reporting requirements, annual meetings and periodic formalities, and detailed record keeping. It is also more expensive to set up with a much higher initial capital requirement.

Once the decision is made which legal form of a company to use for the ESU, the initial capital must be secured and guaranteed by its owners (usually founders for LLCs) or shareholders (founders, investors, and other shareholders for corporations) with a designated number of shares allocated between the parties according to their agreement. With corporations, initial shareholders could be founders (primarily), in-kind shareholders (i.e., university tech transfer offices, incubators, accelerators, and advisors), and cash-for-equity investors (i.e., business angels, some accelerators, some early-stage venture funds). In the case of a corporation, when different investors come in, the share valuation and number of share changes are managed through the *cap tables*. See more on investment types below.

Regardless of the type of the company, the ESU is still founder-focused at the Startup Stage. The company and founder(s) are one of the same in the eyes of ESU ecosystem players, especially investors, even if there is now a new company name.

ESU founders in the Startup Stage need to remain open minded. Flexibility, agility, and iterative incrementality still play a substantial role in this Stage. Except that, these characteristics are now playing in parallel to new venture development (NVD),[11] which adds a little more complexity to the ESU's operating and cost equation. On the one hand, starting a company is an achievement milestone that needs to be celebrated. It generates enthusiasm and creates a positive perception and external value as people, potential customers, and investors take the ESU more seriously under a company name. On the other hand, I have often observed founders' attitude starts changing during and after starting a company, where they become a little more arrogant and overconfident at this Stage. Simon and Shrader (2012) define this optimistic overconfidence as "being certain of success only to end up disappointed, represents a potentially catastrophic error" (p. 291). If anything, it should humble them as now they have more pressure to get their project moving on the right track because the costs multiply and opportunity cost clock starts accumulating.

The Startup Stage ESUs still have limited financial, human, physical, and technological resources. The focus is to continue the path of the developmental stage, except now under a formal (legal) company's name. Even though it is still unpredictable and untested, ESUs continue with the path of direct customer engagement and feedback to get good traction, value proposition testing, and momentum. This is not easy and most of the time it is a roller coaster. There are often the 24–48-hour crises which can lead to the conclusion that "it's over." Somehow, a magical solution pops up in the middle of the night that solves the problem in a different way, requiring changes and pivoting (Dhir et al., 2024; Sala et al., 2022). Perseverance pays especially when founders recalibrate and pivot. Beware of perseverance becoming stubbornness though, where keep pushing something repeatedly that is simply not working could take the project over the cliff (Hunt et al., 2024).

2.3.2 *Approaches, Activities, and Expectations at the Startup Stage*

Lean startup continues with new venture creation with developing, measuring, learning, and validation with incremental development of

[11] In *Chapter 4—Costs and Intellectual Capital Development*, I will cover extensively how successful ESU founders focus on new venture development (NVD) rather than new product/services development, although the latter is a critical part of NVD.

core business value proposition (Ries, 2011). This means going out and knocking on as many doors as possible to test, to listen to customers carefully, and to develop a value proposition that customers need and would pay for. This is super important, and it is a key determinant of survival-or-failure of the ESU. Even though initial positive signals indicate that there may be a market for the value proposition, it is not guaranteed that there is unless it is well-tested and re-tested again with real paying customers, whether businesses or end users or consumers.

At times initial positive signals could be deceiving. Many friends, colleagues, family members, and sometimes potential customers who would be the ESUs' first circle of contacts may provide positive feedback (i.e., signals) indicating that "they will buy such a product or service." This may lead ESU founders to limit their research, overestimate the market, and underestimate the time to acquire customers, timing, and resource needs. When it comes to reality—when friends, family, and potential customers are approached for the sale—founders find out the hard way that "nobody is buying." They are surprised and distraught. This is more common than not. Founders tend to be overconfident with an overestimation of their beliefs and abilities (Moore & Healy, 2008). Because they have received positive signals from close circles, founders may translate this as an easy market entry, overestimating the overall market which is harder to enter (Cain et al., 2015). Therefore, it is imperative that those initial positive signals should not be determined to go on extensively developing, manufacturing, launching, and marketing the products. More factual experimenting and further market testing, realistic resource needs assessment, and sometimes a dose of *humbling feedback* (Mahajan, 1992) are needed to improve accuracy and maintain a healthy level of educated confidence building. More than often, costs associated with overconfident premature market entry end up being wasted on solutions that no one wants to buy or due to excessive competition.

Building a Customer-Driven Consensus

Listening to potential customers for cues, *building a cues consensus*, and pivoting is a major part of this Startup Stage and the successful prioritization, incrementality, and scaling process, as well as the prerequisite to the early Survival Stage. This requires both research orientation and an entrepreneurial mindset. Depending on the ESU's value proposition, listening to customer cues means working directly with them to:

- Understand customer pain points.
- Gather direct feedback by creating a sincere feedback loop.
- Analyze where customers' real needs are and where their frustrations lie.
- Proactively engage with them early in the process.
- Test, test, and re-test again the value proposition from a customer's perspective (not ESU's).
- Work with early adopters from multiple channels (not just one or from close circles).
- Identify their critical experience improvement quotients.
- Determine where there are customer efficiency and effectiveness challenges.
- Measure the customer's current real and opportunity costs in time and money to see how the ESU's value proposition would save them time and money, with positive experiences.
- Define the value proposition from a customer's KPI perspective with acceptable price points and cost-benefit analysis.
- Monitor the marketplace, competitor value propositions, reviews, and ratings.

Listening to customer cues always provides the founders with a different understanding. It moves them from *me-centric* to customer-centric mindset. At times, customer narratives lead to pivoting ideas that founders have never considered. Other times, customers may be complaining about an issue that can be easily resolved by the ESU value proposition but was not considered or included in the original value proposition. Yet it has real value for the customers and could be an important buying trigger point, and hence a selling proposition.

Oftentimes customer narratives lead to pivoting ideas that founders have never considered

As qualitative researchers will attest, each customer will provide a clue or several clues where their issues lie and what is interesting for them to fix in the short- and long-term. And then, one or two test customers will summarize what everybody else is saying. This is what founders need to understand and use the 80–20 model to *build a cues consensus* to recalibrate or totally pivot (Hunt et al., 2024).

Once this consensus is somehow determined, then the focus should be to prioritize the most important and essential components to develop for the first replicable market entry. Then make assumptions on the other priorities and timing, and ensure growth is incrementally planned rather than moving in different directions at the same time. This approach will give time for the ESU to learn from the initial launch experiences and to develop the value proposition further. The learning experiences will also provide opportunities to pivot, where to develop and invest further, and how to save on costs with economies of scale. However, first things first:

- Develop the first problem-solution fit that works from the customers' perspective.
- Determine and prioritize marketing channels to test and validate.
- Identify internal developmental needs and resource requirements, such as people, expertise, and technology.
- Develop a business plan grounded by an innovative, multifaceted, and multidimensional business model.[12]
    - Built on key prioritized assumptions
    - Operationalized and calendarized
    - Incremental milestone driven
    - That financial forecasts tie to the above narrative
    - Where and when to invest
- Seek and secure adequate external financing, ensuring 12–18 months of rolling adequate cash flow to survive.

Mula et al. (2024) found that there are commonalities of how digitalized startups scale, prioritized in four stages: One, "put financial capital in place first ahead of building capacity" (p. 9) and then *build capacity ahead of growth*. Two, developing and testing organizational processes and related technological innovation to handle growth. Three, *pursuing economies scale* with data-driven solutions for cost and capital optimization. And four, reshaping and transforming founders' role to CEO (p. 2).

[12] See *Chapter 5—Costs and Three-Dimensional Business Models* for more details on how to achieve this.

One of the challenges that ESUs have is a lack of knowledge, experience, and expertise in the above challenges. In many cases, they either don't need to have permanent full-time or part-time people or have the funds to pay people to do some of the tasks. Above, I had suggested that an option would be to initially hire motivated interns, either full- or part-time. However, interns may be able to carry on some of the required tasks, but not all tasks or the high-level of expertise needed. Incubators and accelerators are another source for mentors and sometimes advisors. They are helpful but temporary remedies to the ongoing challenges facing ESUs, especially after graduating from programs. There are coaching services offered either privately or as a reward from such organizations. Some of these coaches follow specific processes that are prescribed by their organizations and do not necessarily address the real needs of the ESU.

The Role of Mentors and Advisors

There are distinctions between mentors and advisors. Mentors focus more on the professional and personal development of ESU founders, such as how to lead, make decisions, and develop specific skills. It is more informal, broad, and individually focused. Advisors focus more on the business, its strategy, value proposition development, market entry, marketing, financial planning, and fund raising. Advisors are more structured and transactional, offering general or specialized knowledge. Mentors are empathic towards the individual founder's needs (i.e., subjective), whereas advisors are more objective towards business needs, including human capital (i.e., objective). Although both play important roles to support ESUs, advisors offer better expertise to the ESU's development.

To fill the gap for the knowledge and experience shortfalls, it would be prudent for an ESU to find and engage an advisory board composed of experts with experience in different functions, such as entrepreneurial, business modeling, strategic, large corporate, financial, business development, sales and marketing, supply chain, and operations. Such advisors could be current or ex-founders of startups that have grown their ESUs into larger companies and exited. They could be generalists or specialists or a combination of both.

At the Startup stage, it is advisable to keep the board small, such as two or three, consisting mostly of generalists with some specialized functional areas but mostly strategic and financial. Their advice could be invaluable to the ESU founders. If specialists are needed, such as specific technological, digital marketing, or supply chain, ESU founders can then seek such specialists on a *need to have basis* and upon advice from the other members of the advisory board. The main board would be on a longer-term basis, such as two to three years; and specialist advisors, on a shorter-term basis unless it is determined to have them on board for a longer term. The key is finding the right advisors who align with the mission, vision, and values of the ESU to add real value to the ESU's business.

The compensation for the advisory board members could be in cash or advisory shares (i.e., equity) or a combination of both. As at the Startup Stage ESUs don't have the funds to compensate in cash, they may opt for offering advisory shares vested over a short or long period of time. At later stages, they may compensate in both cash and equity. If only with equity, then the percentage offered may be initially higher than with cash or in combination. These compensation amounts and equity percentages are negotiable and depend on the amount of dedicated time of the advisors. If, for instance, it is half a day once a quarter, the equity percentage may be anything below one percent. If it is half a day once or twice a month with additional just-in-time support, then that percentage could be anywhere between 2% and 10%. The details of the relationship should be drawn up on an Advisory Services Agreement stipulating the terms and conditions, including separation clauses.

There are pros and cons to advisory boards. The biggest pro is that founders can get top advice that they can only gain from long-term experiences for a very reasonable cost. Other benefits include:

- Top expertise and knowledge.
- Strategic guidance on business modeling, planning, and financing.
- Networks and networking opportunities.
- Fundraising, approaches, and advice.
- Added credibility to the ESU.
- Accountability and governance to ensure staying focused on goals and maintaining good governance.

There could also be cons with advisory boards. They include:

- Personality conflicts between the founders and advisors.
- Overreliance on advice, stifling the founders' own skills development.
- Meeting and reports preparation time away from the founders to run the business.
- Equity dilution (for in-kind compensation) and costs (if paid in cash).
- Conflicting advice creating confusion.
- Founders are not coachable or do not listen to the advisors.

To reduce such challenges, ESU founders should make the most of Advisory Board meetings by focusing on key strategic subjects where they can get the most value from the advisors. It also should be noted that advisors provide advice and would not do the management work of the ESU. Networking and fundraising opportunities, for instance, would be guidance and possibly connecting the founders with people within the advisors' network, rather than running customer meetings or facilitating deals. Once these topics are cleared, an Advisory Board could add tremendous value and credibility to an ESU from the Startup Stage onward. Good advisors, for instance, would be tremendously valuable in helping founders with prioritization, pivoting, and incremental growth strategies. They can support how to establish a public presence and when. How to test markets and build relationships with customers to understand their needs.

Developing the Pitch

Finally, the Startup Stage is characterized by developing a solid pitch with constant pitching to different audiences, including incubators, accelerators, investors, customers, and other stakeholders. Effective pitches, founders' narration, and *informational signaling* to solicit financial and social resources (Huang & Knight, 2017; Wesley et al., 2022) are art and science. It will make or break an ESU no matter how good its value proposition is. In the earlier chapter, I mentioned that *a pitch is the window to the soul of the startup*. This is so true. It tells a great deal about how ESU founders are thinking, what they've worked on, how they are framing their narrative, and to what audiences they are addressing.

Pitches are also the beginning of creating a positive *trust perception* with the first impressions of ESU founders (Konya-Baumbach et al., 2019). This is true especially when founders use *substantive signals* related to the firm and its value proposition jointly with proper and appealing *rhetorical signals*, such as relevant information, press releases with sponsors, videos, and images (Steigenberger & Wilhelm, 2018). It requires good visuals as a *sense-giving strategy to skeptical audiences*, such as customers and investors, to connect and get them engaged, and to win them over (Henike et al., 2020; van den Broek & Gander, 2024). Adopting from Sull and Eisenhardt's (2015) approach on strategy, in order for ESU pitches to be effective and remembered, they must be easy for the audiences to understand.

There are many pitching techniques, design, and deck models. Here I will only cover the basic topics that are needed to cover:

1. A Cover Introduction—a slide that includes the company name, logo, memorable tagline, presenters name and position, purpose or event, and date.
2. Problem Statement and Definition—a shortened, summarized version of the problem analysis, including how and who is impacted with the problem, including key metrics.
3. Problem-Solution Fit—the unique value proposition through its product and/or services solutions addressing the problem.
4. Market Opportunities and Size—to share specific data on the market size, the market segments and channels, potential growth opportunities, and ESUs prioritization.
5. The Business Model—a compact summarization of what activities ESU would perform, how those activities are offered, to whom, and why they create value.
6. The Revenue Model—how the ESU will make money through what features: products and services, installation, training and development, subscriptions, ongoing services (i.e., MRR and ARR) such as maintenance and similar.
7. Traction To-Date—how much have they achieved so far (i.e., milestones conquered) and where are they today, any customer testimonials, trust, or reputational metrics.
8. Go-to-Market Strategy—short-, medium-, and long-term business development, sales and marketing plans, key channels prioritized, and partnership development.

9. Competition Analysis—a metric of competitors and the ESU's competitive positioning.
10. Financials—past, present, and future forecasts, key assumptions and projections with scenarios (optimistic, realistic, and pessimistic), revenue streams, cost investments to achieve growth, CAC, and similar highlights and KPIs.
11. The Team—the founders with their roles and responsibilities, relevant expertise and background, key or potential future team members, and advisors.
12. Funding Needs—specifically tailored to the investment community, how much financing the ESU is raising and for what purpose: how the ESU is planning to allocate the raised funds (i.e., 45% marketing, 30% R&D, 25% production) with an outline on incremental use of funds at milestones, and potential return on investment in terms of revenue, market share, and growth.
13. Needs, Asks, or Call to Action—specifically tailored to the audience, to specify what the presenter is currently seeking to support ESU's journey and next steps.
14. Q&A.
15. Backup Slides—further details in support of case-specific questions come up during the Q&A related to the above slides.

Key to a successful pitch is to tell the audience a story that is *simple*, *understood*, and *remembered* (Sull & Eisenhardt, 2015). Founders should have a one-minute (i.e., elevator) pitch and a three-minute first impression pitch. Pitches need to be concise with good visuals and pictures (that tell a thousand words). It should be tailored to the precise audience, whether they are investors, incubators, accelerators, customers, industry partners, mentors, and advisors, a competition or media. Once a pitch is developed properly, founders can then use the 80–20 rule where 80% of the pitch remains the same and 20% can be adapted for the audiences.

2.3.3 Cost Considerations and Risk Factors

The ESU at the Startup Stage operates with limited resources, even though it now requires larger sums of cash to cover the company setup and business running costs. The company setup costs are considered *one-off costs* whereas the company running (or operating) costs are considered *recurring cash fixed costs*. Depending on the ESU type and its state at the company startup phase, whether it is advanced to operationalize quickly or needs to spend time developing, networking, testing, and recalibrating. It is usually the latter than the former. The company's one-off setup costs are common for either ESU type or state. Regardless, costs at this stage are *enablers* of value creation. Figure 2.6 illustrates the financing and cost investment focus during the early stages, especially during the Startup State.

One-off startup costs may include (but are not limited to) the following:

- Legal formation fees, including notary, licenses, permits, and other government fees (corporation setup costs are higher than LLC setup costs).
- Professional fees, including lawyer/legal and accountant.
- Insurances, which can be general and professional liability insurance depending on the type of business and risks involved, and mandatory social and health (where required).
- Business setup costs:
  - Office space with initial rent downpayment (i.e., first and last month, plus a deposit), furnishings, equipment (i.e., computers

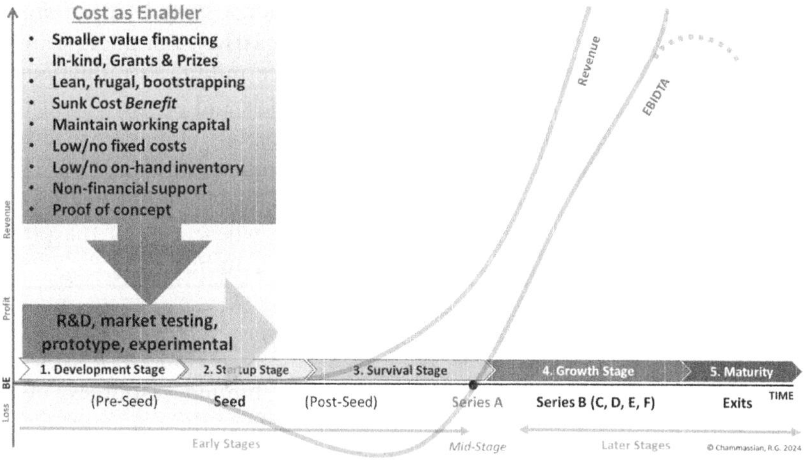

Fig. 2.6 Early stages financing and cost investments

and printers), software, and miscellaneous items such as office supplies and business cards.
  - Initial inventory if product driven. This should be as limited as possible with little or no on-hand inventory. The focus should be very high inventory turnover.
  - Technology infrastructure setups, such as website, domain name, and hosting, subscription software (i.e., CRM, ERP).
  - Initial marketing-related costs, such as logo design and initial branding launch depending on the ESU complexity and strategy.

- Potential initial people costs, whether a paid intern, a part-time temporary assistant, or recruiting someone if the ESU has the means and needs.

The above is an impartial list but most probably represents over 90% of the initial Startup Stage costs involved in most cases. No matter what state the ESU is in, legal formation, professional fees, and insurance are guaranteed. Office space and equipment can be optional. However, a physical location must be registered with the *Company's Registry* whether it is a home address, a co-working space, or an actual office. Some incubators and accelerators, such as university spinoffs, offer low-cost subsidized office space along with professional services for free or with very reasonable fees, such as HR, legal, accounting, and tax reporting.

Most of the time, ESUs in the Startup Stage must still operate as frugally as possible. That means they should avoid or minimize recurring (cash) fixed costs as much as possible, such as rent, utilities, overhead, and outsourced services (i.e., web and marketing services). Such costs are enabling sunk costs that offer limited benefits and are not considered to be investment oriented to offer some future ROI benefit. They play a small enabling role in the jigsaw puzzle of value creation picture. They are purely operating expenses or consumables (at times, capital expenditures if equipment is bought) that neither provides ongoing value in terms of revenue generating or customer acquiring, nor future value for a perceived return on those costs. They are necessary costs to get the business up and running. As prioritization is key, such initial costs should be minimized with low priority. Whereas higher priority should be given to developing a value proposition that customers need and want, and that it captures value for them.

Investors also like ESU founding teams who are frugal at the Startup Stage. They prefer money spent on value-creating activities that lead to improved company valuation. As a word of caution, ESU founders should never ask potential investors to pay for incurred/past company setup costs. Let's remember that *entrepreneurs pay for the past, investors pay for the future* (Leach & Melicher, 2021).

Besides starting a company and establishing a public presence, the key focus of the Startup Stage is to prioritize spending time and money on costs to test markets, to establish customer needs, to determine a holistic value proposition, business model validation, and re-design, while ensuring financial viability. Forecasting and spending prioritization for costs as a combined enabler of value creation ought to be on customer-facing value proposition validation activities. Below is a decent list that covers the majority (>80%) of planning considerations. They would need to be adjusted to the ESU's type of business.

Financial Planning Prerequisites:

- Begin with short-, medium-, and long-term goals. What would you like to achieve and when (milestones)? Remember these goals are iterative and can change, but it's a starting point.
- What would these goals achieve in terms of value creation and capture—for whom and how?
- Based on your market/demand analysis, experimentation, and feedback loop, clearly define your industry and channels, and your target audience (i.e., specific paying customers).
- Define and prioritize your value proposition options, such as physical products vs. services.
  - If both, distinguish between them clearly.
  - Calculate appropriate pricing for both.
  - Identify one-time sales versus repeat sales versus recurring revenue, whether it's physical products or intangible services or both.
  - Determine sales volume, such as quantities that can be sold.
  - Identify any seasonality for sales peaks and valleys: winter, summer, and bank holidays.
- Clearly understand how and when revenue would be recognized. This may sound like an accounting subject, but it is a must to know by ESU founders on how to position their sales proposals, terms

and conditions, and cash flow. This will become a huge issue at mid- and late stages, especially during financing and exit events if it's not clearly understood and defined.

- Determine your direct costs related to each sales quantity (i.e., cost of good/services sold) and your indirect costs related to running your business (i.e., operating expenses: general and administrative, marketing, IT, R&D, and similar).

Pricing Considerations:

- Externally: customer acceptance price points vs. competitive environment
  - *Test different pricing scenarios* with customers, such as market penetration pricing versus premium pricing. Remember that revenue for the ESU is a cost to its customers.
  - *Market penetration pricing* is used for initial market entry, customer acquisition, market share gain, and to create sales volume. This pricing strategy is short term, initially low, and disruptive depending on the competitive landscape. It can be used for both products (i.e., gadgets, tools) and services (i.e., SaaS, subscriptions, streaming).
  - *Premium pricing* is used when offering unique selling (value) proposition based on the multisided business model. This pricing strategy is long term, emphasizing on quality and customer value perception due to its customer cost efficiency and effectiveness.
  - *Discounting* is utilized for volume purchases or long-term customer relationships, retention, and contracts. It should also be used for recurring revenue purposes.
- Internally: profitability per product/service line = price minus costs = gross profit (margin)
  - *Cost of goods sold*: product acquisition price if the supplier is outsourced. If not, then raw material, labor, manufacturing overhead (including warehousing of raw material and work-in-progress products), and freight-in.
  - *Allocation from operating expense* allocation from:
    - General and administrative expenses:

        - Rent, utilities, admin staff wages, insurance, and office supplies.
        - Warehousing, handling (picking and packaging), and shipping.
        - Credit card charges and other payment fees (i.e., PayPal).[13]
    - R&D expenses: development and prototyping.
    - Marketing, sales, and customer acquisition costs (CAC):
        - General advertising, marketing material, website design, development, and maintenance,[14] promotions, and sales commissions.
        - CAC includes focused marketing campaigns and the sales process of obtaining customers (i.e., sales calls/ meetings, follow-ups, free sampling).
- Desired profit margin (a percentage).
- Include VAT, sales taxes, and any statutory charges in the final price, especially if the customer is the end user. Exclude VAT from internal forecasting (and pitching).
- Delivery costs, if product driven, should be incorporated in the final customer price. Otherwise, it may be perceived as a ***hidden cost*** for the customer.

Revenue Determinations:

- *Calculation*: price × quantity per product line or service type.
- *Contracts*: online terms and conditions versus services contracts must be clearly set with all customers, whether testing products and services or with longer-term relationships. As a minimum, they should include the following for each type of business:

[13] Also include or add credit card charges on the price calculus (usually 3%). This becomes an issue if not included because it is incurred for your business as a Selling (Operating) Expense. If not included in the price calculus, then it becomes an out-of-pocket unrecoverable expense.

[14] If initial website design and development is for a major e-commerce or a platform-based business, such as software-as-a-service (SaaS), music or news streaming, which require a substantial initial investment, then these costs are to be classified and capitalized as an intangible (non-current) asset on the balance sheet and amortized over its economic life. If they are for basic marketing purposes, then classify them under Marketing Expenses. Classify all recurring or routine website maintenance costs under Marketing Expenses.

- *Product contracts*:
  - The parties involved (legal names, addresses, and representative).
  - Sold product model, serial number, description, function, features, etc.
  - Price: if shipping costs included or added, plus VAT, and other applicable taxes and fees.
  - Payment terms: credit card, invoiced (i.e., with net 30-day payment).
  - Delivery terms: date, method, and ownership transfer (i.e., upon shipment or delivery).
  - Customer acceptance: when does ownership transfer occur? This is used for revenue recognition purposes; plus buyers' rights to inspect and accept upon delivery (if any).
  - Returns and refunds: timeframe a customer can return a product intact and get a refund, either in cash, credit, or voucher for future purchases.
  - Warrantees and/or guarantees meeting or exceeding manufacturers or legal obligations.
  - Liabilities, dispute resolution and location, and termination conditions.
  - Licensing agreement if there are unique and specific features.
- *Services contracts*:
  - The parties involved (legal names, addresses, and representatives).
  - Service descriptions in detail, itemized including scope, limitations, and exclusions.
  - Service duration: one-time or recurring (monthly, annually, auto-renewal terms).
  - Price: one-time or subscription fees corresponding to each service description line per above with payment schedule, taxes, and charges.
  - Payment terms: credit card (whether one-time or recurring) and invoicing.
  - Service Level Agreement (SLA) for long term or recurring contracts with performance standards and metrics, response times, guarantees, inclusions, and exclusions.

  - Obligations and responsibilities by each party.
  - IP rights: what the customer can do (i.e., reseller) and cannot do.
  - Licenses: terms on limited to number of terminals or users vs. unlimited use.
  - Cancellations and termination conditions with lead-time months.
  - Warranties and/or guarantees with timeframes on functionality, outages, and upgrades.
  - Dispute resolution jurisdiction, governing laws, and methods (i.e., arbitration, litigation).

- Both types of contract general clauses.

  - Amendment/modification processes, timelines, and impact.
  - Formal communication methods (i.e., email or post mail).
  - Force majeure responsibilities and non-liability in case of unforeseeable events (listed).

Revenue recognition practices are an important consideration when it comes to determining profitability periods and generally acceptable accounting practices. It is reviewed by investors, by auditors during due diligence of VCs and during trade sales (i.e., M&A event), and by local tax authorities. It is beyond simply adhering to financial accounting requirements or guidelines. ESU internal policies and practices represent the health of an ESU financial state and business. Playing with vague and inconsistent revenue models will distort financial statements, and create doubt, credibility issues with investors and M&A partners, and potential penalties from local tax authorities. This is especially true for more complex business and revenue models, such as recurring services (i.e., maintenance) and SaaS MRR/ARR.

Beware of value proposition *bundling* where a contract covers several deliverables, such as products, installation, configuration ongoing services, and warranties mixed with unclear delineation. It is imperative to develop value propositions with revenue models that are clearly defined and adhere to these practices from the get-go, especially when growth models are being developed. This is imperative to the survival of the ESU (Coad et al., 2013). Many reputable companies have faced dire consequences when their revenue had to be restated (see Cascini et al., 2014; Huang & Hairston, 2023; Myers et al., 2022; Okaily et al., 2019; Thorps,

2021). The opportunity cost and early failure potential are very high if pricing and revenue recognition practices are not defined clearly before scaling and growth. There are many tools, coaches, online services, and specialized software that assist in developing an ESU's revenue recognition model. It is highly advisable to seek the support of qualified accountants and legal experts to define revenue recognition (and other conditions) on contract and ESU policies for disclosures.

The process of financial planning should be as follows:

1. Begin with assumptions
   - When do you think you will get the first and type(s) of revenue?
   - Reverse engineer on what is needed strategically and operationally to get there?
   - Identify human, organizational, technological, social, and relational resource needs.
2. Allocate costs associated with these requirements, and distinguish between:
   - Enabling costs, which are non-revenue generating such as office space.
   - Moderating costs associated with determining gross margin (i.e., cost of goods/services sold) and profitability.
   - Mediating costs as investment in developing intellectual capital and future growth, such as in human capital, R&D, tech (i.e., hardware and specialized software, e-commerce website, etc.), organizational capabilities, building trust and reputation, and unique relationships.
   - Identify *need to haves* vs. *nice to haves* on costs and investments to prioritize on the most important costs to have.
   - Incrementalize development and growth with clear milestones instead of doing many things at the same time.
3. Operationalize and calendarize both revenue and costs in a monthly forecast.
4. Develop a cash budget with cash inflow and outflow timing to determine and ensure 12–18 months of rolling adequate cash flow to survive and to operate (i.e., cash burn rate).
5. Identify investment milestones within the calendarized financial plans.

6. Determine how to finance the investments, internally and/or externally.

Self-financing through revenue generation is a good way to finance operations. However, most of the time there is no adequate revenue stream at the Startup stage. Therefore, no matter how much founders invest their own time and money, as well as operate frugally, ESUs inevitably need external financing. It is why one of the top reasons ESUs fail is due to running out of cash. The major reasons why they do include:

1. Poor financial planning by being overoptimistic, overestimating revenue generation, and underestimating time and associated costs of developing the business.
    - To mitigate this, it is advisable to have scenario planning with a range of situations and configurations to come up with optimistic, realistic, and pessimistic scenarios.
2. Scaling too rapidly by expanding quickly, hiring too many people, opening branches, and growing into new markets at the same time without adequate financial (cash) resources.
    - To mitigate, incremental growth with milestone achievements is an absolute must.
3. Inadequate cash resources and funding by underestimating the cash needs, timing and time to raise capital, unexpected costs, raising too little without the adequate reserves for cushion, and difficulty to raise new funds from investors.
    - To mitigate, scenario planning, prioritization, and incremental development with milestones are crucial, along with giving sufficient time to raise money from the right financing sources.

At the Startup stage, it is also essential to know what resources to go to raise capital.

- Universities, incubators, and accelerators provide indirect financing with subsidized services and space. In return for their investment in time, resources, and (sometimes) cash, these entities may take direct equity positions with the ESU.

- Government funding agencies and foundations offer grants through needs applications, competitions, or simply loans to be repaid with low or no interest.
- Platforms offer early testing opportunities for the ESU project's viability by providing visibility and fundraising opportunities with multiple small investments from the public on the internet. There are various financing platform business models, such as donations, (non-financial product) reward-based, equity crowdfunding, and crowdlending that offer peer-to-peer lending to businesses.
- Business angels are high net-worth individuals such as serial entrepreneurs, senior executives, or simply wealthy individuals with a passion to invest their own funds into early-stage ESUs. They are an important and popular source of funding:
  - Usually, they invest locally (some internationally) and often in the seed rounds during the Startup Stage.
  - Typically, they invest between 25 and 200 K, but less than 1 million.
  - Their objectives are diverse, not just financial returns.
  - They bring entrepreneurial and business experiences and industry knowledge.
  - They often co-invest with other angels and sometimes with venture funds.
- Early-stage venture capital (VC) firms are private equity setup as partnerships that invest other people's or organizations' money with the goal of cash out through an exit event. Most early-stage VCs invest in high-tech ESUs in early stages.

Next Chapter 3 will cover how investments work, how investors view ESU projects, and determine their investability in Survival, Growth, and Maturity Stages. How ESU founders should position their ESU strategies and pitches to attract and treat their investors as important stakeholders, and in fact another type of customer.

Takeaways

- The first input and characteristic of this stage is creating a legal entity for the ESU.
- Mainly there are two company formats used throughout the world to launch a legal entity: a limited liability company (LLC) or a share corporation.
- Lean startup approaches continue at this stage, except some high-tech ESUs need serious investment capital to continue their R&D.
- For non-high-tech ESUs, initial positive signals from friends, colleagues, and family. They do not constitute what real paying customers may need and pay for.
- It is imperative that founders go out and talk to as many potential customers as possible to build a *customer-driven cues consensus* and develop value propositions (i.e., problem-solution fit) that they need and would pay for.
- Revenue for the ESU is a cost to its paying customers.
- Ensure to define value propositions from a customer's KPI perspective with acceptable price points and cost-benefit analysis.
- Oftentimes customer narratives lead to pivoting that founders never considered.
- ESU founders can solicit mentors and advisors. It is highly recommended that they form an advisory board at this stage and compensate them with advisory shares initially. The benefits of an advisory board outweigh its costs.
- Develop comprehensive pitches for one- and three-minute presentations that create positive trust perception to skeptical audiences; that are simple, effective, understood, and remembered with visuals that tell a thousand words.
- Startup stage costs remain as an enabler of value creation. However, costs need to play a mediating role in value capture during the comprehensive financial planning process at this stage.

Bibliography

Ancillai, C., Sabatini, A., Gatti, M., & Perna, A. (2023). Digital technology and business model innovation: A systematic literature review and future research agenda. *Technological Forecasting and Social Change, 188*, 122307. https://doi.org/10.1016/j.techfore.2022.122307

Andrews, R., Fazio, C., Guzman, J., Liu, Y., & Stern, S. (2022). The startup cartography project: Measuring and mapping entrepreneurial ecosystems. *Research Policy, 51*(104437), 1–18. https://doi.org/10.1016/j.respol.2021.104437

Andries, P., Debackere, K., & Van Looy, B. (2013). Simultaneous experimentation as a learning strategy: Business model development under uncertainty. *Strategic Entrepreneurship Journal, 7*(4), 288–310. https://doi.org/10.1002/sej.1170

Ang, L., & Buttle, F. (2006). Managing for successful customer acquisition: An exploration. *Journal of Marketing Management, 22*(3–4), 295–317. https://doi.org/10.1362/026725706776861217

Bailetti, T. (2012, February). Technology entrepreneurship: Overview, definition, and distinctive aspects. *Technology Innovation Management Review*, 5–12.

Banal-Estañol, A., Macho-Stadler, I., Nieto-Postigo, J., & Pérez-Castrillo, D. (2023). Early individual stakeholders, first venture capital investment, and exit in the UK startup ecosystem. *Journal of Corporate Finance, 80*, 102420. https://doi.org/10.1016/j.jcorpfin.2023.102420

Bojovic, N., Genet, C., & Sabatier, V. (2018). Learning, signaling, and convincing: The role of experimentation in the business modeling process. *Long Range Planning, 51*(1), 141–157. https://doi.org/10.1016/j.lrp.2017.09.001

Brown, T. (2008). Design thinking. *Harvard Business Review, 86*(6), 84–92.

Burnell, D., Stevenson, R., & Fisher, G. (2023). Early-stage business model experimentation and pivoting. *Journal of Business Venturing, 38*(4), 106314. https://doi.org/10.1016/j.jbusvent.2023.106314

Burmaoglu, S., Sartenaer, O., & Porter, A. (2019). Conceptual definition of technology emergence: A long journey from philosophy of science to science policy. *Technology in Society, 59*, 101126. https://doi.org/10.1016/j.techsoc.2019.04.002

Cain, D. M., Moore, D. A., & Haran, U. (2015). Making sense of overconfidence in market entry. *Strategic Management Journal, 36*(1), 1–18. https://doi.org/10.1002/smj.2196

Carroll, L. (2017). A comprehensive definition of technology from an ethological perspective. *Social Sciences, 6*(4), 126. https://doi.org/10.3390/socsci6040126

Cascini, K. T., DelFavero, A., & Bezner, R. (2014). Corporate revenue miscalculations & the impact on stakeholders. *Journal of Business & Economics Research (JBER), 12*(2), 77. https://doi.org/10.19030/jber.v12i2.8521

Cassar, G. (2009). Financial statement and projection preparation in start-up ventures. *The Accounting Review, 84*(1), 27–51. https://doi.org/10.2308/accr.2009.84.1.27

CBInsights. (2022, December 1). The top 12 reasons Startups fail. CBInsights Research. https://www.cbinsights.com/research/report/startup-failure-reasons-top/

Chammassian, R. G. (2016). *Towards a new cost paradigm for technology startup entrepreneurs* [Doctoral Dissertation]. Grenoble Ecole de Management, Grenoble, France.

Clayton, P. (2024). Mentored without incubation: Start-up survival, funding, and the role of entrepreneurial support organization services. *Research Policy, 53*(104975), 1–17. https://doi.org/10.1016/j.respol.2024.104975

Coad, A., Frankish, J., Roberts, R. G., & Storey, D. J. (2013). Growth paths and survival chances: An application of Gambler's Ruin theory. *Journal of Business Venturing, 28*(5), 615–632. https://doi.org/10.1016/j.jbusvent.2012.06.002

Coad, A., & Reid, A., (2012). *The role of technology and technology-based firms in economic development: Rethinking innovation and enterprise policy in Scotland*. Technopolis Group, Scotland.

Cotei, C., & Farhat, J. (2018). The M&A exit outcomes of new, young firms. *Small Business Economics, 50*(3), 545–567. https://doi.org/10.1007/s11187-017-9907-1

Coviello, N., Autio, E., Nambisan, S., Patzelt, H., & Thomas, L. D. W. (2024). Organizational scaling, scalability, and scale-up: Definitional harmonization and a research agenda. *Journal of Business Venturing, 39*(5), 106419. https://doi.org/10.1016/j.jbusvent.2024.106419

Dandis, A. O., Al Haj Eid, M. B., Robin, R., & Wierdak, N. (2022). An empirical investigation of the factors affecting customer lifetime value. *International Journal of Quality & Reliability Management, 39*(4), 910–935. https://doi.org/10.1108/IJQRM-12-2020-0412

Deligianni, I., Sapouna, P., Voudouris, I., & Lioukas, S. (2022). An effectual approach to innovation for new ventures: The role of entrepreneur's prior start-up experience. *Journal of Small Business Management, 60*(1), 146–177. https://doi.org/10.1080/00472778.2019.1698432

Dhir, A., Meenakshi, N., Nawaz, R., & Kaur, P. (2024). How do we pivot? Facilitators, inhibitors, and strategies of tech healthcare startups before, during, and after a crisis. *Technological Forecasting and Social Change, 207*, 123606. https://doi.org/10.1016/j.techfore.2024.123606

Eisenmann, T. R. (2020). Determinants of early-stage startup performance: Survey results. *Harvard Business School*. 21–057, 1–63. https://doi.org/10.2139/ssrn.3725023. Entrepreneurial Management Working paper.
Elkington, J. (1994). Towards the sustainable corporation: Win-win-win business strategies for sustainable development. *California Management Review, 36*(2), 90–100.
Elkington, J. (1997). *Cannibals with forks: The triple bottom line of 21st century business*. Capstone Publishing.
Giones, F., & Brem, A. (2017). Digital technology entrepreneurship: A definition and research agenda. *Technology Innovation Management Review, 7*(5).
Gompers, P. A., Gornall, W., Kaplan, S. N., & Strebulaev, I. A. (2020). How do venture capitalists make decisions? *Journal of Financial Economics, 135*(1), 169–190. https://doi.org/10.1016/j.jfineco.2019.06.011
Graña-Alvarez, R., Gomez-Conde, J., Lopez-Valeiras, E., & González-Loureiro, M. (2024). Management control systems, business financial literacy and financial leverage in business-incubated start-ups. *The British Accounting Review*, 101427. https://doi.org/10.1016/j.bar.2024.101427
Haskel, J., & Westlake, S. (2018). *Capitalism without capital: The rise of the intangible economy*. Princeton University Press.
Henike, T., Kamprath, M., & Hölzle, K. (2020). Effecting, but effective? How business model visualisations unfold cognitive impacts. *Long Range Planning, 53*(4), 101925. https://doi.org/10.1016/j.lrp.2019.101925
Hmieleski, K. M., & Ensley, M. D. (2007). A contextual examination of new venture performance: Entrepreneur leadership behavior, top management team heterogeneity, and environmental dynamism. *Journal of Organizational Behavior, 28*(7), 865–889. https://doi.org/10.1002/job.479
Huang, L., & Knight, A. P. (2017). Resources and relationships in entrepreneurship: An exchange theory of the development and effects of the entrepreneur-investor relationship. *Academy of Management Review, 42*(1), 80–102. https://doi.org/10.5465/amr.2014.0397
Huang, T.-C., & Hairston, S. (2023). Analyst revenue forecasts and firm revenue misstatements. *European Accounting Review, 32*(2), 379–414. https://doi.org/10.1080/09638180.2021.1983447
Hunt, R. A., Townsend, D. M., Lerner, D. A., & Brownell, K. M. (2024). Pivot, persist or perish? Knowledge problems and the extraordinarily tight boundary conditions of entrepreneurs as scientists. *Journal of Business Venturing Insights, 21*, e00459. https://doi.org/10.1016/j.jbvi.2024.e00459
Jiang, H., & Murmann, J. P. (2023). Functional knowledge versus strategic knowledge: What type of knowledge matters most for the long-term performance of startups. *Management and Organization Review, 19*(3), 417–461. https://doi.org/10.1017/mor.2021.77

Karami, M., & Read, S. (2021). Co-creative entrepreneurship. *Journal of Business Venturing, 36*(106125), 1–16. https://doi.org/10.1016/j.jbusvent.2021.106125

Klotz, A. C., Hmieleski, K. M., Bradley, B. H., & Busenitz, L. W. (2014). New venture teams: A review of the literature and roadmap for future research. *Journal of Management, 40*(1), 226–255. https://doi.org/10.1177/0149206313493325

Konya-Baumbach, E., Schuhmacher, M. C., Kuester, S., & Kuharev, V. (2019). Making a first impression as a start-up: Strategies to overcome low initial trust perceptions in digital innovation adoption. *International Journal of Research in Marketing, 36*(3), 385–399. https://doi.org/10.1016/j.ijresmar.2019.01.008

Leach, C., & Melicher, R. (2021). *Entrepreneurial finance* (7th ed.). cengage.

Liedtka, J. (2018). Why design thinking works. *Harvard Business Review, 96*(5), 72–79.

Lukas, E., Mölls, S., & Welling, A. (2016). Venture capital, staged financing and optimal funding policies under uncertainty. *European Journal of Operational Research, 250*(1), 305–313. https://doi.org/10.1016/j.ejor.2015.10.051

Mahajan, J. (1992). The overconfidence effect in marketing management predictions. *Journal of Marketing Research, 29*(3), 329–342.

Mansoori, Y., & Lackéus, M. (2020). Comparing effectuation to discovery-driven planning, prescriptive entrepreneurship, business planning, lean startup, and design thinking. *Small Business Economics, 54*(3), 791–818. https://doi.org/10.1007/s11187-019-00153-w

Marcon, É., Le Dain, M.-A., & Frank, A. G. (2022). Designing business models for Industry 4.0 technologies provision: Changes in business dimensions through digital transformation. *Technological Forecasting and Social Change, 185*, 122078. https://doi.org/10.1016/j.techfore.2022.122078

Marcon, A., & Ribeiro, J. L. D. (2021). How do startups manage external resources in innovation ecosystems? A resource perspective of startups' lifecycle. *Technological Forecasting and Social Change, 171*, 120965. https://doi.org/10.1016/j.techfore.2021.120965

McMullen, J. S., & Dimov, D. (2013). Time and the entrepreneurial journey: The problems and promise of studying entrepreneurship as a process. *Journal of Management Studies, 50*(8), 1481–1512. https://doi.org/10.1111/joms.12049

Min, S., Zhang, X., Kim, N., & Srivastava, R. K. (2016). Customer acquisition and retention spending: An analytical model and empirical investigation in wireless telecommunications markets. *Journal of Marketing Research, 53*(5), 728–744. https://doi.org/10.1509/jmr.14.0170

Moore, D. A., & Healy, P. J. (2008). The trouble with overconfidence. *Psychological Review, 115*(2), 502–517. https://doi.org/10.1037/0033-295X.115.2.502

Mula, C., Zybura, N., & Hipp, T. (2024). From digitalized start-up to scale-up: Opening the black box of scaling in digitalized firms towards a scaling process framework. *Technological Forecasting and Social Change, 202*, 123275. https://doi.org/10.1016/j.techfore.2024.123275

Myers, L. A., Schmardebeck, R., Seidel, T. A., & Stuart, M. D. (2022). The impact of managerial discretion in revenue recognition: A reexamination*. *Contemporary Accounting Research, 39*(3), 2130–2174. https://doi.org/10.1111/1911-3846.12775

Neck, H. M., Neck, C. P., & Murray, E. L. (2021). *Entrepreneurship: The practice and mindset*. Sage.

OECD. (1996). *The knowledge-based economy*. OECD.

Okaily, J. A., Dixon, R., & Salama, A. (2019). Corporate governance quality and premature revenue recognition: Evidence from the UK. *International Journal of Managerial Finance, 15*(1), 79–99. https://doi.org/10.1108/IJMF-02-2018-0047

Read, S., & Sarasvathy, S. D. (2005). Knowing what to do and doing what you know: Effectuation as a form of entrepreneurial expertise. *The Journal of Private Equity, 9*(1), 45–62.

Ries, E. (2011). *The lean startup: How today's entrepreneurs use continuous innovation to create radically successful businesses*. Crown Publishing.

Rizvanović, B., Zutshi, A., Grilo, A., & Nodehi, T. (2023). Linking the potentials of extended digital marketing impact and start-up growth: Developing a macro-dynamic framework of start-up growth drivers supported by digital marketing. *Technological Forecasting and Social Change, 186*, 122128. https://doi.org/10.1016/j.techfore.2022.122128

Sala, P. K., Philbin, S. P., & Barikzai, S. (2022). A qualitative research study of the tech startup journey through entrepreneurial pivoting. *International Journal of Entrepreneurial Behavior & Research, 28*(4), 1050–1074. https://doi.org/10.1108/IJEBR-07-2021-0528

Sarasvathy, S. D. (2001). Causation and effectuation: Toward a theoretical shift from economic inevitability to entrepreneurial contingency. *Academy of Management Review, 26*(2), 243–263.

Sarasvathy, S. D. (2004). Making it happen: Beyond theories of the firm to theories of firm design. *Entrepreneurship Theory and Practice, 28*(6), 519–531.

Schwab, K. (2016). The Fourth Industrial Revolution: What it means, how to respond. *The World Economic Forum*. https://www.weforum.org/agenda/2016/01/the-fourth-industrial-revolution-what-it-means-and-how-to-respond/

Shetty, S., & Sundaram, R. (2020). Two heads are better than one: Multi-founder firms and quality signals to investors and acquirers. *International Journal on Emerging Technologies, 11*(3), 574–578.

Simon, M., & Shrader, R. C. (2012). Entrepreneurial actions and optimistic overconfidence: The role of motivated reasoning in new product introductions. *Journal of Business Venturing, 27*(3), 291–309. https://doi.org/10.1016/j.jbusvent.2011.04.003

Song, Y., Dana, L. P., & Berger, R. (2021). The entrepreneurial process and online social networks: Forecasting survival rate. *Small Business Economics, 56*(3), 1171–1190. https://doi.org/10.1007/s11187-019-00261-7

Steigenberger, N., & Wilhelm, H. (2018). Extending signaling theory to rhetorical signals. *Organization Science, 29*(3). https://doi.org/10.1287/orsc.2017.1195

Sull, D. N., & Eisenhardt, K. M. (2015). *Simple rules: How to thrive in a complex world*. Houghton Mifflin Harcourt.

Tatikonda, M. V., Terjesen, S. A., Patel, P. C., & Parida, V. (2013). The role of operational capabilities in enhancing new venture survival: A longitudinal study. *Production and Operations Management, 22*(6), 1401–1415. https://doi.org/10.1111/poms.12038

Teece, D. J. (2009). *Dynamic capabilities and strategic management: Organizing for innovation and growth*. Oxford University Press.

Teece, D. J. (2012). Dynamic capabilities: Routines versus entrepreneurial action. *Journal of Management Studies, 49*(8), 1395–1401. https://doi.org/10.1111/j.1467-6486.2012.01080.x

Thorps, D. N. (2021). Revenue recognition: 4 top concerns noted by peer reviewers. *Journal of Accountancy, 232*(5), 24–30.

Tzabbar, D., & Margolis, J. (2017). Beyond the startup stage: The founding team's human capital, new venture's stage of life, founder–CEO duality, and breakthrough innovation. *Organization Science, 28*(5), 857–872. https://doi.org/10.1287/orsc.2017.1152

Van Den Broek, A., & Gander, J. (2024). When strategy is a dirty word: The role of visuals in sensegiving strategy to a skeptical audience. *Long Range Planning*,, 102411. https://doi.org/10.1016/j.lrp.2023.102411

Van Le, H., & Suh, M. (2019). Changing trends in internet startup value propositions, from the perspective of the customer. *Technological Forecasting and Social Change, 146*, 853–864. https://doi.org/10.1016/j.techfore.2018.06.021

Van Meeteren, M., Trincado-Munoz, F., Rubin, T. H., & Vorley, T. (2022). Rethinking the digital transformation in knowledge-intensive services: A technology space analysis. *Technological Forecasting and Social Change, 179*, 121631. https://doi.org/10.1016/j.techfore.2022.121631

Voss, G. B., & Voss, Z. G. (2008). Competitive density and the customer acquisition–retention trade-off. *Journal of Marketing, 72*, 3–18.

Waßenhoven, A., Rennings, M., Laibach, N., & Bröring, S. (2023). What constitutes a "Key Enabling Technology" for transition processes: Insights from the bioeconomy's technological landscape. *Technological Forecasting and Social Change, 197*, 122873. https://doi.org/10.1016/j.techfore.2023.122873

Wesley Ii, C. L., Kong, D. T., Lubojacky, C. J., Kim Saxton, M., & Saxton, T. (2022). Will the startup succeed in your eyes? Venture evaluation of resource providers during entrepreneurs' informational signaling. *Journal of Business Venturing, 37*(5), 106229. https://doi.org/10.1016/j.jbusvent.2022.106229

West, G. P., & Meyer, G. D. (1998). To agree or not to agree? Consensus and performance in new ventures. *Journal of Business Venturing, 13*(5), 395–422. https://doi.org/10.1016/S0883-9026(97)00037-2

Zaheer, H., Breyer, Y., Dumay, J., & Enjeti, M. (2022). The entrepreneurial journeys of digital start-up founders. *Technological Forecasting & Social Change, 179*(121638), 1–27. https://doi.org/10.1016/j.techfore.2022.121638

CHAPTER 3

Costs and Entrepreneurial Startup Lifecycles—Mid-to-Late Stages

3.1 Introduction—The Entrepreneurial Startup Survival Stage

An entrepreneurial startup (ESU) by design is a venture that has the potential to develop and grow into a scalable, replicable, and growth-oriented business (Bohan et al., 2024; Heskel & Westlake, 2018; Jansen et al., 2023). Its characteristics are usually developing and executing value propositions with innovative business models that are multisided and multidimensional with a positive impact on tackling a societal, technological, environmental, or business problem. "Value must be coupled with rareness in order to play a significant role in improving competitive advantage, which has an effect on performance by mediating a rareness-performance relationship (Newbert, 2008). In addition, competitive advantage is improved when the firm's capabilities and resources are non-imitable, non-substitutable, and organized, especially when they 'address unmet customer needs in market segments large enough to cover organizational fixed costs' (Hinterhuber, 2013, p. 795). In this case, covering fixed costs simply means a firm must be able to first cash breakeven" (Chammassian, 2016, p. 37).

An ESU usually requires longer-term development and planning with shorter-term survival needs. This means that in the shorter term, it needs a cash infusion not only to stay operational and alive, but also enough

R. G. Chammassian, *Costs, Value, and the Entrepreneurial Venture Journey*, Palgrave Studies in Accounting and Finance Practice,
https://doi.org/10.1007/978-3-031-86216-8_3

cash reserves or funding commitments for the near future to test markets, gain traction, earn revenue, become profitable, and scale for growth.

At the survival stage, *committed funding sources* usually come from external investors, mainly business angels, venture capital (VC), and corporate venture capital (CVC). It is advisable to have enough cash reserves or funding commitments for 12–18 months on a rolling basis, depending on the type of business. Although *one size does not fit all* types of ESUs, such cash requirements are part of *working capital* forecasts and a critical mindset (and pattern) for ESU survival.

The reason for this is foresight. Most of the time it takes much longer to develop the new company and marketable value propositions than originally anticipated. I have seen many times where ESU founders underestimate the time and energy it takes to raise money. Founders are usually overoptimistic and overconfident in their abilities (Simon & Shrader, 2012) and overestimating their sales prospects, revenue generation, and forecasts to self-fund from internally generated cash (Cain et al., 2015; Moore & Healy, 2008). The latter happens rarely. Founders find themselves looking for new money *all their time* (i.e., every three to six months). They spend enormous amounts of time and energy on fundraising instead of focusing on developing, scaling, pivoting, and growing their new venture.

Costs and investment are the flipside of the same coin. ESUs invest in costs to grow their ventures

The majority of the cash needed is for costs to be invested in the ESU's value proposition development. These costs play a *mediating role* in value creation, capture, and eventual extraction of the new venture. *Mediating role* means costs are treated with a *return on cost investment* in mind. Let's recall that *costs and investment are the flipside of the same coin*. ESUs invest in costs to grow their venture. Since the standard financial statements (whether actual incurred, or pro forma) do not capture such cost-value returns, this assessment is relative to the ESU's value creation, capture, and extraction logic, and is captured in off-financial statement disclosures. The ultimate goals on the return on costs are developing markets, and growing the business (top and bottom lines) with proven value propositions that would attract an eventual potential buyer of the ESU during a trade sale.

Takeaways

- An entrepreneurial startup (ESU) by design is a venture that has the potential to develop and grow into a scalable, replicable, and growth-oriented business.
- ESUs usually require longer-term development with shorter-term survival needs.
- New money (i.e., cash) is needed not only to survive but also to develop. The rule of thumb is 12–18 months of financing requirements on a rolling basis.
- These investments are in costs to develop ESUs, playing a mediating role in value creation and capture. Costs and investments are the flip side of the same coin.
- Most ESU founders underestimate both their ability to generate free cash from operations (i.e., sales revenue) and the much longer time it takes to fund raise.

3.2 Value Creation, Capture, and Extraction

Value creation occurs when there is an identified need in the marketplace for the ESU's value proposition. That means the ESU is solving a problem in the marketplace where people and/or companies are willing to pay for it, enough that is worthwhile for both the buying customer and the selling ESU to engage. In other words, there is a *real need* for a problem to be solved in the marketplace that customers *want* to buy. *A real need* is supported with data and acknowledged by the impacted people or organizations. The *want* to buy means that they are willing and able to pay for the value proposition. The customer's *need* and *want* must be aligned. If not, then there may be a *need* in the marketplace, but people may not be convinced enough or willing to buy. In retrospect, people and organizations may *want to* buy something, but the timing may not be right, or they may not be able to afford it currently, or they simply won't need it. This is contrary to most ESU founders' approach I have encountered. They come across as having an idea or a solution to sell but haven't identified the real needs and wants of paying customers. In other words, *they have a solution in search of a problem...*

In earlier stages, when founders approach friends, family, colleagues, and sometimes potential customers about their value proposition, they often get encouraging positive responses or *signals*. People want to be polite, nice, and supportive, not to challenge the founders' initiative per se. However, this could be deceptive. When it comes to actual buying, many shy away from *putting money where their mouth is*. Therefore, it is critical to identify and test the real paying market with value propositions before committing to full development. This *need-want-pay* relationship is critical.

Revenue for the ESU is a cost to its customers

Value capture occurs when the ESU's value proposition is saving time and money, fashioning new positive experiences, championing to make an impact, and improving efficiency and effectiveness for paying customers. The return to the customer is a benefit that outweighs the costs incurred on them or their financial statements. As a reminder, *revenue for the ESU is a cost to its customers*. This means the customer costs' mediating value capture must be greater than its moderating effect on their finances or financial statements. In other words, the costs for the customer must either have a mediating effect with a longer-term value impact or a net positive moderating effect on profitability or both. If the customer is a reseller or a business-to-business (B2B), for instance, that means an improvement to their top line, gross margin, and/or gross operating profits (i.e., EBIDTA) outweigh the costs perceived as an incurred expense. This is how customers define *affordability*. Longer-term value impact means that the customer has a greater positive value extraction in the future measured through metrics on satisfaction, improved reputation, and positive experiences as well as on their (B2B) customers whatever their business focus is.

Affordability for the customer means, costs' mediating value must be greater than their moderating effect

For the ESU, value capture is tangible and intangible. On the tangible side, it is through improved revenue, margin, and profitability, whether one-time or recurring monthly (MRR) or annually (ARR). Intangible means customer satisfaction that establishes and improves long-term relationships, trust, and reputation in the marketplace, leading to social and relational capital.

Value extraction occurs when both ESU's customers and stakeholders extract value in the long run from the endeavor. Customers extract value from their own and/or their customers' satisfaction. ESUs extract value when they can scale and grow a new venture exponentially, leading to high venture valuation, with the ultimate value extraction goal occurring at an exit event (i.e., trade sale M&A). Table 3.1 summarizes the differences in value creation, capture, and extraction between ESUs and their paying customers.

Table 3.1 Value creation, capture, and extraction

	ESU	*Customer*
Value Creation	Developing and testing value propositions that: - Customers need, want, and pay for - That is scalable, replicable, and growth oriented Costs act as a mediator of value creation for a future profitable return	- Solving a critical problem that they need and want to be solved - Solution and associated costs can have an immediate effect on themselves, their businesses, or their own customers - Customer return on costs justifiable as a value mediator
Value Capture	Tangible: Revenue income whether one-time, repeat, or ongoing (MRR/ARR). Costs play a moderator of profitability Intangible: Customer satisfaction, longer-term relationship, trust, and reputation in the marketplace. Costs play a mediator of ESU firm value capture	- Saving time and money - Improving efficiency and effectiveness - Focus on core competencies - Making a positive social, environmental, and economic impact (and to their customers if B2B) - Ushering new positive experiences, trust, and reputation Costs incurred have a net positive mediating effect or benefit for them and their finances (plus their customers if B2B), outweighing the moderating effect as a fixed costs/expense
Value Extraction	- Scalability and long-term growth - multi-year profitability, improved margins - Ultimately higher firm value through an exit event	Gratification, satisfaction, and long-term growth, either for themselves and/or their customers

I use the analogy of building a house in developing an ESU. To build a house from scratch, you first need to find the land that is buildable and has all the tangible and intangible features. Tangibles are the practical features, such as location, accessible road, and utilities (i.e., water, drainage, electricity, gas/wood), where the land is also buildable (geologically) and clean (not contaminated, etc.). Intangibles include environment, neighborhood, views, nature, and similar personal aesthetics. Once you identify and purchase the land at a desirable location, you then need to engage an architect to design the features of the house based on your desires, style, architectural standards, and local rules and regulations. These plans are then valued for reasonability (i.e., costs), affordability (i.e., own funds and budget), and financing (i.e., mortgage) qualification. Once adjusted to the above, the plans are sent for approval from the local or state authorities. During this period, you contact several contractors to get offers to select the best value for money building contractor. You ask for several offers and eventually decide on a contractor. Once the plans are approved (after required adjustments, if any), you engage the contractor, and then work on the building plans and timelines with the builder/contractor. The building process begins first with the foundations of the house. This foundation must be strong enough to build the rest of the house above it. After a strong foundation is laid down, the structure is built (i.e., external and internal supporting walls) and then sub-structures are added (i.e., rooms, kitchen, bathrooms, etc.). Finally, the house is painted, floored, and furnished.

An ESU goes through a similar process. The Developmental and Startup Stages are the project ideation, market attractiveness, and feasibility process: what value proposition the ESU is aiming for (what kind of building), and for whom they are targeting this value proposition (where to build). The survival stage is where the value proposition is finetuned to an innovative business model and business venture that is scalable and growth oriented (what and how to build).

This is why I call the survival stage *mid stage* due to its transformative nature from a seedling idea into a formidable growth-oriented business with a supporting organization. It is a critical milestone and a unique challenge to conquer. There are more peaks (with milestones) and challenges on the horizon, but first, the ESU must survive conquering this critical milestone stage and be prepared enough to build a model supporting organization that is scalable, replicable, and growth oriented. In fact, the survival of the ESU depends on (external) financing its development and growth paths (Coad et al., 2013; Mula et al., 2024). They "put financial capital in place first ahead of building capacity" and then *build capacity ahead of growth* (Mula et al., 2024). Most mid—or survival-stage ESU founders really don't understand the criticality of this stage: what is required of them to change or pivot, to focus on, and to build. Hence, they stretch themselves either too thin or cast a wide multi-directional net where they end up losing control by doing too much will little effect. Here are some examples of how ESU founders are (either/or):

- Acting too frugally where they need to be *investing* heavily on value proposition development while working directly with their customers.
- Developing too many sides of the value proposition at the same time spreading themselves too thin in energy, time, and money—not prioritizing and incrementalizing.
- Growing too fast without building the capacity and infrastructure necessary for growth, such as not hiring enough or hiring the wrong people or too many of them, developing unnecessary infrastructure or venture foundations without viability confirmation, while adding too many fixed costs.
- Underestimating the time and money required to develop and finance this stage. Usually, this occurs due to poor assumptions and planning. Examples include focusing too much on *product features rather* than venture development features; not listening to advice and market signals; and overestimating their ability to generate free cash from selling.
- Spending too much time *surviving* due to money shortage and constantly looking for new money instead of focusing on developing the business and its competencies.

Although one size does not fit all, there are source models or patterns from digitalized startups scaling, for instance, where ESU founders can learn from (Mula et al., 2024, p. 2).

1. A*ttract financial capital first before building capacity* and then *build capacity* with intellectual capital (IC) development *ahead of growth.*
2. Develop and test *organizational processes* and enable *tech innovation* to handle growth.

3. Focus on *economies of scale* with data-driven solutions for cost optimization and return on invested costs.
4. Reshape and transforming founders' roles to C-suite positions.

Thus, this mid stage has two key characteristic components: One, to financially, operationally, and strategically survive while developing a unique value proposition that is customer-focused. Two, to develop a new venture organization with a dramatically different mindset and operating model that requires development and investment in human capital, organizational capital (i.e., capabilities, like processes, technology, innovation, etc.), social capital, and relational capital. *Chapter 4—Costs and Intellectual Capital Development* will specifically cover these investments in more detail.

Takeaways

- Value creation begins with an identified need in the marketplace, solving a real problem that customers need, want, and are willing to pay for.
- Value capture occurs when value propositions are affordable for the customer and profitable for the ESU. As ESU revenue is a cost to its customer, affordability for the customer means, costs' mediating value must be greater than their moderating effect.
- Value extraction means long-term benefits to the ESU customer and higher venture valuation for the ESU, especially when an exit event occurs.
- The survival mid stage requires a completely different mindset to develop value propositions that attract financing, build capacity with intellectual capital (IC) development, focus on economies of scale, and reshape the founders' roles.

3.3 Early Mid Stage—Survival of the Fittest

One key tangible and common characteristic of the early survival or mid-stage is that the ESUs usually do not have enough income or cash to survive in the short—to medium-term. That means it either does not have any revenue or it has some revenue but not enough to survive on its own to cover its costs. It needs to find new financing sources that are external to the ESU.

The reason why I started this section with investment needs for survival in mind is because it is critical to view an ESU from the filters of investors as an important intermediary and customer. If we understand the mindset of the investor as a key financing customer on what they look for and need to see in an ESU, we can then reverse engineer the ESU project to better position it as *investible*.

My research with various mid-to-late-stage startup founders indicated that ESUs have three layers of customers:

1. Paying customers, who pay for ESU's value proposition (products and services) such as B2B or B2C end user of ESU products/ services.
2. Financing customers, who invest into the ESU as *financing suppliers*.
3. Trade sales M&A customers who are the future buyers of the ESU, or ESU's ultimate customer.

In fact, ESUs have three types of potential customers: paying, financing, and trade sales

Innovation comes from both within an organization and external sources. Internal sources of innovation mainly come from ESU's human capital, such as the founders along with the team. Innovation also comes from external sources, such as customers whose needs may be different than what the ESU is proposing. "Hence, listening to the customer's needs and requests or addressing current problems or future issues may motivate an ESU to become more innovative and adaptive to the current and future circumstances" (Chammassian, 2016, p. 47). It is a partnering approach with potential customers as early in the process as possible. "We need to give services and learn from the customers and learn what their needs are and learn even if they don't know that they have a need. It is to find their needs from them so we can propose a few things with the aim of finding much more behind the wall" (Chammassian, 2016, p. 89).

Innovation that comes from external sources can be reactive or proactive. Reactive innovation is when customers and markets are telling the ESU to adapt its value proposition to something else that they need and can afford to pay for. This is key for revenue-generating purposes as well as for survival and growth in the mid-to-late stages.

Proactive innovation may also come from investors who finance ESUs as well as provide additional management advice, access to networks, and to potential customers. In fact, experienced and serial entrepreneurs treat their current and potential investors as key customers in parallel to their paying customers. They listen to the financing supplier as customers' needs, feedback, and advise. They view investors (i.e., financing customers) as intermediaries in the value creation process between the ESU, its paying customers, and the eventual trade sales customers.

Hence, it is as important to listen to and build consensus from the messaging and signaling coming from various types of financing customers while listening to their potential paying customers. In fact, if investors *buy-in* the ESU's value proposition, that means they believe in the ESU's concept and its founder's narrative, as well as in the value proposition which will work both in the paying customer and trade sale customer marketplace. Since paying customers are limited to provide the necessary funding through revenue for ESU to self-finance, external investors as financing customers are as important as paying customers if not more important at this stage.

There are several financing customers at mid stage, mostly made up of platforms, accelerators, business angels, and venture funds: venture capital (VC) and corporate venture capital (CVC). The financing rounds at pre-mid stage are usually referred to as post-seed or pre-Series A financing. That means the ESU needs another financing boost to get further clarity on its business model with additional proof of concept before committing to planning and building a scalable business. Financing rounds at mid-to-early growth stage are referred to as Series A. VCs who invest in Series A rounds are increasingly seeking ESUs who are breaking even (BE) financially. Figure 3.1 depicts the picture of mid-stage ESU financing ecosystem players.

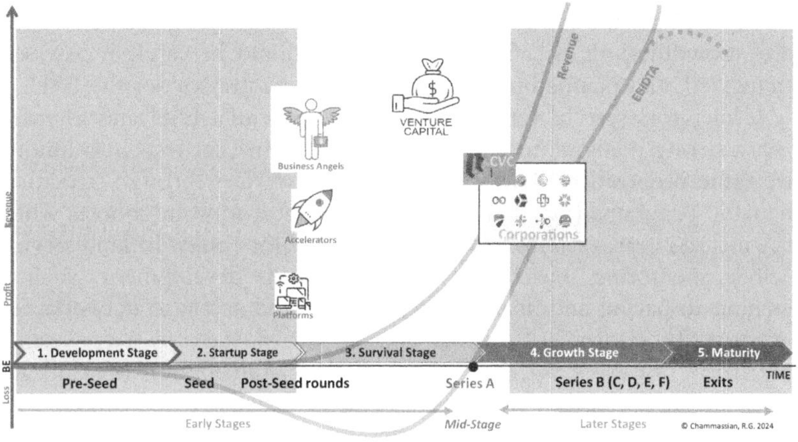

Fig. 3.1 Mid-stage financing customers

3.3.1 Early Survival Stage Financing Options

In the early-to-mid stages, financing options are still diverse beyond the traditional private equity and venture capital. Thanks to digital technologies, platforms have sprung up democratizing investment through crowdfunding and crowdlending platforms to small investors while bringing expanded visibility and early-to-mid stage financing sources for ESUs. These platforms can be reward based with products, equity based with potential future ROI, or debt based with interest payments plus the principal payback in a few years. The opportunity for ESUs is to gain both financing as well as project visibility from a larger audience of micro investors. This is especially effective if the ESU would like to test its value proposition through products and/or services in the marketplace and get direct feedback from financing and paying customers, who could end up being the same. The opportunity for the ESU is the early exposure of the venture's business model business model to a wider audience. The opportunity cost is that the strategy may not generate the right type of response from a pool that may not be the right *crowd* or customer base. Furthermore, whereas the ESU may be using the platforms for feedback to improve and finetune, it may generate negative feedback and reputation too early in the process, although sometimes a fair dose of *humbling feedback* (Mahajan, 1992) is good to improve value propositions. Therefore, crowdfunding as a financing strategy should be carefully assessed, strategized, and planned to ensure it is the right strategy for the ESU.

Accelerators search, vet, and select high-potential ESU and founders with a strong pedigree to develop ESUs initial market tests into innovative value proposition. They provide in-kind services through structured thematic programs (i.e., FinTech, AI, SaaS, or a mix) in cohorts which may include some cash investment in exchange for equity. In-kind services include mentoring, coaching, workshops, skills development (such as pitching to paying and financing customers), and access to networks and investors. In return, accelerators take an equity stake or a convertible (see below) in the ESU, depending on their contribution (in-kind and cash) and negotiation. This may also involve needs-based ongoing in-kind support for a certain period after *graduating* from an acceleration program.

Accelerators work with a pool of startups that go through various steps to be short-listed. The opportunity for the accelerator is having a portfolio of ESUs within a cohort, which reduces its overall financial risks through the risk spread amongst various ESU, say 10–15. If over 80% fail or breakeven and less than 20% make good ROI, then less than 20% would more than offset the losses of the 80%. The challenge with accelerators is in their structured approach of their program design and focus on specific domains, stages, mentor quality and engagement, reputation and trust, and their failure to adapt to rapidly changing trends and technologies. Accelerators are also considered as in-kind and in-cash financing intermediaries, which means they invest with other people's knowledge and monies and can get under pressure by their investors to sell off early or during low financing periods.

For ESUs, the opportunity is to get into diversified programs with experts helping them focus on their projects. They also get good training on how to pitch to investors. The opportunity costs for ESUs include equity dilution, especially when ESUs experience cultural and program fit issues and network limitations. Furthermore, accelerators require time and resource commitment for a specified period taking founders away from running their businesses. Moreover, if the ESUs focus shifts or pivots, the accelerator program and equity dilution may become an expensive sunk cost with future liability. Finally, accelerators may pressure for early exits because the ESU project may no longer suit them instead of the longer-term viability and growth of the ESU.

Business angels (BA) are high net-worth individuals (HNWI)[1] who are looking for ***investible*** ESUs with a strong team (i.e., human capital) to innovate, scale, and grow. They are mostly betting on the team first, then the project and its potential returns. *Investible* means:

1. Is **the team** investible? This includes their entrepreneurial pedigree, human capital, mindset, adaptability, and *coachability*[2] (Johnson et al., 2021; Kuratko et al., 2021). If this first condition is met, then BAs review the next condition.
2. Is **the project** investible? Is there a real market, solving problems with solutions that are scalable, replicable, with sustainable growth, meets customer needs, wants, and affordability, and is within a present and future trend?
3. Would the ESU be attractive enough in a future trade sale marketplace within 3–5 years? Would it be a potentially ***profitable*** investment for a hefty **ROI**?

Although those three criteria are interlinked, they all start with the ESU founders and their human capital. If the team appears to have the pedigree, then the project may become more viable. Let's recall that in earlier to mid stages, people and technology are one and the same.

This is first revealed during the project pitching. Business angels first look at the pitch and then the pitching. Is the team well organized? Do they understand the real problem they are solving? Does the team have drive, passion, and eagerness? How legitimate are they with their information and data? How well do they connect with their audience? Does the project pitch have substance with a well-researched and developed storyline past, present, and future? In fact, such pitching is the ESU

[1] Each country has its own definition of *high net worth*, such as having a *net wealth* of greater than one million Euros/dollars, and an annual income of over 200,000 Euros/dollars. Net wealth means HNWI's Asset Value minus Liabilities equals the investor's net worth.

[2] *Coachability* is one of my personal qualification criteria. Do the founders *listen and act upon advice and feedback* or do they simply *hear* what is said but either dismiss it, brush it aside and do nothing about it? It doesn't mean all advice is good and must be followed. It just means that the advisor/investor shares opinions based on what the founders are saying (i.e., net advice). It is up to the founders to act upon. The winning teams are the ones that not only heed to advice, but also exceed it by following up diligently, researching and finding additional opportunities and challenges.

founders' *informational signaling* on the ESU's strategy and its potential for growth and ROI to seek financial and social resources (Huang & Knight, 2017; Wesley et al., 2022). Signaling can be objective, subjective, informational, and interpersonal (Huang & Knight, 2017; Svetek, 2022).

Majority of the investors at this early mid stage are business angel investors. Since at this stage, there are limited financial data to determine the value of the ESU quantitatively, business angels usually rely on qualitative measures as inputs to predict ESU's value. They also include personal experiences, gut feeling, and connectiveness with the ESU founders. These are all personal and subjective, driving the objectiveness of their investment to predict how the venture would eventually evolve. These criteria diverge tremendously from one investor to another. To demonstrate, based on a major peer-reviewed study, Berre and Le Pendeven (2023) found "36 startup-valuation drivers and cluster[ed] them into five macro-themes: entrepreneur characteristics; firm characteristics; investor characteristics; market Conditions; and deal conditions" (p. 385). In another meta-analysis of journal publications, Ferrati and Muffatto (2021) identified 208 unique criteria divided into 35 specific categories and 11 generic classes. The top three included "characteristics of the entrepreneur and/or the management team, characteristics of the product/service and the marketplace, and investor related factors (i.e., screening focus, expected ROI)" (p. 166). Almost in all cases though, angel investors have their own specific targets based on their cost of capital and discount rate, and plan their own exit from their investments in a future liquidity event (Botelho et al., 2021). In other words, business angels' ultimate goal is to gain a hefty ROI.

3.3.2 *Financing Opportunity Costs and Trust Factors*

Cost of capital refers to what it *costs* a business angel (or any investor) to borrow money from financial markets, which should be equal to the minimum return an angel requires to earn to justify the investment opportunity. For example, if an angel's cost of capital is 5%, this will be the minimum return it needs to get in order to invest in no-/low-risk opportunities, such as a bank savings account. However, basic economic logic dictates that investors must have a much higher return potential than their cost of capital (i.e., income—cost = profit). Since ESUs are high-risk investments, angels (and VCs) would require a much higher return on their investment. This is where their *discount rate* or *internal rate of return (IRR)* comes into play. Discount rates incorporate a higher *risk premium* than its cost of capital to compensate the high risk of ESU investment. It is a rate used to *discount future cash flows* to the ESU investment's present value simply referred to the *discounted cash flow (DCF)* method. In short, the cost of capital is internal to an investor (i.e., an angel or VC), while a discount rate is external to the investor and focuses on the rate of return expected from an ESU.[3]

Besides financial, the business angel *commitment* could be a longer-term interest with the possibility of follow-up on subsequent financing rounds. It could also mean the *lead angel investor* bringing in a network of other angel investors for peer opinion, consensus building, and industry contacts and becoming an advisor on strategic decisions (Bonnet et al., 2022; Wood et al., 2020). There is a trend of business angels investing in a pool with other angel investors as co-investors, for instance, through a *syndicate*,[4] instead of individually (Mason et al., 2019). This is especially viable to attracting future venture funds for the higher rounds. Besides financial sources, it is also important that a strong values connectiveness and vision alignment exist between the business angel (alone or pooled) and ESU founders. If ESU founders make a deal with an angel with deep pockets but have vision alignment issues from the start, this will inevitably lead to future conflicts. For the ESU, the lead investor should be both a financial asset as well as an intangible asset (i.e., networks, human capital, investor social and relational capital) and not a future liability.

> *A lead business angel investor should be a financial asset (i.e., a tangible resource) as well as an intangible asset (i.e., networks, human capital, goal alignment) for the ESU*

There is a great deal of opportunity cost for both angel investors and ESU founders. On the founders' side, the opportunity cost is related to the selection of a lead investor. It is important that founders identify,

[3] For a better understanding cost of capital, discount rates, DCF and similar, refer to a book on the principles of corporate finance (such as by Brealey et al., 2022), or on investment valuations (such as by Damodaran, 2024; or by Koller et al., 2020).

[4] A syndicate is an investment instrument where several investors pool their monies into one investment. This combining allows them to increase the investment ticket amount, have a better negotiating position, and be represented in the cap tables and shareholder board as one voice or voting position. This also helps the ESU's cap tables, making it more manageable by having one syndicate as shareholder instead of several shareholders.

attract, and work with a lead angel investor who has the right background, passion, commitment, and networks, who aligns with the ESU's vision and goals (Cipollone & Giordani, 2019). This *matchmaking process* is critical. Otherwise, personality clashes and unaligned visions and goals could become a major (negative) opportunity cost for the ESU, leading to toxic and lethal situations.

On the business angel side, the opportunity cost of losing their investment is very high as it is known that the vast majority of ESUs do not achieve their initial plans, cannot pivot properly, and in many cases fail within the first few years. It is detrimental that BAs screen the founders for their pedigree, passion, cohesion, diversity, and coachability to get the job done. Furthermore, angel investors need to trust that the ESU founders will do what they say they will do from the start.

The relationship between the angel and founders is built upon the narrative that the founders convincingly *sell* to the investor—the *financing buyer*. This *relational and social trust* can also be culturally relevant depending on a country's cultural high vs. low trust factors that the ESU is incorporated in (Ding et al., 2015). In the United States, for instance, this social trust is higher, than say in some European countries. To build this relationship usually takes time, anywhere from one to six months, depending on the investment round value, ESUs value proposition, and financing and product market conditions. This is why ESU founders should calibrate longer-term financing needs and the time it takes to get the right financing deal with the investor—the financing partner or customer.

3.3.3 Do's and Don'ts of Financing at Early Mid-Survival Stage

Early-to-mid stage is a major evolutionary period of filtering, recalibrating, re-focusing, and pivoting phase (Dhir et al., 2024; Sala et al., 2022), where many novice entrepreneurs discount or underestimate. In most cases, initial positive signals from potential buying customers may be deceiving and do not mean it's time to bet on the value proposition heavily yet. It simply means:

a. There is a good indication that the project is worthwhile to proceed and invest further.

b. This investment should be focused on further developing the value proposition so that it can be scalable and growth oriented leading to sales volume and diversity of customers.
c. Getting closer to several different types of customers and really developing a needs-want-buy based approach to value propositions.
d. Prioritizing what customer channel to focus on in incremental phases.

The filtering involves not only the project development side, but also the project financing side to decipher which type of financing strategy ESUs need to pursue based on their value proposition: crowdfunding (more public/higher visibility), accelerators (with themes and structured programs, but which one), or directly with business angels (more private, what type, who, how to access)? In all cases, this is part of a parallel strategy that takes as much time, effort, and confidence (Huang et al., 2022) as market testing and market entry determinations. It also sets a key foundation for future financing rounds. Not thinking through the financing strategy properly can be a very costly (and sometimes fatal) mistake in the medium to long term. Here are some of the opportunity costs in mid-to-late stages if and when early-to-mid stage financing is not planned properly:

- Dilution of equity can be excessive if the ESU founders are inexperienced or desperate and give away too much equity (i.e., shares) to early-stage investors too early in the ESU lifecycle, it impacts the *capitalization (cap) tables*[5] where equity ownership is accounted for. Early investors may end up having too much control or say into the ESU business and financing strategy. Founders may become demotivated with lower equity stakes in their own company. This also impacts how future investors view the ESUs investability potential. One pharmatech founder I interviewed had only 6% shares in his

[5] A cap table is a balance sheet shareholder sub-ledger that shows who owns what in the ESU. It includes individual ownerships (including founders, vested employees, investors, and other stakeholders), percentage of ownerships, equity valuations, and dilution. It is also used as the basis for future convertibles and in negotiating future financing rounds. Cap tables are one of the first items that a potential investor will ask the ESU to provide during due diligence.

own company by the time his ESU reached the growth stage. He was in a no-win situation and utterly demotivated and demoralized.

- High or hidden debt burdens due to convertible loans or crowdlending. Accounting-wise, convertibles must be recorded as a long-term debt (a non-current liability) on the ESU balance sheet. ESU founders must be transparent with future investors on their debt burden and debt-to-equity conversions in simulated cap tables. Several times, I have encountered ESUs ignoring this or not revealing their debt or conversion burden to future potential investors until it's too late where it becomes a major issue when investors find out about them by accident or after their commitment (i.e., after the fact). This could lead to major trust and legal issues for the ESU. Transparency is key: Founders should never deliberately not tell (or lie to) their investors.
- Future valuation, strategic financing, and exit challenges due to:
  - Complex financing structures with complicated cap tables, different financing actors with misaligned interests and goals, and debt-to-equity ratio issues.
  - Investor conflicts of interest with varying types of ownership, preferred vs. common shares, convertibles, rights and warrants, success-based bonus payment, and future liquidity terms.
  - Not being able to build consensus for follow-up rounds and on exit opportunities.
- Reputational risk if/when the word gets out that the founders have been hiding financial liabilities from investors. The private equity financing, including angel and VCs, is a small well-networked world. People talk especially when soliciting other investors. ESU financial opaqueness not only could lead to negative reputational risks but also could be fatal to ESU survival as no one would invest in them.
- Short-sightedness on cash flow needs for the medium and long term. Founders are usually overoptimistic of their revenue generation forecasts. Most often, it takes much longer to generate free cash flow from sales. ESU founders end up soliciting financing with lower amounts for the short term by overestimating their ability to earn revenue quickly. They end up running out of cash sooner rather than later and must solicit more funding from different sources. Furthermore, some of the debt instruments may mature where the issuer may ask for debt repayment instead of conversion which the ESU

can afford to pay back. This optimistic overconfidence (Cain et al., 2015; Simon & Shrader, 2012) will lead ESU founders to constantly look for new money and running for cover instead of running their business.

Henceforth, understanding what one of the ESU's primary customers, the investors, would look to see in a business plan is a good parallel benchmark to value proposition development. Here are some key areas ESU founders should focus on at this early mid stage:

- Solidifying proof of concept through sales with a diverse multi-customer base, engagement, needs assessment, and feedback loop. This will lead to a more sustainable project with consistent demand, better operational efficiency, and reduced risk during economic downturns.
- Ensuring that the revenue distribution is spread well amongst several customers. Ideally, no single customer should generate more than 10% of ESU's revenue.[6]
- Identifying and understanding key customer acceptance sales triggers that are:
  - Tangible: What direct cost savings and indirect cost benefits can customers gain from the ESU's value proposition?
  - Intangible: What features and experiences would make them buy, remain engaged, and as long-term repeat or recurring customers?
- Developing holistic features with multi-sided platform design thinking.
  - Combining a mix of products, services, networks, relationships, and experiences with users, stakeholders, and triple customers.
  - Utilizing circular value chain and network model.

[6] I have seen ESUs generating > 80% of their revenue from one customer, a grocery chain (for example), and claiming this as absolute proof of concept. While this customer may be a good reference point, it may pose significant risks to the ESU. If such a customer decides to cancel the contract or demand major discounts and concessions due to its negotiating power (which they do), it would severely impact the ESUs major revenue stream and operations, and become a fatal blow to the ESU.

- Putting the necessary conditions around the value proposition for uniqueness, that are valuable for the customer (see above), rare, difficult to imitate, and has the proper organizational design to support for long-term customer engagement.
- Featuring long-term sustainability and impact (social, environmental, and economic), privacy, security, trust legitimacy, customer experiences, access, and empowerment.[7]
- Prioritizing where and when to invest.
- Incrementalizing for a sustainable growth strategy.

- Capturing and extracting intangible value as well as tangible value for the ESU.
- Determining what resources (mainly human capital) are needed to develop, scale, and grow its business, and how founders would reshape their roles vis-a-vis new team members.
- How financing works and who are the players at this early-to-mid stage? Typically, they are:

  - *Seed or Series A*
  - Convertible loans vs. direct equity.
  - Platforms, accelerators, business angels, some early-stage venture capital.
  - Investment new money from 100 K up to two million; lower for non-high tech and higher for high-tech ESUs).

Finally, it is important to note that *costs, time, and money* are interconnected to each other with a major impact, especially on opportunity cost. Based on my interviews, one ESU founder summed it up as “money is less expensive than time.” Another one reassured that “time, which is the biggest money, went into market studies, markets and applications in particular…whatever technology, whatever idea, an important variable is time.” It is *an expensive race with time* from the Startup Stage onwards. The longer it takes to develop the ESU’s value proposition, the costlier and riskier it gets. “The opportunity cost of time also means more money or investment would be needed to finance operations.” Additional quotes: “Time matters! timing matters! So, every week lost is a huge loss because it’s a race.…In our IT consumer-facing business, every week is a huge

[7] How to develop this is discussed more in *Chapter 4—Costs and Intellectual Capital Development.*

loss." "What really increases the expenses, besides manufacturing, is *clinical* [R&D] and time, the two are connected together." "On average, it takes six months between the first meeting with some qualified person in a [sic] company, for example, and the signature of a contract. That means we need to finance six months each time. So that's the reason [why] we are not in the black today." Once a startup, it becomes "a complicated business, very complex. So, you don't want to lose time and make mistakes. You cannot afford to lose time. It's expensive, it's time consuming, and it's risky. So, the best way to do that is get people that have [the right] background." (Chammassian, 2016, pp. 100–101).

Time is money: It is an expensive race with time from the Startup Stage onwards.

Time is money! Therefore, there is an opportunity cost of time not met that is related to ESU's performance and survival. "The first word that comes to my mind is 'time' because performance was, from our point of view, how fast we could actually build the product [value proposition] that we had set out to build. Engineering and product developments delays, which came from the difficulty of the problem that we were solving, increased our costs and led us to a sort of a less independently sustainable position than we would have liked… If things have a way to go wrong, they will, almost certainly will and being able to anticipate those scenarios and be prepared for those when the time comes" (Chammassian, 2016, p. 141).

Takeaways

- Survival means that the ESU does not generate enough revenue and profits to finance its operations or to invest in its growth. It needs external financing.
- It is then important for ESU founders to understand how investors view their project to make the ESU investible.
- In fact, ESUs have three key customers who are paying customers, financing customers, and future trade sales M&A customers.
- It is important to listen to the needs of all customers. Their messaging and signaling lead to external innovation opportunities that could be reactive or proactive.

- Reactive innovation comes from paying customers who react to the ESU's value proposition and offer feedback on their needs and willingness to pay.
- Proactive innovation comes from financing customers who provide proactive feedback (sometimes requirements) on how to position in the marketplace.
- There are several investors at this stage, including platforms (i.e., crowdfunding or lending), accelerators, business angels, and some early-stage venture funds.
- The majority of investors at this early mid stage are angel investors.
- Each one of them has its pros and cons, opportunity and opportunity costs.
- The most important factors are the right matchmaking, trust, and reputation building, not just *selling* the ESU narrative.
- Costs and opportunity costs, time and timing, and money are interconnected to each other.

3.4 Mid-Stage—Surviving the Scale and Early Growth

The mid-stage follows the value proposition logic narrative of early-to-mid stage. It is generally characterized when the ESU has achieved its goal of validating its (prioritized) market channel (i.e., B2B, B2C, P2P), diversified customer base, with good proof of concept, some sales revenue, and a developed unique value proposition. Yet the revenue generated is not enough to sustain the ESU while developing and executing its growth strategy. This means the ESU would need additional financing to invest in developing its team and intellectual capital, (see footnote 6) scaling its operations, and expanding its market base (Bohan et al., 2024). This mid-stage is also a crucial pivotal period in a different way requiring a set of strategic and organizational development with skillsets to build processes that can be replicated to grow the company domestically and internationally.

This stage is sometimes referred to by its financing term as *Series A*. It has a completely different set of requirements and targeted financing, which include developing replicable revenue and operating models, automated processes, and adopting 80–20 rule[8] for sustainable growth. The Time to take between stages depends on how well the venture has an established and sustainable business model, as well as the type of business (i.e., a biotech venture takes a much longer incubation and acceleration period than an agrifood web-based platform). The general characteristics of the mid-stage include:

- To define and acquire necessary resources, mainly human and some organizational.
- To determine investment amounts needed for short—to medium-term (i.e., 12–18 rolling months), to identify financing sources, and to allocate ample time it needs to raise funds.
- To develop and build a scalable, replicable, and growth-oriented organization as a three-dimensional business model that is technology/problem-driven, market/demand-driven, and exit-driven.[9]
- To prioritize scaling and incrementalize growth.
- To plan milestone-driven investment needs in costs based on a growth plan.

Figure 3.2 below illustrates how costs as an investment play a mediating role in the value creation and capture processes of the survival mid stage with long-term ROI mindset. The goal is to design, finance, and develop a scalable business model.

[8] As known as the Pareto Principle.

[9] See Chapter 5—Costs and Three Dimensional (3D) Business Models for more details.

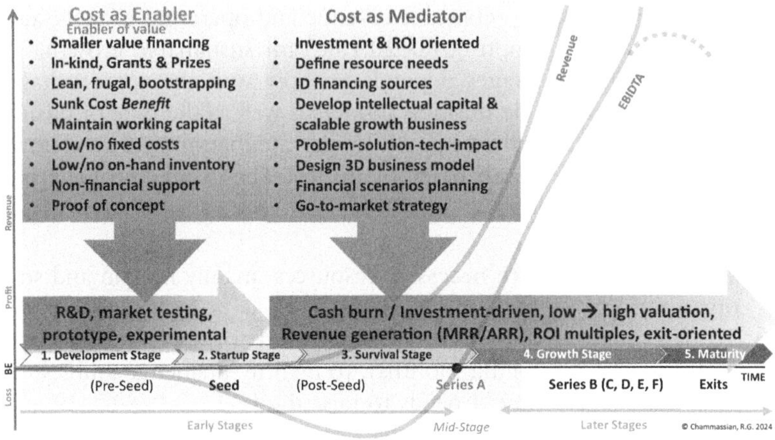

Fig. 3.2 Entrepreneurial lifecycle investment and financing early mid stages

3.4.1 Developing a Scalable Business

To develop a scalable business model requires both physical resources (tangible) and non-physical (intangible) resources with different cost structures and requirements. Follows a general blueprint on the resources that are needed to apply the 80–20 rule where over 80% of such resources are similar for most ESUs, and under 20% are adapted to their line of business. Table 3.2 covers the main tangible (Physical) resource considerations and associated costs including:

Table 3.3 covers the main intangible (non-Physical) resource considerations for intellectual capital development and associated costs which include:

The above are considerations to build an organizational model with assumptions and to plan for its associated costs for a scalable and sustainable business model. Although, business models vary from ESU to ESU, the above listing is the basics of planning and building a multi-sided and multidimensional platform-oriented ESU that establishes a strong basis for value proposition for three types of customers ESUs have. Key is to prioritize and incrementalize the development in order not to spread the ESU too thin in multi-directions at this stage juggling too many topics at the same time.

Table 3.2 Tangible resources and cost considerations using 80–20 rule

	>80% of the time	*<20% of the time*
Facilities and Office Space	• To house a growing team and its culture • To develop a facilities model for future expansion where > 80% is replicable to other locations • To identify facilities that can be expanded modularly to incrementalize fixed costs • To acquire necessary office infrastructure: desks, meeting rooms, and common areas • If direct customer-facing (i.e., B2C), design an experience-driven facilities model that is core to ESU values and is replicable • Location matters! Depending on the ESU's business model: to position as close to key customers or industries as possible • Consumables COSTS: – Furnishings: capital expenditures (CapEx) to be depreciated over its economic life – Facilities rent, utilities, consumables: Operating Expenses (OpEx)	• Key tech developing teams who need to be insourced for IP/IC protection • Determine what could be home based vs. remote work or outsourced work • If producing own products or having own repair centers, ID proper industrial park • Equipment may defer for a food and beverage company (i.e., kitchen equipment) vs. a delivery-based ESU (i.e., vans, robots, bicycles) • R&D facilities/requirement (i.e., a *clean room*) COSTS: – Special equipment: CapEX – Production facilities, R&D, and overhead: Rent, utilities expenses (OpEx)

(continued)

Table 3.2 (continued)

	>80% of the time	*<20% of the time*
Technological infrastructure	• Office equipment: computers, laptops, printers, laptops, shared servers • Telecom: smartphones and mobile devices COSTS: – Majority: CapEx – Outsourced recurring monthly services, such as cloud storage or tech support helpdesk: OpEx	• Engineering and architectural design ESUs require sophisticated software (i.e., CAD, project management) • Considerations to develop its own tech, to buy, or to rent (i.e., license) • Considerations for one-time vs. repeat purchases vs. recurring purchases (i.e., subscriptions) • B2C vs. B2B vs. B2B2B2C vs. P2P and similar COSTS: – Majority: CapEx – Direct revenue-related costs: Cost of Services (var. costs) – Minority: OpEx

	>80% of the time	*<20% of the time*
Operational	For physical product-oriented businesses: • Inbound Supply chain and logistics, whether finished goods or raw material • Warehousing/storage facilities • Out-bound logistics/distribution • Decision to outsource or insource COSTS: • Inbound supply chain: raw material, labor, facilities for own production or finished goods produced elsewhere, PLUS inbound freight, customs duties, and warehousing (working capital):	• Special imbedded proprietary tech in products requires special treatment to safeguard • High-value inventory (>1 K) • Multi SKU[10] modular inventory COSTS: • Same treatment as simpler products, except high-value Inventory may be captured as a long-term asset, esp. if it is reworkable/reusable • Sold inventory: Cost of Goods Sold (var. costs) • If the product is leased,[11] it depends on the country GAAP principle differentiating operating or financial leases – Operating lease—ESU retains ownership: depreciation expense – Finance lease—Ownership eventually transferred to customer: net investment in lease during lease term; interest expense (if any/refinancing) • Specialized facilities and equipment: clean rooms, paint shops • Transportation for delivery and pickup purposes or business: vans, refrigerated, etc COSTS: • Specialized facilities, equipment, and transportation: CapEx

(continued)

10 SKU stands for Stock-Keeping Unit (SKU). It is an alphanumeric scannable bar or QR code printed on the inventory allowing companies to track the type of inventory they have.

11 Leasing business are complex and need to be reviewed by professional accountants and lawyers to ensure service level agreement (SLA) clarity. Generally, there are two types of leases: operating and financial. Leasing has its own value proposition opportunities and challenges. On the one hand, leasing products may generate MRR/ARR with interest income; on the other hand, such products as assets would remain under ESU ownership to depreciate and address wear and tear issues. They will also require a customer support operating model.

Table 3.2 (continued)

	>80% of the time	*<20% of the time*
	– Initially captured as ***inventory***[12] in current assets in the balance sheet – Inventory accounted and valued methods: average, first-in-first-out (FIFO); last in, first out (LIFO), weighted average cost (WAC) – When the product is sold: Cost of Goods Sold/values in inventory account/product SKU or S/N[13] • Outbound logistics: mostly OpEx For Services businesses: 1. Facilities and service delivery infrastructure (i.e., customer sales or care centers) 2. General equipment, hardware, and general software (MS Office) 3. Marketing and sales brochures and branded promotional material COSTS: Inbound: • Equipment, hardware, and software: mostly non-current assets (CapEx) • Facilities: depending on renting (OpEx) buying (CapEx), or leasing (CapEx/OpEx) • Strategic partnerships: OpEx Outbound: • Direct customer support: Cost of Sales (var. costs)	

[12] When it comes to inventory, as the ESU scales and grows the focus should be on working capital generation internally/organically through improved gross margins (i.e., revenue minus cost of goods sold) in order to support the growth and investment in people's productivity through streamlined processes and automation where possible for cost optimization (Tatikonda, Terjesen, Patel & Parida, 2013).

[13] S/N is Serial Number, which is a unique product code often used by manufacturers.

Table 3.3 Intangible resources and cost considerations using 80–20 rule

	> *80% of the time*	< *20% of the time*
People	Human Capital: Senior management, skilled, specialized and experienced team recruitment, training, and development (insourced) Founders' role evolution and reshaping Human Resources: infrastructure and operating support staff (insourced, outsourced) Consultants/subcontractors (outsourced) COSTS: All people related costs are considered OpEx	Specialized software developers and unique process designers (IP development) COSTS: Patents, copyrights, and trademarks: non-current asset/intangibles; otherwise OpEx
Technology or IP	• Website design and brand development depending on the type of business: informational, marketing, online sales driven, or a major multidimensional platform (direct and indirect sales, after-sales services, major help desk, and maintenance) • Specialized software licenses and shared tools (i.e., CRM, ERP) • Outsourced servers/cloud storage • Data sourcing, whether one-time market research or subscription to a database • Big Data development for own use COSTS: One-time development or recurring: OpEx	Development of software-as-a-service (SaaS), licensable Big Data, and similar specialized software development that could be copyright COSTS: Non-current assets—intangibles
Organizational/ Operational	• Process design and development • Service delivery/customer support services: pre-sales, sales, and post-sales (i.e., direct call centers) COSTS: • Process design and development: OpEx • Customer support services: OpEx • Customer-specific dedicated services: Cost of Services Sales (var. costs)	Highly developed and unique/specialized processes COSTS: • If patentable/IP: Non-current assets—intangibles • If not, then OpEx

(continued)

Table 3.3 (continued)

	> *80% of the time*	< *20% of the time*
Relationships	• Strategic partnership – Proprietary manufacturing – Proprietary marketing – Third-party vendors – Universities and research centers – Specialized service providers – Tech platforms (i.e., subcontractors, consultants, web services, white label) and subscriptions • Industry relations and memberships • Customer networks development COSTS: • Proprietary manufacturing: inventory to Cost of Goods Sold • Marketing, industry relations, networks development: OpEx • Third-party vendors, tech platforms, outsourced services: either OpEx or Cost of sales (if direct/revenue driven)	• Strategic joint ventures • Reseller/distributor agreements • R&D projects, joint COSTS: • Joint ventures/creating separate company: Non-current assets—Investments • Reseller/distributor: Cost of Goods/Services Sold • R&D projects, usually OpEx vs. Non-current assets—intangibles if patentable
Social	• Trust and reputation building and maintenance • Social media positioning • Social networks and community building • Stakeholder development and blogs • Non-profit organization contribution • User development and freemium services COSTS: Majority OpEx	Specialized media, news channels, video streaming COSTS: Majority OpEx

ESU's primary financing customers (i.e., its investors) at mid-stages like to see prioritized investments that show profitability along with an incremental replicable growth plan.

ESUs need to make initial (seed) investments judiciously to show proof of concept that is profitable. *Prioritization* should go to *low-hanging fruits*, where ESUs can show the best financial returns on invested costs through business development, and paying customer engagement, feedback, acquisition, and profitable sales. Extensive but prioritized experimentation with market validation and new market or customer segment identification continues as ESUs scale (Sanasi et al., 2023). Although this approach has been key to the survival and success of high-tech ESUs, this *growth hacking* also applies to non-high-tech ESUs that need to scale with external financing support (Bargoni et al., 2024).

Investors as ESU's financing customers very much like to see that ESUs can stand on their own by becoming *financially independent* through profitable sales and some self-financing. *Financially independent* means profitable enough that not only they can survive and cover their operating costs, but also, they can also make enough profit to reinvest into their businesses. This will indicate that ESU's value proposition works and is worthy of further investment for growth. Investors also like to see *incremental growth* that is executed in stages where a set goal is reached. Once those milestones are achieved, then the ESU could plan to execute the next priority in its list, whether it is developing an expanded value proposition or replicating for growth. ESU survival depends on its growth path (Coad et al., 2013).

3.4.2 Financing a Scalable Growth Business

This phase follows the development options of the scalable business model (Bohan et al., 2024; Cavallo et al., 2024; Jansen et al., 2023) with various tangible and intangible consideration in developing and solidifying ESU's value proposition. While the *value logic* remains intact with the tested and identified business model, key characteristics in this phase include developing an executable business plan with the right organizational design that is investible. Iterations and modifications continue to be featured. However, they have more to do with the continuous learning and fine-tuning of the first executable model, the bet on the tested business model to make it a formidable and growth-oriented business. This means the executable business model followed by a plan not only should attract the right financing (customers) but also set the foundation for future financing rounds with larger players, mainly VCs. Growth-oriented organizational development and execution go hand in hand with financing plans.

At the survival stage, the ESU is being developed and centered around *customers*. We identified three key customers: paying, financing, and future trade sales. The Paying customers capture proof of concept value at the ESU firm level. Scalability and growth in revenue, margin, and operating profits are all part of proof that the ESU business model works, especially if this growth is perceived to become incrementally sustainable. Such proof indicates that the project is investible for future growth, which in return attracts financing customers as they seek higher returns (i.e., profits) for their investments. The ultimate value that is extracted by ESU shareholders (mainly founders, investors, and employees) is when ESUs exit through trade sales (or rarely IPOs). In fact, the vast majority of significant wealth extraction for shareholders is generated during an exit event, mainly through trade sales or M&A.

At survival stage, the ESU is being developed and centered around the three customers: paying, financing, and (future) trade sales.

ESU valuations and exit multiples depend on the ESU's industry, market demand for ESU's line of business, and strategic vs. financial value. Early/Mid-stage exits for non-high-tech-driven ESUs may generate 2–10× or more ROI for its early investors based on valuation. For instance, if the ESU valuation is \$10 million during the exit period and the exit value is \$20 million, this equals to 2× returns on the valuation at that point. If a business angel investor had invested \$200K earlier when the pre-investment (i.e., referred to as *pre-money*) valuation was \$2 million, the investor's ownership would be 10% stake in the ESU (to keep it simple). If all things considered equal (i.e., the business angel's shares were not diluted with subsequent investments), the business angel will part with \$2 million as ROI (or 10% of \$20 million) which would have a 10× multiple for the early investor business angel.

For technology-driven high-tech ESUs, such as AI, pharma, nanotech, medtech, and similar, early investors may extract significant returns due to the ESU's high strategic value for its innovation. That is if the high-tech ESU succeeds in proposing value to potential trade sales customers whether it is profitable or not. However, when it does, it creates significant wealth to its shareholders.

It is necessary to position the ESU itself as a value proposition product for a future trade sales customer from mid-survival stage onwards

The reason why I bring up future *trade sales or M&A customers* at this stage is the fact that it now becomes important to also position the ESU as such that it starts treating the company itself as a *value proposition product* for future trade sales to a strategic partner. Although this adds more complexity to the equation of ESUs' mid-stage development, it has a huge significance on how to attract financing customers with a promise of a high exit value in a future trade sales customer. This mindset helps the ESU founders to re-think the positioning of its value proposition to be attractive not only to paying customers in its marketplace for the short—to medium-term, but also to future trade sales customers in the M&A marketplace in the long term. This makes it attractive to financing customers as the mediator of cost investment in the value creation, capture, and extraction process.

To summarize, ESUs need to consider three types of customers while developing their value propositions into a growth business and organization at mid-stage:

1. Paying
2. Financing
3. Trade sales or M&A

Figure 3.3 illustrates the relationship between the three customers within a world of interdependencies on trends, innovation, technological developments, competitive environment, market, and economic conditions.

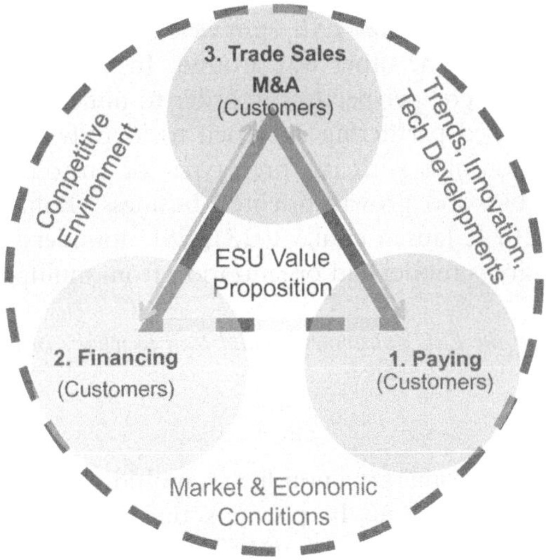

Fig. 3.3 Entrepreneurial startup customer relationship

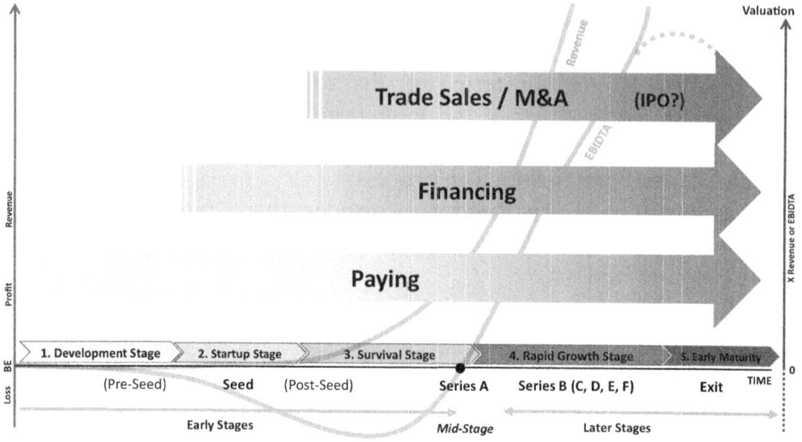

Fig. 3.4 Entrepreneurial startup lifecycle and customers

From the earlier stage and onward, the key to developing a winning ESU value proposition is to address the needs of its customers first and foremost. *What's in it for the ESU customers* should lead to *what's in it for the ESU* and not the other way around. In Fig. 3.4, I break down ESU's three customers' perspectives in order to understand how an ESU should use a focused partnering approach to identify, attract, and form sustainable relationships with its three types of customers. To build a scalable, replicable, and growth-oriented business (Bohan et al., 2024; Cavallo et al., 2024; Jansen et al., 2023), ESU founders need to design their ESU's business model and organization from multiple perspectives.

What's in it for the ESU's customers should lead to what's in it for the ESU

Paying Customers

Acquiring paying customers is a non-linear, multidimensional, networked, and interconnected process. In previous times, business was a linear process: manufacturers and service providers supplied goods and services to a firm and the firm sold to customers. It was highly product driven. Even services were considered *products*. With the knowledge, sharing, circular, and experience economies, advancements in technologies, innovation, digitalization, and sustainability orientation, business models became value driven, not product driven. These shifts have dramatically changed how ESUs offer their core competencies as value propositions with multiple interrelated offerings: products, services, information, expertise, experiences, freemium vs. premium (paid), one-time versus recurring (MRR/ARR), digital vs. in-person, web-based and app-based, impact oriented or sustainability oriented, and many more. Suppliers are now *partners*, sometimes *proprietary* and *unique*, spanning across boundaries with interdependent activities that are non-linear or non-sequential (Amit & Zott, 2012, 2021).

In fact, businesses today must think and operate like *multidimensional platforms* set up as value-chain intermediaries of value propositions to multiple stakeholders, user groups, and customers. There are different variations of business models as a platform (as target models) which can be adapted from technology platform business models (as source models) even though one size does not fit all (see Budde et al., 2024; Cusumano et al., 2019; Hahn, 2020; Ruggieri et al., 2018; Täuscher & Laudien, 2018; Van Alstyne & Parker, 2017). Paying customers are only part of this social and economic network of stakeholders, even though they are the ultimate proof that not only the concept value proposition works, but also people and organizations are willing to pay for it.

To distinguish paying customers from different entrepreneurial ecosystem players, we begin with *Stakeholders*. Stakeholders are anyone who can impact or is impacted by the ESU's value proposition, such as people, groups, and organizations, including social, environmental, economic or business, and governmental. Defining and addressing stakeholders are not easy tasks for ESUs. For simplicity purposes, we can break down stakeholders into four categories: customers, shareholders, employees, and society in various forms. While shareholders and employees followed by customers are relatively easier to identify, societal stakeholders are not. The same value proposition can be viewed differently by different stakeholders where there may be respective goal harmony, goal neutrality, or goal conflict (Whittington et al., 2023). Even though it is important to identify and prioritize key impacted stakeholders, ESUs cannot address and be everything to everybody. Let's recall that entrepreneurship and sustainability are a journey and not a destination. *Impact* is the key word. Which stakeholder is or could be positively (or negatively) impacted by ESUs value proposition? What are negative social, environmental, and economic impacts ESUs could eventually address within their value proposition?

Another way to clarify and differentiate is to identify *users of the ESUs value proposition*. Users can be direct or indirect beneficiaries and not necessarily paying customers. They can be a great source of engagement for informational sharing, value testing, market research, public relations, awareness building, blogs, newsletters that lead to the development of social capital, such as networks, trust, and reputation, and shared experiences. For instance, an ESU as a business-to-consumer (B2C) software-as-a-service (SaaS) provider may develop a *freemium* version of its value proposition to non-paying users to build awareness and user network, to gather data, to improve its value proposition and user experiences, and eventually to convert freemium users into *premium* (i.e., paying) customers with different packages. Various content and streaming companies offer such models, such as Spotify, Amazon, and YouTube. Business-to-business (B2B) ESUs, web—and app-based platforms (Budde et al., 2024; Hahn, 2020) can provide curated information on the ESUs value proposition to users with the latest developments, news, professional articles, and blogs, as well as an access point for paying customers to shop and utilize online proprietary resources. Users are considered as resources to identifying, differentiating, and developing a business with multidimensional offerings and impact.

Paying customers are key stakeholders who pay for the ESU's value proposition through its sales of products and/or services. They could be end-user customers, intermediaries, and/or resellers of ESU value propositions to end users.

While costs are guaranteed; profitability is not.

Financially, revenue viewed from the ESU's perspective will define its gross margin and gross operating profit, commonly known as EBIDTA (Earnings Before Interest Depreciation, Taxes, and Amortization). This leads to net cash flows from the core business activities, which make up part of statement of cash flows. These historical net cash flows will lead to forecasting ESU's growth path and become a key part of the ESU's present valuation of future cash flow potential. This is commonly known as Discounted Cash Flows (DCF) method, which is a quantitative method of ESU valuation even though it is still speculative. Figure 3.5 illustrates a simplified process flow to reaching DCF. While the DCF is a valuation method baseline, qualitative approaches continue to influence valuation. The latter is particularly true when it comes to valuing intangibles, such as intellectual capital (with unlimited potential), along with the DCF method (which is limited to profitability and ***positive net cash flow*** or ***cash build***).

Costs act as a moderator of profitability when it comes to income statement reporting (i.e., margin and EBIDTA). The higher the costs, the lower the profitability, and vice versa. Variable, mixed, and fixed costs moderate profitability. While costs are guaranteed; revenue and profitability are not. Hence, developing a value proposition with an organizational model where the ESU can gain from economies of scale is key to improving profitability with scaling, replicating, and growth (Bohan et al., 2024; Cavallo et al., 2024; Jansen et al., 2023). For instance, ESUs that utilize SaaS for their value proposition initially incur high developmental costs before they can market their value proposition and earn revenue. Once on offer, they can gain from economies of scale by multiplying customer subscriptions with MRR or ARR: the more customers sign up for their services, the lesser the cost per subscription, and the higher the margin and profitability (Haskel & Westlake, 2018). However, they still must build an organization to support its customer base, such as a customer care center. To determine what is reasonable to build such an organization, or determine acceptable margins and profitability, ESUs need to research and benchmark industry averages for their type of business. Although *one size does not fit all*, there are certain benchmarks, patterns, developed, and acceptable practices that ESUs can learn from to build their assumptions.

Income statement-associated costs moderate profitability

As mentioned earlier, revenue for the ESU is a cost to its customers. The tangible and intangible benefits for the paying customers must be

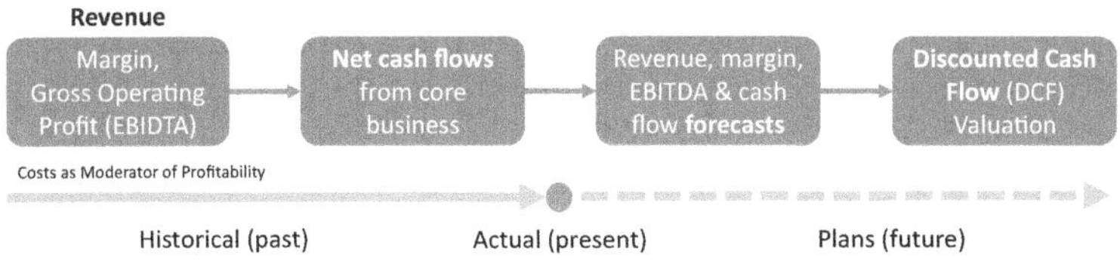

Fig. 3.5 Inputs to Discounted Cash Flow (DCF) valuation

higher than their cost. Designing the ESU value proposition around this concept is super critical. This includes getting closer to the customers, identifying, and highlighting key needed improvement in customer efficiencies and effectiveness, time and cost savings, determining value for money customer perception, and more depending on the type of customer the ESU is engaging.

Overall, customer experiences and perceptions matter. Customers will pay a premium for value propositions that tackle daily problems, improve their lives and businesses, and save time and money. In other words, a customer's costs of ESU services (i.e., ESU revenue) should go beyond being a moderator of customer profitability. It should also be a mediator of intangible value, such as seamless experiences, reduced time and stress, just-in-time issues resolution, their customer' satisfaction (if B2B) so that customers can focus on *their own* core competencies instead of dealing with process issues.

There are exceptions to the revenue-generating model, which represent less than 20% of the 80–20 rule. These are certain types of ESUs that their revenue model relies on other types of income, such as those derived from consulting, licensing agreements (i.e., licensing income), and royalties. These are mostly high-tech ESUs, such as pharma, medtech, biotech, imbedded technologies,[14] and similar ESUs that are heavily R&D driven and may license use of data, tech, and IP (i.e., brand, enzymes, chemical processes) as well as get royalties on each sold item to end users (Ozmel et al., 2013). Such ESUs usually have a longer incubation and development period, operate at a loss, stay longer in survival stage, and require much higher financing to pay for their investments in costs. Some of them are R&D technology transfers from universities who have spun off to become an independent ESUs with high-level of financing dependencies. However, licensing can also apply to non-patented ESUs with novel processes, products, services, big data, and platform networks that combined may offer unique intangible value for people or companies to license to—a spillover value from intellectual capital development. A study by Dang et al. (2022) found that non-patented technologies are licensed to more licensees with lower license fees than patented technologies with

[14] A good example of this is Goretex™ who has positioned its value proposition as a premium brand waterproofing technology imbedded in well-known outdoor garments, shoes, and boots products of higher end outdoor brand names such as Solomon, Reichl, Merrell, and Lowa.

higher licensing fees. Licensing fees and royalties, however, may not be enough to cover all the high-tech ESUs' ongoing R&D costs which are very human capital driven. ESUs need to hire, motivate, and retain knowledge workers with PhDs, engineering degrees, and specialists to develop further.

Financing Customers

At this survival mid stage, there are three predominant financing players (over 80%): business angels (BA), venture capital (VC), corporations and corporate VC (CVC), some equity crowdfunding, and accelerators. There are some others, such as family offices and foundations, but they are a minority (less than 20%). Before I highlight their differences, there are a couple of key characteristics that need to be noted.

First, a *financing customer* for the ESU is an investor in the ESU. ESUs finance their investment needs externally because they cannot generate enough free cash flow from their core business operations. As stated, financing and investment are the flip side of the same coin.

Second, external financing customers (or investors) inject cash into the ESU in exchange for equity in the majority of cases. This cash is to be used by the ESU to invest appropriately into its growth business (costs). This financing/investment round is commonly referred to as *new money* in exchange for *new shares*. The initial valuation prior to new money is called *pre-money value*. When new money is injected in exchange for new shares, the ESU valuation changes into post-money value. The formulas are simple:

$$\text{Pre-Money Value} + \text{New Money} = \text{Post-Money Value}$$

$$\text{Pre-Money Shares} + \text{New Shares} = \text{Post-Money Shares}$$

Third, at each round of financing, ESU founders' and previous investors' share ownership is diluted by the new investment rounds. The share composition, valuations, and dilutions are captured off-balance sheets in a Capitalization Table (as known as *cap tables*).

Fourth, what is not considered as financing or investment within this context is when a new external person or entity purchases the shares of an existing ESU shareholder. In other words, the cash exchanged to buy the shares from an existing investor is not money injected into the ESU development. For instance, a VC purchases 1,000 shares for $200 K from an existing BA in the startup in addition to purchasing 9,000 shares for $1.8 million. The $1.8 million is the actual or true financing for the ESU, whereas the $200 K is not. For the BA, it is an exit in a cash-to-equity trade with the VC.

Fifth, debt financing is mostly limited to *Convertible Loans* that eventually convert to equity, and in rare cases, private loans from family and friends. There is almost no possibility for major debt financing from banks because the high-risk characteristics of the ESU do not match the economic requirements of the bank. With limited historical financial data and little receivables or collection history, it is not economically plausible for banks to deal with the high opportunity cost or high default risk potential of ESUs. There are rare exceptions to this at the growth stage, such as a bridge loan or for the financing of equipment.

Business Angels continue to play a key role when ESUs reach the survival and early growth stage and require larger sums for investment. Financially, at mid stage (Series A), they provide anywhere between 25 and 500 K, sometimes more (i.e., if in high tech). They invest individually or with a group of angels in a *syndicate* (Mason et al., 2019). They can be passive investors who co-finance with VCs with similar terms and conditions, known as *term sheets.* They can also be actively and deeply involved with the ESU either in a strategic advisory capacity or with a role in the ESU board with decision-making and voting rights. They provide further mentorship and coaching to founders and their teams; networks and connections to potential customers, suppliers, and other investors; and a certain level of validation that the ESUs business model is credible to attract other investors, including VCs. Since business angels invest their own money, they have a higher tolerance for risk and investment strategy than VCs for instance. They also can wait longer or exit earlier since the decision is only theirs, usually not dependent on other partners or investors (Botelho et al., 2021). As they invest earlier in the ESU up to mid stage, they tend to take smaller equity stakes, such as 10%, and expect higher returns to their cost of capital (i.e., 20% to 40%).

Venture capital firms are *partnerships* formed and managed by *General Partners* (*GP*) who operate as professional fund managers. They create a thematic fund to attract other investors, known as *Limited Partners* (*LP*). Their business model is sometimes referred to as the 2–20 model: 2% of committed funds are reserved as annual *management fees* and 20% are *carried interest* where 20% of the future profits go to General Partners. VC funds invest in high-risk, high-growth businesses with the goal of maximizing financial returns for the GPs and LPs. They are a strong contributor to innovative and technology-oriented ESUs. Since they invest other people's monies, they have a time limit as to when to exit (i.e., within three to six years). They usually invest in ESUs with a proven business model and value proposition, with annual or recurring revenue and significant growth potential, and (increasingly) after financial breakeven. They screen ESUs through their due diligence metrics, which include:

- Their own internal requirements: investment amount, internal rate of return (IRR), target location or demographics, and cash-out potential to name a few.
- Investability of the team: composition and characteristics.
- The characteristic of the ESU project: its value proposition and execution plan.
- The ESU's industry and market trends.
- ESU's exit potential within trade sales markets.

Usually, VCs come into the picture where larger financing amounts rounds (i.e., Series A, B, C, D, ...) and amounts are needed (i.e., from two million dollars or Euros to over 100 million) in ***staged financing***, over several years (Lukas et al., 2016). Although there are some venture funds that invest in smaller amounts earlier, they are a minority in terms of dollar or euro value.[15] VCs take strategic decision-making roles in the ESU boards and monitor the ESU performance intensely, which can lead to alternative directions, pivoting, or scaling with follow-up investments (Hogrebe & Lutz, 2024). Although their risk tolerance may seem to be lower than that of business angels, due to high fixed costs VCs encourage ESUs to "adopt aggressive scaling and research strategies, characterized by high-potential rewards and commensurate risks of failure" (Norbäck et al., 2024, p.1). They can take a larger equity stake in the ESU (i.e., 20% to 40%) depending on pre-money valuation and the amount invested. Since they invest other people's monies (i.e., LPs) and larger amounts, they have a higher rate of return requirement (i.e., 30% to 60%) due to higher cost of capital and investment risk including

[15] See Pitchbook Venture Reports for up-to-date trends and analysis https://pitchbook.com/news/reports.

an *implied (entrepreneur) optimism discount percentage* (Anshuman et al., 2012). Most ESU entrepreneurs (especially novice or first timers) struggle to understand this and at times agree to VC terms that give VCs too much liquidity rights. VCs in return expect most ESUs not to survive and the few survivors to grow and make a substantially higher return to compensate for the losses of the other ESUs.

Corporate Venture Capital (CVC) is a more specific form of VC a major corporation sets up an autonomous organization as a fund to invest in potential ESUs with similar strategic alignment. Many large corporations have CVC units, such as GE Ventures, Intel Capital, Rober Bosch Venture Capital, Google Ventures, and many more. According to Sauvage et al. (2022), there are four types of CVCs:

1. *Strategic* where they focus on long-term strategic alignment to existing business units.
2. *Financial* whose purpose is explicitly ROI driven. They operate more independently than the parent company since they focus on maximizing ROI.
3. *Hybrid* where they focus on strategic alignment to parent company businesses while prioritizing financial returns.
4. *In-transition* CVCs where they are somewhere in between the above three types.

CVCs usually invest in promising innovative ESUs with unique technologies and approaches, new and unexplored market segments, and complementary value propositions to parent company business models. For *strategic* CVCs, such investments provide the parent company access to emerging trends and markets and foster further innovation. It can also lead to *inbound open innovation* opportunities for corporations especially when they foster a learning culture, innovation appropriation strategies, formal organizational structure, and top management competence (Zhang et al., 2024).

CVC directors often act as mediators of knowledge between ESUs and CVC parent company, facilitating corporate strategic outcomes, positively influencing innovation performance, and providing inputs to improve intellectual capital capabilities as well as innovative outputs through new value propositions (Bendig et al., 2024).

However, where innovation requires openness and lack of boundaries, CVCs become a paradox within a structured corporate culture. Many corporations have a lack of clarity on how a CVC should work, be measured, and be assessed. They also lack the mindset for clear decision-making models, goals and objectives, processes, and attracting and retaining human capital talent where "no two CVCs are organized the same way" (Strebulaev & Wang, 2024, pp. 30–31). It is important for the ESU to determine how the relationship works between the parent company and the CVC, as well as clarify what are the CVCs intentions, expectations, and structures (Sauvage et al, 2022).

There are pros and cons to the different types of CVCs. The pros for ESUs are several folds. Financial support is the obvious one. As non-financial support, CVCs offer a way to test value propositions for validation and added credibility. ESUs also can gain access to resources at the parent company, such as expertise in the supply chain, marketing, R&D, and industry contacts that otherwise would not be available for the ESU or would be very costly to access independently. Not only these could be good non-financial or in-kind support that saves money and time for the ESU, but also can significantly improve ESUs innovation outputs (Wang et al., 2021) and can also lead to a pathway for future exit opportunities with potentially higher takeover premiums for the ESU and higher IPO valuation with financial returns to both ESUs and CVCs (Huang & Madhavan, 2021; Ivanov & Xie, 2010).

The cons for the ESUs are also a few. The most prominent one is the conflict of business interest, especially when the CVC is a potential competitor who invests in the ESU to learn about the value proposition, making the ESU dependent on the parent company, having too many strings attached where other investors shy away, or simply a ploy to "catch and kill." Therefore, trust is a major factor between the ESU and CVC.

Trade Sales M&A Customers

Exits are when ESU shareholders cash out from their investments either partially or fully. This is called the *harvesting* process as majority of ESU shareholder wealth is created during exit. As a reminder, there are internal and external ESU shareholders. Internal include founders and employees with vested stock options; external, investors who provide financing to grow the business (i.e., business angels, VCs, and CVCs). External to ESU financing customers aim at getting their monies out with 3× or more ROI when ESUs exit through trade sales, M&A, and sometimes (but rarely) IPOs.

The ESU exit planning is strategic and long term. Identifying target trade sales customer needs in industries or market segments is a mid-to-late-stage endeavor. This planning should start earlier than later. If founders decide to seek external financing, they need to consider their exit scenarios from the get-go *to position the company as a product for eventual trade sales*/M&A markets[16] in such a way that there would be several bidding options. In other words, exit planning is a proactive and parallel process to scaling and growth planning. During its journey, ESUs may be approached by different *suiters* for mergers, total or partial trade sales. There are different variations to exit events. The reasons for exit planning as early as at mid stage are several folds:

1. It is a major (explicit or implicit) requirement for majority of financing customers.
2. Thinking and planning exit scenarios early creates a *harvesting mindset* and helps to improve positioning of the ESU *as a value proposition product* in the triple-customer competitive marketplace.
3. When ready, exit preparations take time and effort. It usually requires having several items ready to present to potential buyers, mainly documentation, first in a general pitch, followed by secondary and tertiary details during due diligence. They include (but not limited to) business plans, customer lists, financials, IP, license, supplier and customer contracts, any material liabilities, and processes (operational and financial accounting).[17]
4. Once a general term sheet is agreed upon, trade sales customers conduct extensive *due diligence* to determine if what has been shared with them during term sheet negotiations matches with reality. Due diligence is conducted by specialists, such as auditors, lawyers, and subject matter experts. Their task is to identify any mismatches between what they are told and what the ESU documentation indicates, plus any past, present, or future risks and liabilities that could

[16] See Chapter 5—Costs and Three-Dimensional Business Models for further details.

[17] Examples of this include purchasing-to-payables cycle (i.e., how suppliers are identified, selected, chosen, and engaged; approval process, signature authorization, and payment); selling-to-receivables (i.e., customer acquisition processes and costs, engagement and contracts, revenue recognition policies, and cash collection).

have a ***material impact*** (i.e., litigation, vague contracts, revenue recognition issues, undisclosed liabilities, hidden costs). In fact, due diligence is an assurance process by the trade sale customer that the price they are paying matches their expectation as well as if the ESU has a reasonable *operational and financial controls environment*. It is also a way for them to find reasons to re-negotiate the terms usually to lower the purchase price due to identified risks, re-statement of financial statements, weak controls environment, or future cost risks. ESU founders need to ensure they remove such risks and doubts. Let's remember that trade sales customers are also investors paying for future value.

5. Exits are challenging for the ESU founders as they take a lot of time from their daily work and could be very stressful. They face unprecedented questioning and requests by different due diligence specialists for details and explanations. Preparing for exits over the years and being somewhat ready for an exit pay big dividends during the trade sales process. It reduces the risk of lowering the sale price, time spent, opportunity cost of preparation, and work disruption. Hence, early investment in exit strategy, planning, and preparation may cost a little time and money over the years, but it is a major mediator of future value extraction during the exit event.

If ESU founders decide to seek external financing, they need to consider exit scenarios from the get-go to position the company as a product for eventual trade sales in M&A markets

Once the ESU is ready and its board decides to exit, the process to exit could be short, between 6–12 months. This depends on the ESU's strategic and operational situation (past, current, and future growth forecasts), position in the marketplace, ESU's *marketability*, and M&A market and economic conditions. In all cases, strategic planning for exits must begin earlier in the ESUs lifecycle than later when it is in a mature situation. Usually, this stage is mid-stage when ESUs need to attract major financing customers to fund their projects.

Experienced ESU founders know this process well. They plan and position their companies as a value proposition product for sale in the M&A marketplace from the get-go, especially at mid-stages. Although this positioning may change or pivot over time like any value proposition, the mindset is as such ESUs need to research and identify key trade sales target customers earlier in the process. Hence, like the previous two types of customers—paying and financing—ESU founders identify key differentials that trade sales customers would be interested in acquiring the ESU.

There are two major reasons why larger companies purchase or acquire ESUs: strategic and financial. *Strategic acquisitions* focus on long-term strategic alignment to existing corporate businesses with synergies, new innovations, and approaches (including technologies) as *credible alternatives* and *uncertainty reducers* (Mathisen et al., 2022). *Financial acquisitions*, which occur much less than strategic acquisitions, provide an immediate direct financial benefit to the buyer, whether they are top line (i.e., revenue) growth, margin or EBITDA, market share, or new channels.

ESUs need to define what future trade sales customer needs they can satisfy, which is difficult to do in an ever-changing market and economic conditions. Yet, the basics of customer needs assessment is the same as with other types of customers, except that founders need to have a good vision as to where certain industries are heading. What problems can the ESU solve that could eventually address the needs of future trade sales customers?

Finally, *going public* or initial public offerings (IPO) is another way of exiting and raising money at the same time. IPOs are quite rare though and constitute a very small percentage of exits. They are usually reserved for ESUs with rapidly evolving technologies that *substitute for existing technologies*, such as deeptech (i.e., pharmatech, nanotech, and similar) who would like to somewhat remain independent (Bowen et al., 2023). IPOs expose ESUs to larger public financial markets. However, they are long, expensive, and complex procedures which involve expert services of investment banking as intermediaries undertaking the creation, sales, and distribution of the financial assets.

Fundraising

This topic is a major concern for many ESUs. In my experience, over 80% of startups complain that they must put too much time and effort into fundraising. When asked how, the answer usually is time spent in searching databases of potential investors, reviewing lists, shortlisting them, and contacting with emails first. They complain that they hardly get responses or feedback. Many fail to raise money and eventually go into liquidation. *Running out of cash* is one of the top reasons why ESUs fail. The reasons for this should be clearer by now, after the previous sub-section.

Investors align their investment thesis to their defined value, including triple bottom line impact that is social, environmental, and economic (Elkington, 1994, 1997). Just like with paying customers, ESU founders ought to clearly understand financing customer needs to better position their ESUs. Furthermore, ESU founders need to have clarity as to (a) which stage they are currently in, where they want to go, and what they want their ESU to be in X years; (b) what type of investors they would like to attract; and (c) how much equity or shares are they willing to give in exchange for financing?

Founders need to combine the above mix of knowledge of their current situation, strategic direction, and investor type, then filter through the data to find the right fit in investors, values, and then find ways to contact them personally through networking or introductions. For instance, increasingly mid-stage Series A VCs are looking for ESU that are already breaking even financially and they are fundraising to develop into a scalable and growth organization (not just continuing to research and develop, unless they are in high-tech R&D, such as pharma). Otherwise, the opportunity cost of not knowing what type of financing customers would *buy into the ESU value proposition* and invest, or their needs can be severe and devastating to ESU's survival.

Financing markets are much tighter than product markets. They are fragmented but highly networked through professional pools, industry, or investment associations (i.e., business angel clubs), and focused entrepreneurial ecosystem players, such as incubators and accelerators that are screeners of ESUs and their value proposition. To obtain financing by attracting financing customers, ESU founders need to have a proper level of financial literacy and social trust (Fernandez, 2021; Graña-Alvarez et al., 2024; Skica et al., 2022) in addition to the ESUs value proposition and intellectual capital.

Triple bottom line impact is also important for investors, especially for impact investors. At times, most ESUs ignore the financials and focus on impact only, believing that their mission will be sufficient to attract financing customers. This is a major misjudgment. Impact investors want a double return: impact with financial returns combined. They might want a smaller return or forgo major returns, but still, they focus on returns on their investment.

One major consideration prior to fundraising is how much equity are founders willing to give up. Of course, this will depend on valuation and negotiation. During Seed financing, pre-money valuations range from \$1 to \$10 million as a general range. That means, raising \$100 K to \$1 million will be equivalent to around 10% in equity. During mid-stage Series A, ***usually*** pre-money valuations range between \$10 million and \$50 million. That means raising \$1 M to \$15 million would issue another 10% to 30% of equity (i.e., new shares). This would dilute both founders' shares as well as early investor's share percentages. If valuations can get higher during fundraising discussions, then ESUs can raise similar amounts as per above while giving away less equity. Besides profitability and free cash flow determinations, one major way to improve valuations is through intellectual capital valuation, which consists of intangibles and its sustainable business model.

In early-to-mid stages, valuations are sometimes difficult to calculate due to a lack of real historical financial data. ESU founders may have an idea of how much their ESU is worth (usually higher); while financing customers, may differ (usually lower). The latter may walk away if founders keep insisting on a higher valuation. However, like with all customers, if several financing customers are suggesting a similar ballpark of ESU valuation, then the ESU valuation is within that range. Founders should work within the suggested range.

Finally, it is important to note that ESUs should reserve circa 10% of their equity pool to Employee Stock Options Pool (ESOP) and for sweat equity, such as advisory shares. This will indicate to both financing customers and potential employees that the ESU is ensuring that the current and future team (will) have a stake in the company, which is a major motivational tool to attract human capital talent.

Takeaways

- At the survival stage, the ESU is being developed and centered around the three customers (paying, financing, and future trade sales).
- What's in it for the ESU's customers should lead to what's in it for the ESU.
- First and foremost, ESU founders need to develop a scalable business model that requires the acquisition of tangible and intangible resources.

- Then, founders need to plan to finance this model's resources and development.
- Financing requires the search and selection of the primary financing customers. ESU costs associated with developing their business are mediators of future value.
- In parallel, ESU founders need to identify and work with paying customers. ESU direct costs associated with selling are moderators of profitability.
- Revenue for the ESU is a cost to its paying customers.
- While costs are guaranteed, profitability is not for both the ESU and its paying customers.
- Financing customers are the investors for the ESU, who are usually business angels, VC, and CVC with some exceptions, such as foundations.
- Every financing round brings in new money into the ESU in exchange for new shares. This will dilute previous share owners' percentages on the ESU cap tables.
- Each type of financing customer has its own characteristics, needs, and goals.
- Trade sales customers follow the same customer needs-value logic that ESUs need to understand along with market and economic trends.
- ESU founders need to consider exit scenarios from the get-go to position the company as a product for eventual trade sales in M&A markets.
- There are two types of acquisitions: strategic (majority) and financial (minority).
- Actual exit transactions are cumbersome and complicated.
- Fundraising takes a long time and effort and is usually underestimated by ESU founders until it's too late.

3.5 Late Mid Stage—Preparing for a Growth Business and Organization

Mid-stage is where the challenges change dramatically. This is when an ESU must scale. It must develop replicable models using the 80–20 rule to expand into new markets, geographies, channels, and possibly industries. At this stage costs play a mainly mediator role, where there is an initial investment to develop for expansion with a perceived return. Here cost effectiveness is defined to show how it meets and exceeds the ESU's objectives with the investment. The biggest challenge most ESUs face is the fact that they do not pivot, change approaches, and dramatically adapt to a scalable business model (Bohan et al., 2024; Cavallo et al., 2024; Jansen et al., 2023). ESUs need to also build processes and organizational capabilities (i.e., organizational capital) to replicate and grow ("copy and paste") by using the 80–20 rule, where over 80% of the processes are the same ("think global") and under 20% adapted to local circumstances ("act local").

Many ESUs do not make it through this super important stage as they remain in early-stage mindset and mind trap, repeating the same habits as if they are in the early stage. This also effects an ESUs financing options with Series A, where the deal structure must be the baseline and foundation for later stage Alphabet Series (B, C, D, ...). In other words, even though the mid-stage is a continuation of the early stages, it is the start of a new lifecycle and approach, as we begin transforming the ESU from an enclosed limited environment to a more exposed external environment with different conditions, environmental challenges, markets, competitions, etc. I have noticed a colossal mindset failure with many ESUs when they reach this stage, they keep forgetting three main things:

1. They need to have a replicable model before scaling, with a one-two punchline:
    a. invest/expand into a new market (80–20 rule) and treat new entry costs as investment (cost effectiveness) as a mediator of future value extraction, and
    b. become profitable, with cost efficiency as a moderator of profitable value.
2. They are in a new hybrid lifecycle, where they need to think completely differently, such as developing a business organization with streamlined documented processes, hiring experienced professionals to run value-chain primary functions (R&D, operations, business development, sales, and marketing, after-sales support activities), and support functions (HR, finance and accounting, supply chain, procurement, logistics, distribution). Unless experienced, this is unknown territory for most founding teams. They tend to get stuck in early-stage mindset continuing with the same approaches

such as focusing too much on new product development (NPD) or R&D, instead of organizational and capabilities development, and remain too frugal where they need to bet higher.

3. They lose touch with the fact that they need to review, recalibrate, and renew their exit-driven business models with different scenarios of firm value extraction. This is when Series A financing structuring becomes very important to set the foundation for later financing (alphabet) Series if desired as well as making the financing attractive and competitive to different financing customers.

The mid-stage is the start of a new lifecycle and approach, transforming the ESU from an enclosed internal environment to a more exposed external environment with different market conditions

At mid-stage and thereafter, ESU founders need to change their entire approach to developing and managing a growth organization. In addition, ESU founders need to re-define their value proposition as a multi-sided and multidimensional platform addressing stakeholders, users, and (triple) customers' needs in a focused way, develop intellectual capital (especially human capital), reconfigure and reshape their roles vs. newcomers', in a prioritized and incremental way. Developing a multi-sided comprehensive offering depends on the complexity of the business.

For instance, if an ESU is developing an online digital platform business, founders need to understand their value (services) distribution strategy to determine how to go to a market with millions of users, and then replicate and multiple to other locales. If developing a financial SaaS company to solve a financial problem, they need to attract several talented team members from various industries and functions. This could include the finance and banking industry, payment solutions, web interface software development, digital marketing, and regulations. In majority of the cases, the requirement patterns are the same.

First, scalable and replicable: how to develop a scalable and growth-oriented business model that can be replicated? Scalability provides *competitive advantage* during a *phase of exponential growth*, sometimes referred to as *growth hacking* (Bargoni et al., 2024). The driver for scalability is digitalization supported by a well-organized and innovative team (Bohan et al., 2024).

Scalability provides competitive advantage during a phase of exponential growth hacking

This is where *standardization of value proposition* comes into play. Using the 80–20 rule, founders need to develop an organizational model that can replicate their value propositions at scale. This means to *copy and paste* the same organizational model in different locations, countries, etc. over 80% of the time. Whereas they can adapt less than 20% of the time to local conditions to appeal *culturally relevant customer experiences* (Weiger, 2023). The design of replicable business platforms leads to cost-efficient scaling and growth. It could also lead to economies of scale, hence scaling, from initial developmental investments, experiences, and processes. These investments in developmental costs mediate value capture and eventual value extraction. Also, they can gain on reduced fixed costs, which would have a moderating effect on profitability. Whereas localization adds cultural aspects for improved customer experiences and sales.

Second, sustainable value propositions: ESU accountability should focus not only on economic returns but also on social and environmental impact where applicable. Designing organizations with triple bottom line impact for sustainable value propositions is a must, not an option. I find many ESUs that have a good value proposition also have a poorly defined and executed sustainability impact. For many ESUs, it is not difficult to re-define their sustainability and impact. The reason is that good value propositions are there to improve efficiencies and effectiveness in the way we live and conduct business, especially when innovative digital technologies are applied (Bähr & Fliaster, 2023). Hence, most ESUs have a strong sustainability value proposition by default. Re-defining, re-designing a little, and eventually *living* these sustainable value propositions through the lens of sustainability impact add huge value to all three customer groups (Ilyas & Osiyevskyy, 2022).

The focus is *to walk the sustainability value talk* and avoid just having a glossy web page declaring how socially, environmentally, and economically responsible the ESU is. The latter leads to *sustainability washing*, which is a major reducer of trust and reputation value in the triple-customer marketplace. *Sustainability transparency* is also key to market encroachment where "customer awareness, unique experience and customer contribution are all needed to enact transparency" (Nijhof et al., 2019, p. 2126). Stakeholder and customer engagement and partnering are necessary to improving sustainability *value flow dimensions: value intention, proposition, creation, delivery, and capture* (Attanasio et al., 2022).

Third, reshaping of roles: pivotal to scaling is re-defining ESU's value chain, reconfiguring and reshaping of founders' own roles, and re-crafting ESU joiners' roles (Mathias & Williams, 2018; Van Lancker et al., 2023). In fact, "scaling-specific paths through which the role-crafting of joiners shapes founders' roles" (Van Lancker et al., 2023, p. 1). In the early stages, founders play many roles. In mid-stage scaling and beyond, they need to pass many responsibilities to newly hired talent (i.e., human capital) to take over certain tasks for them to focus on strategy, business development, and fundraising. These involve breaking up the multi-tasks that ESU founders are doing into clusters or groupings and hiring the right talent into these tasks with key responsibilities. Key is to distinguish what roles create *dynamic capabilities* that generate long-term ESU value that needs to be acquired, developed, maintained, and owned internally; and what are *ordinary capabilities*, such as administrative assistance, bookkeeping, order processing, customer inquiries, and similar that can be relatively easily sourced, either to maintain in-house, to outsource or to automate. These can be grouped into organizational, functional, and founder roles:

Organizational and functional roles:

- Development of value propositions (through a platform of products, services, technologies, and software) and organizational, social, and relational capital.
- Operations: supply chain, logistics, distribution whether online, virtual, or physical product
- Marketing and sales, including business development.
- Finance and accounting.

Founder (basic) roles:

- Chief Executive Officer (CEO) responsible for overall strategy and ESU leadership.
- Chief Operating Officer (COO) addressing everything that is operational, including finance responsibilities in early stages.
- Chief Technology Officer (CTO), Chief Information Office (CIO), or Chief Digital Information Officer (CDIO) for overall ownership and shaping of value creation through its own

developed (i.e., core), adopted or adapted (enabling) technologies, technology landscaping, and road mapping, including organizational processes.
- Chief Marketing Officer (CMO) who encompasses everything involving marketing and sales strategy, from web design, digital and sales campaigns, and social media presence.
- Business Development Officer (BDO) depending on the type of business to develop unique partnerships, corporate key accounts, and joint projects (aka relational capital).
- Chief Financial Officer (CFO), which is essential in mid to later stages, focusing on both strategic, managerial, and operational aspects of finance and accounting.

In the early—to late-mid stages, ESUs do not need or should not justify a CFO's role as there is no need for one. Usually, the COO or the CEO can play that role. This is why it is essential for the founding team to have or acquire proper financial literacy (Graña-Alvarez et al., 2024; Skica et al., 2022). The financial responsibilities can eventually split separately into a CFO role when the operations grow domestically and internationally, where financial strategies, processes, and controls need to be put in place, documented, and automated where feasible. This is also important for future due diligence purposes during an exit scenario.

Allocated costs to this organizational reconfiguration and development must be aligned according to the value hierarchy. The highest cost priority should go to roles that generate and *mediate* the most ESU venture value through ESU's dynamic capabilities and intellectual capital development. Any repetitive tasks associated that require ordinary capabilities must be assessed to determine either to keep in-house, to outsource, or to automate, whichever option *moderates* value for money better.

Takeaways

- It is the start of a new lifecycle and approach, transforming the ESU from an insulated environment to an externally exposed environment.
- ESUs need to have in place scalable, replicable, and growth business models, sustainable value propositions, and reshaping of roles.

- Scalability provides competitive advantage during a phase of exponential growth hacking, which requires unique processes, innovation, and organizational capabilities, especially human capital.
- Sustainable value propositions must include transparency, realistic triple bottom line impact assessment, and stakeholder engagement.
- Reshaping of founders' roles involve role-crafting of new positions while reconfiguring the strategic roles the founders will play.
- Cost investments into the growth organization should be seen as ESU value mediator; while cost optimization through scaling, as value moderator.

3.6 Late Stage—Fast Growth with Multiplication Effect

Later stage ESUs are characterized by their financing requirements as in *Alphabet* Series B, C, D, E, F, and so on. This does not mean that every ESU needs to go through each of these fundraising Series. It just means that ESUs need to raise further financing to build, scale, grow, and expand into newer geographic territories and market channels, and to prepare for mainly trade sales exits (or IPOs in the minority of cases). The strategic goal at later stages is attention to operational efficiency, while discovering new market opportunities, expanding, and growing. It usually involves expanding through new subsidiaries and international growth; developing more structure through efficient and effective processes; and hiring specialists and experts, such as in digital marketing and supply chain.

The late stage is also characterized with proven business models, higher revenue, margin, and improved profitability where the net cash flows from operating activities are reinvested into the business, and yet it needs additional financing to fund its further growth and expansion activities. For instance, Series B financing is sometimes referred to as further *Build* the ESU's growth with proven traction and capability to scale. They are underwritten by VCs and CVCs specialized in later stage financing with some inclusion of early investors who opt for follow-up investment. The goal for the financing customers is improved valuation with profitable growth and intangibles mainly intellectual capital (IC) for a future exit scenario with high ROI.

As Fig. 3.6 illustrates, investments into ESU IC development costs mediate ESU firm value. Whereas investment into streamlined, replicable, efficient, and effective processes *moderate* improved margin (through the cost of revenue) and profitability or EBIDTA (through operating expenses).

Where needed, follow-on financing through Series C and beyond, continue to develop the scaling, growth, further improvements of operational efficiencies, and preparation for an exit scenario (acquisition or IPO in rare cases). This leads to a level of ESU maturity that founders and shareholder boards need to decide if or when to exit or to remain more independent through an IPO. Majority of the time (over 80%), financing customers prefer to exit via trade sales or M&A in order to get certain multiple returns on their invested capital. In rare cases (under 20%) where ESUs opt to remain independent (and not to exit), they either have to plan for this in mid-stage or to inform their intention to prospective investors as early in the process as possible. There are some investors who could opt to receive dividends as a form of income from their investments.

Late stages carry different risks. However, they are considered less risky than early and mid stages with improved predictability due to replicable processes, better understood and moderated cost structures, established

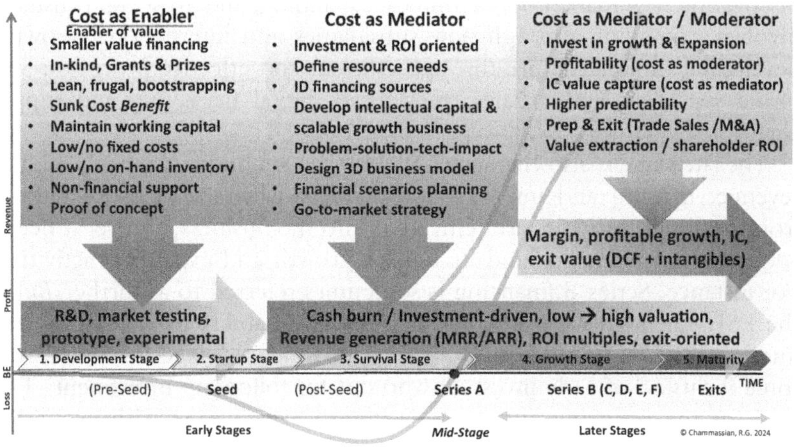

Fig. 3.6 Entrepreneurial lifecycle investment and financing mid-late stages

pricing mechanisms, and historical precedence. In Later stages, where there is rapid growth, in addition to cost-effectiveness in growth investments and improved valuation, the effort tends to move more into cost efficiency. The ESUs focus is on building reliable processes using the 80–20 rule:

>80% of the time establishing replicable models capitalizing from economies of scale with:

- Well-designed, tested, and documented processes
- Digitalized and centralized tech platforms
- Streamlined production methods with automation where possible

<20% of the time developing localized approaches for efficiency, effectiveness, and sustainability for social, environmental, and economic impact, such as:

- Sourcing talent locally, empowering them, and offering ESOP
- Adapting value propositions to local cultural norms, tastes, preferences, and experiences
- Reducing lead times and improving environmental footprint by localizing the supply chain wherever possible

These late rapid growth stages are characterized with major revenue and profitability growth multiples. They are also known to become more *corporatized* with standardized processes and documented procedures while remaining continuously innovative and disruptive in the marketplace. Teece (2012) differentiates these as ordinary versus dynamic capabilities. Ordinary capabilities are grounded on *routines* of known, measured, and repeated practices learned from individual skills and collective learning. They usually include operational, administrative, and compliance-related tasks. Whereas dynamic capabilities involve the speed of *sensing*, *seizing*, and *transforming* opportunities into sustained and above-normal growth and returns (Teece, 2012).

To achieve these steps, founders need to change tact and management style to sustain and build a growth-oriented company. They need to step back from day-to-day operations and focus on strategic dimensions and continuous innovation (i.e., dynamic capabilities) while creating and delegating a leadership team of expert talent to develop and execute operational, administrative, and compliance processes (i.e., ordinary capabilities) through the growth period. This requires attracting, hiring, retaining, motivating, and compensating experienced and seasoned professionals in a leadership team specialized in business functions, such as supply chain, business development, marketing and sales, finance, and HR. Since the innovation direction is set at later stages, onboarding key talent as human capital becomes a hallmark at this stage. In return, human capital with its dynamic capabilities plays a stronger role in developing a strong venture culture (Shepherd et al., 2023) and addressing complex problems associated with growth. Whereas in earlier stages, the focus is on exploration and survival, in later stages, the focus is on *investments*, *competitive maneuvers*, *market entry*, and *acquisitions* (Margolis & Tzabbar, 2020). In return, the dynamic capabilities of the human capital become a major attraction for trade sales customers as a means of *acqui-hiring* talent (Chatterji & Patro, 2014).

The vast majority of costs are invested in people. Attracting, hiring, motivating, and retaining talented individuals require a compensation package that includes a market-based salary as well as employee stock options (i.e., ESOP). Costs invested in Human capital as an intangible asset have a mediating effect on higher organizational value for a future trade sale. It is people who develop organizational, social, and relational capital.[18]

However, from a financial accounting perspective, people costs are considered fixed costs in the income statement rather than an intangible assets amortized on the balance sheet. This is where a balancing act comes into play between purely profitability-based valuation and intangible value-driven valuation. DCF approach is an ESU valuation method based on future profitability and free cash flow from operating activities. As people's costs are considered fixed costs, they moderate profitability and free cash flow negatively. Whereas human capital with its dynamic capabilities that develop ESU's intellectual capital further mediates higher firm valuation than a purely DCF calculation. Such intellectual capital and

[18] Chapter 4—*Costs and Intellectual Capital Development* specifically covers how such capital collectively creates, captures and extracts additional ESU value than purely DCF-derived valuation from free cash flow, which is based on EBIDTA from the income statement.

organizational capabilities value are tracked in off-balance sheet disclosures. This is why ESUs with little or no profitability end up exiting with much higher valuations.

People costs (i.e., salaries) as an expense are a moderator of profitability and free cash flow. Whereas human capital costs as an intangible asset are a mediator of venture value.

However, not all ESU growth goes according to plan. Many issues and challenges arise during the growth stage, including competitive environment, changes in market and economic conditions; new trends, innovation, and tech disruptions (see Fig. 3.3); with all three types of customers (paying, financing, and trade sale/M&A); and shareholder needs and requirements (i.e., external investors, ESU founders and employees). When it comes to valuations and exits, just like value proposition and market entry, timing is everything. Knowing when to exit, how to harvest, and how much are all key considerations.

Takeaways

- The characteristics of late-stage fast growth are building, scaling, growing, and expanding into newer geographic territories and market channels, and preparing for mainly trade sales exits.
- The strategic goal at later stages is attention to operational efficiency, while discovering new market opportunities, expanding, and growing.
- This stage is known by its fundraising *alphabet series B, C, D, E, ...*
- It has proven business models, fundamentally higher revenue and profitability, and generating free cash flow, with improved predictability.
- The focus on investments, competitive maneuvers, market entry, and acquisitions.
- This is a prime stage for trade sales exits.
- The biggest risk at this exit is the timeliness of an exit event and market and economic conditions.

3.7 Late Stage—Maturity and Harvesting

Ideally, an ESU should exit at its prime: when valuation is in its highest level, market conditions are ripe, M&A is a sellers' market, and shareholders are aligned for an exit. However, this ideal alignment does not happen most of the time and *one size does not fit all*. There are many determinants of exit motivation (i.e., intrinsic vs. extrinsic; buyer vs. seller; various conditions) and exit categories (i.e., financial, stewardship, or cessation through systemic liquidation) (DeTienne et al., 2008, 2015; Hohen & Schweizer, 2021).

Financial harvesting is most prevalent and desired when external investors are involved (i.e., financing customers) who believe in the founding team, the project and its growth stage, and profits and potential ROI. Each of these key players addresses financial harvesting through their own opportunity cost prism. The founders are motivated by the financial rewards with the wealth created at the exit. Investors are motivated by the financial returns they will get against their cost of capital employed in their investment, commonly known as ROI. Financial harvesting is the ultimate desire for ESU, that are scalable and growth oriented, requiring external financing.

Financial harvesting is the most desired outcome by external investors

Exits with financial harvesting have several forms, including M&A trade sales and IPOs. Acquisitions occur when a larger company acquires a smaller ESU to create, capture, and extract value for the larger corporation. IPOs occur when the ESU has a strong market position, would like to remain somewhat independent, and could extract higher value by going public (fully or partially).

3.7.1 Mergers & Acquisitions (M&A)

There are two main types of acquisitions: strategic and financial. *Strategic acquisitions* occur when a larger company buys an ESU for its intangibles, mainly people, innovation capabilities, and intellectual capital. ESU is simply better at innovation than R&D department of larger corporations. Such acquisitions also fit within the strategic long-term corporate plans to integrate ESU's new technologies and approaches (i.e., cost savings), new market opportunities (i.e., growth), competitive advantage, standalone capabilities or synergies, unique partnership (i.e., relational capital), and expanded networks and reputation (i.e., social capital), within a larger context. Well-known examples of strategic acquisitions include Google's purchase of YouTube for $1.65B in 2006, Facebook's acquisition of Instagram for $1 billion in 2012, and WhatsApp for $19 billion. Reynolds (2017) at Wired Magazine characterized this as "if you can't build it; buy it." Majority of acquisitions are strategic. Both ESU founders and early or existing investors benefit from the value extraction of the exit with wealth and ROI.

Long-term value is incorporated into the existing corporate strategies, projects, and value propositions through products and services. With tech-oriented ESUs, *acqui-hiring* (or buying the ESU for its people) plays a key role. Although there is calculable book value for an ESU (i.e., based on EBIDTA), usually strategic acquisition bidders' valuations are higher and primarily based on intangibles (i.e., intellectual capital) which is not easily calculable using traditional accounting methods. The most prevalent intangible valuation goes to IP, mainly patents, which is deemed to be directly related to revenue. Therefore, on a *cost basis*, assuming that the ESU is integrated, acquiring companies record a majority of the acquisition price paid under intangibles. They include:

- *IP*, such as specifically valued patents. IPs are *amortized* through their deemed economic life and directly impact profitability. Amortization (like depreciation) is a non-cash non-operating cost, which does not impact EBIDTA.
- *Acquisition* if the ESU is kept independent, or
- *Goodwill* is the difference between fair or market value (paid) and calculated book value (i.e., IP or otherwise). Goodwill is regularly revaluation and *impaired*. Unlike amortization, impairment is based on fair market value rather than economic life. *Impairment*, like amortization, is a non-cash non-operating expense.

Financial acquisitions occur when the acquiring firm is looking for financial growth through an acquisition and eventual re-sell. Usually, these firms are private equity, some VCs, and hedge funds that acquire an ESU to generate a good ROI. They contribute to the deal financial resources and expertise (i.e., debt financing), and management insights for operational efficiencies with an objective view of improved value extraction. In many cases, financial acquirers bid lower or underprice their targets, especially when it comes to financially strained, under-performing, or under-valued ESUs, in order to turnaround and re-sell in an exit (Salva & Zhang, 2022).

Financial acquirers focus on generating a substantial ROI for their investors (i.e., LPs). Their costs are mainly related to the cost of capital and investment management. In order to motivate founders or the management team (if they are not replaced), financial acquirers offer additional financial incentives and ways to get engaged in the business. However, due to ESU bad performance, negative market conditions, or investment timing constraints, such returns may not occur. In such cases, financial acquirers resort to either ***staged investment***, such as additional financing, or ***systemic liquidation*** by divesting or abandoning the investment to secondary VC markets (Andrieu & Groh, 2021).

For the ESU founders, the opportunity is getting further financing to survive and grow, and expertise and networks from the acquirer. However, there is a high opportunity cost of losing control as well as not getting the returns they wished for. Early stage and current investors may benefit from the transaction. It is a way out, perhaps with a lower return, if not a loss. Usually, ESU founders and early or existing investors extract some value from the transaction even though it may be discounted. A minority of ESU exits are financial acquisitions.

3.7.2 Initial Public Offering (IPO)

Vast majority of ESU exits are through strategic and financial acquisitions, and a minority through IPOs, either partial or full. When it comes to overall valuations, however, the small number of exits via IPOs have a higher deal value than trade sales acquisitions (Moore et al., 2024). IPOs are usually beneficial when ESU historical and future growth potential are substantial and public financing offers a better return than private exits through acquisition. IPOs also maintain a sense of ESU independence to go it alone instead of becoming part of a larger company. Investors of all stages benefit from IPOs. In fact, later stage investors (Series C and onwards) specifically finance for exit preparation, and Series E and onwards, especially IPOs. Late-stage VCs play a key role in financing such series. IPOs can be partial or full (exit) from a private to a public company.

However, IPOs require complex procedures with vast amount of time and money to prepare for (Ball & Gefter, 2016). Investment banks play an intermediary role to prepare for the valuation starting with an in-depth due diligence, eventual sale, and distribution of financial securities through public (stock) markets. Investment bankers are considered experts in determining the value of the newly issued shares.

Although IPOs are romanticized in social media, they are much harder, complex, and complicated to achieve. Besides time and money, transparency and disclosure requirements put the founders and leadership team into a different limelight. What they have said and done in the past and promise for the future become public. Founder and management *accountability* requirements are much higher and more scrutinized than in private markets, besides being compliant with legal disclosure requirements. Public trust and reputation in the ESU play key roles in maintaining or growing the firm valuation that they started with the IPO. Public markets reward companies that meet and exceed their forecasts. *Predictability* is what publicly traded ESUs are measured by. Indeed, we all know that usually there are fluctuations in ESU quarterly results, which is the variance between forecasts and actuals. Hence, at times publicly traded ESU share prices tend to fluctuate tremendously with the ups and downs. Therefore, even though it is hard work to prepare for IPOs and to go public, it is as hard to maintain ongoing predictable results. Hence, the vast majority of ESUs opt to exit via acquisitions rather than IPOs.

3.7.3 ESU Maturity

One cannot easily predict that the high-growth stage will continue or stagnate or that M&A buyers are willing to pay a high premium. ESU maturity depends on many variables. Harvesting through exits via trade sales (M&A) is a desired outcome of ESUs and their financing customers. Where experienced entrepreneurs live with this credo, novice entrepreneurs are ill-prepared to understand the importance, intricacies, and complexities of harvests through exits. Founders' maturity, entrepreneurial human capital, and financial literacy can be an indicator and a predictor of attracting financing and growing the ESU to its maturity and exit (Kato & Honjo, 2015; Graña-Alvarez et al., 2024; Skica et al., 2022; Xie, 2024).

Exit scenarios must be strategized from mid-stage (Series A) to position the ESU as a value proposition product for sale in the trade sales/ M&A (or IPO) marketplace. This requires an understanding of and positioning in the M&A and IPO landscape. Although market and economic conditions change during the ESU's journey, so can its exit strategy iteration.

However, what is even more difficult to do is deciding *when* to exit. In fact, *maturity* is not an end, but a means of *transition* into a larger context, whether corporate or public. Exits facilitate the ESU's maturity transition into a larger setting. Many ESUs opt for the corporate setting through an acquisition. In either case, timing is everything. There is no magic formula as to when to exit. Although an ESU's ultimate *success* may be measured by its exit (whether M&A or IPO), many ESUs are not likely to exit many years after its funding due to a lack of readiness (Yimfor & Garfinkel, 2023). This could be objective (i.e., low valuation, not enough growth, or other challenges) or subjective (i.e., founder or shareholder unwillingness).

Often ESUs reach early maturity before an exit scenario. This means growth stagnates and scaling options are limited. The reasons for this are many, including economic and market conditions, new and competing technologies, or simply *optimistic overconfidence* of the founding team (Simon & Shrader, 2012). This could lead to mediocre results, an unattractive value proposition for financing customers for further funding, and undesirable alternatives, such as a merger with another ESU, management team takeover (i.e., management buyout), or liquidation due to ESU failure.

In early maturity situations, if a rival ESU or a larger company can accept incorporating the ESU's value proposition, a merger could lead to some form of continuity. A merger usually means that the ESU will have to liquidate and merge its company's value proposition and possibly team into the other company. This could be complex in terms of shareholder agreements with the ESU's existing shareholders versus the merging company ownership.

Management buyout could be another scenario where the ESU continues its operation but as a small company owned by the management team, who often on a token compensation to the investors to take over and run the ESU as a small business.

Liquidation simply means wind down and closure of the company through bankruptcy or solvency, with some salvaging of its assets, such as equipment, properties, and intangible assets (i.e., IP) if any.

Takeaways

- ESUs should exit when its valuation is in its highest level, market conditions are ripe, M&A is a sellers' market, and shareholders are aligned for an exit.
- Financial harvesting is the most desired outcome by external investors.
- Larger firms acquire innovative ESUs for their innovation, mainly IC.
- There are two types of M&A by larger firms: strategic and financial acquisitions.
- The majority of M&A are strategic, acquiring ESU for their IC capabilities, especially human capital
- A minority of M&A are financial, acquiring ESUs for direct financial growth or re-structuring and eventually reselling by some hedge funds.
- ESU IPOs are rare complex transactions that require vast amount of time and costs to prepare for. Investment banks are the intermediaries facilitating the IPO.
- ESUs may reach a maturity stage where its growth is substantially lower than before: growth stagnates and scaling options are limited.
- Maturity periods may lead to re-structuring, mergers, employee or management buyouts, or solvency in extreme cases.

Bibliography

Amit, R., & Zott, C. (2012). Creating value through business model innovation. *MIT Sloan Management Review, 53*(3), 40–50.

Amit, R., & Zott, C. (2021). *Business model innovation strategy*. John Wiley & Sons.

Andrieu, G., & Peter Groh, A. (2021). Strategic exits in secondary venture capital markets. *Journal of Business Venturing, 36*(2), 105999. https://doi.org/10.1016/j.jbusvent.2019.105999

Anshuman, V. R., Martin, J., & Titman, S. (2012). An entrepreneur's guide to understanding the cost of venture capital. *Journal of Applied Corporate Finance, 24*(3), 75–83. https://doi.org/10.1111/j.1745-6622.2012.00391.x

Attanasio, G., Preghenella, N., De Toni, A. F., & Battistella, C. (2022). Stakeholder engagement in business models for sustainability: The stakeholder value flow model for sustainable development. *Business Strategy and the Environment, 31*(3), 860–874. https://doi.org/10.1002/bse.2922

Ball, J. H., & Gefter, A. (2016). The IPO exit: A practical legal guide for financial sponsors. *The Journal of Private Equity, 19*(4), 69–73. https://doi.org/10.3905/jpe.2016.19.4.069

Bähr, K., & Fliaster, A. (2023). The twofold transition: Framing digital innovations and incumbents' value propositions for sustainability. *Business Strategy and the Environment, 32*(2), 920–935. https://doi.org/10.1002/bse.3082

Bargoni, A., Santoro, G., Messeni Petruzzelli, A., & Ferraris, A. (2024). Growth hacking: A critical review to clarify its meaning and guide its practical application. *Technological Forecasting and Social Change, 200*, 123111. https://doi.org/10.1016/j.techfore.2023.123111

Bendig, D., Göttel, V., Eckardt, D., & Schulz, C. (2024). Human capital in corporate venture capital units and its relation to parent firms' innovative performance. *Research Policy, 53*(6), 105003. https://doi.org/10.1016/j.respol.2024.105003

Berre, M., & Le Pendeven, B. (2023). What do we know about startup-valuation drivers? A systematic literature review. *Venture Capital, 25*(4), 385–429. https://doi.org/10.1080/13691066.2022.2086502

Bohan, S., Tippmann, E., Levie, J., Igoe, J., & Bowers, B. (2024). What is scaling? *Journal of Business Venturing, 39*(1), 106355. https://doi.org/10.1016/j.jbusvent.2023.106355

Bonnet, C., Capizzi, V., Cohen, L., Petit, A., & Wirtz, P. (2022). What drives the active involvement in business angel groups? The role of angels' decision-making style, investment-specific human capital and motivations. *Journal of Corporate Finance, 77*, 101944. https://doi.org/10.1016/j.jcorpfin.2021.101944

Botelho, T., Harrison, R., & Mason, C. (2021). Business angel exits: A theory of planned behaviour perspective. *Small Business Economics, 57*(1), 583–602. https://doi.org/10.1007/s11187-019-00292-0

Bowen, D. E., Frésard, L., & Hoberg, G. (2023). Rapidly evolving technologies and startup exits. *Management Science, 69*(2), 940–967. https://doi.org/10.1287/mnsc.2022.4362

Brealey, R. A., Myers, S. C., Allen, F., & Edmans A. (2022). *Principles of corporate finance* (14th ed.). McGraw-Hill Education.

Budde, L., Hänggi, R., Laglia, L., & Friedli, T. (2024). Leading the transition to multi-sided platforms (MSPs) in a B2B context—The case of a recycling SME. *Industrial Marketing Management, 116*, 106–119. https://doi.org/10.1016/j.indmarman.2023.12.002

Cain, D. M., Moore, D. A., & Haran, U. (2015). Making sense of overconfidence in market entry. *Strategic Management Journal, 36*(1), 1–18. https://doi.org/10.1002/smj.2196

Cavallo, A., Cosenz, F., & Noto, G. (2024). Business model scaling and growth hacking in digital entrepreneurship. *Journal of Small Business Management, 62*(4), 2058–2085. https://doi.org/10.1080/00472778.2023.2195463

Chammassian, R.G. (2016). Towards a New Cost Paradigm for Technology Startup Entrepreneurs (Doctoral Dissertation). Grenoble Ecole de Management, Grenoble, France.

Chatterji, A., & Patro, A. (2014). Dynamic capabilities and managing human capital. *Academy of Management Perspectives, 28*(4), 395–408. https://doi.org/10.5465/amp.2013.0111

Cipollone, A., & Giordani, P. E. (2019). Entrepreneurs meet financiers: Evidence from the business angel market. *Journal of Business Venturing, 34*(5), 105913. https://doi.org/10.1016/j.jbusvent.2018.11.003

Coad, A., Frankish, J., Roberts, R. G., & Storey, D. J. (2013). Growth paths and survival chances: An application of Gambler's ruin theory. *Journal of Business Venturing, 28*(5), 615–632. https://doi.org/10.1016/j.jbusvent.2012.06.002

Cusumano, M. A., Gawer, A., Yoffie, D. B. (2019). *The business of platforms: Strategy in the age of digital competition, innovation, and power.* Harper Business.

Damodaran, A. (2024). *The little book of valuation: How to value a company, pick a stock, and profit* (2nd ed.). Wiley.

Dang, J., Motohashi, K., & Huo, D. (2022). Get Pennies from many or get a Dollar from one? Multiple licensing in markets for technology. *Technovation, 113*, 102423. https://doi.org/10.1016/j.technovation.2021.102423

DeTienne, D. R., McKelvie, A., & Chandler, G. N. (2015). Making sense of entrepreneurial exit strategies: A typology and test. *Journal of Business Venturing, 30*(2), 255–272. https://doi.org/10.1016/j.jbusvent.2014.07.007

DeTienne, D. R., Shepherd, D. A., & De Castro, J. O. (2008). The fallacy of "only the strong survive": The effects of extrinsic motivation on the persistence decisions for under-performing firms. *Journal of Business Venturing, 23*(5), 528–546. https://doi.org/10.1016/j.jbusvent.2007.09.004

Dhir, A., & N., M., Nawaz, R., & Kaur, P. (2024). How do we pivot? Facilitators, inhibitors, and strategies of tech healthcare startups before, during, and after a crisis. *Technological Forecasting and Social Change, 207*, 123606. https://doi.org/10.1016/j.techfore.2024.123606

Ding, Z., Au, K., & Chiang, F. (2015). Social trust and angel investors' decisions: A multilevel analysis across nations. *Journal of Business Venturing, 30*(2), 307–321. https://doi.org/10.1016/j.jbusvent.2014.08.003

Elkington, J. (1994). Towards the sustainable corporation: Win-win-win business strategies for sustainable development. *California Management Review, 36*(2), 90–100.

Elkington, J. (1997). *Cannibals with forks: The triple bottom line of 21st century business*. Capstone Publishing.
Fernandez, V. (2021). The role of trust and social commitment in start-up financing. *International Review of Financial Analysis, 75*, 101722. https://doi.org/10.1016/j.irfa.2021.101722
Ferrati, F., & Muffatto, M. (2021). Reviewing equity investors' funding criteria: A comprehensive classification and research agenda. *Venture Capital, 23*(2), 157–178. https://doi.org/10.1080/13691066.2021.1883211
Graña-Alvarez, R., Gomez-Conde, J., Lopez-Valeiras, E., & González-Loureiro, M. (2024). Management control systems, business financial literacy and financial leverage in business-incubated start-ups. *The British Accounting Review*, 101427. https://doi.org/10.1016/j.bar.2024.101427
Hahn, G. J. (2020). Industry 4.0: A supply chain innovation perspective. *International Journal of Production Research, 58*(5) 1425–1441. https://doi.org/10.1080/00207543.2019.1641642
Haskel, J., & Westlake, S. (2018). *Capitalism without capital: The rise of the intangible economy*. Princeton University Press.
Hinterhuber, A. (2013). Can competitive advantage be predicted?: Towards a predictive definition of competitive advantage in the resource-based view of the firm. *Management Decision, 51*(4), 795–812. Retrieved from http://doi.org/10.1108/00251741311326572
Hogrebe, F., & Lutz, E. (2024). The sunk cost fallacy in venture capital staging: Decision-making dynamics for follow-on investment rounds. *Journal of Corporate Finance, 86*, 102589. https://doi.org/10.1016/j.jcorpfin.2024.102589
Hohen, S., & Schweizer, L. (2021). Entrepreneurs' exit strategy intentions and their final exit paths. *Schmalenbach Journal of Business Research, 73*(3–4), 443–477. https://doi.org/10.1007/s41471-021-00123-7
Huang, L., & Knight, A. P. (2017). Resources and relationships in entrepreneurship: An exchange theory of the development and effects of the entrepreneur-investor relationship. *Academy of Management Review, 42*(1), 80–102. https://doi.org/10.5465/amr.2014.0397
Huang, P., & Madhavan, R. (2021). Dumb money or smart money? Meta-analytically unpacking corporate venture capital. *Strategic Entrepreneurship Journal, 15*(3), 403–429. https://doi.org/10.1002/sej.1369
Huang, W., Vismara, S., & Wei, X. (2022). Confidence and capital raising. *Journal of Corporate Finance, 77*, 101900. https://doi.org/10.1016/j.jcorpfin.2021.101900
Ilyas, I. M., & Osiyevskyy, O. (2022). Exploring the impact of sustainable value proposition on firm performance. *European Management Journal, 40*(5), 729–740. https://doi.org/10.1016/j.emj.2021.09.009

Ivanov, V. I., & Xie, F. (2010). Do corporate venture capitalists add value to start-up firms? Evidence from IPOs and acquisitions of VC-backed companies. *Financial Management, 39*(1), 129–152.

Jansen, J. J. P., Heavey, C., Mom, T. J. M., Simsek, Z., & Zahra, S. A. (2023). Scaling-up: Building, leading and sustaining rapid growth over Time. *Journal of Management Studies, 60*(3), 581–604. https://doi.org/10.1111/joms.12910

Johnson, M. J., Kim, K. H., Colarelli, S. M., & Boyajian, M. (2021). Coachability and the development of the coachability scale. *Journal of Management Development, 40*(7/8), 585–610. https://doi.org/10.1108/JMD-06-2020-0174

Kato, M., & Honjo, Y. (2015). Entrepreneurial human capital and the survival of new firms in high—and low-tech sectors. *Journal of Evolutionary Economics, 25*(5), 925–957. https://doi.org/10.1007/s00191-015-0427-3

Koller, T., Goedhart, M., & Wessels, D. (2020). *Valuation: Measuring and managing the value of companies* (7th ed.). Wiley.

Kuratko, D. F., Neubert, E., & Marvel, M. R. (2021). Insights on the mentorship and coachability of entrepreneurs. *Business Horizons, 64*(2), 199–209. https://doi.org/10.1016/j.bushor.2020.11.001

Lukas, E., Mölls, S., & Welling, A. (2016). Venture capital, staged financing and optimal funding policies under uncertainty. *European Journal of Operational Research, 250*(1), 305–313. https://doi.org/10.1016/j.ejor.2015.10.051

Mahajan, J. (1992). The overconfidence effect in marketing management predictions. *Journal of Marketing Research, 29*(3), 329–342.

Margolis, J., & Tzabbar, D. (2020). Leveraging founding team human capital for innovative new ventures. *Organizational Dynamics, 49*(4), 100749. https://doi.org/10.1016/j.orgdyn.2019.100749

Mason, C., Botelho, T., & Harrison, R. (2019). The changing nature of angel investing: Some research implications. *Venture Capital, 21*(2–3), 177–194. https://doi.org/10.1080/13691066.2019.1612921

Mathias, B. D., & Williams, D. W. (2018). Giving up the hats? Entrepreneurs' role transitions and venture growth. *Journal of Business Venturing, 33*(3), 261–277. https://doi.org/10.1016/j.jbusvent.2017.12.007

Mathisen, M. T., Shankar, R. K., Widding, Ø., Rasmussen, E., & McKelvie, A. (2022). Enablers of exit through trade sale: The case of early-stage research-based spin-offs. *Small Business Economics, 59*(2), 521–535. https://doi.org/10.1007/s11187-021-00484-7

Moore, C., Chadwick, F., & Hull, L. (2024). Venture pulse. In *KPMG Private Enterprise*. https://assets.kpmg.com/content/dam/kpmg/xx/pdf/2024/04/venture-pulse-q1-2024.pdf

Moore, D. A., & Healy, P. J. (2008). The trouble with overconfidence. *Psychological Review, 115*(2), 502–517. https://doi.org/10.1037/0033-295X.115.2.502
Mula, C., Zybura, N., & Hipp, T. (2024). From digitalized start-up to scale-up: Opening the black box of scaling in digitalized firms towards a scaling process framework. *Technological Forecasting and Social Change, 202*, 123275. https://doi.org/10.1016/j.techfore.2024.123275
Newbert, S. L. (2008). Value, rareness, competitive advantage, and performance: A conceptual-level empirical investigation of the resource-based view of the firm. *Strategic Management Journal, 29*(7), 745–768. http://doi.org/10.1002/smj.686
Nijhof, A., Bakker, M., & Kievit, H. (2019). The role in encroachment of the sustainability aspects of value propositions. *European Journal of Marketing, 53*(10), 2126–2145. https://doi.org/10.1108/EJM-11-2017-0879
Norbäck, P.-J., Persson, L., & Tåg, J. (2024). Risky business: Venture capital, pivoting and scaling. *Small Business Economics*. https://doi.org/10.1007/s11187-024-00944-w
Ozmel, U., Robinson, D. T., & Stuart, T. E. (2013). Strategic alliances, venture capital, and exit decisions in early stage high-tech firms. *Journal of Financial Economics, 107*(3), 655–670. https://doi.org/10.1016/j.jfineco.2012.09.009
Reynolds, M. (2017, November 25). If you can't build it, buy it: Google's biggest acquisitions mapped. *WIRED*. https://www.wired.com/story/google-acquisitions-data-visualisation-infoporn-waze-youtube-android/
Ruggieri, R., Savastano, M., Scalingi, A., Bala, D., & D'Ascenzo, F. (2018). The impact of digital platforms on business models: An empirical investigation on innovative start-ups. *Management & Marketing, 13*(4), 1210–1225. https://doi.org/10.2478/mmcks-2018-0032
Sala, P. K., Philbin, S. P., & Barikzai, S. (2022). A qualitative research study of the tech startup journey through entrepreneurial pivoting. *International Journal of Entrepreneurial Behavior & Research, 28*(4), 1050–1074. https://doi.org/10.1108/IJEBR-07-2021-0528
Salva, C., & Zhang, X. (2022). Financial versus strategic bidders and underpricing as an acquisition motive. *Journal of Business Finance & Accounting, 49*(9–10), 1830–1862. https://doi.org/10.1111/jbfa.12609
Sanasi, S., Ghezzi, A., & Cavallo, A. (2023). What happens after market validation? Experimentation for scaling in technology-based startups. *Technological Forecasting and Social Change, 196*, 122839. https://doi.org/10.1016/j.techfore.2023.122839
Sauvage, N., Zeisberger, C., & Varadan, M. (2022). Is corporate venture capital right for your startup? How entrepreneurs can decide whether to pursue

corporate funding, and if so, which CVC to pick. *Harvard Business Review Digital Articles*, 1–8.

Shepherd, D. A., Breugst, N., & Patzelt, H. (2023). A founding-team model of creating a venture's culture. *Journal of Business Venturing, 38*(2), 106286. https://doi.org/10.1016/j.jbusvent.2022.106286

Simon, M., & Shrader, R. C. (2012). Entrepreneurial actions and optimistic overconfidence: The role of motivated reasoning in new product introductions. *Journal of Business Venturing, 27*(3), 291–309. https://doi.org/10.1016/j.jbusvent.2011.04.003

Skica, T., Mikuš, J., & Holienka, M. (2022). Financial literacy and new business entry. *Financial Internet Quarterly, 18*(2), 42–66. https://doi.org/10.2478/fiqf-2022-0012

Strebulaev, I. A., & Wang, A. (2024). Steer clear of corporate venture capital pitfalls. *MIT Sloan Management Review, 65*(3), 30–35.

Svetek, M. (2022). Signaling in the context of early-stage equity financing: Review and directions. *Venture Capital, 24*(1), 71–104. https://doi.org/10.1080/13691066.2022.2063092

Tatikonda, M. V., Terjesen, S. A., Patel, P. C., & Parida, V. (2013). The role of operational capabilities in enhancing new venture survival: A longitudinal study. *Production and Operations Management, 22*(6), 1401–1415. https://doi.org/10.1111/poms.12038

Täuscher, K., & Laudien, S. M. (2018). Understanding platform business models: A mixed methods study of marketplaces. *European Management Journal, 36*(3), 319–329. https://doi.org/10.1016/j.emj.2017.06.005

Teece, D. J. (2012). Dynamic capabilities: Routines versus entrepreneurial action. *Journal of Management Studies, 49*(8), 1395–1401. https://doi.org/10.1111/j.1467-6486.2012.01080.x

Van Alstyne, M., & Parker, G. (2017). Platform business: From resources to relationships. *NIM Marketing Intelligence Review, 9*(1), 24–29. https://doi.org/10.1515/gfkmir-2017-0004

Van Lancker, E., Knockaert, M., Collewaert, V., & Breugst, N. (2023). Preparing for scaling: A study on founder role evolution. *Journal of Business Venturing, 38*(4), 106315. https://doi.org/10.1016/j.jbusvent.2023.106315

Wang, L., Huang, H., & An, Y. (2021). Technological fit, control rights allocation, and innovation performance of corporate venture capital-backed enterprises. *Venture Capital, 23*(3), 229–255. https://doi.org/10.1080/13691066.2021.1905931

Weiger, W. H. (2023). Engaging business customers through online experiences in different cultures. *Journal of International Marketing, 31*(3), 59–79. https://doi.org/10.1177/1069031X231165234

Wesley Ii, C. L., Kong, D. T., Lubojacky, C. J., Kim Saxton, M., & Saxton, T. (2022). Will the startup succeed in your eyes? Venture evaluation of resource providers during entrepreneurs' informational signaling. *Journal of Business Venturing, 37*(5), 106229. https://doi.org/10.1016/j.jbusvent.2022.106229

Whittington, R., Angwin, D., Regner, P., Johnson, G., & Scholes, K. (2023). *Exploring strategy* (13 ed.). Harlow, United Kingdom: Pearson.

Wood, M. S., Long, A., & Artz, K. (2020). Angel investor network pitch meetings: The pull and push of peer opinion. *Business Horizons, 63*(4), 507–518. https://doi.org/10.1016/j.bushor.2020.03.008

Xie, Y. (2024). Founder premiums, venture capital investments and acquirer benefits. *Journal of Business Finance & Accounting, 51*(5–6), 943–1014. https://doi.org/10.1111/jbfa.12737

Yimfor, E., & Garfinkel, J. A. (2023). Predicting success in entrepreneurial finance research. *Journal of Corporate Finance, 81*, 102359. https://doi.org/10.1016/j.jcorpfin.2023.102359

Zhang, H., Ma, Z., Liang, X., & Garrett, T. C. (2024). Antecedents and outcomes of open innovation over the past 20 years: A framework and meta-analysis. *Journal of Product Innovation Management, 41*(4), 793–815. https://doi.org/10.1111/jpim.12710

CHAPTER 4

Costs and Intellectual Capital Development

4.1 Introduction—The Transformative Knowledge Economy

The Knowledge Economy first coined by Peter Drucker (1969) has been the bulwark of growth in developed economies (and increasingly in developing economies) where there has been a high reliance on knowledge, information, and high-skilled labor. Drucker stated that with the advancement of new technologies and the fundamental increases in knowledge from mass education availability, international business transformed into a networked world economy with major implications to the way we live and work. This knowledge combined with technological advancements has led to major sources and shifts in competitive advantage.

Haskel and Westlake (2018) define knowledge as "connections made between pieces of information, supported by evidence, to form a coherent understanding. Knowledge cannot exist without information, and knowledge is required to fully understand and interpret information. Knowledge can, therefore, include theories, hypotheses, correlations, or causal relationships observed from information constituted by analyzable data" (p. 64). They further deduce that knowledge as an intangible is scalable much more than physical products. Unlike physical (tangible) products where they can only be used in one location at a time, intangibles can be used and re-used in multiple locations and for multiple purposes at the

R. G. Chammassian, *Costs, Value, and the Entrepreneurial Venture Journey*, Palgrave Studies in Accounting and Finance Practice,
https://doi.org/10.1007/978-3-031-86216-8_4

same time. Hence, knowledge has a scalability quotient much higher than any physical product. This scalability can be *supercharged with network effects.* Although physical products can also have a networked effect when everyone uses them (like a mobile phone), intangibles have a much bigger network effect due to their flexibility and potential gain from economies of scale.

A good example of this is banking transactions, such as paying bills and withdrawing or depositing cash. Before the introduction of ATMs (Automatic Teller Machines), banking customers had to physically go to a bank to conduct basic financial transactions, including cash withdrawals. Most of the costs associated with these transactions were human, physical asset, and overhead costs related (whether rented or owned space). Tellers earned a monthly salary year after year. Customers had to travel to a bank at a designated location, park (if they had to drive), and then wait in line to withdraw cash. The opportunity cost was a timely and expensive endeavor for all parties.

With the introduction of ATMs, banks invested in these *automated tellers* (known as *cash machines*) whose costs were eventually offset by the elimination of teller salaries. ATMs took up less space and were available 24 h per day, unlike a bank branch. Furthermore, ATMs could be set up at any key physical location (such as shopping malls) without the higher costs incurred by setting up a bank branch. This service made banking transactions *available* to customers at multiple locations for their *convenience* and *satisfaction.* With the advancement of technologies (hardware and software), these ATMs began providing additional services, such as making deposits, payments, money transfers, purchases, and similar. ATM manufacturers and bank customers saw the opportunity to expand their services by replicating the process.

Demand for ATMs and additional automated service offerings increased. Different banks offered similar services, including at international locations. ATM manufacturers, such as the NCR Corporation, had to re-design their ATM models for different markets, countries, and languages. This meant physical re-design and localization, such as localized keyboards for different languages and banking transactions. This added additional costs in R&D, components, and spare parts for maintenance (i.e., language keyboards). With the advancement of smart screen technology and software, ATM manufacturers re-designed their ATMs with touch screens with multiple language offerings in one machine or market with numerical keyboards only. Software replaced physical keyboards for different languages. This reduced ATM manufacturing costs, purchase price, and maintenance costs.

Tech advancements with cloud data storage and retrieval, high-speed networks, and data processing led to further digitalization of financial services along with less use of cash and ATMs. Banks began to offer cashless online services to businesses and consumers through home computers and mobile devices (i.e., smart phones and tablets). Banking customers could now conduct their financial transactions at their own leisure and choose virtually, even though they could still go to an ATM to withdraw or deposit cash when needed. Cash, a tangible asset, became *digital* and *virtual*. We can now transfer cash and pay for products and services *cashless* and sometimes *touchless*. We call this digital commerce, mobile point-of-sale (POS) payments, and digital remittances. Digital payments transaction value for 2024 is targeted to be $11.5 trillion and it is estimated to grow by 9.52% CAGR[1] by 2028, reaching $16.6 trillion in 2028 (Statista Market Insights, 2023). This evolution is led by financial technology (FinTech) driven entrepreneurial startups (ESU) who are setting new standards with the advancement of trends and technologies. "There are three major trends affecting the payment industry with sustainable long-term impacts: seamless commerce, mobile payments, and blockchain technology" (Statista, 2023, p. 8). Safety standards, security, and social trust play a pivotal role in the advancement and use of digital commerce evolution, hallmarks of both *technological* and *social capital*.

ATMs continue to play a role and evolve into Interactive Teller Machines (ITMs) sometimes referred to as *video remote tellers* (VRT) where customers could opt for personalized services to interact with human tellers virtually (NCR Atleos, n.d.). This may lead to a *spillover effect* and development where VRTs could become available on home and mobile devices. This scalability, spillover, and network effect has led to unlimited banking services availability and experiences, empowering banking customers with convenience, choice, access, trust, value, safety, security, privacy, and loyalty. The basic banking services have not changed. They are still related to financial transactions. What has changed is the way we efficiently and effectively use banking services, as NCR Corporation's motto stated, *transforming transactions into relationships*. Although we still use physical devices and equipment to access banking services,

[1] Compounded Annual Growth Rate.

the transformation is with the customer relationship. Customer empowerment and experiences, including convenience, access, privacy, safety, and trust legitimacy (Van Le & Suh, 2019), have led to strong customer loyalty, which is an invaluable intangible asset called *social capital*. In addition, the need to devise and develop new features in service offerings has led to unique partnerships between banks and producers of hardware and software, which is also a vital intangible asset called *relational capital*.

The banking services transformation from tangible to intangible value with unlimited opportunities is just an example of how everyday activities have been transformed with the advancement of technological infrastructure and developments (such as generative AI), network effects, and spillovers in the knowledge economy. Hence, intangibles and investment in intangibles have become the hallmark of twenty-first-century Knowledge Economy (Haskel & Westlake, 2018; OECD, 1996). Over 90% of S&P 500 market value is made of intangible assets,[2] mainly in intellectual capital. In fact, in almost all facets of life and business, this transformation has been powered by advances of technology, democratizing availability of information, knowledge sharing, and choices. In most cases, technology has enabled these intangible facets to be complementary value drivers and not necessarily all replacements. Except that, these complementaries have superseded pure profitability KPIs in ESU value capture and eventual extraction from trade sales. Figure 4.1 illustrates how these complementaries have shifted value drivers.

For instance, while products and services still create value, the shift has been towards intangible intrinsic value through experiences, access, availability, and choices since the early part of the twenty-first century. This is now followed by a sense of sharing, sustainability, impact, security, and trust in the 2020s and beyond. While profitability is still desired, intangible and sustainable value creates, captures, and extracts much higher enterprise value than profitability by itself. This has led to the shifts from a shareholder mindset to a stakeholder mindset.

Prior to 2000, costs played mainly a moderator role for margin and profitability even though investments were made in new product development (NPD). With the Knowledge Economy, costs are mainly invested in intangibles and play a mediator role of enterprise value, even though costs still have a moderating element on margin and profitability.

[2] Source: Ocean Tomo in Haskel and Westlake (2018).

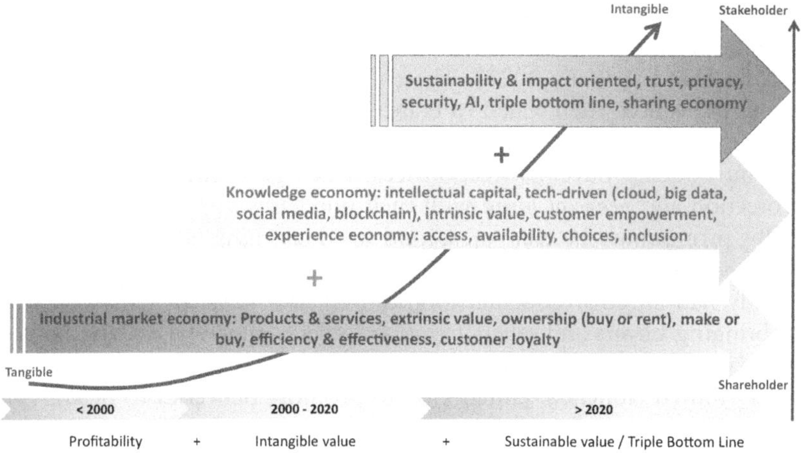

Fig. 4.1 Fundamental marketplace changes with the knowledge economy

Figure 4.2 further illustrates this transition with specific examples of innovation areas.

An example of this evolution from tangible to intangible value is Vinted, an ESU based in Lithuania that made second-hand fashion a consumer-to-consumer (C2C) marketplace. The idea started in the small Baltic country of Lithuania where its two founders came up with the

INNOVATION	< 2000		2000 - 2020		> 2020
Business models, Problem-Solution fit	Product/Services driven	+	Value driven, Experience oriented	+	Values driven w/ impact
Technology	*Build or buy*	+	Big data, Cloud, Blockchain, Platforms, Social Media	+	White label, Gen AI Tech-as-a-service (TaaS)
Products / Services	Ownership, rental/leasing	+	Multi-Access, Options/Choice	+	Sharing & networks
Value	Mainly extrinsic	+	Mainly intrinsic	+	Impact oriented
Customer	Sales / revenue genearting	+	Shareholders	+	Financing & future M&A
Customer relations	Loyalty focused	+	Empowerment, partnership	+	Values, privacy, trust safety/security
Investment	Mainly tangibles	+	Mainly intangibles	+	Sustainability
Costs	Moderator of profitability	+	Mainly mediator of value	+	Mixed, mainly mediator of value
ROI	Profitability, free cash flow	+	Firm value extraction, intangibles, IC	+	Triple Bottom Line

Fig. 4.2 Transformation of innovation examples with the knowledge economy

concept "to create a platform where individuals could buy and sell clothing from each other's wardrobes" (15 Years of Vinted, Empowering Second-Hand at Scale, 2023). The company was launched in 2008 with women's fashion, then scaled to France in 2013, which became its largest market. In 2016, it changed its business model by removing seller fees and introducing buyer protection fees which gave buyers the choice of protection and *peace of mind* with their purchases.

By promoting the sale of second-hand clothing which was mainly confined to very fragmented, hidden, and private sales, Vinted had already had an environmental footprint. It also *democratized* such sales by bringing buyers and sellers together under a *platform*, making fashion affordable, available, with a positive environmental and social impact. In 2021, Vinted launched Vinted Go "to promote deliveries to pickup and drop-off points as a solution with a lower impact on the climate compared to in-home delivery." In 2023, it added a new *item verification service*[3] for trading higher-price second-hand merchandise. Internationally, it grew organically and via acquisition, such as Homerr in the Netherlands.[4] In 2019, Vinted became the first Lithuanian unicorn, with a valuation of over one billion euros.

Vinted's business model is value(s) driven even though they *facilitated the sales* as an intermediary of second-hand products between sellers and buyers. Vinted solved a social and environmental problem by initially making second-hand clothing available and affordable to people willing to sell and buy (later scaling to other types of merchandise); reducing waste by reselling second-hand merchandise with a circular economy approach; and improving its environmental footprint with their *Vinted Go* launch. Technological advances with online platforms and cloud computing, big data, blockchain, and similar technologies enabled Vinted to facilitate its problem-solution fit efficiently and effectively.

These digital platforms are multi-sided, they are highly oriented towards data analytics and adopted both by ESUs and established companies as part of the Industry 4.0 *platform economy* (Budde et al., 2024; Hahn, 2019; Schwab, 2016). A platform acts as an ecosystem by itself, a *meta-organization or "organizations of organizations"* (Kretschmer et al.,

[3] https://company.vinted.com/newsroom/vinted-introduces-item-verification-service.

[4] https://company.vinted.com/newsroom/homerr-vinted-go-join-forces.

2022) to motivate and incentivize stakeholders, customers, and users alike to participate, contribute, share, learn, buy and sell.

Like Vinted, entrepreneurial startups (ESUs) play a vital role in this transformation.[5] The majority of ESUs that seek external financing are designed for an eventual exit scenario mainly through trade sales/M&A (and sometimes IPO) so that its shareholders can earn a return on their investment (ROI). As the majority of exits through trade sales are strategic in nature, many larger firms acquire smaller firms for their intangible assets for strategic positioning. On the flipside, this means to extract a higher premium value from exits, ESUs must develop unique value propositions (UVP) for their M&A customers. For these ventures, this UVP is extracted through the development of Intellectual Capital (IC), which is made of human, organizational, relational, and social capital.

This chapter will focus on the transformation of the Knowledge Economy *product* lifecycles from the standard industrial model with a focus on NPD to the ESU model where the focus is New Venture Development (NVD) with intellectual capital being its core value creation, capture, and eventual extraction through exits.

Although this model has been initially developed from my research with high-tech startups, it can also apply to non-high-tech problem-driven ESUs that need to develop a scalable business model with a growth-oriented company that seeks external financing to do so. To clarify, the distinction between high-tech and non-high-tech ESUs is as follows:

- High-tech startups by default are technology-driven, solving *core technological* problems through mainly R&D (Bailetti, 2012; Burmaoglu et al., 2019; Giones & Brem, 2017; Van Meeteren et al., 2022). They can be university R&D technology transfer spinoffs or ESUs specialized in developing disruptive technologies that transform the way scientific and medical industries operate, industries perform, and lives improve and extend. Examples of this are pharma,

[5] I use an adaptation of Leach and Melicher's (2021) definition of *entrepreneurial ventures* from their inception as entrepreneurial startups (ESU) as a form of new venture development (NVD), through its different lifecycle stages, with the ultimate purpose of high value extraction through exits. These ESUs' performance is reflected in value creation, capture, and extraction with scalable growth over time. In most cases, they require a staged, sometimes substantial amount of external financing to invest in their development and growth strategy. This contrasts with lifestyle and salary-replacement micro-businesses.

nanotechnology, artificial intelligence (AI), medical devices, and similar.

- Non-high-tech or Mid and low-tech startups in contrast are usually solving a societal, environmental, business, governance, or economic problem. They use digital *enabling technologies* and *application domains* (or *general-purpose technologies*) as a means, an enabler, and a mediator (or a tool) to solve the problem they are solving more efficiently and effectively (Ancillai et al., 2023; Carroll, 2017; Coad & Reid, 2012; Van meeteren et al., 2022; Waßenhoven et al., 2023). Their technologies either exist, are adopted, or adapted to their problem-solution fit. Examples include AI, social media, cloud computing, block chain, white-label SaaS,[6] online platforms, and hybrid technologies.

Takeaways

- The knowledge economy with tech advancements has led to a major sources and shifts in competitive advantage.
- Knowledge as an intangible is much more scalable than physical products. It can be used and re-used in multiple locations and purposes at the same time.
- This scalability can be supercharged with network effects and spillovers.
- It has shifted from shareholder to stakeholder mindset; from tangible to intangible value; from product-driven to value(s)-driven business models.
- Financial value-wise, profitability has been supplemented by intangible and sustainable values and valuations.
- Entrepreneurial startups (ESU) have been key drivers of this transformation from new product development (NPD) to new venture development (NVD).
- Initially driven by high-tech ESUs developing core technologies and increasingly by (non-high tech) social, environmental, and economic problem-driven ESUs utilizing enabling technologies, application domains, or general-purpose techs.

[6] Software as a Service.

4.2 Knowledge Economy *Product* LifeCycles

Entering the *Fourth Industrial Revolution*, "we stand on the brink of a technological revolution that will fundamentally alter the way we live, work, and relate to one another. In its scale, scope, and complexity, the transformation will be unlike anything humankind has experienced before. We do not yet know just how it will unfold, but one thing is clear: the response to it must be integrated and comprehensive, involving all stakeholders of the global polity, from the public and private sectors to academia and civil society" (Schwab, 2016, pp. 2–3).[7]

This transformation towards the fourth (post-)industrial knowledge economy has seen dramatic shifts in business model design from product driven to value(s) driven. Value creation is mainly driven by the *use of intellectual capital by the most innovative companies in the* world (Li et al., 2021). Within the previous industrial model, investments were made in new product development (NPD)[8] either for a new market entry (whether a startup or a larger corporation) or to expand existing product offerings in the marketplace. These investments were made in product R&D which are then tested, refined, and marketed.

New ventures are now created by founders based on the *knowledge context* of their background whether an (ex)employee, an academic researcher, or a user (Agarwal & Shah, 2014). *(Ex)employee* entrepreneurial context is based on their knowledge gained throughout their employment within a firm. They transform their knowledge into innovative products whether their existing employers accept or reject. In the latter case, employees leave their employment to create a new venture based on their new idea. *Academic researchers* establish new ventures as a spinoff from their research context to develop further, commonly known as academic entrepreneurs (Giunti & Duberley, 2023; Hayter et al., 2022). Whereas *user entrepreneurs* innovate with the context of their usage of products and services (Baldwin et al., 2006; Oo et al., 2019).

As illustrated in Fig. 4.3, within the standard industrial economy, value creation is based on NPD. Business models are product-driven to capture

[7] https://www.weforum.org/agenda/2016/01/the-fourth-industrial-revolution-what-it-means-and-how-to-respond/.

[8] In this context, the word *product* applies to a combined *product and/or services*.

traditional economic value where revenue minus expenses leads to profitability. R&D costs are treated as expenses in the income statement and are considered to be sunk costs. Whereas product costs play a moderating role in profitability. The ultimate value capture is profitability, which has a one-year horizon due to the way financial accounting and reporting work. Venture value is assessed according to the discounted cash flow (DCF) method using future net cash flows at present value. DCF has limited valuation multiples based on single digit multiples of revenue and EBIDTA.[9] It also depends on the market position of the product and strategic fit for any future acquiring company. Startups who focus on product-driven business models have a lesser chance of attracting investors due to shorter product lifecycles compared to ***value-driven cycles***.

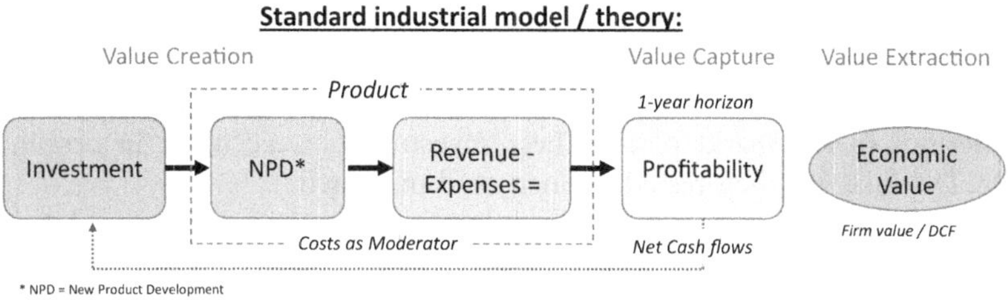

Fig. 4.3 Standard industrial model of value creation, capture, and extraction[10]

[9] Earnings Before Interest Depreciation Taxes and Amortization, commonly known as cash-oriented Gross Operating Income (or loss).

[10] Chammassian (2016) and Chammassian and Blum (2018).

With technological advancement and the emergence of the knowledge economy, ***tangible product life cycles*** become shorter, whereas intangibles add a new dimension with their scalability, spillover, and network effect. With the latter, value creation focuses on non-physical product lifecycles. Business models become value driven (not product-driven), with value creation focusing on new venture development (NVD) through entrepreneurial startups (ESU) instead of simple NPD, even though sellable products are part of the new venture's value proposition. The Vinted C2C-oriented platform business model proves this. Even though they are facilitating the sale of second-hand merchandise, their ***product*** is the C2C facilitation of the sale of existing second-hand merchandise with different lifecycles through a double-sided platform. It could be any merchandise as long as there is a seller and a buyer, and the transaction is legitimate.

Knowledge economy's ESU's approach is more holistic. It incorporates intangible value creation, capture, and extraction in its value proposition with multiple offerings addressing stakeholder needs through a portfolio of products, services, experiences, and choices. Stakeholders include three types of customers (i.e., paying, financing, and future trade sales), shareholders, communities of interest (i.e., social, environmental, governance, economic), and users (i.e., informational, freemium, influencers). In fact, ESUs act as a multi-sided platform addressing customer, stakeholder, and user needs simultaneously through information sharing, blogs, videos, stories, freemium, and premium offerings (Kretschmer et al., 2022).

The ESU business model focuses on sustainable long-term development, scalability, and growth with triple bottom line impact considerations, that are social, environment, and economic (Elkington, 1994, 1997). It has a multi-year horizon with various scalability, growth, spillover, and network effects that lead to future venture value based on profitability and intellectual capital capabilities. Although NPD plays a moderating role of profitability, intellectual capital plays a mediating role of enterprise value. The ultimate value extraction is from enterprise value through a trade sales exit scenario. Figure 4.4 illustrates the ESU model in the knowledge economy.

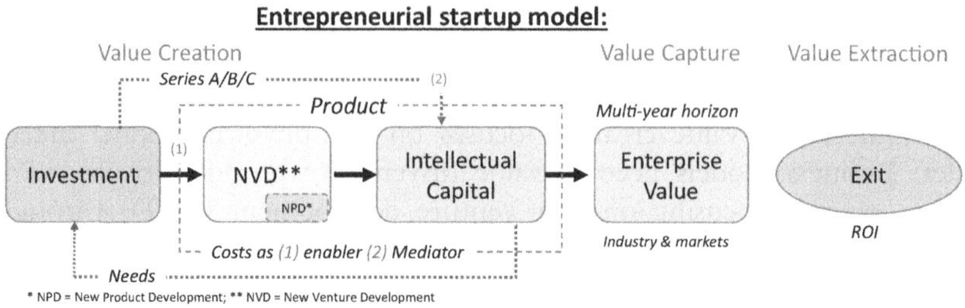

Fig. 4.4 Knowledge economy model of value creation, capture, and extraction[11]

Costs within the ESU business model act as mainly an enabler and mediator of value, even though costs play a moderating role with NPD. What is interesting about this model is that intangible value propositions through intellectual capital will lead to a positive effect on triple-customer attraction, repeat and recurring revenue generation, and enterprise value.

Takeaways

- We have entered the 4th Industrial Revolution with a dramatic shift in business model design from product driven to value(s) driven.
- Value creation is mainly driven by intellectual capital (IC) development.
- New ventures or ESUs are created by ex-employees, academic researchers, or user entrepreneurs.
- Standard industrial model and theory have been traditionally based on NDP for value creation, annualized profitability for value capture, and economic firm value through discounted cash flow (DCF) models.
- The knowledge economy ESU model is based on NVD and IC development for value creation, annualized NPD profitability and multi-year enterprise value for value capture, and ROI through exit (mainly trade sales) for value extraction.

[11] Chammassian (2016) and Chammassian and Blum (2018).

4.3 Intangible Assets and Costs

Intangible assets have been the hallmark of the twenty-first century and the majority of investments in companies. It is commonly referred to as the non-physical aspects of a company that creates, captures, and extracts value for its stakeholders with a competitive advantage. All larger companies and high-tech-driven ESUs recognize this. These aspects include anything that can be recognized, documented, and measured as part of a company's competitive advantage in the marketplace. Examples of intangibles include market share; brand recognition; customer lists; big data; unique software and technology; company and brand reputation; internal knowledge and expertise; intellectual property (IP, such as patents, copyrights, and trademarks); unique processes and relationships; and social networks.

4.3.1 Costs, Intangibles, and International Accounting Standards

When it comes to capturing intangibles as a capital asset with long-term financial accounting value in a company, intangibles must be identifiable, non-physical, and with clear ownership. The International Accounting Standards (IAS) 38 on Intangible Assets defines it as "an identifiable non-monetary asset without physical substance. Such an asset is identifiable when it is separable, or when it arises from contractual or other legal rights. Separable assets can be sold, transferred, licensed, etc. Examples of intangible assets include computer software, licenses, trademarks, patents, films, copyrights and import quotas" (IFRS—IAS 38 Intangible Assets, n.d.).

The key words here are *identifiable when separable or arises from contractual or other legal rights.* However, unless it is clearly identifiable, such as pharmaceutical drug patent with a unique R&D discovery, it is very difficult to determine the economic value of an internally generated intangible asset. IAS 38 further adds two additional considerations to meet the definition of a financially accountable intangible asset: One, "that there will be future economic benefits from the asset;" and Two, that "the cost of the asset can be reliably measured." If this criterion is met, then an intangible can be *accounted for* and *classified as a non-current asset* on the balance sheet. An example of this would be an approved pharmaceutical patent as IP whose development costs can be accounted for an intangible asset and then amortized over its considered economic life, which for such patents, the maximum is 20 years. For such assets, the research component is usually expensed and considered *sunk costs*, while the development component can be recognized as part of the intangible assets on a cost basis (IAS 38).

However, if it is difficult to reliably measure both its costs and future economic benefits, which is in the majority of cases, then costs associated with generating intangible value are to be recognized as an expense in the income statement. IAS 38 further establishes that "the cost of generating an intangible asset internally is often difficult to distinguish from the cost of maintaining or enhancing the entity's operations or goodwill. For this reason, internally generated brands, mastheads, publishing titles, customer lists, and similar items are not recognized as intangible assets" on the balance sheet. In most cases, IAS 38 does not allow for internally generated intangibles to be captured as an asset on the balance sheet, but allows externally generated intangibles to be classified as such when they are acquired either through a purchase or M&A.

Here is where an important distinction lies. Although intangible assets may not be recognized as an *accountable* non-current assets, they still will carry a very large portion of a company's value, especially when it comes to ESU valuations.

From an investment perspective, costs associated with generating intangible value are often considered to be a *sunk cost* with the goal of deriving a *benefit*. Sunk cost by itself may have a negative perception, but *sunk cost benefit* is how it should be addressed.[12] Investments into intangibles have very *different economic characteristics* than investment into tangible assets. Tangible assets are physically identifiable, quantifiable (i.e., a building or a car), with a pre-defined and determined useful economic life.[13] According to IAS 16, the useful life is either the number of years an asset is (expected) to be useful or the units of production or similar it can obtain (i.e., a printer may have a useful life of one million printed pages). The useful life determines the economic life of a tangible asset. Economic life is determined by the assets' usefulness where income generated from it exceeds its costs.

[12] See Chapter 1—*The meaning of costs—Insights from tech startup founders and ecosystem* for further details.

[13] See *IAS 16 Property, Plant and Equipment* for further details.

4.3.2 *Spillovers of Intangible Cost Investments*

It is easier to measure benefits or *rents* from tangible assets than intangible assets. We can use units of productivity to form a tangible asset. However, it is very difficult to assess the usefulness of an intangible asset to determine its economic life. Intangible assets can generate *spillovers*,[14] are more likely to be *scalable* (Bohan et al., 2024), and can create *synergies* or complementaries to each other (Haskel & Westlake, 2018). This means with its spillover effects, it would be very difficult to estimate the future value of intangible investments. However, with the right combination of synergies and scalability, intangibles create uniqueness and potentially much higher enterprise value than pure profitability-based valuation. This applies not only for high-tech -driven ESUs, but also non-high-tech ESUs that utilize technologies as a tool to solve problems in the marketplace with UVPs. On the flip side, due to the sunken nature of its costs, intangible asset value would be worth much less if the project does not work.

As an example of spillovers, Vinted uses a cloud-based platform model to match buyers and sellers of second-hand fashion. The matchmaking platform model that Vinted uses is a spillover from Amazon and similar matchmaking technology platforms allowing multiple parties to sell and buy products and handle payments. Amazon may have perfected the buyer–seller matchmaking services and maintains a high company valuation due to its synergies, networks, and brand recognition; it does not have a monopoly on the specific matchmaking technology. In other words, technologies supporting such platforms are no longer unique to Amazon. There are many third-party technology-as-a-service providers that offer a variation of cloud-based services, such as platform-as-a-service (PaaS), infrastructure-as-a-service (IaaS), and software-as-a service (SaaS) that facilitate the setup of such platforms for ESUs like Vinted. In fact, Vinted's platform model is not only a technology model. It is a business model of supporting large number of participants to exchange secondhand goods and services (i.e., the problem that Vinted is solving) where platform-based technologies not only *enable* Vinted to make the

[14] *Spillovers* are tendencies of private investments into intangibles where other firms may benefit from an approach or a trade secret by reverse engineering, mimicking, or replicating what are meant to be private.

exchanges possible but also *mediate* its double-sided exchanges efficiently and effectively.

Over time, Vinted has added new complementary features or synergies, such as *item verification service* for trust, legitimacy authentication, and security, and *Vinted Go* to improve its environmental footprint to its value proposition. Combined Vinted has created a unique value proposition to its triple customers, who are paying for products and services (revenue-generating customers for Vinted); financing its growth (i.e., investors), and making it attractive for eventual trade sales markets or for an IPO.

Finally, Vinted's business model is also *scalable*. They started as a platform matching second-hand fashion sellers to buyers. It has now scaled to other types of second-hand merchandise and operates in different countries with different cultural norms, demand, and supply for such second-hand merchandise sales. Costs initially invested into its intangibles have mediated scalability. In fact, scalability of intangibles means they can be ***duplicated with little or no marginal costs*** (see Bohan et al., 2024; Cavallo et al., 2024; De Ridder, 2024; Haskel & Westlake, 2018; Jansen et al., 2023). Vinted can scale to other countries and second-hand merchandize matchmaking in different markets with little adjustments, for instance, only in localization (i.e., native languages), whereas the core of their business model and mediating technologies changes little. Hence, their growth increases with little marginal cost increase per unit sold, leading to higher margin and profitability due to economies of scale. In fact, their scaling investment into other markets or countries switches from intangible infrastructure to the development of in-country or growth operations. This includes investment into local human capital, organizational capital, social capital, and relational capital—combined called *intellectual capital*. These investments are made into *fixed costs* rather than into (variable) marginal costs per unit sold (De Ridder, 2024). Once these fixed-cost investments are made, then revenue growth and margin per fixed costs will also increase.

4.3.3 Intangible Capital Costs Versus Value

Various studies have attempted to measure intangible asset value with its tradeoffs, opportunity costs, investment and returns, productivity, and valuations from accounting and economics perspective (see works by Brynjolfsson & Yang, 1997; Crouzet & Eberly, 2023; Crouzet et al.,

2022a, 2022b; De Ridder, 2024; Dinh et al., 2019; Haskel & Westlake, 2018; Kanodia et al., 2004; Van Criekingen et al., 2022).

To start with, the consensus is that it is not easy to measure intangibles from a financial accounting perspective. Since most *investments in intangibles* are captured as operating expenses, they do not truly reflect their value as an asset. Furthermore, with spillovers, network effects, scalability, and complementary synergies, it is very difficult to measure what is accounted for as intangibles (whether rarely in the balance sheet or as operating expenses) with its productivity, output, and market value (Kanodia et al., 2004; Van Criekingen et al., 2022). Even though financial inputs such as salaries (as human capital costs) can be captured on the income statement, their overall outputs as productivity can be difficult to measure (McGrattan, 2020). While intangibles can be scaled to be simultaneously copied, stored, and used in different locations (i.e., economies of scale), they are very challenging to create and prove exclusive rights (Crouzet et al., 2022a). Hence, when comparing market valuations with operating expenses, due to multiple-year actuals, forecasts and forecast revisions, "the capital market only partially recognizes the intangible asset value created by SG&A expenditure" (Banker et al., 2019, p. 61).

There appears to be a large gap between investments and valuations of firms in the public financial markets—an excess in returns that cannot be computed through standard accounting valuations such as price per earnings (P/E) ratio. We see this consistently with the major tech firms, such as Apple, Amazon, and Alphabet. Crouzet and Eberly (2023) conducted a study on why when investment by larger U.S. firms were lower, valuations were still rising? They concluded that the excess gap was about the continuous benefits these firms were receiving from their existing intangibles. Instead of having to invest further to grow, they were gaining from little or no marginal costs. That means, once established the focus was more on investing in inputs to intangibles with fixed costs (i.e., for growth) instead of the process or maintenance of intangibles unlike tangibles (De Ridder, 2024; Haskel & Westlake, 2018).

4.3.4 *Intangibles and ESUs*

With high-tech ESUs, the early and mid-stages are all about developing their business model and value propositions through intangibles. Majority of investments go into R&D costs where some may be eventually captured as an intangible asset on the balance sheet (i.e., drug patents) whereas most may not (i.e., research component). Most of the costs are associated with high human capital as they need specialists, researchers, technicians, doctors, and PhDs to conduct the R&D. If and when intangibles are established, then the focus moves more into investing in the inputs to scale (i.e., promoting and selling the drugs in different markets), rather than the process itself since the intangibles are already established.

For the non-high-tech ESU,[15] the focus in early stages is to really define the problem and its impact; to understand the real customer needs, critical mass and competitor landscape; to identify the problem-solution fit scenarios with their impact and the type of technologies it needs to facilitate them; to prototype and price; to develop a plan on how to establish the new venture company, including prioritized resources and investments it needs incrementally; to identify its triple-customer base, at least with paying and financing customers (i.e., investor profile). The goal here is the innovative business model design that leads to its organizational design and resourcing needs through its value configuration (Fjeldstad & Snow, 2018). Costs at early stages should be purely related to these developments. The vast majority of (if not all) costs are associated with developing its new venture landscape (i.e., NVD), which is the foundation of its intangible assets, whether or not the ESU has physical products on offer. In fact, its new business model that creates unique value propositions through scalability and complementaries (i.e., synergies), becomes an intangible asset by itself.

A new venture business model that creates unique value propositions through scalability and complementaries or synergies, becomes an intangible asset by itself.

Once there has been good traction and proof of concept measured by the interest and commitment of financing customers and some identified target market Paying customers, the next step from early to mid stage ESUs is to transform its business model into a formidable venture by investing in the development of its intellectual capital.

[15] That are attempting to solve societal, environmental, economic, or business problems with matching solutions where they use different technologies as tools to enable and mediate the solution delivery.

Takeaways

- Intangible assets are difficult to measure from a financial accounting perspective as International Accounting Standards (IAS) have very tight rules.
- Majority of ESU *cost investments* are in intangible assets.
- Costs associated with creating intangible assets are captured as *operating expenses* in the income statement.
- Additional economic benefits of value creation through spillovers, network effects, and scalability are even more difficult to measure accounting-wise.
- Value created through intangible asset investments has a much longer effect on value capture and extraction due to benefits from low or no marginal costs.

4.4 Developing Intellectual Capital[16] (IC)

The original definition and intention of Intellectual Capital (IC), first coined by Thomas Stewart (1997, 2010), is meant to be a specific part of intangible assets that are *related to knowledge*, beginning with its founders. Thus, intellectual capital is "knowledge-based equity that a company possesses" (Cooper, 2000, p. 22). This is sometimes referred to as the *knowledge-based view* (Grant, 1997), in which knowledge is "the overwhelmingly important productive resource in terms of its contribution to value added and its strategic significance" (Grant, 1997, p. 451) and people are the main agents of value creation through knowledge.

Intellectual capital is "knowledge-based equity that a company possesses"

There are two models that are often mentioned: IC model (Stewart, 1997) and the Comprehensive IC Management model (Bontis, 1998, 2001). They both address human capital as the key to developing internal and external structures and relationships. These structures have to do with *internal knowledge* and know-how, either human or organizational,

[16] Intellectual capital (IC) research and development has been originally grounded with larger industrialized companies and some with SMEs. Here I link those developments to ESU, both from research and professional experiences.

that create, capture, and extract venture value with its innovation through unique value proposition (UVP) in the *external marketplace*. Sometimes the external marketplace has been referred to as *customer capital* which includes all the external to ESU relationships and networks, such as with paying customers, suppliers, partners, and distributors.

Intellectual capital is directly related to knowledge of ESU, beginning with its founders

Over time, IC definition expanded to include an interrelationship between different types of intangible capital actors that combined to create a much higher ESU market value than its book value and/or profitability-driven valuation. For instance, "a complex interplay between human capital and social capital leading to experiences of inclusion and exclusion. Inclusion was most frequently associated with social capital and involvement in association activities, whereas exclusion was attributed to (a lack of) both human capital and social capital" (Metz et al., 2022, p. 122).

To build a formidable venture, ESU founders relentlessly focus on value creation from its early stage. This value is primarily defined by the problem the ESU is trying to solve, the size of the problem, and its triple bottom line impact (social, environmental, and economic). It is followed by the ESUs problem-solution fit and value proposition, market size and impact; the value it is creating for its stakeholders and shareholders alike; along with the technologies it intends to use to solve the defined problem efficiently and effectively. ESU founders identify new or potential applications, commercial uses, and markets through an exploratory process. Sarasvathy (2001) defined this as an *effectuation process*, "to take a set of means as given and focus on selecting between possible effects that can be created with that set of means" (p. 245). Effectuation is further reinforced and made real by the fact that the majority of ESUs operate in a world of great uncertainty, with "non-predictive control" when they are in the process of creating ESUs and evolving ideas into new, marketable products (Sarasvathy, 2008).

During this process of value creation, resource requirements, identification, and acquisition of unique resources and their proper utilization become key. This is commonly known as the resource-based view (RBV). The origins of RBV aimed to view larger industrialized "firms in terms of their resources rather than in terms of their products" to address *strategic options* (Wernerfelt, 1984, p. 179). RBV evolved to address using resources *to sustain competitive advantage* (Barney, 1991), and its performance outputs as a matter of unique inputs and capabilities (Conner, 1991). In simple words, resource capabilities and inputs developed through organizational processes affect outputs. In short, there is an input → process → output relationship.

RBV's relationship to entrepreneurship began a decade later in the 2000s, adding the fact that cognitive abilities of individual entrepreneurs are key inputs to opportunity recognition and resource utilization (Alvarez & Busenitz, 2001). Furthermore, in the process of creating economic value, entrepreneurs must first focus on value creation and value appropriation (Alvarez & Barney, 2005).

However, value must be coupled with rareness in order to play a significant role in improving *competitive advantage*, which has an effect on performance by mediating a *rareness-performance relationship* (Newbert, 2008). In addition, competitive advantage is improved when the firm's capabilities and resources are not easily imitable and substitutable, and properly organized, especially when ESUs are addressing specific customer needs within larger market segments that at the least can cover their fixed costs (Hinterhuber, 2013).

4.4.1 Dynamic Capabilities of Human Capital

To mediate a firm's resources that are rare, valuable, non-imitable and organized, *dynamic capabilities* are required. Dynamic capabilities are defined as a firm's ability to anticipate, direct, and capture opportunities and reduce risks by avoiding threats and by reconfiguring tangible and intangible resources and capabilities to adapt to the changing environment (Lin & Wu, 2014; Pavlou & El Sawy, 2011; Teece, 2009, 2012). To do this, a firm needs to have certain capabilities, such as "sensing the environment, learning, coordinating, and integrating" (Pavlou & El Sawy, 2011, p. 239). This requires building a linkage between decisions on resource planning and firm performance through creative conceptualization and required resource development to implement strategy (Kunc & Morecroft, 2010). The approach and effects make a difference and could be a critical determinant of ESU exit rates (Geroski et al., 2010). Hence, dynamic capabilities of the ESU are strategic by design and allow ESUs to recognize and evaluate an opportunity *(sensing)*; mobilize resources (*seizing*); and to renew continuously (*transforming*). These dynamic capabilities are distinct from *ordinary capabilities*, which are characterized as the day-to-day running of the firm efficiently (Teece, 2012, 2014).

Dynamic capabilities of the ESU are strategic by design and allow ESUs to recognize and evaluate an opportunity (sensing); mobilize resources (seizing); and to renew continuously (transforming).

The dynamic capabilities of ESUs begin with its founders as the first and main resources. Founders bring with them knowledge, passion and skills that initially form the ESU's *human capital*. In some cases, such as with high-tech ESUs, this knowledge is quite rare and valuable because it is specific and scientific based on their education, know how, social networks, and experiences (for example, pharmaceutical products). However, competitive advantage is amplified when such knowledge and skills are learned and developed within the firm, thus becoming *firm-specific, inimitable, and non-substitutable* (Crook et al., 2011; Hatch & Dyer, 2004), which leads to organizational capital. Crook et al. (2011) further suggest that human capital affects performance strongly "when researchers use operational performance measures that are not subject to profit appropriation" and recommend to "invest in programs that increase and retain firm-specific human capital" (p. 443). Another study has concluded that success in human capital investment should be focused more on the outcome of the investment rather than the investment itself, and firms should focus on "the processes of learning, knowledge acquisition, and the transfer of knowledge to entrepreneurial tasks" (Unger et al., 2011, p. 341) to achieve it as a recipe for ESU development and growth.

Hence, human capital is the first and foremost resource of the ESU which develops the interrelated organizational, social and relational capitals that offer unique value propositions through its business model, referred to as intellectual capital (see Fig. 4.5). This will lead to value creation for its revenue-generative customers (i.e., initially proof of concept; eventually scalable growth and profitability), and value capture and extraction for its financing (i.e., investment for ESU development and growth) and future trade sales customers (i.e., ROI for ESU shareholders; value acquisition for M&A customers.

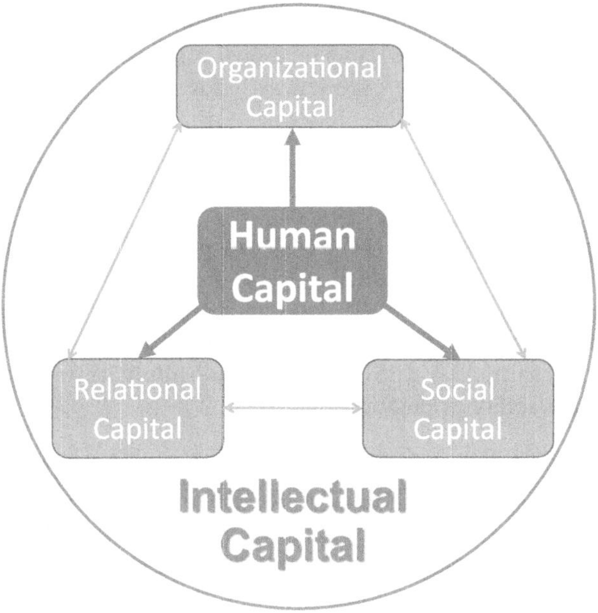

Fig. 4.5 Interrelationship of intellectual capital

Human capital is the first and foremost ESU resource which develops the interrelated organizational, social and relational capitals that offer unique value propositions through ESU's business model, better known as intellectual capital.

4.4.2 Internal and External Capital of IC

IC can also be categorized as internal and external capital, consisting of human capital and organizational capital as internal, and social and organizational capital as external.

1. Internal Capital

a. *Human capital* and its unique dynamic capabilities that create organizational, social and relational capital capabilities; founding team and diversity; experiences, education, know-how, passion, drive, attitude, entrepreneurial grit, coachability; functional knowledge (i.e., financial literacy) and individual social and relational capital contributing to ESU organizational, social and relational capital development.
b. *Organizational capital* which comprises ESU's organizational dynamic capabilities such as know-how and innovation; its business model and UVP; unique processes; R&D and IP (if any); combined technologies utilized (aka tech capital: big data, blockchain, AI)[17]; ESU's culture and (internal) social capital, and sustainability orientation mindset.

2. External Capital

a. *Social capital*, including social networks and social media presence; number of active users; paying customers (i.e., CRM) and financing customers (investors) lists, networks and stakeholder relationships; ESU reputation and trust legitimacy or authenticity, and its social impact.
b. *Relational Capital* with strategic partnerships; proprietary manufacturing and/or marketing; unique relationships with R&D centers, universities and sponsors (i.e., well-known personalities, firms or influencers); joint ventures; and licensing partnerships.

4.4.3 IC and Financial Reporting Standards

Financially, when we use the word *capital* to describe IC and its components, we mean an intangible asset that has a longer-term value. Financial accounting-wise this means at least over one year. From a non-accounting and ESU valuation perspective, it would mean an intangible asset that

[17] For high-tech ESUs, Technological Capital can be listed as a separate category to capture all the R&D, IP, and tech innovation capabilities. Whereas, for non-high-tech ESUs, tech capital can be captured under org capital.

captures and extracts improved future venture value over time (i.e., within three-to-five-year horizon and longer for high-tech ESUs). Due to the limitations of financial accounting, IC as an asset could not be captured in standard balance sheets where Assets = Liabilities + Owner's Equity. However, IC needs to be:

- Voluntarily disclosed, presented and reported as an extra-financial or supplemental schedule specifying its merits. This is particularly important for future growth considerations and valuation purposes when fundraising with financing customers.
- Identified, planned and tracked qualitatively and quantitatively.
- Materially valued on how the ESU is creating short-, medium- and long-term value.
- Externally focused on stakeholders and shareholders, including for financing and future M&A customers.
- Impact oriented, social, environmental, economic and governance.
- Treated and measured as a KPI.

Over the years, IC reporting and frameworks gained momentum and popularity. An Integrated Reporting (<IR>) framework was established, which has become a standard. The International Financial Reporting Standards (IFRS) foundation[18] assumed responsibility over the IC Framework to make <IR> a standard by working with key foundation members (International Integrated Reporting Council [IIRC], 2021). Although <IR> framework was initially designed for larger industrialized companies, ESUs can adapt key <IR> framework aspects for its IC reporting purposes.

The significance of IC is better understood, exercised and reported (through <IR>) by larger companies and high-tech ESUs than non-high-tech ESUs. With the latter group it is generally not well understood, employed and appreciated by ESU founders. However, adapting from high-tech ESU approaches and developing key IC components will lead

[18] "The IFRS Foundation is a not-for-profit, public interest organisation established to develop high-quality, understandable, enforceable and globally accepted accounting and sustainability disclosure standards. [Its] Standards are developed by our two standard-setting boards, the International Accounting Standards Board (IASB) and International Sustainability Standards Board (ISSB)" (IFRS—Who We Are, n.d.).

to a much higher value for all three non-high-tech ESUs customers: paying, financing and eventual trade sales M&A.

4.4.4 IC Inputs, Process, and Outputs

IC Researchers generally define IC as structural, human, and relational capital. Based on my research and experience, I have expanded this breakdown to encompass human, organizational, social, and relational capital that are interrelated. The best way to view how to develop IC is to look at it from an input (purpose) → development (process) → outputs (value) perspective as an iterative and continuous process. Figure 4.6 provides an overview of how value is created, captured, and extracted with IC development.

Inputs to IC development start with the founders' human capital. That is, the co-founding team's background, composition and diversity, their dynamic capabilities, and founders' networks and relationships or founders' social capital (see Sect. 4.5—*The Role of Human Capital* for more details). Furthermore, key inputs to strategic IC development include:

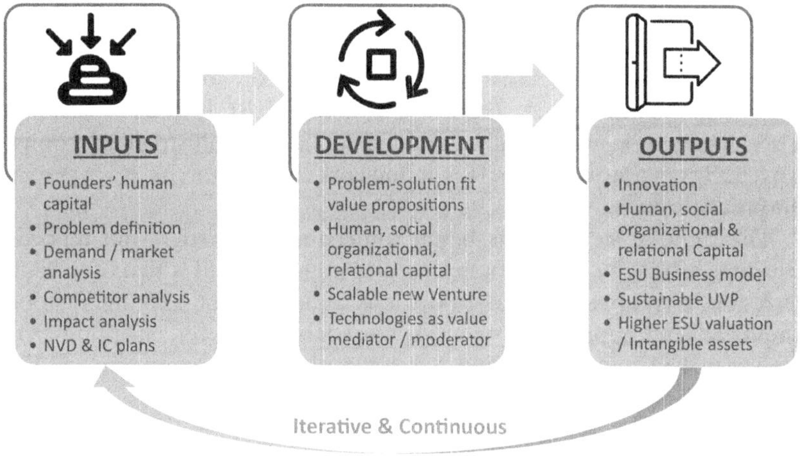

Fig. 4.6 Intellectual capital strategic development

- Extensive, well-researched, and understood *problem definition.*
- Real *needs, demand, and market analysis* from a triple customers' perspective, including market testing and feedback loops.
- Extensive current landscape of *competitors.*
- Determination of the defined problem's triple bottom line *impact* (social, environmental, and economic).
- *New venture development (NVD) plan* with assumptions, incremental development, and growth plans, IC development resource needs and operational financial plans (calendarized), investment requirements with milestones, and financing needs and the type of investor sought (i.e., financing customers).

The **Development** process is mostly related to the new venture development with IC playing the key mediating role in the ESUs overall problem-solution fit value proposition.

- *Human capital development* is the single most important component of IC development, especially when its dynamic capabilities are developed in-house to create specific, inimitable, and not easily substitutable value propositions (Crook et al., 2011; Hatch & Dyer, 2004). Then, human capital develops organizational, social, and relational capital.
- *Organizational capital development* includes ESU's unique value proposition (UVP) through its innovative business model that is scalable and growth oriented (see Sect. 4.6—*All-in-One Organizational Capital* for more details). It contains all the internal aspects of ESU's development, both tangible and intangible, including technologies developed or utilized.
- *Social Capital development* is associated with trust and reputation building in the marketplace through networks development with stakeholders, users, and triple customers (paying, financing, and future trade sales/M&A) with positive social impact.
- *Relational Capital development* is mainly associated with strategic partnerships and unique relationships built with various other organizations, public and private. These relationships are unique and not easily duplicable.
- *Scalable new venture development* is the incremental growth business model using 80-20 approach. Over 80% of the organizational growth can be replicated into other markets, internationally with a well-designed and developed organizational setup and resourcing

model. Less than 20% of this model can be adapted to local market conditions and cultures. This business model becomes solidified at mid-stage.

- *Technological development* is not only related to technical developments, such as new technologies, platforms, or new products, but also associated with unique efficient and effective internal processes that are tested and are cost moderated.

The vast majority of costs associated with IC development are human capital related, especially in the early and mid stages. They are considered to be fixed costs from an accounting perspective since most people's costs (i.e., salaries and benefits) are not capitalized as intangible assets and not part of the cost of sales (i.e., labor input for manufacturing or direct services). This is why it is imperative to properly identify the type of desired human capital in order to plan, attract, develop, motivate, and appropriately compensate them. The ultimate productivity output of human capital is developing ESU's short-, medium- and long-term value and valuation. Let's recall that the majority of trade sales M&A customers acquire ESUs for strategic purposes with acqui-hiring in mind.

The main **output** of IC is about creating enterprise value, which has a multi-year horizon to capture ESU venture value with the ultimate goal of an exit scenario through trade sales M&A or IPO as value extraction for its shareholders (i.e., investors, founders, employees, and similar). Part of this achievement includes ESU's developed innovation and future capabilities, its sustainable business model, and UVP. Most research has shown that IC has a tremendous positive influence (as a process) on innovation (as an output) and vice versa. In fact, within this iteration "innovation fully mediates the relationship between IC and competitive advantage" (Chahal & Bakshi, 2015, p. 376).

Overall, research on IC alludes to the fact that ESUs invest in developing IC with know-how, experience, organizational dynamic capabilities, networks, trust, reputation, and partnerships. This investment and its returns are neither identified nor quantified as a cost, whether an incurred cost or an opportunity cost. However, it is qualified as a factor of success or avoidance of early failure. Such investment in IC requires significant amounts of time, effort, and money and comes with varying opportunity costs and performance outcomes. Costs may not be explicitly included in the scientific debates, but they are implicitly mentioned and form a crucial link in the RBV value chain.

Takeaways

- IC is *knowledge-based equity that a company possesses.*
- People as human capital are the main agents of IC value creation through their knowledge, know-how, experiences, and education.
- ESU founders develop IC through an effectuation process in an uncertain, unpredictive, and ambiguous environment.
- IC forms part of resource-based view (RBV) value logic addressing strategic options to develop and sustain competitive advantage in the marketplace.
- Competitive advantages must include rareness, (triple) customer value, inimitability, and organizational (dynamic) capabilities.
- Dynamic capabilities are strategic by design to allow founders to sense, seize, and transform ideas into unique value propositions (UVP).
- Human capital is the main ESU resource to develop interrelated organizational, social, and relational capitals that offer UVPs through their business model.
- Human and organizational capital are internal; Social and relational capital are external to the ESU.
- Since IC is not captured directly on financial statements, they need to be voluntarily disclosed, qualitatively and quantitatively, materially valued and justified for its future economic benefits, externally focused and impact oriented.
- There is an established integrated reporting (<IR>) framework that has become a standard with the International Financial Reporting Standards (IFRS) foundation.

4.5 The Role of Human Capital

People play the most important role in all ESU stages, especially in the early to mid to late development. A "combinations of human and social capital are related to [new venture] survival while overreliance on financial capital is not" (Linder et al., 2020, p. 910). Even though the latter is also crucial for ESU survival, *overreliance* is the key word.

In the early stages, it is all about the founders, their background, passion, and dynamic capabilities. In the case of a single founder, all responsibilities of ESU developments fall on that one founder. On the one hand, it is easier to make decisions on their own. On the other hand, single founders would lack the diversity of thought, experiences, and capabilities of multi-founder teams. Whereas, with multiple founder ESUs with diverse backgrounds, the responsibilities of ESU project development and division of labor are spread amongst its founders. Most investors prefer multi-founder teams to single-founder ESUs (Shetty & Sundaram, 2020).

In survival and mid stage when business models are formalized and business plans are executed, where the focus is on new venture development for the growth phase, human capital development expands from founder-centric to ESU team-centric in need of talent acquisition and development of ESU dynamic capabilities and IC. In later stages, it's all about the team and its value, both in costs (i.e., salaries being one of the highest fixed costs) and ESU valuation.

People and technologies are one and the same in early-stage ESUs

During my research interviews with ESU founders, the most important word that was inferred was about people. How to attract, retain, compensate, and invest in people and the ESU team. For high-tech ESUs, people and technology are one and the same, especially at ESU's early and mid-stages. Follows some direct quotes from ESU founders that were spontaneously shared when a general topic of costs was discussed (Chammassian, 2016, pp. 81–85):

- "Our experience confirms that team and people, for a startup, is key." "Having a good team, good people, with a good background knowledge, excited for what so they are not just there for making 8 h per day. To live their experience is key." "The first thing is the money. Without it, you can't do anything [sic]. But the second and even more important probably, is the people that you are around. And we put really a lot of importance on the choice of the people and especially at the beginning for the development of the product" (ESU 1).
- "Having the right people in the team is key, and you can't compromise on this." "We are lucky enough that what we do is extremely motivating to the team. So people are working very hard and doing a lot" (ESU 2).
- "It's not because you are a start-up that you should discount the salaries" (ESU 4).

- "It was a people story before a project... The team was really the core of the story." "Team is core. Team is essential...having a team allowed us to make sure that we are balanced, in terms of what is important—money, market, technology." "The biggest issue when you're a small team and you're growing is to hire someone and there's a risk of hiring someone, meaning will the person fit in the team and will the person be up to the job as much as the other guys...you can't allow for the team to have any underperformance element in the team because then you break the whole momentum of the team" (ESU 5).
- Talented people "want to go in trendy buzzing, 'we change-the-world.com' type of business." "People is [sic] investment" and "retention plans is [sic] clearly an investment for us" (ESU 6).
- "I don't think that there is a massive difference between technology and people....People and technology in a technology start-up are exactly the same" (ESU 7).
- If "you need to build a really ambitious product, you need to solve really hard problems, you need to hire the best people and very often, a lot of them, and therefore, you need to incur really high-fix costs." "You don't know how soon or how late you are actually going to reach the goals you have and so you know your costs are primarily, if not totally, driven by the amount of money you're paying your team" (ESU 10).
- "[Our] industry requires large sums and human capital, but also very high [cash] burn rate...To solve this really difficult problem, you needed some exceptionally good people." "This wasn't going to be solved by a few students." "You could have gotten lucky. You could have hired a junior person who was just exceptional and so forth. But, in the end, I felt that the safer route to solving the problem was to hire these people with experience and the record of solving problems" (ESU 11).
- "To convince people, high-quality people, to go working in a start-up business is not always easy." "Older managers have extensive industry experience" (ESU 12).
- "You need to start with people with some professional experience; so not to hire people too young. Two years ago, I changed radically how to hire people. I prefer to hire people with more experience, that means with an age around 35 and [with] international experience too....We need to work with employees who have the

experience of working with others who have international skills. It's very important" (ESU 13).

- "[I have] an enormous responsibility to my employees because, as you know, with start-ups, it's not just a job. People come, and when they join an organization like this, they're working really hard, and it becomes part of their life. So, I feel an emotional connection with them and a very big responsibility that I treat them right. And I make this the best possible decision they could have made emotionally, psychologically, financially, etc." "my investment. So, if I go and hire when you first do it, all you do is the cost." "To me, you can't build something great without a team of great people around you" (ESU 14).
- "I did not think [just] shares really motivate. I think what motivates lots of them were the type of job, tasks they were given; their potential influence on the product; seeing what impact it had on education within a country or throughout Europe … I think it's more related to the impact they have on the world, or on the society more so than the money." "The biggest assessment [for us] … was investing in people" (ESU 15).

From RBV perspective, founders define the firm and its performance to create competitive advantages that are hopefully inimitable and non-substitutable. Founders bring with them knowledge, experiences and skills that initially form the core of the ESU value configuration. These founder characteristics are general and/or specific, such as business, entrepreneurial, management, industry or sector specific, technical, and scientific.

For starters, there needs to be a fit "between entrepreneurs' personal characteristics and the requirements of being an entrepreneur," such as "self-efficacy, ability to recognize opportunities, personal perseverance, human and social capital, superior social skills" (Markman & Baron, 2003, p. 281). Founders' human capital determines significantly the size of the high-tech startups (Colombo et al., 2004) and their growth potential (Colombo & Grilli, 2005). "Moreover, the value of founder knowledge is relative to the type of opportunity exploited: high-risk opportunities favor founders with managerial experience, whereas low-risk opportunities favor founders with industry experience" (Dencker & Gruber, 2015, p. 1035). Founders' motivation to initiate, grow and exit is not only an input but also a process of ESU development that is directly linked to financial outcomes (Debrulle et al., 2021; Murnieks et al., 2020). Founders' strong (or weak) financial skills have a positive (or negative) influence on operational and financial outcomes when they are juggling between *taking risks and controlling their operations* (Graña-Alvarez et al., 2024). Within this process it also includes the development of the ESU's culture through the founders' *cognitive diversity* (Shepherd et al., 2023).

4.5.1 General and Specific Human Capital

Human capital knowledge, education, experiences, and skills can be classified into two different categories: general and specific human capital. They have different effects on ESU's development, growth, and size, attracting financing customers, and success or failure.

General Human Capital

General human capital means their background could be applied to different situations, conditions, businesses, roles, and industries but not necessarily or directly attributable to an ESU development (Rauch & Rijsdijk, 2013).

- It has a better *propensity to attract financing* more so from sources outside their industry's network and contributes much more towards the firm's growth than specific human capital (Bosma et al., 2004).
- *Industry experience* tends to raise more resources from friends, family, and fools (Kotha & George, 2012) and breakeven faster (Oe & Mitsuhashi, 2013).
- *University degrees, general working experience, and the age* of its human capital have a positive effect on firm size (Gottschalk et al., 2009). Highly educated people produce more profits (Bosma et al., 2004).
- *Experience in business ownership* leads to a positive effect on a firm's survival (Bosma et al., 2004).
- *Entrepreneurial and startup experience* "(especially financially successful experience) increases both the likelihood of VC funding via a direct tie and venture valuation" (Hsu, 2007, p. 722). It also has the tendency to grow a business disproportionally by identifying different markets and opportunities that are outside the ESU's specific domain. For instance, "serial entrepreneurs have learned

through prior startup experience to generate a 'choice set' of alternative market opportunities before deciding which one to pursue in their new firm creation" (Gruber et al., 2008, p. 1652). This growth mindset combined with entrepreneurial experience reduces failure risks.
- "Founder's *business management expertise and academic status* attracted external investment, but founder's general technological expertise did not" (Gimmon & Levie, 2010, p. 1214).

Specific Human Capital:

Specific human capital background is related to specialized domains, industry-specific experiences, skills, and knowledge. They are not easily transferrable to other domains, roles, and industries (Rauch & Rijsdijk, 2013).

- It has a larger *impact on firm size* due to the industry contacts, knowledge of niche markets, and specific networks (Gottschalk et al., 2009).
- *Industry experience* acquired prior to starting up "significantly reduces learning performance" (Hatch & Dyer, 2004, p. 1155). It is also vital in addressing issues inherent with startups, especially when they "commit more resources to information distribution and interpretation [and facilitate reaching the firm] break-even point faster" (Oe & Mitsuhashi, 2013, p. 2193).
- It is not known or related to ESU growth and has "direct negative effects on business failure" (Rauch & Rijsdijk, 2013, p. 923).

4.5.2 Human Capital Development: Inputs, Process, and Outputs

As with IC, a good way to view how human capital value is developed is to look at it from inputs (background) → development (process) → outputs (value) perspective. Figure 4.7 illustrates how value is created, captured, and extracted with human capital development.

As **inputs**, founders' background diversity, networks, motivation, and passion initially drive the entire development of the new venture intellectual capital and value (Abecassis-Moedas et al., 2021; Akroyd & Kober, 2020), including their:

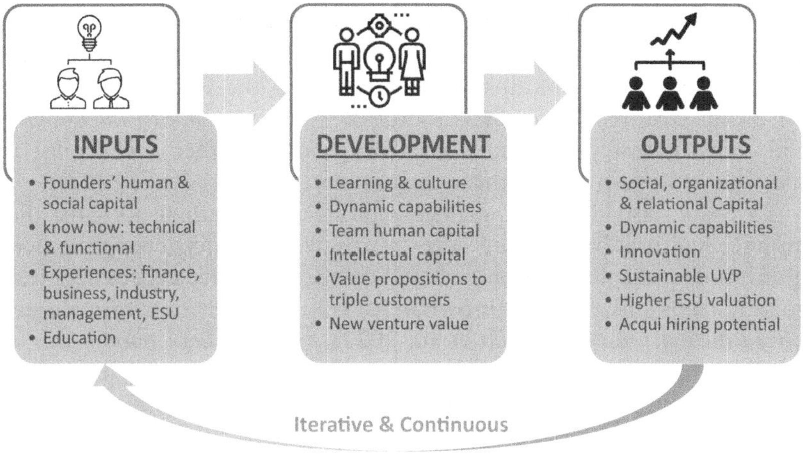

Fig. 4.7 Human capital development process

- Knowledge and know-how, whether technical (i.e., engineering, technological) or functional (i.e., marketing, supply chain, finance, IT).
- Experiences: entrepreneurial startup and exits, fundraising, business in general, management, industry-specific (i.e., food and beverage, automotive, etc.), international.
- Education: business and/or specific trade, degrees.
- Own social capital through networks and relationships in industry, business, finance, social, and international (Devarakonda et al., 2022).
- Capabilities: functional (i.e., finance, marketing, sales, IT), dynamic, or ordinary.
- Mindfulness, learning, attitude, and coachability.

Diversity of founder background as input plays a critical role in the **development** of ESU human capital. Diversity means that founders have multiple category characteristics, neither too specialized nor too generalist. It also means complementary backgrounds where one founder has the technical know-how and industry knowledge or experience with strong social networks (for instance); whereas another, has strong entrepreneurial, startup, and functional (i.e., marketing and financial literacy) background (Banal-Estañol et al., 2023). Entrepreneurial knowledge can lead to adoption and adaption of technologies, such as AI, that lead to frugal innovation instead of reinventing the wheel (Qin, 2024). Financing customers also assess founders'[19] diversity *multidimensionally* with both industry and functional backgrounds, either a generalist or specialist at least in one of those dimensions (Souitaris et al., 2022).

Diversity also includes gender, cultural, and ethnic origins. For instance, cultural background may determine if founders engage in open innovation and collaboration or based on their negative experiences (i.e., coming from authoritarian or patriarchal cultures) they *engender a generalized lack of trust* (Wyrwich et al., 2022), whether *hope trumps fear* or not (Huang et al. 2019). How founders interact with and learn from their peers (either internal or external) to create a *learning-by-interacting* culture (Tubiana et al., 2022).

Finally, mindfulness, learning capacity, and coachability are very high determinants of developing dynamic capabilities. With the fast-evolving knowledge and digital landscape, *whoever learns fast wins* (McGrath, 2023). Founders' willingness to learn and their innovation development and output also depend on their coachability by experts, mentors, advisors, and investors (Johnson et al., 2021; Marvel et al., 2020; Kuratko et al., 2021). Coachable founders who adhere to advice tend to overcome their resistance to change, pivot parts of their business model, grow their ESUs larger, and are less likely to fail (Burnell et al., 2023; Chatterji et al., 2019).

The ultimate **outputs** or goals for human capital are:

- Social, organizational, and relational capital.
- Strong ESU innovation and dynamic capabilities.
- An innovative and all-encompassing business model.
- Sustainable UVP are firm-specific, inimitable, and not easily substitutable (Crook et al., 2011; Hatch & Dyer, 2004).
- Higher ESU valuation that would attract diverse financing customers.
- To prepare for potential exit scenarios where acqui-hiring may play an important consideration for trade sales M&A customers.

[19] To remind, financing customers prefer to invest in multi-founder ESUs than single-founder ones.

4.5.3 *Human Capital Characteristics and Associated Costs in Different Stages*

ESU's founding team's human capital diversity, composition, functional capacities (i.e., technological, financial literacy, marketing skills), capabilities to develop relationships, strategic thinking, and abilities to grow the organization depend on the lifecycle stage of the ESU. For instance, in the earlier stages, it's all about the ESU founders and their abilities to develop the ESU and its human capital dynamic capabilities. In mid stages, it is the founders' ability to let go of some of the functions and assign it to the professional new hires who develop the ESU's human capital and social capital capabilities. These reshaping of roles during the ESU's lifecycle stages and decision-making structure will have a tremendous impact on the ESUs success (Tzabbar & Margolis, 2017). Associated costs with human capital development also highly depend on the lifecycle stage.

Although most research on human capital (whether general or specific) has been based on high-tech ESUs. There are many lessons that can be drawn from this research for non-high-tech ESUs. High-tech ESUs need to develop their human capital-intensive strategies from their earlier stages, whereas for non-high-tech startups it becomes much more important during their survival and early growth mid-stage which is a period of complexity, and resource and capital intensive. In other words, non-high-tech ESUs can have a similar configuration for their intellectual capital development through human capital from its early stages planning to prepare for their mid-stage.

From this, we can also ascertain that founders with specific or general human capital would have different perceptions towards costs simply because they come from different backgrounds, experiences, and approaches to running a business (or not) even though they may be operating within the same ESU organizational context. These perceptions include a major subjective component (Felin et al., 2017) due to the ESU founders' *perceptive capacity* (Bylund & Packard, 2022), which comes with the founder's experiences (or the lack thereof), learning and adaptations (Sarasvathy, 2001, 2004) no matter how objective the founders' goals are. Table 4.1 highlights ESU human capital characteristics and associated costs, which could be a general guide for ESU founders on how to treat human capital and costs within the three entrepreneurial stages:

Table 4.1 ESU human capital characteristics and associated costs

Human Capital (HC)	*Characteristics*	*Associated costs*
Early stage	• Founding team composition and complementary backgrounds • Founders' functional capacities and capabilities to develop relationships • Advisory support from ecosystem players (i.e., incubators and accelerators) • Possibly paid interns and early employees • Developing HC plan for IC development and financing purposes • Seeking seed financing	• Founder share distribution • Equity dilution/financing customers • High tech: – Very high costs of PhD, engineers and similar – Value ***mediator*** • Non-high tech: – Frugal, avoidance of salaries/ fixed costs – Value ***enabler*** • Very high opportunity cost if not executed properly
Mid stage	• Founding team completion • Recruitment of management team members with dynamic capabilities • Professionalization of roles • Founder role evolution and reshaping • Organizational, social, and relational capital development • HC growth planning and justification • Seeking further external financing with Series A	• Highest fixed costs for high and non-high-tech ESUs • High risk with unpredictable results • Investment oriented for long-term ESU valuation • ***Mediator*** of value • Employee stock option plans (ESOP) • Further equity dilution with new financing/Series A • Seeking reasonable ROI if an exit occurs
Late stage	• Growth team recruitment/ planned 80-20 rule with expansion • Further professionalization and focus on team ***dynamic capabilities*** • Determine to insource, outsource or automate ***ordinary capabilities*** • Further external financing with Series B, C, D, ... (if/when needed) • Preparation of exit scenarios, including acqui-hiring potential	• Mainly fixed costs with improved predictability • Marginal costs reduction for improved margin • ***Mediator*** of value invested in ***dynamic capabilities*** • ***Moderator*** of value related to ***ordinary capabilities*** with cost optimization • High ROI expectations

In the early stages, it is all about the founding team and its heterogeneity with different and complementary backgrounds. It is up to the founding team:

- To recognize their strengths and where they lag.
- To identify key HC skill set required to attract another strategic founder.
- To differentiate their roles to make them complementary to each other.
- To harmonize individual goals with strategic direction.
- To plan for future human capital resourcing needs and incremental acquisition.

At mid-stage, founders' goal is to seek key management team members to take over certain specialized roles and functions, to continue with prioritized market validation and experimentation (Sanasi et al., 2023), and to run day-to-day business. The management team must be professionals with industry experience and functional expertise to develop organizational, social, and capital. They would also design and plan for a scalable model, while founders can focus on strategy and financial capital raising. This *growth hacking* is not only for high-tech ESUs (Bargoni et al., 2024), but also for growth-oriented non-high-tech ESUs who seek external financing with eventual exit in mind. Costs are to be treated as investment or mediator of value creation and capture through human capital dynamic capabilities.

At later stages, the focus is purely on growth, scaling, and replication by continuous human capital value acceleration. However, the distinction at this stage is the differentiation between dynamic capabilities (i.e., costs as mediator of future value) and ordinary capabilities (i.e., costs and moderator of margin and operational expenses) to see what to keep in-house, to outsource or automate. Any process that is repetitive and measurable can be either automated or outsourced.

Takeaways

- During early-stage ESUs, it's all about the founders. In fact, people and technology are one and the same in early-stage ESUs.
- In survival mid stage and early growth stages, human capital development expands from founder centric to ESU team centric.
- The value of human capital in founders (and later, the team) is their dynamic capabilities (vs. ordinary capabilities).
- They consist of their background (education, knowledge, experiences), functional capabilities, and capacities to learn, develop, network, and build relationships.
- Multi-founder teams are preferred over single-founder ESUs, esp. by investors.
- Human capital (HC) can be general and/or specific.
- General HC includes general industry experience, education, and work experience in business, management, entrepreneurial, and startups.
- Specific HC includes specific industries, domains skills, knowledge, and experiences.
- HC development is also an iterative process of inputs → development → outputs.
- Founders' diversity includes background, networks, motivation, gender, and culture; plus their mindset, learning, perceptive capacity, and coachability.
- Majority of cost investments in ESUs are in human capital.

4.6 All-in-One Organizational Capital

Organizational capital, sometimes referred to as *structural capital*, is mainly concerned with the ESU's mostly non-human intangible assets, such as its:

- Organizational dynamic and innovation capabilities (versus ordinary capabilities).
- Business model and UVP.
- Unique business processes.
- Technologies utilized, either their own innovation or hybrid combination of existing ones.
- R&D, technological capital, and IP (if any).

- Databases/Big Data.
- Company culture and its internal social capital (i.e., interrelationships).
- Sustainability orientation.

It comprises mainly of what is *owned* by the ESU and how they are *utilized* that defines its existence—to create, capture, and extract value. Although technically it would include tangible assets, ESUs rarely own such assets with material value. Tangible assets would include computers and servers, furniture, and any fixed assets that are owned by the ESU, which it rarely does, especially in the early stages. The majority of ESU's organizational capital comprises intangible assets.

When combined in a cohesive way, these intangible assets collectively create and capture unique value in the marketplace and for the ESU. They represent how ESU's core business activities and values are developed, proposed, and managed. In a way, organizational capital us ESU's core engine or driver of value proposition, its *value narrative in action*. These narratives have been repeatedly shared by ESU entrepreneurs as a persuasive argument to tell their stories and to legitimize their distinctiveness (van Werven et al., 2015). They convey ESU's ideas and concepts in action to potential paying and financing customers; business partners, including other entrepreneurs and companies with whom they would partner; scientific communities to collaborate with; other businesses to license technology to or from. In return, potential partners use these narratives to analyze the ESUs value proposition, originality, collaboration opportunity, and investment requirements (Martens et al., 2007).

Organizational Capital puts the ESU's value narrative into action

Figure 4.8 captures the process of Organizational Capital development from inputs to development to desired outputs.

As **inputs**, ESU's human capital with its dynamic capabilities develops its organizational dynamic capabilities through unique processes, procedures, and technologies, whether through its own R&D (including IP) or adapted from spillovers, such as PaaS, SaaS, or IaaS, blockchain, AI, big data, cloud computing, and similar. For high-tech-driven ESUs, these technologies are tracked and valued separately as technological capital since they are solving technological problems from the get-go. Whereas

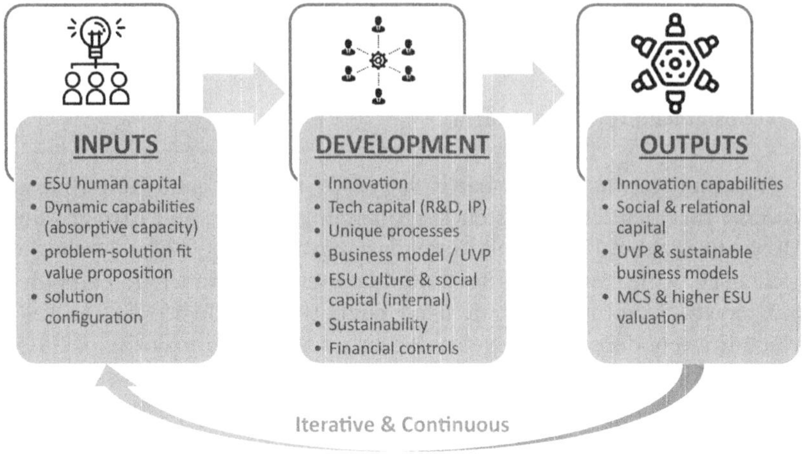

Fig. 4.8 Organizational capital development process

non-high-tech ESUs are usually solving problems that are initially non-tech but with the collective use of various technologies defined above, they are solving such problems much more efficiently and effectively than currently done.BM & UVP; R&D; company culture; org social capital; sustainability orientation.

Developing dynamic (management or organizational) capabilities, ESUs require absorptive capacity and resource mobilization. *Absorptive capacity* (Cohen & Levinthal, 1990) is the ESU's "ability to identify, assimilate and exploit external knowledge; ... [track] dynamic environmental changes, boost innovation speed, product adoption, and firm growth" (Xiong & Bharadwaj, 2011, p. 88). It starts with ESU's human capital which first broadly identifies, assimilates, transforms, and exploits external knowledge to create and capture organizational capital at the ESU level (Bedford et al., 2022). This absorptive capacity includes (but is not limited to) knowledge gained from financing customers (Shuwaikh & Dubocage, 2022), paying customers, and existing business models which have an impact on ESU's own business model innovation (Bhatti et al., 2021). However, such organizational capabilities need to be aligned and deployed with existing (and planned) resources in order to create ESU value (Gruber et al., 2010) with its problem-solution fit configuration to capture external (market) value as a competitive advantage (Wilden et al., 2013).

These human capital absorptive capabilities also apply to developing a strong ESU culture and internal social capital. Specific human capital alone could lead to "well-worn paths" and "competence traps, whereas knowledge-related learning capabilities enable a firm to deal with dynamic environments" (Winkelbach & Walter, 2015, p. 98). Hence, founders and ESU management team need to be self-aware and mindful of these specific knowledge traps and be more open to new ideas, invest in general human capital, learn from the experiences, and embrace new opportunities to maximize performance (outputs). This, in return, will improve the absorptive capacity of the ESU (Chammassian, 2016).

When it comes to technology, I define technology in a much broader sense adopting various but comprehensive definitions, such as Bailetti's (2012), Carroll's (2017), and Coad and Reid's (2012) as an example "to capture not only the equipment, software or instruments used to produce a good or service but also the (tacit) knowledge, techniques, organizational methods, etc. used to design, develop and market the products and services by businesses (and the public and not for profit sector), in cooperation with other actors in the innovation system" (p. 1).

Technology for high-tech ESUs is their main value driver and can be classified separately as technological capital. These ESUs develop core technologies based on R&D (Bailetti, 2012; Burmaoglu et al., 2019; Giones & Brem, 2017; Van Meeteren et al., 2022). Technology for non-high-tech EUS is the mediator of ESUs' problem-solution fit value proposition that determines how efficiently and effectively the ESU is executing its narrative. These ESUs use *enabling technologies* and *application domains* (known as *general-purpose technologies*) as a means or a tool to solve the problem they are solving more efficiently and effectively (Ancillai et al., 2023; Carroll, 2017; Coad & Reid, 2012; Van meeteren et al., 2022; Waßenhoven et al., 2023).

4.6.1 Costs of Organizational Capital Development

Parallel to the development of organizational capital processes, ESUs need to establish proper financial processes and controls as the moderators of value capture and value extraction. Besides good business practices and governance, this is a key requirement for financial and trade sales customers. These processes and controls must be both strategic and operational.

For starters, costs play a pivotal role as an enabler, mediator, and moderator of ESU value creation, capture, and extraction processes. Strategic Cost Management (SCM) approaches were first developed with industrialized companies (Shank, 1989, 1996) to address how costs play a strategic role in developing and extracting value through investments, including from a value-chain perspective (see Shank & Govindarajan, 1992a, 1992b, 1993). However, SCM should be treated more than a management control tool; it needs to be “a philosophy, an attitude, and a set of techniques to contribute to shaping the future of the company” (Kumar & Kumar, 2011, p. 118). In other words, perceptions towards costs can formulate a strategy as much as data could drive strategy, whether financial or non-financial in nature. SCM approaches can be adopted by ESUs for both internal and external assessment.

Internally, costs can be divided into two components: *structural* (what is owned) and *executional* (how it is executed) exemplified by Anderson and Dekker (2009a, 2009b). *Structural costs* have to do everything with design, whether organizational, product, or process (i.e., supply chain) that is part of the overall strategy. This aligns well with the ownership component. Structural costs should be treated as an investment and mediator for ESU future value with ROI in mind.

Whereas *executional costs* include how those owned assets are executed or operationalized, especially when it comes to scaling and growth (Bohan et al., 2024; Cavallo et al., 2024; Jansen et al., 2023). Executional cost management “employs measurement and analysis tools (e.g., cost driver analysis, supplier scorecards) to evaluate supply chain performance and sustainability” (Anderson & Dekker, 2009b, p. 289). It should also employ developing scaling and growth-related cost models where there is an initial organizational setup model, for instance for country expansion, followed by an operational expenditure model using the 80-20 rule (>80% similar, <20% adapted to local circumstances). Besides design, the initial organizational setup costs should be treated as an initial investment in growth and as a mediator of value with per growth location ROI in mind. Whereas the operational costs, which includes running day-to-day operations or business, should be treated as a moderator of profitability. Below is a summary of structural and executional organizational capital costs. Table 4.2 summarizes the differences between the two cost types.

Table 4.2 Organizational capital cost types

Organizational capital cost types	*Characteristics*	*Treated as …*
Structural	Development of the main organizational capital: innovation, technologies, unique process design, product design, financial controls	Investment, mediator of ESU value, with ROI in mind
Executional	Operational, associated with running the ESU's business operations, including scaling and growth: 1. Initial setup 2. Running growth units, subsidiaries, and other country operations	Mainly operational expenses, moderator of profitability 1. Growth setup, mediator of value, growth ROI in mind 2. Cost of sales and operational expenses as moderator of profitability

4.6.2 ESU Lifecycles and Organizational Capital Costs

Organizational Capital costs also have different characteristics and associated costs in ESU lifecycles. Table 4.3 summarizes these differences in characteristics and costs.

4.6.3 Management Control Systems (MCS)

Costs, whether strategic investment or operational oriented, are part of financial as well as management control systems (MCS) which are critical to the development, well-functioning, and valuation of ESU especially when it comes to financing and future trade sales M&A customers (Davila et al., 2015). MCS was originally referred to as maintaining or altering formalized routines when controlling costs and being cost-effective were part of these routines (Simons, 1987, 1990). Hence, costs should be identified, tracked, controlled, reduced, or eliminated to be effective (Chammassian, 2016).

However, MCS is not purely financial. It incorporates strategy, founders' beliefs, core values and motivational drivers, diagnostic controls, competitive landscape, environmental and contextual variables,

Table 4.3 Organizational capital characteristics and associated costs per ESU stage

Organizational capital	*Characteristics*	*Associated costs*
Early stage	• Founders' dynamic capabilities • R&D oriented to define the problem • Problem-solution fit and configuration • Developing organizational development plans • Human capital and Resource needs • Financing requirements	• Frugal, avoidance of fixed costs and tangible assets • Human capital as a value *enabler* • R&D: high with tech-driven; lower for mid/low tech • Very high opportunity cost
Mid stage	• Leadership team capabilities • Business model and UVP • Unique processes and organizational capabilities development • ESU culture, Social and relational capital development • Growth plans using 80-20 rule • Seeking further external financing with Series A	• Mostly structural and intangible, some tangible • Technologies • Unpredictable results • Investment oriented for long-term ESU valuation • *Mediator* of value • Reasonable ROI
Late stage	• Growth team recruitment/ planned 80-20 rule with expansion • Focus on innovation capabilities • HC development • Insource, outsource, or automate ordinary capabilities • Further external financing with Series B, C, D, ... (if/ when need be) • Preparation of exit scenarios, including for acqui-hiring potential	• Structural: fixed costs with higher predictability • Executional/growth – Setup: *Mediating* value – Cost of Sales and operational expenses: *moderating* profitability • Cost optimization with ordinary capabilities • Goal: High ROI

from assumptions to operating plans, budgets, and financial controls, addressing complexity with growth (Chenhall, 2003; Davila & Foster, 2005, 2007; Simons, 1994). Specifically, ESU founders' financial literacy (Eisenmann, 2020) and *commitment blueprint* have a strong imprint and design in the way MCS is designed, tracked, and controlled, including ESU cultural controls (Akroyd & Kober, 2020; Cugueró-Escofet & Rosanas, 2013; Graña-Alvarez et al., 2024). With the paradigm shift of knowledge economy ESUs with innovative value propositions, MCS have adapted to address uncertainty, complexity, and evolving environments of technological development with formal and informal controls (Davila et al., 2009; Chenhall & Moers, 2015).

Sustainability has added another dimension to MCS. Sustainability of the ESU's (internal) value chain, coupled with external sustainability requirements with paying customers and other stakeholders has been influencing how ESUs create, capture, and extract value. This has had a profound effect on how ESU founders and teams regard and integrate sustainability into the ESU's strategy and imbed in its culture with clear responsibilities and stakeholder engagement in order not to be marginalized in the marketplace (Albertini, 2019; Beusch et al., 2022; Bezuidenhout et al., 2023).

Properly integrated MCS with disclosure of its intangible assets has a positive impact on an ESU's value in the marketplace, its financial performance, and on its valuation by financing and future trade sales M&A customers (Braune et al., 2020; Davila et al., 2015). There are many different MCS models, combining and integrating with <IR>, that ESU founders can utilize. They include, but are not limited to:

- Balanced Scorecard (Kaplan, 2010; Kaplan & Norton, 1992, 1993–2004), covering financial and operational aspects of ESU, and aligning it with its measurable strategic goals.
- Lean Startup Methodology (Ries, 2011), with product and market experimentation, customer feedback loop, and iterative learning and development (build-measure-learn) to identify minimum viable products (MVP), to pivot or continue, in order to develop their business models (Bocken & Snihur, 2020; Ghezzi, 2020; Shepherd & Gruber, 2021).
- Agile performance management linking strategic goals to business and individual objectives, becoming highly networked, empowered and autonomous, receiving continuous feedback, and making rapid

decisions and improvements (Darino et al., 2019; de Souza et al., 2022).
- Integrated Reporting <IR> (IIRC, 2021).

Takeaways
- Organizational capital (OC) puts the ESU's value narrative into action.
- It includes org dynamic and innovation capabilities; business model and UVP; unique processes; any R&D, tech or IP; big data; ESU culture and internal social capital; and sustainability orientation.
- As the majority of ESU's OC comprises intangible assets, it creates and captures high ESU and marketplace value when combined cohesively.
- OC dynamic capabilities require absorptive capacity and resource mobilization.
- Even though most ESU costs are in HC, OC costs can be divided into structural and executional.
- Structural costs are related to design—organizational, product, and process.
- Executional costs include operationalization, scaling, and growth.
- OC cost investments and tracking are part of management control systems (MCS).
- MCS incorporates strategy; founders' beliefs, core values, and motivational drivers; diagnostic controls; competitive landscape; financial assumptions to operating plans, budgets, and financial controls, addressing scaling and growth.
- IC KPIs can be tracked via various means, including <IR>, lean startup methodology, and balanced scorecard.

4.7 Social Capital and Purpose

The importance of social capital came into prominence in the 1990s after the sociologist James Coleman highlighted how key cultural characteristics, especially in high-trust countries, could lead to prosperity. Social capital is "the component of human capital that allows members of a given society to trust one another and cooperate in the formation of new groups and associations" (Fukuyama, 1995, p. 90). Such *high-trust cultural attributes* have had a major positive impact on innovation especially when our economies moved from an industrial-based to knowledge-intensive economies. However, this form of trust is distinctly modern, referred to as *reflective trust*, instead of the traditional patriarchic *blind trust* which societies were used to. Reflective trust is more community oriented between various marketplace actors that promotes interpersonal (social) and interfirm (market) relationships (Adler, 2001). The value of these relationships depends on substance, sources, or effects based on how they are developed and maintained collectively (Adler & Kwon, 2002). Nahapiet and Ghoshal (1998) identified three social capital dimensions: cognitive, relational, and structural.

- *Cognitive* dimension is associated with narratives, construction of communication, and shared motives, such as shared experiences, values, beliefs, understandings, cultural aspects, and attitudes towards a common good.
- *Relational* dimension acts as the behavioral basis between two collaborating firms during social exchanges and attributes (i.e., trust, exchange basis, expectations, and obligations).
- *Structural* dimension is the network configuration, organization, roles, rules, and frequency of exchanges (i.e., distinction between users, stakeholders, and paying customers).

Fast forward, today social capital is a critical intangible asset for ESUs that embodies relationships and trust within certain norms, environment, and the marketplace. It is the basis of a sharing economy (Schwab, 2016) where it promotes and strengthens a complex cocktail of cooperation, inclusion, learning, bonding, coordination, social value, exchanges, innovation, reciprocity, goodwill, and connectiveness between the ESU and its stakeholder communities with measurable (social) impact (Davlembayeva et al., 2020; Lee et al., 2019; Ortiz et al., 2016). Developing social capital as a strategy is to mediate trust legitimacy in the marketplace in order to gain external resources, survive, and grow (Delmar & Shane, 2004; Zimmerman & Zeitz, 2002).

A strong social capital leads to ESU knowledge seeking, resource acquisition, and eventual value proposition improvement as a form of circular knowledge economy.

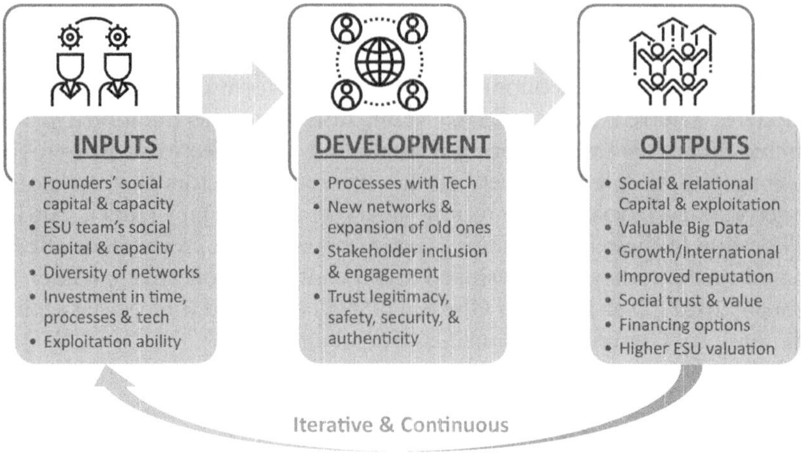

Fig. 4.9 Social capital development process

A strong social capital leads to ESU knowledge seeking, resource acquisition, and eventual value proposition improvement as a form of *circular knowledge economy*. Social capital creates means to organizational learning (new and improved knowledge) from the markets and social networks and advances ESU value proposition. It also promotes internal vs. external social belongingness, a sense of connecting between the outside and inside worlds of ESUs. ESU's social capital can lead to developing communities where they can comment and contribute to ESU venture product development. Figure 4.9 illustrates how social capital is developed.

4.7.1 Social Capital and Technology

The internet as a technological medium combined with *voluntary associations* by users, stakeholders, sellers, and buyers has democratized social relationship building. It has played a moderating role in social trust, *lowering the cost of cooperation and enhancing bridging networks* (Chung et al., 2024). The internet has fostered sharing experiences, collaboration, and engagement on social, environmental, and economic issues leading to potential changes and impact. Digitalization with online social platforms, communities and networks have led to improved market-oriented innovation, fundraising and growth through internationalization and digital marketing (see also Eiteneyer et al., 2019; Han et al., 2024; Rizvanović et al., 2023; Sanz-Blas et al., 2021). Social trust and socially committed ESUs increase their chances of attracting financing customers and obtaining external financing (Fernandez, 2021). Social media and platform technologies play critical roles in marketing, public relations, accumulating knowledge, and developing social trust. In fact, the "effect on social trust is highest under the joint influence than it is under the individual influence" (Chung et al., 2024, p. 1). Thus, the internet becomes a key *socio-relational trust capital* for an ESU. Examples of this include ratings of services such as hotels on Booking.com or restaurants on Tripadvisor.com; online user communities of games, music, and movies where members exchange knowledge, perceptions, information, experiences, and ideas on existing and new products (Pyo et al., 2023).

4.7.2 Moderators and Mediators of Social Capital

There are moderators and mediators of social capital value creation and capture. For instance, entrepreneurial ecosystem players, such as universities, incubators, and accelerators (private or public), and governmental support organizations are great networking and social capital development mediators, especially when it comes to high-tech-driven ESUs and their survival (Bandera & Thomas, 2019). This can also apply to non-high-tech ESUs. Being in or working within an innovation hub dramatically improves an ESU (especially novice) founders' experiences, whether commercial or technical; attitude towards risk-taking; networking skills and building social capital; fundraising; and gaining critical insights on technological and market developments that otherwise would not be available in such concentration (Cooper & Park, 2008). However, there is no guarantee that such ecosystems will provide magical results. It is up to the ESU founders to moderate relationships. Conversely Heirman and Clarysse (2007) found that firm alliances do not significantly speed up innovation, and university collaborations slow development times (Chammassian, 2016).

'What you know' (human capital) influences 'who you know' (social capital) and 'how good you are at interacting

with strangers' (an aspect of social competence) and ultimately determines 'whom you choose' (network utilization)

Early-stage ESU founders' industry reputation and experience (i.e., specific human capital) enable the founders to employ existing networks effectively through existing ties to solicit and attract financing. The effectiveness of these ties is fundamentally improved when the founders' background also includes managerial skills and social competence (i.e., general human capital). In fact, "'what you know' (human capital) influences 'who you know' (social capital) and 'how good you are at interacting with strangers' (an aspect of social competence) and ultimately determines 'whom you choose' (network utilization)" (Zhang et al., 2008, p. 594[20]). Social capital exists due to personal social networks and business networks that facilitate ESU founders and their startups to move towards their goals and utilize those ties to their benefit by taking action (Huang et al., 2012). However, initial social networks and the size of networks are not as important as the diversity and types of networks for growth and development or the combination thereof (Lechner et al., 2006).

4.7.3 *Investing in Social Capital Development*

To develop social and relational capitals takes time and effort over long periods. There is no rule or known benchmark as to how much time and/or resources should be dedicated to building relational or social capital. They will certainly be different but ongoing over the different ESU lifecycle stages. It is also unclear what qualitative and quantitative performance measures and ROI should be from time and cost investments.

It would be highly relative to the business and ultimate purpose of this investment in social capital development time, processes, and technology costs. However, the purpose must be coupled with the founders' (and later the ESU teams') ***capacity to build*** networks, relationships, and reputation, and their ***ability to exploit*** them for market and business development, building unique relationships and partnerships, to grow locally and

[20] Zhang et al. (2008, p. 594).

internationally and to finance for growth. Invariably, social capital development combines sharing and circular knowledge economy variables, including users, stakeholders, and triple customers (i.e., paying, financing, and trade sales M&A). Although ESUs' investment in developing social capital is critical, eventually exploitation becomes more important than investing as it could lead to better ESU survival (Brüderl & Preisendörfer, 1998). Figure 4.10 summarizes how social capital development requires three variables:

- **Investment in time**, processes, and technology **costs** (new, existing, hybrids, platforms)
- **Capacity to build** relationships, networks, reputation, and trust in the marketplace.
- **Ability to exploit** existing and new networks for the go-to-market, to develop business and unique relationships, to grow internationally, and to finance this growth.

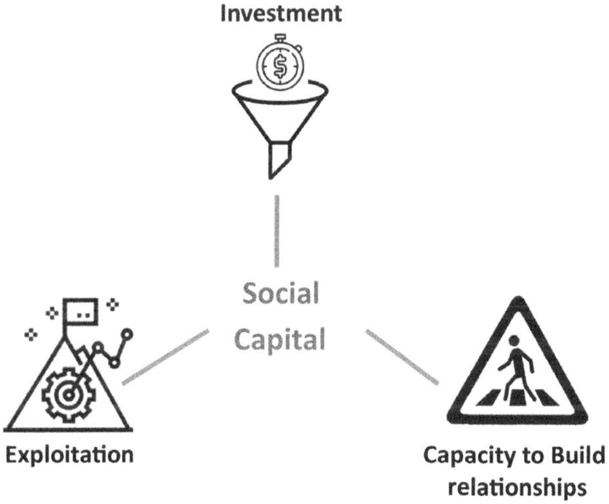

Fig. 4.10 Social capital development variables

4.7.4 *Social Capital Development and Founders' Experience*

There are different approaches to building social capital through human capital networks and capacity. These approaches vary between novice and experienced entrepreneurs. For instance, novice entrepreneurs who come from university or research programs use direct networks such as their alma maters and contacts from incubators and indirect networks through industry associations and memberships. Experienced entrepreneurs employ mostly direct industry contacts that are client focused on niche industries (Gately & Cunningham, 2014). These relationships eventually develop social capital in the form of resources as part of the entrepreneurs' personal networks (Stam et al., 2014), which have a positive influence on ESU performance from its exploitation. Stam et al. (2014) found that "network connections enable entrepreneurs to identify new business opportunities, obtain resources below the market price, and secure legitimacy from external stakeholders" (p. 152). A study by Hsu (2007) indicated Founders' own social networks and their ability to attract and recruit senior managers have a positive effect on ESU valuation. Although network diversity has the most positive impact on performance, investment in social capital must be specific in order to get higher returns on investment, which is defined as a contribution to the firm survival and profits (Bosma et al., 2004). Table 4.4 summarizes the characteristics and associated costs of social capital development by ESU founders and teams.

Table 4.4 Social capital characteristics and associated costs per ESU stage

Social capital	*Characteristics*	*Associated costs*
Early stage	• Founders' own social capital and capacity to build relationships • Exploitation of founders' networks • Founders' background—specific and/or general human capital • Entrepreneurial and networking skills • Demand and competitor analysis • Investment in time and effort • Advise and support from university faculty, mentors, and advisors	• Financially frugal • Major time consumption to develop real social capital • Founder human capital as a value *enabler* • Experimentation, learning, and recalibration • Unpredictable results • Very high opportunity cost

(continued)

(continued)

Social capital	*Characteristics*	*Associated costs*
Mid stage	• ESU team human and social capital and capacity to build relationship • Development of processes and tech • Exploitation of new networks and expanding old ones • Identification, inclusion, and engagement of different users, stakeholders, and triple customers • Building social trust, legitimacy, authenticity, and relational capital • International growth and networks • Financing for growth development	• Developing and/or adopting technologies and platforms • Intangible to build trust, reputation and big data • Investment oriented for long-term ESU valuation • Fixed costs as *Mediator* of value creation and capture • Seeking validation and predictability • Reasonable ROI • High opportunity cost
Late stage	• International growth through exploitation of networks • Scaling social and relational capital development • Capture and extract value through big data and customer relationship management (CRM) technologies • Some external financing required • Exit preparation through social networks and contacts	• Lower investment in platform infrastructure • Cost optimization through economies of scale and further automation • Enabling tech development or subscriptions • International growth team • Expected high ROI • Higher ESU valuation • Lower opportunity cost

Takeaways

- Social capital (SC) is a component of ESU human capital that builds valuable trust and reputation within a given society and community.
- SC is an intangible asset within the context of the sharing economy promoting cooperation, inclusion, learning, bonding, coordination, social value and impact, exchanges, innovation, reciprocity, goodwill, and connectiveness.
- A strong social capital leads to ESU knowledge seeking, resource acquisition and improved value proposition within the circular knowledge economy.

- Examples of valuable social capital include market social trust and reputation (i.e., legitimacy, rankings), authenticity, impact orientation, and social networks.
- The internet is an important moderator, democratizing social relationships by combining voluntary associations between users, buyers, seller and stakeholders.
- SC development requires investment in time, ESU founder and team capacity to build relationship and networks, and their ability to exploit them.
- Developing SC depends on founders' and team experiences: "what you know" (human capital) influences "who you know" (social capital) determines "whom you choose" (network utilization).

4.8 Uniqueness of Relational Capital

Relational capital deals with the value created through *unique relationships* built with paying and financing customers, suppliers, shareholders, stakeholders, users, specialized ecosystem players (i.e., incubators and accelerators), universities, R&D centers, public and private foundations, and similar. These relationships could be internal and external (Cooper, 2000; Hormiga et al., 2011a, 2011b; Friesl, 2012; Gately & Cunningham, 2014; Teece, 2011). They are pathways to gaining further market and management knowledge and building legitimacy through *interorganizational collaboration* (Delmar & Shane, 2004; Friesl, 2012; Zimmerman & Zeitz, 2002). However, in order to make these relationships *valuable*, they need to be *distinctive* and *proprietary*. Building such distinctive proprietary relationships is a difficult process. It requires a combination of strategic need, creative and innovative approaches, time and dedication, competence, *resourceful narratives*, and judgment calls (Fisher et al., 2021; Oftedal et al., 2024). A good example would be how ESUs with products as part of their value proposition form relationships with suppliers. Figure 4.11 illustrates the relational capital developmental process.

4.8.1 Building Relationships with Suppliers

By default, it is generally accepted that ESUs don't have the buying power of larger companies, especially during their early and mid-stages. It is a known fact that larger suppliers prefer to pick and choose their customers

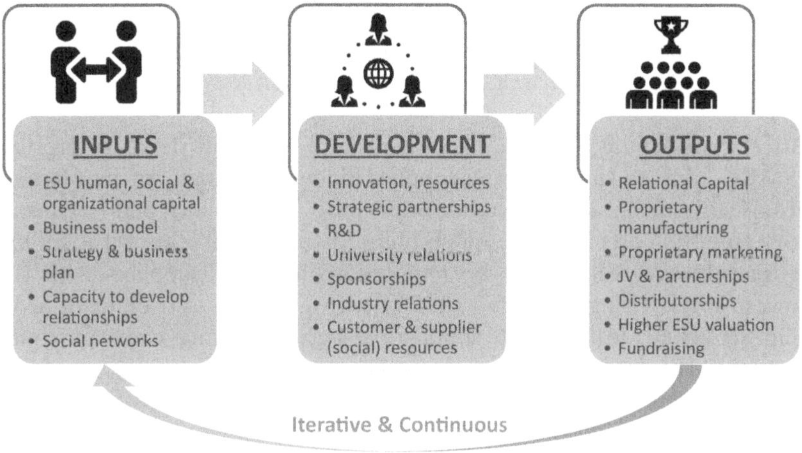

Fig. 4.11 Relational capital development process

as they see fit and attractive for them (Schiele et al., 2012). It is also known that ESUs lack developed processes (especially in early to mid stages), management capabilities and regular or repeat customers to have consistent orders for suppliers. However, ESUs are also sources of innovation and aspire to grow significantly through disruptive value propositions, attracting paying and financing customers. This means they have an innovative and pioneering mindset that needs to partner with suppliers who can be open to working with innovative ESUs where they may also leverage and learn from the new experiences (Wagner, 2021). In order to attract suppliers and become partners, Tessaro et al. (2023) suggest ESUs to employ seven factors: "strategic compatibility, innovation potential, startup network, credible growth opportunity, profitability, memorable experiences, and purchaser sellership" (p. 100). With their capacity to build relationships, exploit their social capital, and be innovative, Wagner (2021) advocates that ESUs could position themselves as *lead users* with their suppliers. Wagner uses Al-Zu'bu and Tsinopoulos' (2012) definition of *lead users* as "a special group of customers that experience needs unknown to the public, which they address by creatively using their technical expertise" (p. 671). This supplier collaboration with ESUs as *lead users* during their new product and services development could improve product variety to supplier and improve performance for both parties.

By bartering knowledge and know-how, ESUs and smaller suppliers can learn from each other's capacity to innovate and improve their respective processes.

After prototyping, ESUs, like small and medium-sized enterprises (SMEs), need to start ordering supplies in low quantities. As these orders are usually small, (a) they are not interesting for suppliers, and (b) inventory (supply) costs could be much higher than what the market is willing to pay. Hence, ESUs may be tempted to look for suppliers with the lowest costs. Using Wagner's (2021) analogy, ESUs can emulate SME mindset when dealing with suppliers, especially during early and mid-stages. SMEs prefer dealing with smaller suppliers with similar mentality who they can trust (see Ellegaard, 2006; McGowan, 2018). ESUs can research and identify such suppliers domestically (where possible) or *near abroad* (closer proximity or country) to be able to work with. Such smaller suppliers may also appreciate to work with innovative ESUs as *lead users*. From mid-stage onwards when ESUs begin growing, especially internationally, ESUs can learn from this relationship and be able to replicate in other countries using local suppliers there using the 80-20 rule. This will also make their supply chain more sustainable with lower environmental impact and higher local socio-economic impact by working with local suppliers. This concurs with Bustamante's (2019) assessment that in any case during international growth ESUs make different types of decisions when it comes to insourcing vs. outsourcing. To summarize:

- <u>Early-to-mid stage</u> ESUs, through their capacity to build relationships and exploit their social capital, should identify and work with smaller local suppliers who are willing to work with a startup as a *lead user*.
  - They should employ novel approaches, such as "strategic compatibility, innovation potential, startup network, credible growth opportunity, profitability, memorable experiences, and purchaser sellership" (Tessaro et al., 2023, p. 100).
  - This experience could be beneficial for both ESU and the supplier as they can learn from each other's capacity to innovate and improve their respective processes by *bartering knowledge and know how.*

- Upon mid-stage to growth stages, ESUs may design and replicate supplier profile and processes to other countries (using the 80-20 rule) as it may no longer be possible to work with the original local supplier for international growth.
  - Using the 80-20 rule, ESUs can design processes from learned experiences that can be replicated over 80% of the time in other countries and localized less than 20% of the time to address local conditions.
  - This is also critical from a sustainability perspective. It improves the ESU's environmental footprint and local socio-economic impact.

4.8.2 Characteristics and Development Costs of Relational Capital

ESUs seek to acquire resources, knowledge, and relationships with ***interorganizational collaboration*** with market and non-market actors differently during the three ESU lifecycles (Friesl, 2012; Marcon & Ribeiro, 2021). Table 4.5 summarizes the relational capital development in different ESU lifecycles:

In the ESU's early stages, there is a higher propensity, reliance, and vulnerability to socio-relational networks. This also depends on the previous entrepreneurial and startup experiences of ESU founders. Experienced founder ESUs have lesser vulnerabilities than inexperienced ones (Wesley Ii et al., 2022). Furthermore, high-tech-driven ESUs require different types of relationships in attaining intellectual capital in their early stages than non-high-tech-driven ESUs. For high-tech ESUs, earlier stages are a period of complexity, resource and capital intensive due to front-end investment requirements in R&D. They are highly reliant on support from unique ecosystems, such as universities, their research and technology transfer offices, early financing customers, and potentially industry partners, such as pharmaceutical companies for tech development, testing, and licensing. Technologies first conceived within universities are usually transferred to a commercial entity by researchers or students, who then become promising entrepreneurs. In this case, universities excel mostly in research innovation and facilitate the transfer of the technology to a more value creation stage (Ho et al., 2014).

For all types of ESUs, incubators, and accelerators provide an extensive network of knowledge, resources, and valuable services, such as space

Table 4.5 Relational capital characteristics and associated costs per ESU stage

Relational capital	*Characteristics*	*Associated costs*
Early stage	• Founders' own social capital and capacity to build relationships • Exploitation of founders' networks • Partnerships with universities, R&D centers, incubators, and accelerators • Associations with industry and events • Prototyping and developing supplier relations • Networking, needs/demand analysis • Competitor analysis • Investment in time and effort • Seeking sponsorships and public grants	• Financially frugal • Major time consumption • Founder social capital as value *enabler* • Experimentation, learning, and recalibration • Grants may have a positive moderating effect on ESU's perceived partner value • Sponsorships are enablers • Prototyping and supplier engagement • Unpredictable results • High opportunity cost
Mid stage	• ESU team social capital and capacity to build relationship • Exploitation of stakeholder networks: new and expanding old ones • Development of processes on partnership programs with triple bottom-line impact • Business development with key account customers • International growth alliances: supply chain, JVs, larger companies • Financing partnerships for growth	• Customer acquisition costs (CAC) development to scale • Intangible value to build trust, reputation, and big data • Investment in platforms for long-term ESU valuation • Fixed costs as *Mediator* • MCS & <IR> • Reasonable ROI • High opportunity cost
Late stage	• International growth through exploitation of networks • Scaling social and relational capital development • Unique and proprietary marketing and manufacturing partnerships • Big data and customer relationship management (CRM) technologies • Some external financing needed • Higher growth due to competitive advantage • Exit preparation through social networks and contacts	• Initial investment with partners • Investment in scientific and functional human capital • Cost optimization through economies of scale and further automation • International growth team • MCS & <IR> • Enabling tech development or subscriptions • Expected high IC valuation, ESU exit, and ROI • Lower opportunity cost

(i.e., offices, laboratories), training and development, networking opportunities, coaching and advising, and functional services, such as HR, legal, and accounting (Banal-Estañol et al., 2023). These ecosystems, which are usually country- and sometimes industry-specific, have grown significantly in the past decades (Cooper, 2000; Gately & Cunningham, 2014).

These relationships lead to a culmination of socio-relational value (capital) through the development of "four types of relational capital activities, namely, development of networks and contacts, relationship building, accessing and leveraging knowledge experts and members of associations" (Gately & Cunningham, 2014, p. 516). Invariably, these relationships also improve their personal entrepreneurial capabilities as well as ESU performance (Huynh & Patton, 2014).

On the other hand, such relationships can lead to a high opportunity cost as at times they could lead ESUs towards wrong paths or may not significantly speed up innovation. For instance, university collaborations may slow down development times (sometimes significantly) due to bureaucratic hurdles or diverging incentives (Heirman & Clarysse, 2007). Stronger ties with lockdown relationships may hinder ESU development and performance. They could also lead to the "danger of misappropriation, which will pull partners apart" (Hallen et al., 2014, p. 1078). Key to reducing opportunity costs is developing network and *interorganizational relational diversification*. Weaker ties combined with social network diversity and social defenses have a more positive effect on performance and can moderate weaknesses while ESUs are organizing and deploying resources (Hallen et al., 2014; Stam et al., 2014).

4.8.3 Transforming Challenges into Relational Capital

It needs to be noted that in early-to-mid stages core *ESU power* is limited to its innovation capabilities and capacity to build relationships. They simply lack human, technological, marketing, and financial resources. When they try to form partnerships and alliances, established or larger organizations recognize this *lack of power* and may try to extract much more value from the ESU than its affordable for the ESU. This is evident with early-stage financing customers and sometimes accelerators when they try to extract more shares during negotiations on their investments. To mitigate this *power gap risk*, ESUs can employ certain tactics while still seeking the support of and benefits from key relationships (Oukes et al., 2019). These tactics may include:

- Seeking public financing, such as grants, for their ESU's R&D. This would give more legitimacy and flexibility for ESUs to seek key relationships (Islam et al., 2018).

- Seeking sponsorship from a key industrial player, a known expert or academic, or a successful entrepreneur with networks who can vouch for the ESU. This can increase the ESU's *perceptive value* in the eyes of potential partners and customers. To achieve this, ESU founders need to be entrepreneurial and act resourcefully *to transform actions into (winner) narratives* (Fisher et al., 2021) to get sponsorships.
- ESU's location may matter. If the ESU is located within or working through a government supported hub or well-established incubator or accelerator, they may receive more legitimacy, protection and negotiating power through its network position, in addition to knowledge sharing interactions. This will help them with their *structural power position* through *their network centrality and hierarchical authority* (Oukes et al., 2019).

In mid-stages, where ESUs have survived, developing a growing organization and either have the proper financing or seeking it, ESUs have more room to maneuver with partnerships due to their experiences, focus and potentially strengthened power through their innovation. For instance, with the supplier example above, as ESUs seek higher volume from their supply chain, they can extract better deals with different suppliers. They can also leverage from their experience with earlier suppliers to replicate the model during international growth. However, ESUs should be mindful not to over-exert their buying power as it may backfire on them. "A partner is more likely to respond well to collaboration, persuasion, coalition, integration and exchange" (Oukes et al., 2019, p. 80) than intimidation and playing suppliers against each other.

4.8.4 Proprietary Relational Capital

Having said this, the transition to industry 4.0, sharing and circular economy, and sustainability have impacted ESUs as well as large manufacturing firms and suppliers. Many industrialized companies are transforming or have transformed their business models and corporate strategies to incorporate these traits (Kurpjuweit & Wagner, 2020; Parida et al., 2019). To do so, they must search for partnerships and alliances for new innovations and exchanges. Within this world, ESUs play a dual role in this transition:

1. A resource of innovation and a supplier to larger firms. Established firms are actively searching for ESUs as suppliers of innovation for their *outside-in startup-supplier programs* in order to increase their competitiveness (Kurpjuweit & Wagner, 2020). Knowing this trend, ESUs actively can develop unique partnership models specifically designed to address this business-to-business (B2B) customer need.
2. A customer or buyer of supplies. In this case, larger manufacturing firms have increasingly incorporated modern technologies, such as artificial intelligence (AI), blockchain, 5G technology, big data, and similar into their value chain for sustainable manufacturing, efficiency, effectiveness, risk management, and improvement of their operational productivity (Cui et al., 2020; Madanaguli et al., 2024; Mangla et al., 2024; Rodríguez-Espíndola et al., 2022). ESUs can benefit tremendously from these trends by partnering with willing producers to develop their value propositions' value chain for proprietary manufacturing and sustainable scaling.

The word *proprietary* means something valuable (i.e., a property) that we own that is unique and valuable. Proprietary manufacturing means producing something tangible with unique processes, blends, technologies, techniques, and methods that are unique, sometimes protected by patents, owned and controlled by a manufacturer or jointly with customer. These proprietary manufacturing methods could lead to unique products that are difficult to replicate or reverse engineered by competitors, that could give its owners a competitive advantage in the marketplace.

An example of *proprietary manufacturing* would be the design and manufacture of a gadget that could be discreetly attached to a smart phone monitoring temperature and air quality around us. The value proposition of this gadget is the detection of air particles and is linked to software that detects, analyzes, and provides just-in-time information to the smart phone owner. The data is also anonymously captured[21] into a large database. The detections related to air quality, humidity, (unwanted) smells, smoke, chemicals, gas, pollution, pollen, and many other items. If reverse-engineered, one can replicate the general technology within 6–12 months. The owners of the technology form a partnership with an

[21] Being General Data Protection Regulation (GDPR) compliant. See https://gdpr-info.eu/.

SME manufacturer in a country with high ethical and sustainability standards. The manufacturer may involve unique design formulation through specialized machinery with custom-built software that would make the gadget work only with the client's software and would be rendered useless through some self-destruct nanotechnology that when it is disassembled or broken down, it will make the gadget useless and not possible to reverse engineer. The goal is to own exclusivity to the gadget design with an eventual (pending) patent, to prevent others from replicating without the gadget owner's permission or licensing. The partnership with the manufacturer is considered to be a relational capital because the methods and the ownership rights have a very high long-term value.

Proprietary marketing has a similar logic to proprietary manufacturing, except it is more intangible. It involves the utilization of unique big data, networks, branding, and marketing strategies that combined with a client's value proposition create exclusivity and competitive advantage through replicability and international expansion (for instance). The approach is not just the input of information, but also the process of using data analytic tools, including AI curation methods, to segment and target customers in a very efficient and effective way. This would lead to a competitive advantage, higher revenue and earnings, and a strong brand identity that would be very difficult to copy, replicate, or imitate. This proprietary marketing would have a long-term value and is considered to be a valuable relational capital to the ESU.

When it comes to financing customers, selecting and partnering with passive investors versus active investors may make a difference in the speed of growth depending on the ESU market and competitive environment (Inderst & Mueller, 2009). In addition to traditional ways of attracting financing with business angels and venture capital firms, ESUs can also raise funds at project-level with strategic alliances and partnerships, such as licensing agreements and possibly loyalties with larger. This is particularly true with higher-tech ESUs, such as licensing agreements with pharmaceutical or biotech companies (Ozmel et al., 2013). Generally, patented technologies are licensed more likely than not as a complementary financial benefit from an intangible asset. However, licensing is not simply reserved for high-tech ESUs with patents. It can also apply for ESUs with non-patented novel processes, products, services, big data, and platform networks that combined may offer unique intangible value for people or companies to license—a spillover value from intellectual capital development. A study by Dang et al. (2022) found that non-patented patented technologies are licensed to more licensees with lower license fees than patented technologies with higher licensing fees.

Takeaways

- Relational capital (RC) deals with the value created through unique relationships built with customers, suppliers, shareholders, stakeholders, users, specialized ESU ecosystem players, universities, R&D centers, foundations, and similar.
- RC is a unique interorganizational collaboration that is distinctive and proprietary.
- Examples include proprietary manufacturing and marketing, joint ventures and strategic partnerships (i.e., distributors), and financial partnerships.
- For instance, by bartering knowledge and know-how, ESUs and smaller suppliers can learn from each other to innovate and improve their respective processes.
- By building partnerships, alliances and sponsorships, ESUs can become both a resource and supplier of innovation to larger companies as well as customers and buyers of supplies.
- Proprietary relationships, meaning valuable and unique, can lead to special ways of manufacturing and marketing products and services that is not easily replicable or reverse engineered.

4.9 Conclusion

The knowledge economy has been human-inspired and driven which has led to the development of the Fourth Industrial Revolution where technology has altered the way we live, work, play, relax, and relate to each other. The speed of technological discoveries, increase in capabilities, and reduction in computing costs have led to a scale and scope of transformation that we never experienced as human beings. The knowledge economy was made possible not only as the result of human capital inputs and processes but also of its outputs for learning, sharing, and democratizing information through the availability of knowledge, through videography (i.e., YouTube, influencers), blogs, webpages, generative AI, data curation, etc.

Coupled with the knowledge of sustainability, this has come to be known as the sharing economy. Although tech advances have made daily life more efficient and effective, our human adaptation, adoption, and acceptance have been and will get slower as people try to catch up and adapt with the changes. Examples are AI and its impact, electrification, and autonomous technologies. This challenge has also led to the notion of sustainability. There seems to be an unspoken social contract with ourselves whereas we have accepted these advancements with the condition that it needs to make a positive social, environmental, and economic impact to make our world a better place to live.

Human capital, combined with organizational capital, social capital, and relational capital, plus incorporating social, environmental, and economic values into the ESU's value proposition, will create and capture tremendous new venture enterprise value that has a multi-year horizon, with the ultimate value extraction through a liquidation exercise, such as trade sales M&A or IPO exit.

Bibliography

Abecassis-Moedas, C., BenMahmoud-Jouini, S., Manceau, D., & Pereira, J. (2021). Imprinting of founders' entrepreneurial motivations on enterprises' practices and processes: The context of creative industries. *Creativity and Innovation Management, 30*(1), 182–197. https://doi.org/10.1111/caim.12421

Adler, P. S. (2001). Market, hierarchy, and trust: The knowledge economy and the future of capitalism. *Organization Science, 12*(2), 215–234. https://www.jstor.org/stable/3086057

Adler, P. S., & Kwon, S.-W. (2002). Social capital: Prospects for a new concept. *Academy of Management Review, 27*(1), 17–40. https://www.jstor.org/stable/4134367

Agarwal, R., & Shah, S. K. (2014). Knowledge sources of entrepreneurship: Firm formation by academic, user and employee innovators. *Research Policy, 43*(7), 1109–1133. https://doi.org/10.1016/j.respol.2014.04.012

Akroyd, C., & Kober, R. (2020). Imprinting founders' blueprints on management control systems. *Management Accounting Research, 46*, 100645. https://doi.org/10.1016/j.mar.2019.07.002

Al-Zu'bu, Z. M. F., & Tsinopoulos, C. (2012). Suppliers versus lead users, examining their relative impact on product—Al-Zu'bi & Tsinopoulos. *Journal of Product Innovation Management, 29*(4), 667–680. https://doi.org/10.1111/j.1540-5885.2012.00932.x

Albertini, E. (2019). The contribution of management control systems to environmental capabilities. *Journal of Business Ethics, 159*(4), 1163–1180. https://doi.org/10.1007/s10551-018-3810-9

Alvarez, S. A., & Barney, J. B. (2005). How do entrepreneurs organize firms under conditions of uncertainty? *Journal of Management, 31*(5), 776–793.

Alvarez, S. A., & Busenitz, L. W. (2001). The entrepreneurship of resource-based theory. *Journal of Management*, *27*(6), 755–775. https://doi.org/10.1177/014920630102700609

Ancillai, C., Sabatini, A., Gatti, M., & Perna, A. (2023). Digital technology and business model innovation: A systematic literature review and future research agenda. *Technological Forecasting and Social Change, 188*, 122307. https://doi.org/10.1016/j.techfore.2022.122307

Anderson, S. W., & Dekker, H. C. (2009a). Strategic cost management in supply chains, part 1: Structural cost management. *Accounting Horizons, 23*(2), 201–220. https://doi.org/10.2308/acch.2009.23.2.201

Anderson, S. W., & Dekker, H. C. (2009b). Strategic cost management in supply chains, part 2: Executional cost management. *Accounting Horizons, 23*(3), 289–305. https://doi.org/10.2308/acch.2009.23.3.289

Bailetti, T. (2012, February). Technology entrepreneurship: Overview, definition, and distinctive aspects. *Technology Innovation Management Review*, 5–12 (2012)

Baldwin, C., Hienerth, C., & Von Hippel, E. (2006). How user innovations become commercial products: A theoretical investigation and case study. *Research Policy, 35*(9), 1291–1313. https://doi.org/10.1016/j.respol.2006.04.012

Banal-Estañol, A., Macho-Stadler, I., Nieto-Postigo, J., & Pérez-Castrillo, D. (2023). Early individual stakeholders, first venture capital investment, and exit in the UK startup ecosystem. *Journal of Corporate Finance, 80*, 102420. https://doi.org/10.1016/j.jcorpfin.2023.102420

Bandera, C., & Thomas, E. (2019). The Role of innovation ecosystems and social capital in startup survival. *IEEE Transactions on Engineering Management, 66*(4), 542–551. https://doi.org/10.1109/TEM.2018.2859162

Banker, R. D., Huang, R., Natarajan, R., & Zhao, S. (2019). Market valuation of intangible asset: Evidence on SG&A expenditure. *The Accounting Review, 94*(6), 61–90. https://doi.org/10.2308/accr-52468

Bargoni, A., Santoro, G., Messeni Petruzzelli, A., & Ferraris, A. (2024). Growth hacking: A critical review to clarify its meaning and guide its practical application. *Technological Forecasting and Social Change, 200*, 123111. https://doi.org/10.1016/j.techfore.2023.123111

Barney, J. B. (1991). Firm resources and sustained competitive advantage. *Journal of Management, 17*(1), 99–120.

Bedford, D., Bisbe, J., & Sweeney, B. (2022). Enhancing external knowledge search: The influence of performance measurement system design on the absorptive capacity of top management teams. *Technovation, 118*, 102586. https://doi.org/10.1016/j.technovation.2022.102586

Beusch, P., Frisk, J. E., Rosén, M., & Dilla, W. (2022). Management control for sustainability: Towards integrated systems. *Management Accounting Research, 54*, 100777. https://doi.org/10.1016/j.mar.2021.100777

Bezuidenhout, S., De Villiers, C., & Dimes, R. (2023). How management control systems can enable, constrain, and embed integrated reporting. *Accounting & Finance, 63*(4), 4251–4273. https://doi.org/10.1111/acfi.13092

Bhatti, S. H., Santoro, G., Khan, J., & Rizzato, F. (2021). Antecedents and consequences of business model innovation in the IT industry. *Journal of Business Research, 123*, 389–400. https://doi.org/10.1016/j.jbusres.2020.10.003

Bocken, N., & Snihur, Y. (2020). Lean Startup and the business model: Experimenting for novelty and impact. *Long Range Planning, 53*(4), 101953. https://doi.org/10.1016/j.lrp.2019.101953

Bohan, S., Tippmann, E., Levie, J., Igoe, J., & Bowers, B. (2024). What is scaling? *Journal of Business Venturing, 39*(1), 106355. https://doi.org/10.1016/j.jbusvent.2023.106355

Bontis, N. (1998). Intellectual capital: An exploratory study that develops measures and models. *Management Decision, 36*(2), 63–76.

Bontis, N. (2001). Assessing knowledge assets: A review of the models used to measure intellectual capital. *International Journal of Management Reviews, 3*(1), 41–60. https://doi.org/10.1111/1468-2370.00053

Bosma, N., Van Praag, M., Thurik, R., & De Wit, G. (2004). The value of human and social capital investments for the business performance of startups. *Small Business Economics, 23*(3), 227–236.

Braune, E., Sahut, J.-M., & Teulon, F. (2020). Intangible capital, governance and financial performance. *Technological Forecasting and Social Change, 154*, 119934. https://doi.org/10.1016/j.techfore.2020.119934

Brüderl, J., & Preisendörfer, P. (1998). Network support and the success of newly founded business. *Small Business Economics, 10*(3), 213–225.

Brynjolfsson, E., & Yang, S. (1997). The intangible benefits and costs of investments: Evidence from financial markets. *ICIS Proceedings*. http://aisel.aisnet.org/icis1997/10

Budde, L., Hänggi, R., Laglia, L., & Friedli, T. (2024). Leading the transition to multi-sided platforms (MSPs) in a B2B context—The case of a recycling SME. *Industrial Marketing Management, 116*, 106–119. https://doi.org/10.1016/j.indmarman.2023.12.002

Burmaoglu, S., Sartenaer, O., & Porter, A. (2019). Conceptual definition of technology emergence: A long journey from philosophy of science to science policy. *Technology in Society, 59*, 1–11. https://doi.org/10.1016/j.techsoc.2019.04.002

Burnell, D., Stevenson, R., & Fisher, G. (2023). Early-stage business model experimentation and pivoting. *Journal of Business Venturing, 38*(4), 106314. https://doi.org/10.1016/j.jbusvent.2023.106314

Bustamante, C. V. (2019). Strategic choices_ Accelerated startups' outsourcing decisions. *Journal of Business Research, 105*, 359–369. https://doi.org/10.1016/j.jbusres.2018.06.009

Bylund, P. L., & Packard, M. D. (2022). Subjective value in entrepreneurship. *Small Business Economics, 58*(3), 1243–1260. https://doi.org/10.1007/s11 187 021 00451-2

Carroll, L. (2017). A Comprehensive definition of technology from an ethological perspective. *Social Sciences, 6*(4), 126. https://doi.org/10.3390/socsci6040126

Cavallo, A., Cosenz, F., & Noto, G. (2024). Business model scaling and growth hacking in digital entrepreneurship. *Journal of Small Business Management, 62*(4), 2058–2085. https://doi.org/10.1080/00472778.2023.2195463

Coad, A., & Reid, A. (2012). *The role of technology and technology-based firms in economic development: Rethinking innovation and enterprise policy in Scotland*. Technopolis Group.

Cohen, W. M., & Levinthal, D. A. (1990). Absorptive capacity: A new perspective on learning and innovation. *Administrative Science Quarterly, 35*(1), 128–152.

Colombo, M. G., Delmastro, M., & Grilli, L. (2004). Entrepreneurs' human capital and the start-up size of new technology-based firms. *International Journal of Industrial Organization, 22*(8), 1183–1211.

Colombo, M. G., & Grilli, L. (2005). Founders' human capital and the growth of new technology-based firms: A competence-based view. *Research Policy, 34*(6), 795–816. https://doi.org/10.1016/j.respol.2005.03.010

Cooper, S. Y., & Park, J. S. (2008). The impact of 'incubator' organizations on opportunity recognition and technology innovation in new, entrepreneurial high-technology ventures. *International Small Business Journal: Researching Entrepreneurship, 26*(1), 27–56. https://doi.org/10.1177/0266242607084658

Conner, K. R. (1991). A historical comparison of resource-based theory and five schools of thought within industrial organization economics: Do we have a new theory of the firm? *Journal of Management, 17*(1), 121–154.

Corrado, C., Haskel, J., Jona-Lasinio, C., & Iommi, M. (2022). Intangible capital and modern economies. *Journal of Economic Perspectives, 36*(3), 3–28. https://doi.org/10.1257/jep.36.3.3

Chahal, H., & Bakshi, P. (2015). Examining intellectual capital and competitive advantage relationship: Role of innovation and organizational learning. *International Journal of Bank Marketing, 33*(3), 376–399. https://doi.org/10.1108/IJBM-07-2013-0069

Chatterji, A., Delecourt, S., Hasan, S., & Koning, R. (2019). When does advice impact startup performance? *Strategic Management Journal, 40*(3), 331–356. https://doi.org/10.1002/smj.2987

Chammassian, R. G. (2016). *Towards a new cost paradigm for technology startup entrepreneurs* (Doctoral Dissertation). Grenoble Ecole de Management, Grenoble, France.

Chammassian, R. G., & Blum, V. (2018). *Costs, value creation, and early stage technology startups: It's all about intellectual capital.* Paper submitted for presentation at the Association Francophone de Comptabilité (AFC) 39ème Congrès, Nantes, France. 15–16 May 2018.

Chenhall, R. H. (2003). Management control systems design within its organizational context: Findings from contingency-based research and directions for the future. *Accounting, Organizations and Society, 28*(2), 127–168.

Chenhall, R. H., & Moers, F. (2015). The role of innovation in the evolution of management accounting and its integration into management control. *Accounting, Organizations and Society, 47*, 1–13. https://doi.org/10.1016/j.aos.2015.10.002

Chung, K. H., Shim, D. C., & Park, H. H. (2024). Revisiting theory of social capital: Can the internet make a difference? *Technological Forecasting and Social Change, 202*, 123282. https://doi.org/10.1016/j.techfore.2024.123282

Cooper, J. (2000). Turning knowledge into value. *CMA Management, 74*(8), 22–26.

Crook, T. R., Todd, S. Y., Combs, J. G., Woehr, D. J., & Ketchen, D. J. (2011). Does human capital matter? A meta-analysis of the relationship between human capital and firm performance. *Journal of Applied Psychology, 96*(3), 443–456. https://doi.org/10.1037/a0022147

Crouzet, N., & Eberly, J. (2023). Rents and intangible capital: A Q+ framework. *The Journal of Finance, 78*(4), 1873–1916. https://doi.org/10.1111/jofi.13231

Crouzet, N., Eberly, J. C., Eisfeldt, A. L., & Papanikolaou, D. (2022a). The economics of intangible capital. *Journal of Economic Perspectives, 36*(3), 29–52. https://doi.org/10.1257/jep.36.3.29

Crouzet, N., Eberly, J., Eisfeldt, A. L., & Papanikolaou, D. (2022b). Intangible capital, non-rivalry, and growth. *SSRN Electronic Journal*. https://doi.org/10.2139/ssrn.4264886

Cui, Y., Kara, S., & Chan, K. C. (2020). Manufacturing big data ecosystem: A systematic literature review. *Robotics and Computer-Integrated Manufacturing, 62*, 101861. https://doi.org/10.1016/j.rcim.2019.101861

Cugueró-Escofet, N., & Rosanas, J. M. (2013). The just design and use of management control systems as requirements for goal congruence. *Management Accounting Research, 24*(1), 23–40. https://doi.org/10.1016/j.mar.2012.11.001

Dang, J., Motohashi, K., & Huo, D. (2022). Get Pennies from many or get a Dollar from one? Multiple licensing in markets for technology. *Technovation, 113*, 102423. https://doi.org/10.1016/j.technovation.2021.102423

Darino, L., Sieberer, M., Vos, A., & Williams, O. (2019). Performance management in agile organizations. McKinsey & Co.

Davila, A., & Foster, G. (2005). Management accounting systems adoption decisions: Evidence and performance implications from early-stage/startup companies. *Accounting Review, 80*(4), 1039–1068.

Davila, A., & Foster, G. (2007). Management control systems in early-stage startup companies. *Accounting Review, 82*(4), 907–937.

Davila, A., Foster, G., & Jia, N. (2015). The valuation of management control systems in start-up companies: International field-based evidence. *European Accounting Review, 24*(2), 207–239. https://doi.org/10.1080/09638180.2014.965720

Davila, A., Foster, G., & Li, M. (2009). Reasons for management control systems adoption: Insights from product development systems choice by early-stage entrepreneurial companies. *Accounting, Organizations and Society, 34*(3–4), 322–347. https://doi.org/10.1016/j.aos.2008.08.002

Davlembayeva, D., Papagiannidis, S., & Alamanos, E. (2020). Sharing economy: Studying the social and psychological factors and the outcomes of social exchange. *Technological Forecasting and Social Change, 158*, 120143. https://doi.org/10.1016/j.techfore.2020.120143

De Ridder, M. (2024). Market power and innovation in the intangible economy. *American Economic Review, 114*(1), 199–251. https://doi.org/10.1257/aer.20201079

De Souza, M. L. P., De Souza, W. C., Freitas, J. S., Filho, L. D. R. D. M., & Bagno, R. B. (2022). Agile roadmapping: A management tool for digital entrepreneurship. *IEEE Transactions on Engineering Management, 69*(1), 94–108. https://doi.org/10.1109/TEM.2020.3027918

Debrulle, J., Maes, J., & Gardiner, E. (2021). How entrepreneurs think: Financial decisions for the long or short term. *Journal of Business Strategy, 42*(4), 233–239. https://doi.org/10.1108/JBS-04-2020-0068

Delmar, F., & Shane, S. (2004). Legitimating first: Organizing activities and the survival of new ventures. *Journal of Business Venturing, 19*, 385–410.

Dencker, J. C., & Gruber, M. (2015). The effects of opportunities and founder experience on new firm performance: Opportunities, founder experience and new firm performance. *Strategic Management Journal, 36*(7), 1035–1052. https://doi.org/10.1002/smj.2269

Devarakonda, R., Reuer, J. J., & Tadikonda, H. (2022). Founder social capital and value appropriation in R&D alliance agreements. *Research Policy, 51*(4), 104474. https://doi.org/10.1016/j.respol.2022.104474

Dinh, T., Sidhu, B. K., & Yu, C. (2019). Accounting for intangibles: Can capitalization of R&D improve investment efficiency? *Abacus, 55*(1), 92–127. https://doi.org/10.1111/abac.12149

Drucker, P. (1969). *The age of discontinuity: Guidelines to our changing society*. New York: Harper & Row.

Eisenmann, T. R. (2020). *Determinants of early-stage startup performance: Survey results* (Harvard Business School. 21–057, 1–63. Entrepreneurial Management Working paper). https://doi.org/10.2139/ssrn.3725023

Eiteneyer, N., Bendig, D., & Brettel, M. (2019). Social capital and the digital crowd: Involving backers to promote new product innovativeness. *Research Policy, 48*(8), 103744. https://doi.org/10.1016/j.respol.2019.01.017

Elkington, J. (1994). Towards the sustainable corporation: Win-win-win business strategies for sustainable development. *California Management Review, 36*(2), 90–100.

Elkington, J. (1997). *Cannibals with forks: The triple bottom line of 21st century business*. Capstone Publishing.

Ellegaard, C. (2006). Small company purchasing: A research agenda. *Journal of Purchasing, 12*, 272–283. https://doi.org/10.1016/j.pursup.2006.08.004

Felin, T., Koenderink, J., & Krueger, J. I. (2017). Rationality, perception, and the all-seeing eye. *Psychonomic Bulletin & Review, 24*(4), 1040–1059. https://doi.org/10.3758/s13423-016-1198-z

Fernandez, V. (2021). The role of trust and social commitment in start-up financing. *International Review of Financial Analysis, 75*, 101722. https://doi.org/10.1016/j.irfa.2021.101722

Fisher, G., Neubert, E., & Burnell, D. (2021). Resourcefulness narratives: Transforming actions into stories to mobilize support. *Journal of Business Venturing, 36*(106122), 1–17. https://doi.org/10.1016/j.jbusvent.2021.106122

Fjeldstad, Ø. D., & Snow, C. C. (2018). Business models and organization design. *Long Range Planning, 51*(1), 32–39. https://doi.org/10.1016/j.lrp.2017.07.008

Friesl, M. (2012). Knowledge acquisition strategies and company performance in young high technology companies. *British Journal of Management, 23*(3), 325–343. https://doi.org/10.1111/j.1467-8551.2011.00742.x

Fukuyama, F. (1995). Social capital and the global economy. *Foreign Affairs, 74*(5), 89. https://doi.org/10.2307/20047302

Gately, C. G., & Cunningham, J. A. (2014). Building intellectual capital in incubated technology firms. *Journal of Intellectual Capital, 15*(4), 516–536. https://doi.org/10.1108/JIC-07-2014-0087

Geroski, P. A., Mata, J., & Portugal, P. (2010). Founding conditions and the survival of new firms. *Strategic Management Journal, 31*(5), 510–529. https://doi.org/10.1002/smj.823

Ghezzi, A. (2020). How entrepreneurs make sense of lean startup approaches: Business models as cognitive lenses to generate fast and frugal heuristics. *Technological Forecasting and Social Change, 161*, 120324. https://doi.org/10.1016/j.techfore.2020.120324

Gimmon, E., & Levie, J. (2010). Founder's human capital, external investment, and the survival of new high-technology ventures. *Research Policy, 39*(9), 1214–1226. https://doi.org/10.1016/j.respol.2010.05.017

Giones, F., & Brem, A. (2017). Digital technology entrepreneurship: A definition and research agenda. *Technology Innovation Management Review, 7*(5), 44–51. http://timreview.ca/article/1076

Giunti, G., & Duberley, J. (2023). Academic entrepreneurship: Work identity in contexts. *Entrepreneurship & Regional Development, 35*(5–6), 532–552. https://doi.org/10.1080/08985626.2023.2178676

Gottschalk, S., Niefert, M., & Muller, K. (2009). *Founder's human capital, entry strategies and start-up size* (ZEW–Centre for European Economic Research discussion Paper [09-030]). http://papers.ssrn.com/sol3/papers.cfm?abstract_id=1433285

Graña-Alvarez, R., Gomez-Conde, J., Lopez-Valeiras, E., & González-Loureiro, M. (2024). Management control systems, business financial literacy and financial leverage in business-incubated start-ups. *The British Accounting Review*, 101427. https://doi.org/10.1016/j.bar.2024.101427

Grant, R. M. (1997). The knowledge-based view of the firm: Implications for management practice. *Long Range Planning, 30*(3), 450–454.

Gruber, M., Heinemann, F., Brettel, M., & Hungeling, S. (2010). Configurations of resources and capabilities and their performance implications: an exploratory study on technology ventures. *Strategic Management Journal, 31*(12), 1337–1356. https://doi.org/10.1002/smj.865

Gruber, M., MacMillan, I. C., & Thompson, J. D. (2008). Look before you leap: Market opportunity identification in emerging technology firms. *Management Science, 54*(9), 1652–1665. https://doi.org/10.1287/mnsc.1080.0877

Hahn, G. J. (2019). Industry 4.0: A supply chain innovation perspective. *International Journal of Production Research, 58*(5) 1425–1441. https://doi.org/10.1080/00207543.2019.1641642

Hallen, B. L., Katila, R., & Rosenberger, J. D. (2014). How do social defenses work? A resource-dependence lens on technology ventures, venture capital investors, and corporate relationships. *Academy of Management Journal, 57*(4), 1078–1101. https://doi.org/10.5465/amj.2012.0003

Han, X., Goxe, F., & Freeman, S. (2024). Internationalization through social networks: A systematic review and future research agenda. *International*

Business Review, 33(4), 102292. https://doi.org/10.1016/j.ibusrev.2024.102292
Haskel, J., & Westlake, S. (2018). *Capitalism without capital: The rise of the intangible economy*. Princeton University Press.
Hayter, C. S., Fischer, B., & Rasmussen, E. (2022). Becoming an academic entrepreneur: How scientists develop an entrepreneurial identity. *Small Business Economics, 59*(4), 1469–1487. https://doi.org/10.1007/s11187-021-00585-3
Hatch, N. W., & Dyer, J. H. (2004). Human capital and learning as a source of sustainable competitive advantage. *Strategic Management Journal, 25*(12), 1155–1178. https://doi.org/10.1002/smj.421
Heirman, A., & Clarysse, B. (2007). Which tangible and intangible assets matter for innovation speed in start-ups? *Journal of Product Innovation Management, 24*(4), 303–315. https://doi.org/10.1111/j.1540-5885.2007.00253.x
Hinterhuber, A. (2013). Can competitive advantage be predicted? Towards a predictive definition of competitive advantage in the resource-based view of the firm. *Management Decision, 51*(4), 795–812. https://doi.org/10.1108/00251741311326572
Ho, M.H.-C., Liu, J. S., Lu, W.-M., & Huang, C.-C. (2014). A new perspective to explore the technology transfer efficiencies in US universities. *The Journal of Technology Transfer, 39*(2), 247–275. https://doi.org/10.1007/s10961-013-9298-7
Hormiga, E., Batista-Canino, R. M., & Sánchez-Medina, A. (2011a). The role of intellectual capital in the success of new ventures. *International Entrepreneurship and Management Journal, 7*(1), 71–92. https://doi.org/10.1007/s11365-010-0139-y
Hormiga, E., Batista-Canino, R. M., & Sánchez-Medina, A. (2011b). The impact of relational capital on the success of new business start-ups. *Journal of Small Business Management, 49*(4), 617–638.
Hsu, D. H. (2007). Experienced entrepreneurial founders, organizational capital, and venture capital funding. *Research Policy, 36*(5), 722–741. https://doi.org/10.1016/j.respol.2007.02.022
Huang, H.-C., Lai, M.-C., & Lo, K.-W. (2012). Do founders' own resources matter? The influence of business networks on start-up innovation and performance. *Technovation, 32*(5), 316–327. https://doi.org/10.1016/j.technovation.2011.12.004
Huang, T. Y., Souitaris, V., & Barsade, S. G. (2019). Which matters more? Group fear versus hope in entrepreneurial escalation of commitment. *Strategic Management Journal, 40*(11), 1852–1881. https://doi.org/10.1002/smj.3051
Huynh, T., & Patton, D. (2014). The performance of university spin-offs: The impact of entrepreneurial capabilities and social networks of founding teams

during start-ups. In *The United States Association for Small Business and Entrepreneurship (USASBE)* (pp. 1–27).

IFRS—IAS 38 Intangible assets. (n.d.). https://www.ifrs.org/issued-standards/list-of-standards/ias-38-intangible-assets/#about. Retrieved on 1 August 2024.

IFRS—Who we are. (n.d.). https://www.ifrs.org/about-us/who-we-are/

Inderst, R., & Mueller, H. M. (2009). Early-stage financing and firm growth in new industries. *Journal of Financial Economics, 93*(2), 276–291. https://doi.org/10.1016/j.jfineco.2008.07.004

Insights | The new interactive teller machines: where convenience meets the human element | NCR Atleos. (n.d.). https://www.ncratleos.com/insights/what-is-an-interactive-teller-machine

International Integrated Reporting Council (IIRC). (2021). International framework. In *International framework*. https://www.integratedreporting.org

Islam, M., Fremeth, A., & Marcus, A. (2018). Signaling by early stage startups: US government research grants and venture capital funding. *Journal of Business Venturing, 33*(1), 35–51. https://doi.org/10.1016/j.jbusvent.2017.10.001

Jansen, J. J. P., Heavey, C., Mom, T. J. M., Simsek, Z., & Zahra, S. A. (2023). Scaling-up: Building, leading and sustaining rapid growth over time. *Journal of Management Studies, 60*(3), 581–604. https://doi.org/10.1111/joms.12910

Johnson, M. J., Kim, K. H., Colarelli, S. M., & Boyajian, M. (2021). Coachability and the development of the coachability scale. *Journal of Management Development, 40*(7–8), 585–610. https://doi.org/10.1108/JMD-06-2020-0174

Kanodia, C., Sapra, H., & Venugopalan, R. (2004, January 3). Should intangibles be measured what are the economic trade-offs. *Journal of Accounting Research, 42*(1), 89–120.

Kaplan, R. S. (2010). Conceptual foundations of the balanced scorecard. *Harvard Business Review, 10*(74), 1–36. Working paper.

Kaplan, R. S., & Norton, D. P. (1992, January–February) The balanced scorecard: Measures that drive performance. *Harvard Business Review*, 71–79.

Kaplan, R. S., & Norton, D. P. (1993–2004). Putting the balanced scorecard to work. In *The economic impact of knowledge* (pp. 315–324). Elsevier. https://doi.org/10.1016/B978-0-7506-7009-8.50023-9

Kotha, R., & George, G. (2012). Friends, family, or fools: Entrepreneur experience and its implications for equity distribution and resource mobilization. *Journal of Business Venturing, 27*(5), 525–543. https://doi.org/10.1016/j.jbusvent.2012.02.001

Kretschmer, T., Leiponen, A., Schilling, M., & Vasudeva, G. (2022). Platform ecosystems as meta-organizations: Implications for platform strategies.

Strategic Management Journal, 43(3), 405–424. https://doi.org/10.1002/smj.3250

Kumar, A., & Kumar, S. (2011). Strategic cost management–suggested framework for 21st century. *Journal of Business and Retail Management Research, 5*(2), 118–130.

Kunc, M. H., & Morecroft, J. D. W. (2010). Managerial decision making and firm performance under a resource-based paradigm. *Strategic Management Journal, 31*(11), 1164–1182. https://doi.org/10.1002/smj.858

Kuratko, D. F., Neubert, E., & Marvel, M. R. (2021). Insights on the mentorship and coachability of entrepreneurs. *Business Horizons, 64*(2), 199–209. https://doi.org/10.1016/j.bushor.2020.11.001

Kurpjuweit, S., & Wagner, S. M. (2020). Startup supplier programs: A new model for managing corporate-startup partnerships. *California Management Review, 62*(3), 64–85. https://doi.org/10.1177/0008125620914995

Leach, C., & Melicher, R. (2021). *Entrepreneurial finance* (7th ed.). Cengage.

Lee, R., Tuselmann, H., Jayawarna, D., & Rouse, J. (2019). Effects of structural, relational and cognitive social capital on resource acquisition: A study of entrepreneurs residing in multiply deprived areas. *Entrepreneurship & Regional Development, 31*(5–6), 534–554. https://doi.org/10.1080/08985626.2018.1545873

Lechner, C., Dowling, M., & Welpe, I. (2006). Firm networks and firm development: The role of the relational mix. *Journal of Business Venturing, 21*(4), 514–540. https://doi.org/10.1016/j.jbusvent.2005.02.004

Li, X., Nosheen, S., Haq, N. U., & Gao, X. (2021). Value creation during fourth industrial revolution: Use of intellectual capital by most innovative companies of the world. *Technological Forecasting and Social Change, 163*, 120479. https://doi.org/10.1016/j.techfore.2020.120479

Lin, Y., & Wu, L.-Y. (2014). Exploring the role of dynamic capabilities in firm performance under the resource-based view framework. *Journal of Business Research, 67*(3), 407–413. https://doi.org/10.1016/j.jbusres.2012.12.019

Linder, C., Lechner, C., & Pelzel, F. (2020). Many roads lead to Rome: How human, social, and financial capital are related to new venture survival. *Entrepreneurship Theory and Practice, 44*(5), 909–932. https://doi.org/10.1177/1042258719867558

Madanaguli, A., Sjödin, D., Parida, V., & Mikalef, P. (2024). Artificial intelligence capabilities for circular business models: Research synthesis and future agenda. *Technological Forecasting and Social Change, 200*, 123189. https://doi.org/10.1016/j.techfore.2023.123189

Mangla, S. K., Luthra, S., Garza-Reyes, J. A., Jabbour, C. J. C., & Brem, A. (2024). Sustainability and Industry 4.0: The role of social, environmental and technological factors in the development of digital manufacturing. *Technological Forecasting and Social Change*, 123223. https://doi.org/10.1016/j.techfore.2024.123223

Marcon, A., & Ribeiro, J. L. D. (2021). How do startups manage external resources in innovation ecosystems? A resource perspective of startups' lifecycle. *Technological Forecasting and Social Change, 171*, 120965. https://doi.org/10.1016/j.techfore.2021.120965

Markman, G. D., & Baron, R. A. (2003). Person–entrepreneurship fit: Why some people are more successful as entrepreneurs than others. *Human Resource Management Review, 13*(2), 281–301. https://doi.org/10.1016/S1053-4822(03)00018-4

Martens, M. L., Jennings, J. E., & Jennings, P. D. (2007). Do the stories they tell get them the money they need? The role of entrepreneurial narratives in resource acquisition. *Academy of Management Journal, 50*(5), 1107–1132.

Marvel, M. R., Wolfe, M. T., & Kuratko, D. F. (2020). Escaping the knowledge corridor: How founder human capital and founder coachability impacts product innovation in new ventures. *Journal of Business Venturing, 35*(6), 106060. https://doi.org/10.1016/j.jbusvent.2020.106060

McGowan, P. (2018). The impact of effectuation on small firm buying decisions. *Journal of Business & Industrial Marketing, 12*(3), 444–459. https://doi.org/10.1108/IMP-05-2017-0019

McGrath, R. G. (2023). Who learns fastest, wins: Lean Startup and discovery driven growth. *Journal of Management*, 1–21. https://doi.org/10.1177/01492063231204870

McGrattan, E. R. (2020). Intangible capital and measured productivity. *Review of Economic Dynamics, 37*, S147–S166. https://doi.org/10.1016/j.red.2020.06.007

Metz, I., Stamper, C. L., & Ng, E. (2022). Feeling included and excluded in organizations: The role of human and social capital. *Journal of Business Research, 142*, 122–137. https://doi.org/10.1016/j.jbusres.2021.12.045

Moro-Visconti, R. (2024). *The valuation of intangible assets: An introduction in artificial intelligence valuation.* Palgrave Macmillan. https://doi.org/10.1007/978-3-031-53622-9_2

Murnieks, C. Y., Klotz, A. C., & Shepherd, D. A. (2020). Entrepreneurial motivation: A review of the literature and an agenda for future research. *Journal of Organizational Behavior, 41*(2), 115–143. https://doi.org/10.1002/job.2374

Nahapiet, J., & Ghoshal, S. (1998). Social capital, intellectual capital, and the organizational advantage. *The Academy of Management Review, 23*(2), 242. https://doi.org/10.2307/259373

Newbert, S. L. (2008). Value, rareness, competitive advantage, and performance: A conceptual-level empirical investigation of the resource-based view of the firm. *Strategic Management Journal, 29*(7), 745–768.

Oe, A., & Mitsuhashi, H. (2013). Founders' experiences for startups' fast break-even. *Journal of Business Research, 66*(11), 2193–2201. https://doi.org/10.1016/j.jbusres.2012.01.011

OECD. (1996). *The knowledge-based economy*. Paris: OECD.

Oftedal, E. M., Foss, L., & Rutherford, M. (2024). From propriety to validity in new ventures: A nine-year study of three startup companies. *Technovation, 131*, 1–13.

Oo, P. P., Allison, T. H., Sahaym, A., & Juasrikul, S. (2019). User entrepreneurs' multiple identities and crowdfunding performance: Effects through product innovativeness, perceived passion, and need similarity. *Journal of Business Venturing, 34*(5), 105895. https://doi.org/10.1016/j.jbusvent.2018.08.005

Ortiz, B., Donate, M. J., & Guadamillas, F. (2016). Relational and cognitive social capital: their influence on strategies of external knowledge acquisition. *Procedia Computer Science, 99*, 91–100. https://doi.org/10.1016/j.procs.2016.09.103

Oukes, T., Von Raesfeld, A., & Groen, A. (2019). Power in a startup's relationships with its established partners: Interactions between structural and behavioural power. *Industrial Marketing Management, 80*, 68–83. https://doi.org/10.1016/j.indmarman.2017.12.007

Ozmel, U., Robinson, D. T., & Stuart, T. E. (2013). Strategic alliances, venture capital, and exit decisions in early stage high-tech firms. *Journal of Financial Economics, 107*(3), 655–670. https://doi.org/10.1016/j.jfineco.2012.09.009

Parida, V., Burström, T., Visnjic, I., & Wincent, J. (2019). Orchestrating industrial ecosystem in circular economy: A two-stage transformation model for large manufacturing companies. *Journal of Business Research, 101*, 715–725. https://doi.org/10.1016/j.jbusres.2019.01.006

Pavlou, P. A., & EI Sawy, O. A. (2011). Understanding the elusive black box of dynamic capabilities. *Decision Sciences*, *42*(1), 239–273. https://doi.org/10.1111/j.1540-5915.2010.00287.x

Pyo, T.-H., Tamrakar, C., Lee, J. Y., & Choi, Y. S. (2023). Is social capital always "Capital"? Measuring and leveraging social capital in online user communities for in-group diffusion. *Journal of Business Research, 158*, 113960. https://doi.org/10.1016/j.jbusres.2023.113690

Qin, W. (2024). How to unleash frugal innovation through internet of things and artificial intelligence: Moderating role of entrepreneurial knowledge and future challenges. *Technological Forecasting and Social Change, 202*, 123286. https://doi.org/10.1016/j.techfore.2024.123286

Rauch, A., & Rijsdijk, S. A. (2013). The effects of general and specific human capital on long-term growth and failure of newly founded businesses. *Entrepreneurship Theory and Practice, 37*(4), 923–941. https://doi.org/10.1111/j.1540-6520.2011.00487.x

Ries, E. (2011). *The lean startup: How today's entrepreneurs use continuous innovation to create radically successful businesses*. New York: Crown Publishing.

Rizvanović, B., Zutshi, A., Grilo, A., & Nodehi, T. (2023). Linking the potentials of extended digital marketing impact and start-up growth: Developing a macro-dynamic framework of start-up growth drivers supported by digital marketing. *Technological Forecasting and Social Change, 186*, 122128. https://doi.org/10.1016/j.techfore.2022.122128

Rodríguez-Espíndola, O., Chowdhury, S., Dey, P. K., Albores, P., & Emrouznejad, A. (2022). Analysis of the adoption of emergent technologies for risk management in the era of digital manufacturing. *Technological Forecasting and Social Change, 178*, 121562. https://doi.org/10.1016/j.techfore.2022.121562

Sanasi, S., Ghezzi, A., & Cavallo, A. (2023). What happens after market validation? Experimentation for scaling in technology-based startups. *Technological Forecasting and Social Change, 196*, 122839. https://doi.org/10.1016/j.techfore.2023.122839

Sanz-Blas, S., Buzova, D., & Pérez-Ruiz, P. (2021). Building relational worth in an online social community through virtual structural embeddedness and relational embeddedness. *Technological Forecasting and Social Change, 162*, 120350. https://doi.org/10.1016/j.techfore.2020.120350

Sarasvathy, S. D. (2001). Causation and effectuation: Toward a theoretical shift from economic inevitability to entrepreneurial contingency. *Academy of Management Review, 26*(2), 243–263.

Sarasvathy, S. D. (2004). Making it happen: Beyond theories of the firm to theories of firm design. *Entrepreneurship Theory and Practice, 28*(6), 519–531.

Sarasvathy, S. D. (2008). *Effectuation: Elements of entrepreneurial expertise*. Northampton, MA: Edward Elgar.

Schiele, H., Calvi, R., & Gibbert, M. (2012). Customer attractiveness, supplier satisfaction and preferred customer status: Introduction, definitions and an overarching framework. *Industrial Marketing Management, 41*, 1178–1185. https://doi.org/10.1016/j.indmarman.2012.10.002

Schwab, K. (2016). The fourth industrial revolution: What it means, how to respond. *The World Economic Forum*. https://www.weforum.org/agenda/2016/01/the-fourth-industrial-revolution-what-it-means-and-how-to-respond/

Shank, J. K. (1989). Strategic cost management: New wine, or just new bottles? *Journal of Management Accounting Research, 1*, 47–65.

Shank, J. K. (1996). Analysing technology investments—From NPV to strategic cost management (SCM). *Management Accounting Research, 7*(2), 185–197.

Shank, J. K., & Govindarajan, V. (1992a). Strategic cost analysis of technological investments. *Sloan Management Review, 34*(1), 39–51.

Shank, J. K., & Govindarajan, V. (1992b). Strategic cost management: The value chain perspective. *Journal of Management Accounting Research, 4*, 179–197.

Shank, J. K., & Govindarajan, V. (1993). *Strategic cost management*. New York, NY: The Free Press.

Shepherd, D. A., & Gruber, M. (2021). The Lean Startup Framework: Closing the Academic–Practitioner Divide. *Entrepreneurship Theory and Practice, 45*(5), 967– 998. https://doi.org/10.1177/1042258719899415

Shepherd, D. A., Breugst, N., & Patzelt, H. (2023). A founding-team model of creating a venture's culture. *Journal of Business Venturing, 38*(2), 106286. https://doi.org/10.1016/j.jbusvent.2022.106286

Shetty, S., & Sundaram, R. (2020). Two heads are better than one: Multi-founder firms and quality signals to investors and acquirers. *International Journal on Emerging Technologies, 11*(3), 574–578.

Shuwaikh, F., & Dubocage, E. (2022). Access to the corporate investors' complementary resources: A leverage for innovation in biotech venture capital-backed companies. *Technological Forecasting and Social Change, 175*, 121374. https://doi.org/10.1016/j.techfore.2021.121374

Simons, R. (1987). Accounting control systems and business strategy: An empirical analysis. *Accounting, Organizations & Society, 12*(4), 357–374.

Simons, R. (1990). The role of management control systems in creating competitive advantage: New perspectives. *Accounting, Organizations and Society, 15*(1–2), 127–143.

Simons, R. (1994). How new top managers use control systems as levers of strategic renewal. *Strategic Management Journal, 15*(3), 169–189.

Souitaris, V., Peng, B., Zerbinati, S., & Shepherd, D. A. (2022). Specialists, generalists, or both? Founders' multidimensional breadth of experience and entrepreneurial ventures' fundraising at IPO. *Organization Science, 34*(2), 557–588. https://doi.org/10.1287/orsc.2022.1581

Stam, W., Arzlanian, S., & Elfring, T. (2014). Social capital of entrepreneurs and small firm performance: A meta-analysis of contextual and methodological moderators. *Journal of Business Venturing, 29*(1), 152–173. https://doi.org/10.1016/j.jbusvent.2013.01.002

Statista Market Insights. (2023, May). *Digital payments—Market data and analysis 2023*. Statista. https://www.statista.com/study/41122/fintech-report-digital-payments/

Stewart, T. A. (1997, 2010). *Intellectual capital: The new wealth of organization*. Crown Currency.

Teece, D. J. (2009). *Dynamic capabilities and strategic management: Organizing for innovation and growth*. New York, NY: Oxford University Press.

Teece, D. J. (2011). Dynamic capabilities: A framework for profitability. *Ivey Business Journal, 18*(7), 509–533.

Teece, D. J. (2012). Dynamic capabilities: Routines versus entrepreneurial action. *Journal of Management Studies, 49*(8), 1395–1401. https://doi.org/10.1111/j.1467-6486.2012.01080.x

Teece, D. J. (2014). The foundations of enterprise performance: Dynamic and ordinary capabilities in an (economic) theory of firms. *Academy of Management Perspectives, 28*(4), 328–352. https://doi.org/10.5465/amp.2013.0116

Tessaro, J. A., Harms, R., & Schiele, H. (2023). How startups become attractive to suppliers and achieve preferred customer status: Factors influencing the positioning of young firms. *Industrial Marketing Management, 113*, 100–115. https://doi.org/10.1016/j.indmarman.2023.05.024

Tubiana, M., Miguelez, E., & Moreno, R. (2022). In knowledge we trust: Learning-by-interacting and the productivity of inventors. *Research Policy, 51*(1), 104388. https://doi.org/10.1016/j.respol.2021.104388

Tzabbar, D., & Margolis, J. (2017). Beyond the startup stage: The founding team's human capital, new venture's stage of life, founder–CEO duality, and breakthrough innovation. *Organization Science, 28*(5), 857–872. https://doi.org/10.1287/orsc.2017.1152

Unger, J. M., Rauch, A., Frese, M., & Rosenbusch, N. (2011). Human capital and entrepreneurial success: A meta-analytical review. *Journal of Business Venturing, 26*(3), 341–358. https://doi.org/10.1016/j.jbusvent.2009.09.004

Van Criekingen, K., Bloch, C., & Eklund, C. (2022). Measuring intangible assets—A review of the state of the art. *Journal of Economic Surveys, 36*(5), 1539–1558. https://doi.org/10.1111/joes.12475

Van Le, H., & Suh, M. (2019). Changing trends in internet startup value propositions, from the perspective of the customer. *Technological Forecasting and Social Change, 146*, 853–864. https://doi.org/10.1016/j.techfore.2018.06.021

Van Meeteren, M., Trincado-Munoz, F., Rubin, T. H., & Vorley, T. (2022). Rethinking the digital transformation in knowledge-intensive services: A technology space analysis. *Technological Forecasting and Social Change, 179*, 121631. https://doi.org/10.1016/j.techfore.2022.121631

van Werven, R., Bouwmeester, O., & Cornelissen, J. P. (2015). The power of arguments: How entrepreneurs convince stakeholders of the legitimate distinctiveness of their ventures. *Journal of Business Venturing, 30*(4), 616–631. https://doi.org/10.1016/j.jbusvent.2014.08.001

Wagner, S. M. (2021). Startups in the supply chain ecosystem: an organizing framework and research opportunities. *International Journal of Physical Distribution & Logistics Management, 51*(10), 1130–1157. https://doi.org/10.1108/ijpdlm-02-2021-0055

Waßenhoven, A., Rennings, M., Laibach, N., & Bröring, S. (2023). What constitutes a “Key Enabling Technology” for transition processes: Insights from the bioeconomy’s technological landscape. *Technological Forecasting and Social Change, 197*, 122873. https://doi.org/10.1016/j.techfore.2023.122873

Wernerfelt, B. (1984). A resource-based view of the firm. *Strategic Management Journal, 5*(2), 171–180.

Wesley Ii, C. L., Kong, D. T., Lubojacky, C. J., Kim Saxton, M., & Saxton, T. (2022). Will the startup succeed in your eyes? Venture evaluation of resource providers during entrepreneurs’ informational signaling. *Journal of Business Venturing, 37*(5), 106229. https://doi.org/10.1016/j.jbusvent.2022.106229

Wilden, R., Gudergan, S. P., Nielsen, B. B., & Lings, I. (2013). Dynamic capabilities and performance: Strategy, structure and environment. *Long Range Planning, 46*(1–2), 72–96. https://doi.org/10.1016/j.lrp.2012.12.001

Winkelbach, A., & Walter, A. (2015). Complex technological knowledge and value creation in science-to-industry technology transfer projects: The moderating effect of absorptive capacity. *Industrial Marketing Management, 47*, 98–108. https://doi.org/10.1016/j.indmarman.2015.02.035

Wyrwich, M., Steinberg, P. J., Noseleit, F., & De Faria, P. (2022). Is open innovation imprinted on new ventures? The cooperation-inhibiting legacy of authoritarian regimes. *Research Policy, 51*(1), 104409. https://doi.org/10.1016/j.respol.2021.104409

Xiong, G., & Bharadwaj, S. (2011). Social capital of young technology firms and their IPO values: The complementary role of relevant absorptive capacity. *Journal of Marketing, 75*(6), 87–104.

15 Years of Vinted, Empowering Second-Hand at Scale. (2023, November 29). https://company.vinted.com/newsroom/15-years-of-Vinted_ Retrieved on 31 July 2024.

Zhang, J., Souitaris, V., Soh, P., & Wong, P. (2008). A contingent model of network utilization in early financing of technology ventures. *Entrepreneurship Theory and Practice, 32*(4), 593–613. https://doi.org/10.1111/j.1540-6520.2008.00244.x

Zimmerman, M. A., & Zeitz, G. J. (2002). Beyond survival: Achieving new venture growth by building legitimacy. *Academy of Management Review, 27*(3), 414–431.

CHAPTER 5

Costs and Three-Dimensional (3D) Business Models

5.1 An Introduction to Three-Dimensional Business Models

Value is in the eye of the value beholder. Experienced entrepreneurial startup (ESU) founders adopt a stakeholder value alignment approach from their entrepreneurial venture's journey from early stages onwards. This value is viewed through the lens of three types of customers: paying (i.e., revenue-generating), financing (i.e., investors), and trade sales (i.e., M&A exits). Value is then created, captured, and extracted through three-dimensional (3D) business models (BMs) that are technology/problem-driven, market/demand-driven, and exit-driven which are designed to work simultaneously. Within these business models, costs play enabling, moderating, and mediating roles.

The value narrative begins with the characteristics of ESUs and their business models in the Fourth Industrial Revolution (Schwab, 2016) through ESU lifecycles where intellectual capital (IC) development leads to value proposition through multiple offerings. This value proposition is created, captured, and extracted three-dimensionally, which leads to higher venture valuations than traditional valuation models, such as discounted cash flow (DCF). Hence, BMs are value-driven and not product-driven (Amit & Zott, 2012, 2021), countering populist misconceptions of BMs being B2B or B2C (i.e., channel), a technology (i.e.,

R. G. Chammassian, *Costs, Value, and the Entrepreneurial Venture Journey*, Palgrave Studies in Accounting and Finance Practice,
https://doi.org/10.1007/978-3-031-86216-8_5

blockchain/FinTech), a subscription model, or a monthly recurring revenue (MRR) or annual recurring revenue (ARR) (i.e., revenue models) to name a few.

The focus of a business model is defining (inputs), developing (processes), and executing value propositions where products and services are outputs of their value proposition platforms (Kretschmer et al., 2022). These platforms are need-based and externally viewed through the lenses of ESUs' three customer groups: those paying for value propositions, those financing ESU value development, and those ultimately interested in acquiring the ESU through a trade sale (i.e., M&A). Financing customers play a crucial mediating role by investing in these high-risk ventures with the belief that eventually the ESUs will develop, grow, and exit through a liquidation scenario where they can reap high returns on their investments (ROI). Convincing financing customers to invest means that ESUs need to produce *real evidence* with data that their projects are viable. This *evidence* includes in-depth problem definition, problem–solution, and technology fit with positive triple bottom line impact, proof of concept with go-to-market strategies, and high-growth potential through the ESU's lifecycles.

Costs play a pivotal role in 3D BM development. Costs are omnipresent throughout all lifecycles and the only certainty throughout the ESUs lifecycles, especially during its BM design. There are no guarantees to success, growing from one stage to another or developing a cohesive BM. What is guaranteed, however, is costs in all ESU lifecycle stages and steps of BM development (Chammassian, 2016). How costs are perceived and treated is key to ESU survival, advancement, and avoidance of early failure. Experienced ESU founders, entrepreneurs, and investors know this *secret*: how to treat costs as enabler, moderator, and mediator of value, as an input, process, and output for each dimension of the 3D BM (Chammassian, 2016; Chammassian & Sabatier, 2020).

This work is based on research and developed from the experiences of high-tech entrepreneurs who have started and successfully exited (or failed to progress) after a substantial amount of external fundraising. The research findings culminated into the development of the 3D BM and its characteristics on how these ESU founders formulate and design their value propositions addressing the needs of their triple customers from the early stages. The 3D BM was derived as a generalized design pattern from high-tech ESU that can be adapted to non-high-tech ESUs.

Takeaways

- Value is in the eyes of the value stakeholders.
- Experienced entrepreneurial startup (ESU) entrepreneurs view this value through the lens of three types of customers who are paying (i.e., revenue-generating), financing (i.e., investors), and future trade sales (i.e., M&A exits).
- Value is created, captured, and extracted through three-dimensional (3D) business models that are technology/problem-driven, market/demand-driven, and exit-driven.
- Within 3D business models, costs play enabling, mediating, and moderating roles.
- Costs are the only certainty throughout all ESU lifecycles.
- 3D BMs apply to high-tech and non-high-tech ESUs alike.

5.2 Cost Investments in the Knowledge Economy

The Knowledge Economy (Drucker, 1969) transformed developing economies from the industrialized manufacturing-oriented economies into a high reliance on knowledge, information, and high-skilled labor. This was enabled and mediated by new and advanced technologies that have made the world's economy into a highly networked, information-driven, open, and scalable one. Over 90% of investments made in Standard and Poor's (S&P) 500 companies[1] (for instance) have been in intangible assets (Heskel & Westlake, 2018; OECD, 1996). Knowledge combined with technological advancements has led to the Fourth Industrial Revolution (Schwab, 2016) with major shifts in value chains and competitive advantage. Knowledge as an intangible asset is more scalable than physical products. It can be scalable and replicable many times more (even unlimited times) than physical products or tangible assets (Bohan et al., 2024; Haskel & Westlake, 2018; Jansen et al., 2023). Intangibles also have a much larger network effect than tangible products due to their flexibility and potential gain from economies of scale. This has led to a major evolution of business models grounded on value (and values) rather than products (Amit & Zott, 2021).

[1] *Source* Ocean Tomo in Haskel & Westlake (2018)

Business models in the knowledge economy
are value driven, not product driven

The knowledge economy's innovation output has been predominantly led by entrepreneurial startups (ESU) with business models as narratives telling their stories on how they create, capture, and extract value (Amit & Zott, 2012, 2021). These narratives usually start with an idea or a hypothesis that is tested and re-tested until the narrative test aligns with the financial test (Magretta, 2002) that could lead to a formidable, scalable, and growth-oriented business. The majority of investments are made into costs orchestrating intangible assets, mainly driven by intellectual capital (IC)[2] development which creates, captures, and extracts most value for innovative companies (Li et al., 2021). The purpose of these investments has been in new venture development (NVD) instead of new product development (NPD), even though products can form part of an ESU's value proposition, with the ultimate goal being to extract value through a liquidation event—an exit via trade sales M&A or IPO.

Before diving into the business models, it is important to elaborate on the characteristics of ESUs, ESU lifecycles, and the role IC plays in developing ESU as a new venture and as a product for eventual sale through trade sales M&A.

Takeaways

- The knowledge economy has transformed developing countries from industrial manufacturing-oriented to knowledge, information, and high-skilled labor one.
- Knowledge coupled with technological advancements have led to the fourth industrial revolution, which is characterized by highly networked, information-driven, open, and scalable BMs.
- Majority of investments (i.e., over 90%) have been made in intangible assets, specifically in intellectual capital (IC) development.
- Intangible assets have a much larger network effect than tangible assets due to their flexibility and potential gain from economies of scale.

[2] IC consists of human, organizational, social, and relational capital combined. IC development is covered extensively in Chap. 4—*Cost Planning and Intellectual Capital Development.*

- The ultimate goal of these investments is value extraction through an exit event (i.e., trade sale M&A) as a return on investment (ROI).
- This has led BMs to become value driven than product driven.

5.3 Entrepreneurial Startups (ESU)

An entrepreneurial startup (ESU) by design means a startup that has the potential to develop and grow into a scalable, replicable, and growth-oriented business. This process is sometimes referred to as the entrepreneurial journey (McMullen & Dimov, 2013; Zaheer et al., 2022) with growing organizational lifecycles (Phelps et al., 2007). ESU characteristics usually include:

- Founder and human capital driven with their dynamic capabilities (Teece 2009, 2012) to develop intellectual capital (Li et al, 2021)
- Tackling societal, environmental, technological, business, legal, financial, and similar problems.
- Defining customer needs and treating stakeholders as peers, providing resources, and driving benefits (Karami & Read, 2021; Van Le & Suh, 2019).
- Disruptive to existing markets and the ways we live, work, interact, and relate to each other, offering unique values to its stakeholders, (triple) customers, and users.
- Developing and executing value propositions through innovative business models with positive impact (Amit & Zott, 2012, 2021).
- Being scalable, replicable, and growth-oriented (Bohan et al., 2024; Cavallo et al., 2024; Jansen et al., 2023).
- Requiring external financing from different sources to develop and grow in several stages, from development to maturity and eventual harvest through a liquidation exit scenario (Leach & Melicher, 2021).
- Having a high risk and high financial return (or loss) profile, where the majority of wealth is extracted upon an exit event.

ESU's success is 100% dependent on ESU's founding team human capital and its dynamic capabilities (Teece 2009, 2012). They include:

- Founding team composition and diversity;
- Knowledge, know-how, and education;
- Experiences in business, industry, and entrepreneurship;
- Functional capacities, such as technological, marketing, supply chain, and financial literacy (Eisenmann, 2020; Graña-Alvarez et al., 2024), especially *cost literacy;*
- Capabilities to develop social relationships;
- Strategic thinking and abilities to grow the organization (Jiang & Murmann, 2023);
- Decision-making structures which depend on the lifecycle stage of the ESU (Tzabbar & Margolis, 2017).

5.3.1 The Two Categories of ESUs

An ESU is created to solve societal, technological, environmental, business, economic, legal, financial, and similar problems through holistic value propositions to improve efficiency and effectiveness sustainably by employing advanced technologies whether existing, hybrid, or newly developed. I would distinguish two ESU categories (Habtay, 2012; Zott & Amit, 2010):

High technology-driven ESUs that are solving specific technological problems through R&D. They can be university R&D discoveries, technology transfer spinoffs, or employee discoveries leading to creating their own ESUs. They specialize in developing technologies into disruptive innovations through patentable processes, blended formulas, and products that transform the way scientific, medical, and technology-heavy industries operate and improve their environmental footprint and lives. These are sometimes referred to as developing *core technologies* (Bailetti, 2012; Burmaoglu et al., 2019; Giones & Brem, 2017; Van Meeteren et al., 2022). Examples of this are pharma, nanotechnology, medical devices, hydrogen fuel cells, transportation electrification, artificial intelligence (AI), generative AI, robotics, and similar.

Non-high-tech (or market-driven) startups that are solving a societal, environmental, business, governance, or economic problem. They are problem driven and seek solutions with the use of technology as a means, an enabler, or a mediator (i.e., a tool) to solve the problem they are addressing more efficiently, effectively, and sustainably. They use digital *enabling technologies* and *application domains*, at times referred to as *general-purpose technologies* (Ancillai et al., 2023; Carroll, 2017; Coad & Reid, 2012; Van meeteren et al, 2022; Waßenhoven et al., 2023). The technologies they use usually either exist, are adopted, or adapted (as a hybrid) to the problem–solution fit. Examples include software, social media, cloud computing, digital platforms and infrastructure, blockchain, and big data analytics.

Both types of ESUs need to identify key customers to reframe their narrative through pitches for *informational signaling* to the right audience accordingly. In general, when we invoke the word *customer*, we immediately think a customer is someone who pays for products and services. Yet, for ESUs such revenue-generating or *paying customers* are part of a triple-customer triangle. By default, it is imperative for the ESUs to understand, identify, and seek paying customers in order to generate revenue and become profitable—from proof of concept to rapid growth. Yet in the early through mid stages, such paying customers will not generate enough revenue for the ESU to survive, develop, and grow. What they need is investments to survive and develop their value propositions. This investment usually comes from external financing sources. Therefore, they would need to reframe their pitch narratives convincingly to these *financing customers* who would eventually be interested in investing in ESUs with the hope of very high ROI. The only way financing customers can gain a hefty ROI is through a liquidation or exit event. This means that the ESU will need to have the potential for value growth and attractiveness for a future buyer of their ESU through a trade sales M&A scenario, usually with a larger established company. Therefore, ESU founders also need to position their companies as *attractive products for a future trade sale*, potentially being attractive to multiple *trade sales customers* for high and competitive trade sale offers. To summarize, ESUs actually have three types of customers:

1. Paying customers,
2. Financing customers,
3. Trade sales customers.

5.3.2 ESUs' Value Development Financial Requirements

ESUs are external financing dependent entities. They must attract different types of external financing from investors (i.e., financing customers)[3] during their various lifecycle stages. ESUs have a fundamental need to develop their project narratives around financing customers, which by design must also cover paying and trade sale customer needs. ESUs must have the potential for higher returns on investments due to higher risk, more than traditional investment instruments in public markets or in real estate. The majority of the time high-tech ESUs require much higher investment in the earlier stages than non-high-tech ESUs. The latter usually must employ lean startup methods to develop and survive (Eisenmann, 2020; Ries, 2011).

ESUs are external financing dependent entities

Early-stage investors come from the public (i.e., government, universities, foundations) and private sources (i.e., friends and family, business angels, and early-stage venture funds). In the earlier stages, the unpredictability and associated risk are much higher due to many unknowns, limited or no historical precedent, founders' human capital, development costs, and market risks.

In the pivotal mid-stages, BMs are solidified with unique value propositions and replicable models to leverage and gain from economies of scale. Investment and external financing requirements change. They become much larger. ESUs must seek and attract different types of financing customers who are more institutional such as venture capital (VC), corporate venture capital (CVC), and some business angel groups.

In later stages, as predictability improves and risks tend to be lower than in earlier and mid stages, investments are still needed to grow the ESU and prepare for an exit. These growth-oriented financing predominantly come from institutional financing customers, such as VC, CVC, family offices, and other private equity.

[3] I deliberately call these investors as *financing customers* because they invest in cash. Investors as a general category can invest in-kind and in cash. An *in-kind investor* is someone who exchanges services with equity. Examples of in-kind investing include an advisory board member or a contributor to the ESU development (i.e., an unpaid team member) who provides expertise in exchange for equity (shares), referred to *sweat equity*.

In almost all cases, the majority of investments are made into costs to develop intellectual capital (i.e., intangibles) and a small percentage on tangibles (i.e., equipment, facilities, country operations). There are no certainties for success or growth. The only certainty that is guaranteed is costs.

5.3.3 ESUs as Value Proposition Platforms

ESUs' value propositions are offered in multiple formats that can be a mix of products, services, information sharing, blogs, networking, and similar designed to be scalable and growth oriented. In fact, ESUs must develop as multi-sided platforms (albeit digital ones) acting as ecosystems by themselves, *a meta-organization or "organizations of organizations"* (Kretschmer et al., 2022) to motivate and incentivize stakeholders, customers, and users alike to participate, contribute, share, learn, buy, and sell as part of the *platform economy* (Budde et al., 2024; Hahn, 2019). Such platform mindset and business models help ESUs gain valuable insights through big data analytics to determine real customer needs, identify new opportunities to scale with faster time-to-market, guarantee end user and partner satisfaction, attract investors, and develop new capacities (Battisti et al., 2022).

The knowledge sharing and exchanges on such platforms can also generate social, environmental, and economic impact value directly and indirectly. By integrating stakeholder feedback, gained knowledge, and expertise, platforms enable ESUs to gather valuable information on how they can develop their value propositions with social, environmental, and economic benefits. This can also lead to improved trust and reputation, which are valuable social capital.

Takeaways

- ESUs are designed to be scalable, growth oriented, and replicable businesses. Their narratives are derived through their lifecycles with common characteristics.
- The ESU narratives and success are 100% dependent on the founding teams human capital and its dynamic capabilities.
- There are two categories of ESUs: high-tech and non-high-tech-driven.

- High-tech-driven ESUs solve technological problems through R&D and similar discoveries that lead to the developing core technologies.
- Non-high-tech ESUs solve societal, environmental, and business problems where digital enabling technologies and application domains act as a means, enabler, or mediator of efficiency and effectiveness.
- Both ESU categories must identify their key customers to reframe their narratives and informational signaling accordingly.
- ESUs have three types of customers: paying, financing, and future trade sales.
- As ESUs are external financing dependent entities, they have a fundamental need to develop their project narratives around financing customers, which by design must also cover paying and trade sale customers' needs.
- ESU value propositions are multifaceted. They include a mix of products, services, information, blogs, networking opportunities, and similar.
- To develop such value propositions, ESUs must employ a multi-sided platform mindset (albeit a digital one).

5.4 Business Models

Business models are strategically crucial for ESUs in positioning their firms into a cohesive narrative and value proposition to attract (triple) customers. There are various definitions of (and what is meant by) business models. For the most part, business models are defined as evolving narratives with a dynamic consistency of various components that are holistic in their ability to convert intellectual capital into economic value (Amit & Zott, 2012, 2021; Beattie & Smith, 2013; Demil & Lecocq, 2010; George & Bock, 2011; Magretta, 2002; Teece, 2009). A business model is also considered to be a key intangible asset in addition to know-how (Teece, 2011) and a *calculative device* to explore, learn from the marketplace and recalibrate in order to be a key source of competitive advantage and organizational capital (Doganova & Eyquem-Renault, 2009; Velu, 2015).

Transforming problem-solving ideas and concepts into innovative narratives with technology as the mediator is a process that requires a deep understanding and analysis of the ESU's value proposition. Whereas a strategy defines what an ESU would like to become, business models describe the *what*, *how*, *who,* and *why* (Amit & Zott, 2012, 2021; DaSilva & Trkman, 2014):

- **What** a company really does at a given point in time?
- **Who** are the business model's main stakeholders?
- **How** it is designed to create and capture value for its customers as well as stakeholders within its ecosystem?
- **Why** does it create value for them?

Business model experimentation and pivoting begin in the early stages of ESU development. To gain a deep understanding of the problem ESUs are trying to solve, it is necessary to listen to signals (positive and negative) from advisors and potential customers (paying and financing), to pivot their business models either partially and sometimes completely if necessary, and to convince potential customers of the ESU's business model legitimacy (Bojovic et al., 2018; Burnell et al., 2023; Hunt et al., 2024).

5.4.1 The Main Drivers of ESU Business Models

Business models could be either technology driven solving a technological problem, or market-driven where ESUs are solving societal, environmental, or economic problems in the marketplace. Technology-driven business models focus on innovation and R&D experimentation to solve a technological problem before market opportunities are identified (Habtay, 2012; Zott & Amit, 2010). However, R&D, technology, and innovation must include business models, which supersedes any idea, concept, or technology (Chesbrough, 2007). Within known technology-driven business models, especially those with a commitment to R&D, experimentation, and discovery, ESUs consider developing more than one business model at the same time as an adaptive platform (Chesbrough, 2007), as *parallel plays* (McDonald & Eisenhardt, 2020), or as a *plan B* (Gruber, 2010). These may lead to *parallel business models* for improved innovation that may become a necessity for commercialization of discovered technologies, contingency planning, or alleviating risks (Clausen & Rasmussen, 2013). With the inclusion of stakeholders and users, it may lead to new tech product functionalities, benefits to end users and third parties, and potential cross-selling for third parties (Kesting & Gunzel-Jensen, 2015). Sometimes, this is referred to as ***discovery-driven business models*** (McGrath, 2010).

Tech-driven business model approaches also support the notion of contingency theory (from configuration, complexity, and creativity) assuming "that any proposition that contains a moderating variable is a contingency theory" (Van de Ven et al., 2013, p. 396) can also apply to multiple business model designs. As difficult as it is to address and plan for uncertainty—an environment that the majority of ESUs live in—contingency planning is always part of addressing uncertainty, especially external uncertainties (Chenhall, 2003). Costs are an enabler of value creation in the early stages (i.e., sunk cost benefit) and a mediator of venture value creation and capture in mid-to-late stages (i.e., investment).

Market-driven business models are demand and needs driven in which consumers define the demand and pay for as customers. These business models are focused on cost structure, pricing, revenue, margin, and profitability (Habtay, 2012; Zott & Amit, 2010). Costs in market-driven business models are more of a by-product of causation rather than effectuation in Sarasvathy's (2001, 2004) parlance. For instance, because of technological advancements, such as cloud computing, product, and service development costs end up being less than before due to the lower cost of computing and the lower capacity demanded by entrepreneurs (Teece, 2009). Therefore, costs have a moderating effect on profitability: the lower the costs, the higher the profit potential.

Market-driven BMs also address customer willingness to pay. ESU founders must realize that revenue for them is a cost to their paying customers. Therefore, as costs are moderators of profitability for the ESU, they are a mediator and moderator of value for paying customers; and a mediator of ROI for external financing customers (i.e., cost of capital and internal rate of return—IRR). Therefore, getting close to and understanding the needs and willingness to pay by either type of customer is crucial in developing value propositions for all customer types.

Both types of business models require investment in developmental costs, which are usually in human capital, especially for tech-driven ESU from its earliest stages. What is most challenging is knowing how cost investments as inputs lead to the business model value creation and capture for the desired outcome, which is mainly speeding up the value creation process, especially to critical ESU stakeholders such as its founders and triple customers (paying, financing, and trade sales).

5.4.2 Business Models as a Platform vs. Platform Business Models

Platform business models are not new. *Souks* in older times and modern shopping malls connected traders, buyers, and sellers of merchandize at a common physical location. Print newspapers and magazines connected reporters, professionals and experts, readers, and advertisers through a common paper print and distribution format. Digital platforms became an alternative where Amazons of this world connected multiple market players together virtually through the internet. It made trading more open, accessible, available, and connected to a far larger audiences—a hallmark of the sharing economy business model and *an important building block for transitions to sustainability* (Ritter & Schanz, 2019). Although sharing and bartering are also not new, the role of digitalization made it much more efficient and scalable to much larger audiences and networks to collaborate, trade, and share within their ecosystem.

There is an ongoing debate whether it is the algorithms, platform, or the technology that made the sharing economy business model possible. What is clear is that platform business models are a culmination of *flexibility, matchmaking, extending reach, transaction management, trust building, and collectivity* (Sutherland & Jarrahi, 2018). It is the push and pull of supply (i.e., knowledge, resources, and IC) and market demand (Guo et al., 2020) and stakeholder needs addressing social, environmental, and economic trends. In fact, platform business models are commonly known as *multi-sided platforms*, even though in their pure form multi-sided platform business models evoke notions of traditional vertically integrated, resellers or input suppliers (Hagiu & Wright, 2015). Digital platform-based business models have become a mediator of value creation, value delivery, and value capture (Rohn et al., 2021) espousing firms to become a *network of (social) contracts*—a hallmark of the twenty-first century (Rahman & Thelen, 2019), transforming resources into relationships (Van Alstyne & Parker, 2017).

What was once reserved for a few pioneering companies like Amazon, has now become standard in both general business model parlance and as a specific type of platform business model. What has driven this trend is mainly the cost of building a platform. First, there is no need to invest in physical infrastructure or develop its own technologies. Second, information and communication technologies (ICT), cloud storage, and Platform-as-a-Service (PaaS) software have become *commoditized* and much less costly, with more computing power, and simpler to use (i.e., user-friendlier). Third, integrated systems can handle vast amounts of (big) data, coupled with AI/ML algorithms, curation software, and customer relationship management (CRM) tools to retrieve and analyze market information much easier and just-in-time.

5.4.3 The Business Model as an ESU Ecosystem Platform

The word *platform* has become synonymous with innovative ESU business models that are designed as a multidimensional networked ecosystem—*a meta-organization or organizations of organizations* (Kretschmer et al., 2022)—for scaling and growth through their IC capabilities instead of simple differentiation (Van Alstyne et al., 2016). Business models as ecosystem platforms for scaling can lead to multiple business models, either as a core but adaptive, discovery oriented, for cross-selling, parallel, or for contingency as a plan B (Chesbrough, 2007; Clausen & Rasmussen, 2013; Gruber, 2010; Kesting & Gunzel-Jensen, 2015; McGrath, 2010). This is particularly true for digital startups and is referred to as business model scaling (Cavallo et al., 2024). For instance, a business-to-consumer (B2C) business channel may eventually evolve into a business-to-business (B2B) channel or a combination thereof (Muzellec et al., 2015).

Both types of ESUs (High-tech and non-high-tech-driven) solve a specific problem in the marketplace that is economically viable for both the ESU and its customers.

For paying customers, ESUs must offer value propositions through products, services, and knowledge sharing that:

- They have a need for it and are willing to pay for it.
- Make things more efficient and effective for them,
- Capture value for money spent.[4]
- Create positive experiences and build trust, and
- Have a positive social, environmental, and/or economic impact.

[4] Let's recall that *revenue* for an ESU is a *cost* for a paying customer.

For financing customers, it is important that:

- The founders' (initial) and the ESU team's (eventual) human capital has the dynamic capabilities to develop the capacity to lead the project into a profitably growth business (Teece, 2009, 2011). *Trust perception* begins with the first impressions of ESU founders and their pitches (Konya-Baumbach et al., 2019).
- The project makes sense as a growth business based on the criteria mentioned for paying customers, and
- The ESU can eventually get them a large ROI in a future exit event (i.e., trade sale or IPO).

For trade sales customers, acquiring the ESU should:

- Create strategic value and competitive advantage with the acquisition of ESU's IC.
- Lead to eventual financial value.
- Be better and more cost effective than internal R&D (i.e., *buy vs. make scenario*).

It is fundamental that ESUs develop their triple-customer acquisition strategies parallel to each other or three-dimensionally (see below for more details). To design business models as platforms and make them economically viable, ESUs need to focus on estimating cost investment into the platform structure with revenue and profit potential from paying customers (Chesbrough, 2010); financing and cost of financing for financing customers; and ESU venture value and valuation costs for trade sales customers. Although the latter value will develop over time, if ESU founders begin with the exit mindset from the early and mid-stages, ESU venture value discovery would become more objective like a strategic goal. This will also make ESUs much more attractive to financing customers.

ESUs with business models as an ecosystem platform "must create economic incentives for ecosystem members to invest in creating complementary innovation and to keep doing so over time" (Gawer & Cusumano, 2008, 2014, p. 30). It is necessary to transform platform ecosystem participants (triple customers, users, and stakeholders) into relationships (Van Alstyne & Parker, 2017). To do so, however, ESUs need to carefully manage the platform's openness to promote network effects equally beneficial to all without losing control. ESUs need to pick and choose who to engage and how to control these engagements and interactions to create and capture value for the participants and eventually for the ESU.

Another condition is that the *ESU as the platform owner* needs to benefit financially from its investment in the (digital) platform. As platform owners, ESUs must first solve a fundamental problem in the marketplace that is scalable with *internal* spillover effects benefiting the ESU. High-tech ESUs solve a technological problem and non-high-tech ESUs must solve a non-tech problem that will create and maintain incentives for multiple stakeholders, users, and potential customers who will eventually revert to paying for the value proposition. A problem–solution fit combined with proper IC development, including complimentary technologies, platforms would maintain uniqueness that would have a *high switching cost* that will not be easy to copy and replicate.

A platform approach would require incentivizing stakeholders, users, and customers to join, get engaged, contribute, benefit, and eventually convert to paying customers. An ESU may not need to become a *platform for standards* per se, like MS Windows is for office software or smart phones are for apps. They can become a platform for their own innovation combining various direct and indirect value chain and domain ecosystem players as a network. The key to success in thinking and becoming a platform is to:

- Identify the various players within the problem–solution fit formulation and ESU ecosystem.
- Using *design thinking* draw the interconnectedness and exchanges between the players that build a network effect (He & Ortiz, 2021; You, 2022). In other words, how does the pipeline work? Remember that "when a platform enters the market of a pure pipeline business, the platform virtually always wins" (Van Alstyne et al., 2016, p. 5).
- Identify and distinguish between direct and indirect players—stakeholders, users, and customers, such as people, organizations, and resources (knowledge, supply chain).
- Define whom to allow to participate and what to allow each participant to do (van Alstyne et al., 2016).
- Prioritize investment in first, second, and third levels, focusing on simplification, user experiences, and ease of use.

This platform mindset, design thinking, and development pattern cannot be realized overnight. It needs to be researched, planned, and developed over time over different entrepreneurial lifecycles.

Takeaways

- Business models are evolving narratives that convert IC into economic value.
- They define transforming ideas and concepts into innovative value propositions by describing the what, who, how, and why.
- There are two known business model drivers: technology and markets.
- Tech-driven BMs are experimental, R&D, and discovery oriented. They may develop multiple BMs as adaptive, parallel, plan B, or contingency.
- Market-driven BMs focus on customer needs and market demand.
- Costs in tech-driven BMs act as an enabler (i.e., sunk cost–benefit) in the early stages and mediators for mid-to-late stages (i.e., investment) for both ESUs and financing customers.
- Costs in market-driven BMs act as moderators of profitability for the ESU, value mediator, moderator for paying customers, and mediator of ROI for financing customers.
- Platform BMs are marketplaces where stakeholders exchange, match make, transact, buy and sell, and build trust.
- They have become a source model for developing BMs as a multi-sided platform mediating value creation, value delivery, and value capture.
- BMs as ecosystem platforms can lead to scaling with multiple parallel BMs (i.e., core, adaptive, discovery oriented, for cross-selling, or for contingency).
- Examples include B2C, B2B, P2P, products, services, customer services and support, virtual and in-person maintenance, and similar services.

5.5 ESU Lifecycles and Business Model Development

Adapted from Leach and Melicher's (2021) entrepreneurial lifecycle model, the ESU lifecycles begin with ideation in its development stage followed by the Startup, Survival, Growth, and Maturity stages with incremental progress. Although *one size does not fit all*, each of these lifecycle stages has its own characteristics and developmental patterns. Figuratively and practically, ESUs must be ready to consider moving from one stage to the next. These moves are determined by the ESU's developmental and financing needs, market (paying customer) proof of concept, and investor (financing customer) acceptance. There are many "go/no-go" decisions that are made within and throughout each stage to the next. Jumping from one stage to the other without completing certain tasks and validation will lead to false premises, conclusions, and starts backtracking and reconfiguration, even though the latter is common when developing an innovative business model (described above). For every experiment, development, and decision, there are both actual and opportunity costs involved. Figure 5.1 illustrates an overall picture of the flow of these stages.

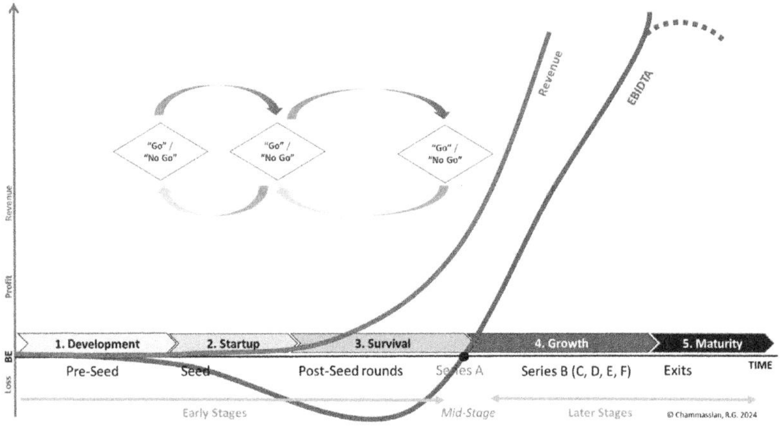

Fig. 5.1 Entrepreneurial startup lifecycles

For every experiment, development, and "go/no-go" decision, there are both actual and opportunity costs involved. Table 5.1 summarizes the ESU lifecycle stage characteristics[5] aligned with business model inputs to create value, process on value capture development, and outputs to extract value.

These lifecycle stages are like a video game where once one stage is successfully concluded, ESUs enter a new stage (in the game) with mostly different, bigger, and costlier challenges. Each of these stages has its unique characteristics, approaches, and cost challenges that start with assumptions, then lead to operational planning, financial forecasting, and cash budgeting, to investment milestones, and financing requirements—all in that order. There are no certainties to go from one stage to another. What is certain, however, is costs in all stages. At each stage, cost requirements and characteristics change to dramatically higher value (and associated risks) when ventures pivot, scale, and grow.

One size does not fit all. There are no limits to time and timing as to when an ESU moves from one stage to the other. It all depends on the type of problem the ESU is solving, and the duration of the development and execution. For instance, developing a value proposition with delivery of farm-to-table agricultural products will require less time and costs, than a technology-driven ESU specialized in hydrogen-powered fuel cell batteries. It also all depends on how well the ESU develops its value proposition through experimentation, learning, recalibrating, pivoting, and executing. Maturity from one stage to the other depends on the readiness, feedback from peers, advisors, and investors, and positive (or negative) signals from potential paying and financing customers and the trade sales marketplace.

Earlier ESU lifecycle stages are the input to the business model value creation

Earlier (development and startup) stages are a period of market research, testing, building, measuring, learning, and validation for most ESUs. They are the inputs to business model value creation. In the earlier stages, high-tech ESU development characteristics and financial needs defer from non-high-tech ESUs. Primarily this has to do with their value creation inputs. With high-tech ESUs, development requires

[5] Chapters 2 and 3 cover extensively on how these ESU lifecycle stages work.

Table 5.1 ESU lifecycle and business model development characteristics

Stage	*Characteristics*
Development	**Input to business model value creation** <u>High tech:</u> • Tech R&D oriented and experimental at a university, R&D center, or incubator • Identifying and solving a technological problem as business model input • Seeking IP protection if/where possible • Specific human capital driven: founders are specialists, scientists, engineers, and similar with strong know-how, education, and talent • Seeking sponsors and financial backers, both public and private • Limited, borrowed resources from ecosystem: labs and incubators, advisors, foundations, government grants • **Costs:** – Opportunity cost of students, scientists, and professor labor – Lab/incubator costs of development, samples, testing, overhead – Early investor ESU company share dilution/negotiating power – Sunk cost ***benefits*** as ***enabler*** of value creation <u>Non-high tech:</u> • Primarily solving a societal, environmental, or economic problem • Entrepreneur-founder driven • Focus on problem analytics with real data • Customer/demand/market needs analytics • Competitor analytics • Impact analysis and determination • Prototyping problem–solution fit • Technology adoption modeling as mediator • Very limited resources: human, financial, physical, and tech • Support from entrepreneurial ecosystem • **Costs**: – Founders' opportunity cost/time – Project opportunity cost if/when not done developed properly – Bootstrapping, lean, and frugal – Market research, analysis, prototyping, sampling – Sunk costs as ***benefits*** and ***enabler*** of value creation *"Go/No-Go" decision to next stage*

(continued)

Table 5.1 (continued)

Stage	*Characteristics*
Startup	**Further input to business model value creation** <u>High tech:</u> • University spinoff to incorporate as a company • Technology transfer (i.e., IP) to the established legal entity • Solidifying IP protection if/where possible • Acquisition of human and organizational resources: specialists, scientists, engineers, space/location, equipment, data • Development of intellectual capital (IC) • Seeking larger Seed financing from private investors (i.e., business angels and VCs) and public grants • Support from entrepreneurial ecosystem: government, universities, incubators, accelerators, mentors, advisors, and service providers • No or very limited revenue to generate cash, possibly consulting, and licensing • **Costs**: – Company setup (one-off) – Large investment in people (i.e., human capital) if/when hiring and onboarding researchers, developers, and technicians (recurring and high costs) – Overhead: office space, lab, and equipment – Subscription and licensing of data, external tools and analysis, enzymes, etc – Financial planning, cash management, and high spending burn rate prioritization on best return on costs/cost–benefit analysis – High opportunity cost of failure – R&D sunk costs as enabler & mediator of value creation <u>Non-high tech:</u> • Establishment of a legal entity • Founder driven • Limited resources: Prototyping, testing, engaging, planning, and developing • Some/low acquisition of human and organizational resources • Seeking smaller seed financing from private investors (i.e., business angels, crowdfunding, friends, and family, some early-stage VCs and public grants) • Pitching to various stakeholders and receiving feedback • Support from entrepreneurial ecosystem: government, universities, incubators, accelerators, mentors, advisors, and service providers • **Costs**: – Company setup (one-off) – Low fixed costs/simple company operating costs: accounting, shared space, and services, overhead – Founders' and project opportunity cost if/when not done developed – Bootstrapping, lean, and frugal; maintain working capital; low/no inventory or high inventory turnover if product-based business – Market research, analysis, prototyping, sampling, paying customer engagement, and market testing – Sunk costs as ***enabler*** and ***mediator*** of value creation *"Go/No-Go" decision to next stage*

(continued)

Table 5.1 (continued)

Stage	*Characteristics*
Survival	**Development of business model value capture** Both ESU types: • Solidifying problem–solution fit with positive impact • Utilization of technologies to enable efficiencies and effectiveness • Developing and testing holistic value propositions through: – Unique processes for positive experiences, reputation, and trust – Identifying and defining the market with proof of concept on products, services, subscriptions, licensing, royalties, networks, and partners – Revenue modeling for scale, one-time vs. recurring revenue (MRR/ARR) – Users, stakeholders, and triple customers (paying, financing, and trade sales) – Scalable and growth markets with 80–20 replication rule • Investment in IC: human, organizational, tech, social, and relational capital – A major shift from frugality to investment orientation, especially for non-high-tech ESUs – Prioritized and incremental investment, financing, and growth milestones – Distinction of dynamic capabilities (to invest) from ordinary capabilities (to cost optimize with outsourcing and automation vs. insourcing) • Major reshaping of founder roles; delegation of responsibilities to the expert management team • Limited revenue: revenue and profits would not cover development needs • Seeking mid-stage Series A investment from mainly VCs (some CVCs) • Exit strategy to ID potential trade sales M&A customers and markets • Some support from entrepreneurial ecosystem facilitators, mainly accelerators, advisors, investors, and service providers • **Costs**: – Mainly in intangibles: People (human capital), organization, platform technologies, social networks, and strategic partnerships – Streamlining marginal and variable costs as ***moderator*** margin and profitability – Leveraging high fixed costs to gain from economies of scale – Costs as ***investment and mediator*** of value capture for higher ESU valuation *"Go/No-Go" decision to next stage*

(continued)

Table 5.1 (continued)

Stage	*Characteristics*
Growth	**Business model value Extraction** • Innovative, scalable, and sustainable business model execution through: – Unique Value Propositions that are replicable and growth oriented – Market-driven multi-sided platform of products, services, networks, and relationships of users, stakeholders, and triple customers • Growth replication using 80–20 model into different international markets • Higher growth revenue, margin, and EBIDTA multiples • Greater IC value, including improved market position, reputation, trust legitimacy, strategic partnerships, impact orientation • Improved/higher valuation with combined profitability and intangible assets • Further need for investment in growth through Series B, C, D, ... mainly from VCs, CVCs, private equity, bridge financing, and institutional investors • Ideal period for an Exit with scenario planning and preparation with different options: trade sales or IPO • **Costs**: – Investment in intangible, IC, and organizational dynamic capabilities as ***mediator*** of value capture and extraction – Streamlining ordinary capabilities with insourcing, outsourcing, or automating as ***moderator*** of margin and profitability – Opportunity cost on when and how to exit (full/partial trade sales or sIPO) *When to "exit/not exit" decision*
Maturity	**Business Model recalibration and pivoting** • Growth oriented but not as high as in high-growth stage – Expansion and revenue are not same level as growth stage – High IC value may be maintained • Need to recalibrate business model to pivot, diversifying and growing organically, to acquire or merge with other companies, or to exit • ESU valuation may be impacted • Bridge financing for own M&A, full or partial exit through trade sales or IPO • **Costs**: – Same as in growth stage – Higher opportunity cost due to missed exit window

technical knowledge and expertise to solve technological problems with longer-term incubation requirements for R&D by expert human capital. Developmental and startup costs are front-loaded due to high-value human capital costs of scientists, technicians, engineers, and similar in order to solve complex problems. Whereas developmental and startup costs for non-high-tech ESUs are usually much lower. These stages require the initial work, capacity, and drive of its founders to define and solve societal, environmental, and economic problems while being frugal utilizing lean startup approaches.

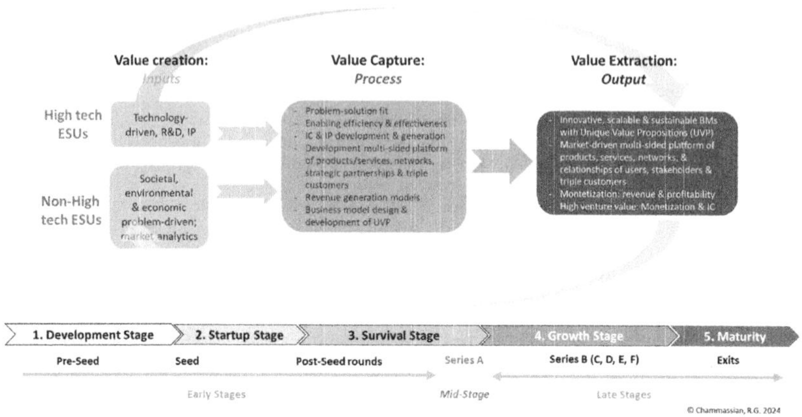

Fig. 5.2 ESU lifecycle and business model development

At mid- and later stages, usually high-tech and non-high-tech ESUs converge in their business model value capture development process. ESUs enter the process of developing business model value capture and value extraction from their business models. See Fig. 5.2—ESU Lifecycle & business model development for an illustration. The mid-stage is a period where both ESU types have to solidify their problem–solution fit to further develop into a growth oriented and profitable organization. The focus is on value capture through IC development, such as multi-sided platforms and UVP, and revenue generation models that are scalable and growth oriented. Later stages are a period of harvest through monetization (i.e., revenue, margin, and profit generation) in multiples, and higher venture valuation. The ultimate goal is to exit through a liquidation event, usually trade sales M&A and less so with an IPO.

Takeaways

- Although one size does not fit all, ESUs go through lifecycle stages that include development, startup, survival, growth, and maturity.
- ESUs need to figuratively and practically move from one to the next stage.
- Each stage has its own characteristics, approaches, cost investment needs, and *go/no-go* decision to move to the next stage.

- Maturity from one stage to the other depends on the readiness, feedback from peers, and positive (or negative) signals from triple customers in the marketplace.
- Business model development is a set of iterative activities of value creation *inputs* → value capture *process* → value extraction *outputs.*
- While value creation inputs differ for tech-driven ESUs and non-tech-driven ESUs, the value capture process and value extraction output characteristics are similar.
- Value creation process includes problem–solution-technology fit enabling marketplace efficiencies and effectiveness with a positive impact of BM UVP.
- Value extraction outputs include innovative, scalable, and sustainable growth-oriented BMs, value propositions, monetization, and (high) venture valuation.

5.6 Intellectual Capital and Business Model Design

Intellectual capital (IC), first coined by Thomas Stewart (1997, 2010), is a specific type of intangible asset that combines human capital, organizational capital, social capital, and relational capital under one generalized term. It is *knowledge-based equity that a company possesses* (Cooper, 2000). The central actors are people as the main agents of value creation, capture, and extraction through knowledge. For ESUs, it begins with its founders and their human capital with their relentless focus on value creation from the ESU's early stages, value capture process during mid-stages, and value extraction during the later stages.

Intellectual capital is knowledge-based equity that a company possesses

During the process of business model value creation and capture, ESUs need to identify, acquire, and utilize key resources, such as human, financial, organizational, social, and relational (i.e., partnerships). This is commonly known as the resource-based view (RBV). ESU founders first need resources and capabilities as inputs to utilize and develop *strategic* options for their opportunities, and to capture and *sustain competitive advantage* (Alvarez & Barney, 2005; Barney, 1991; Conner, 1991; Wernerfelt, 1984). For ESUs, competitive advantage is captured when they develop innovative business models that are rare, unique, valuable, not easily imitable, and well organized through their *dynamic capabilities* as opposed to ordinary capabilities (Lin & Wu, 2014; Pavlou & El Sawy, 2011; Teece, 2009, 2012). Dynamic capabilities of the ESU are strategic by design. They allow ESUs to recognize and evaluate an opportunity (*sensing*); mobilize resources (*seizing*); and renew continuously (*transforming*). These dynamic capabilities are distinct from ordinary capabilities, which are characterized as the day-to-day running of the firm efficiently (Teece, 2012, 2014).

For ESUs, dynamic capabilities begin with the founders as the first and main resources. They are made up of the founders' knowledge, know-how, education, experiences (business, entrepreneurial, managerial, industry), business functional literacy (financial, marketing, IT, supply chain), passion, drive, mindfulness, attitude, and individual social capital (networks). ESU founders are the main inputs in developing ESU's IC, which includes its non-founder human capital, organizational capital, and social and relational capitals. For high-tech ESUs, people and technology are one and the same at the early stages. It is people that develop the technology. This is why high-tech ESUs biggest costs by far are people-related since they need high-salaried scientists, researchers, engineers, and technicians. Figure 5.3 highlights the key characteristics of each type of IC:

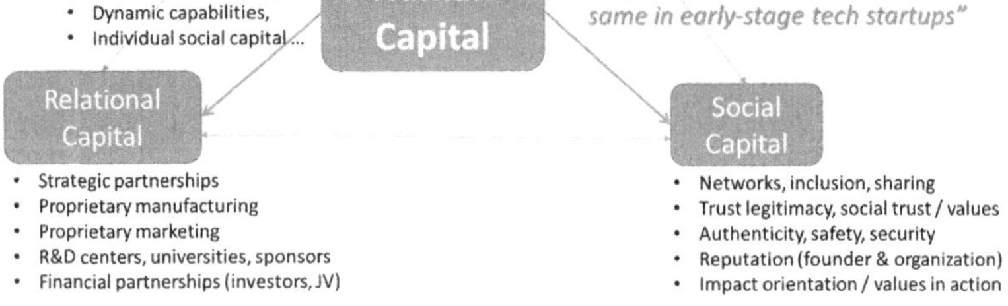

Fig. 5.3 ESU intellectual capital characteristics

With the knowledge economy and Industry 4.0, there have been dramatic shifts in business model design away from pure product development and into firm-level value creation, capture, and extraction. Value creation is mainly driven by the *use of intellectual capital by the most innovative companies in the* world (Li et al., 2021). Hence, business models have become value driven through intellectual capital development (and not product driven). ESU founders are the key drivers to designing and developing business models. Founders design business models through experimentation with multiple configurations for contingency, which eventually leads to organizational design (Fjeldstad & Snow, 2018), resourcing, and financing requirements. In fact, innovative business models that create unique value propositions through scalability and complementaries/synergies become an intangible asset by itself.

Takeaways

- Intellectual capital (IC) is knowledge-based equity that a company possesses.
- IC is made of human, organizational (including tech), social, and relational capital which are needed to identify, acquire, and utilize resources for BM development.
- People play a central role with their dynamic capabilities in developing IC.
- Dynamic capabilities are strategic that allow ESUs to recognize and evaluate opportunities (sensing), mobilize resource (seizing), and develop (transforming).
- They begin with the founders' knowledge, know-how, education, experiences, business functional literacy (i.e., financial), passion, drive, and social capital.
- People and technologies are one of the same in early-stage ESUs.
- Founders design BMs through experimentation and configurations for contingency, which lead to organizational design, resourcing, and financing requirements.
- An innovative BM that is rare, unique, valuable, not easily imitable, and well organized becomes an intangible asset by itself.

5.7 Three-Dimensional (3D) Business Models

From the earliest developmental stage, ESU foundations are grounded in ideas and concepts derived from the experiences, discoveries, and narratives of its founders to *sense*, *seize*, and *transform* it into a scalable and growth-oriented company (Bohan et al., 2024; Cavallo et al., 2024; Jansen et al., 2023; Teece, 2012, 2014). With high-tech ESUs, it is driven by a technological or scientific discovery that needs to be further researched and developed to determine whether viable markets exist for its value proposition. For non-high-tech ESUs, the focus is on solving a societal, environmental, and economic problem that is not properly addressed in the marketplace. The well-analyzed problem needs to be big enough that the proper problem–solution fit options with the use of technologies can be scalable and growth oriented. For both types of ESUs, these identified discoveries must be developed into innovative business models to create, capture, and extract value with users, stakeholders, and customers (whether paying, financing, or eventual trade sales).

The discovery transformation into an innovative and investible business model begins with the development of the ESUs' technologies and intellectual capital through a business model that is rare, unique, valuable, not easily imitable, and well organized through their *dynamic capabilities* as opposed to ordinary capabilities (Lin & Wu, 2014; Pavlou & El Sawy, 2011; Teece, 2009, 2012). Business model discovery and design is iterative, made of value creation *inputs*, value capture *process*, and value extraction *outputs*. Even though innovative business model design is iterative, it can and will change over time, the pattern of development is similar during ESUs' lifecycle stages (See Fig. 5.4—Drivers of the three-dimensional business models). They form a *portfolio* of three parallel business models that work together simultaneously over the ESUs lifecycle development (Chammassian, 2016; Chammassian & Sabatier, 2020) as follows:

- Value creation *inputs* are usually made in the earlier developmental and startup stages.
  - Ideas, concepts, and problems (whether tech or non-tech) are analyzed and properly defined to form the foundational input for the holistic IC development.

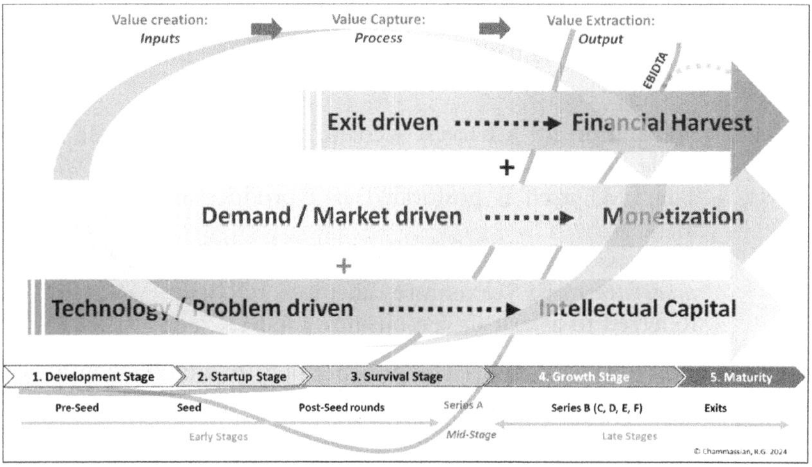

Fig. 5.4 Drivers of the three-dimensional business models

- As a precedent, these inputs as *drivers* are reviewed and revised consistently during the development of ESU IC and technologies development throughout the follow-up lifecycle stages.
- Costs associated with the value creation are mostly *enablers* of value creation, which eventually become *mediators* of value capture, and venture value extraction.
- Referred to as Tech/problem-driven business models.

• Value capture *process* is when the technology-market fit (for high tech) or problem–solution fit (for non-high tech) is identified and developed during the early- to mid-stages.

- This is when proof of concept is solidified, go-to-market strategies are developed, revenue, margin, and profitability models and scenarios are tested and established.
- IC is vigorously developed with a multi-sided platform mindset.
- Costs associated during the value capture are mostly *mediators* of ESU venture value capture and *moderators* of profitability.
- Referred to as demand/market-driven business models.

- Value extraction *output* is generated at the later (growth) stages due to improved ESU valuation from a combination of intangible IC and monetization.
  - Preparation for a harvest scenario through a trade sale exit is made.
  - The ESU itself is positioned as a product for sale in M&A markets.
  - Costs associated during the value extraction are *mediators* and *moderators* of ESU venture valuation.
  - Referred to as exit-driven business model.

These three business model components operate simultaneously and cohesively, converging within a three-dimensional framework to create a unified business model platform. Each one of these business model components has its own value creation *inputs*, value capture *processes*, and value extraction *outputs*.

5.7.1 Technology- or Problem-Driven Business Model Inputs

Before delving into the specifics of technology- or problem-driven business models (i.e., high tech or non-high-tech ESUs respectively), it is important to define what is meant by *technology*. There are many definitions and interpretations as to what technology is. Follows some examples:

- "Technological emergence [is] a cyclic process in highly creative scientific networks that demonstrates qualitative novelty, qualitative synergy, trend irregularity, high functionality, and continuity aspects in a specified time frame" (Burmaoglu et al., 2019, p. 1).
- "To capture not only the equipment, software or instruments used to produce a good or service but also the (tacit) knowledge, techniques, organizational methods, etc. used to design, develop and market the products and services by businesses (and the public and not for profit sector), in cooperation with other actors in the innovation system" (Coad & Reid, 2012, p. 1).
- "Something created through ordering exhibiting organization, whose aspects function with a purpose that can provide some benefit, or something that is organized (implying creation of order) whose

aspects function with a purpose that can provide some benefit" (Carroll, 2017, p. 6).

Technology by itself may have many interpretations, applications and contextual meanings. Like the *meaning of costs* (see Chap. 1), technology must be accompanied by another adjective to define its meaning or purpose. In the world of ESUs, one such combination could be *technology entrepreneurship*, for instance, which Bailetti (2012) defines as a "collaborative experimentation and production of new products, assets, and their attributes, which are intricately related to advances in scientific and technological knowledge and the firm's asset ownership rights" (P. 5). It could also be "new products based on breakthroughs in research; science-based advances through specific knowledge in an academic field," that could lead to "technology proof of concept; first customer validation; [to] activate a global but niche market" (Giones & Brem, 2017, p. 45).

Broadly and commonly speaking, when we mention the word technology, we usually think of some kind of scientific discovery (i.e., pharma), highly technical processes (i.e., 3D printing), or innovative engineering development (i.e., IoT, AR/VR, smart products) as *core technologies* (Van Meeteren et al., 2022) powered by computing, analytical and digital technologies such as blockchain, AI, big data, cloud computing, digital platforms, infrastructure, SaaS and similar as known as *enabling technologies* and *application domains* (Van Meeteren et al., 2022) or *general purpose technologies* (Waßenhovenet al., 2023). Based on the above, here is how I make the distinction between high-tech-driven ESUs and problem-driven (or non-high tech) ESUs.

- High-Tech ESUs utilize tech and scientific discoveries through R&D as the driver or input to value creation or *core technologies* (Bailetti, 2012; Burmaoglu et al, 2019; Giones & Brem, 2017; Van Meeteren et al., 2022).
- Problem-driven (non-high tech) ESUs aim to solve societal, environmental, or business problems through the use of digital *enabling technologies* and *application domains* (or *general-purpose* technologies) as a mediator, a tool, or an intermediary to value capture (Ancillai et al., 2023; Carroll, 2017; Coad & Reid, 2012; Van meeteren et al, 2022; Waßenhoven et al., 2023).

For problem-driven ESUs, innovative technologies may include unique processes, techniques, and methods created through dynamic capabilities by its human and organizational capital that could lead to digital-driven business model innovation (BMI) archetypes (Ancillai et al, 2023). These BMI must be rare, not easily imitable, valuable, and well organized with strong organizational, social, and relational capital features. To be innovative, reconfigured business models need to feature a minimum of two *non-trivial changes* to existing business model elements that are new to the industry or markets (Amit & Zott, 2021; Bock & George, 2017).

Although both types of ESUs are people or human capital driven with their dynamic capabilities, high-tech ESU is highly human capital intensive (i.e., founding team including employees) from the earliest stages requiring larger investments into the high costs of human capital. Whereas problem-driven (non-high-tech) ESUs are mainly founder (human capital) driven in its early stages and need to be frugal and lean. In both cases, costs are considered *sunk* or *unrecoverable* in the value creation process.

At mid-stages, while the trend of high-cost investments into human capital continues with high-tech ESU, the dynamics shift significantly with non-high-tech ESUs, where frugal approaches developing their IC are no longer sufficient for scaling and growth—requiring substantially greater investment. Figure 5.5 below illustrates how the iterative process of value creation, value capture and value extraction is achieved over the ESU lifecycles.

Value Creation: *Inputs*

In the early-stage value creation *inputs*, the focus is *what is the identified technological, social, environmental, and/or economic problem all about.*

- For high-tech ESUs, it is their R&D-driven *core technologies*, such as new and emerging techs, IP, unique discoveries, and scientific processes
  - R&D Costs are mainly the team's human capital related that are generally very high.
  - R&D costs are generally considered sunk costs (Mañez & Love, 2020).
- For non-high-tech ESUs, the inputs are societal, environmental, and economic problem-driven. They also include in-depth analysis of the

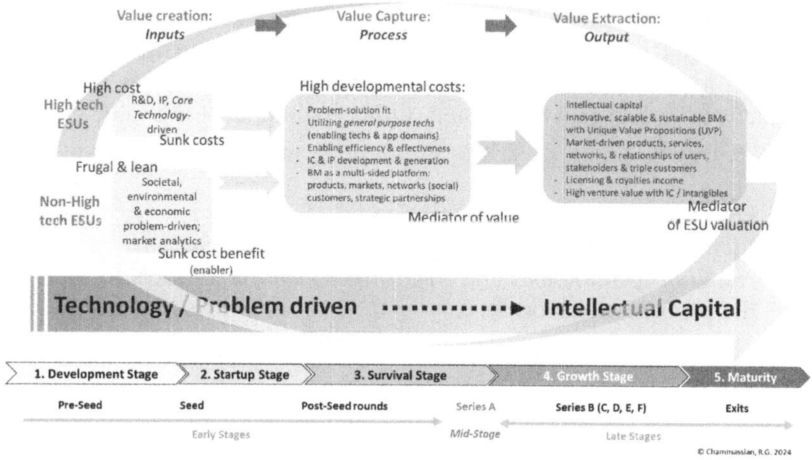

Fig. 5.5 Technology/problem-driven business model components

problem, with demand and market analysis, competitor analysis with prototyping, and initial proof of concept.

- These ESUs operate frugally utilizing lean methods to control expenditures (Ries, 2011), such as maintaining operating capital with low or no inventory levels and avoiding fixed costs where possible.
- Most of the costs are related to the market and competition research and analytics.
- Cost outlays must have some returns in mind to make them *sunk cost benefits* (Datar & Rajan, 2021; Duxbury, 2012).

Value Capture: *Process*

The value capture process answers the question on *how the identified problem is solved* which creates tremendous value in the marketplace of its triple customers (paying, financing, trade sales). For both types of ESU, the process of value capture is enabling efficiency and effectiveness, identifying markets and customer needs, and solving tech or non-tech problems through IC development (human, organizational, social, and relational capital). It also captures the *who are the beneficiaries of the value proposition* (i.e., triple customers). By simply having social media presence or a website will not be enough. There needs to be some ways of optimizing user, stakeholder, and customer engagement, interaction, sharing, intuitive and user friendly, with positive experiences that keep the network participants interested. Other highlights of the value capture process include:

- Formulizing the problem–solution fit.
- Identifying and utilizing *general-purpose technologies*, such as *enabling* technologies and *application domains* as tools to mediate the problem–solution fit.
  - For high-tech-driven ESUs, these would be in addition to their R&D-driven *core technologies*.
- Developing unique processes to mediate efficiency and effectiveness.
- Focus is on IC development and securing IP where possible.
- Designing innovative business models and value propositions as a multi-sided platform of products, services, channels, social networks, diverse user, partner, and customer groups.
- Transforming knowledge networks into relationships with immersive experiences catered to evolving preferences.
- Pitching convincingly the ESU narrative to financing customers to attract investment.

Value Extraction: *Outputs*

Value extraction outputs must answer two fundamental questions: *what is the value output* and *what's in it for the value beholder*? First and foremost, the ESU needs to extract enterprise value (i.e., ROI, future valuation) through its developed IC and for its triple customers:

Figure 5.6 summarizes what questions tech- or problem-driven ESU business models must answer in simplified form:

- Paying customers: addressing a real need and problem to solve, improving efficiency and effectiveness, savings costs and time, with positive experiences, and gaining knowledge.
- Financing customers: improved ESU valuation for a better ROI.
- Future trade sales customers: strategic (and financial) value through ESUs developed IC and for its business and customers.

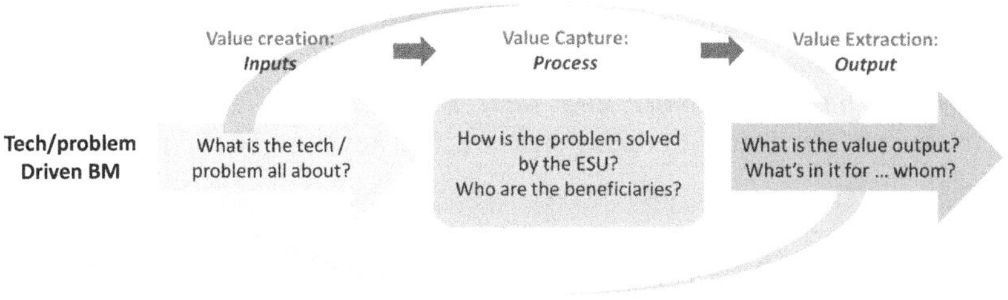

Fig. 5.6 Technology/problem-driven business model development questions

5.7.2 Demand- and Markets-Driven Business Models

Demand- and market-driven business models play a parallel role to tech- or problem-driven business models. They represent classic well-known approaches to value creation ***inputs*** from markets, customers, and competitive environment; value capture ***process*** with value proposition and value delivery; and value extraction ***outputs*** through monetization for all three types of customers. Figure 5.7 illustrates the flow of demand/ market-driven business models through the ESU lifecycle.

Value Creation: *Inputs*

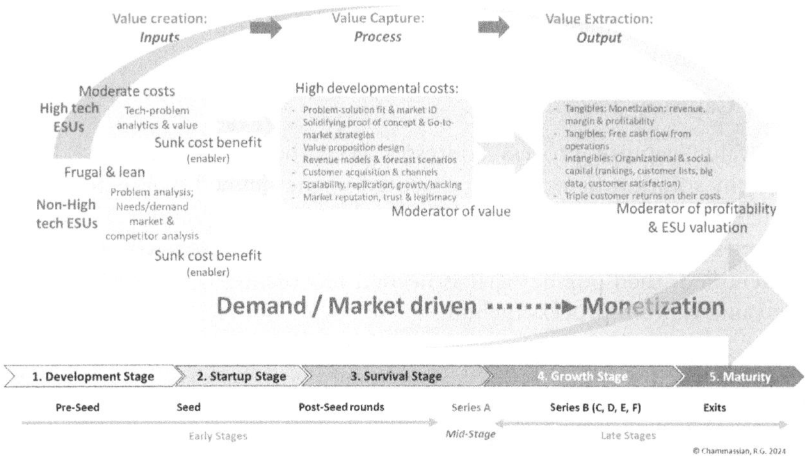

Fig. 5.7 Market/Demand-driven business model components

When it comes to market- or demand-driven business models, the focus is on *what is the market demand or customer need, how big is the market, who is the paying customer and what is the competitive landscape*. The marketplace need and demand size are the key inputs for this business model.

- For high-tech ESUs, although it is still driven by their core technologies, the key is to find the appropriate markets and pay customers for their technologies.
    - Determining market size and potential for growth.
    - Identifying market partners to experiment with.
    - These market trial and error are sunk costs benefits.
- For non-high-tech ESUs, the inputs are driven by the market/demand analysis from the get-go. A deep understanding of market and customer needs, market size, and competitive landscape are major inputs for the value creation step.
    - Frugality and lean approaches continue with a focus on operating capital, low or no inventory levels, and avoiding fixed costs where possible.
    - Most of the costs are related to the market and competition analysis.
    - Cost outlays must have some returns in mind to make them sunk cost benefits.

Value Capture: *Process*

The value capture process addresses how the market/demand-driven problem–solution fit would be executed in the defined marketplace. For both types of ESU, the process of value capture includes identifying market signals and customer willingness to pay for its services. Once this is identified, then pursue what is needed to execute. Other highlights of the value capture process include:

- Identifying different markets, channels, customer types and acquisition methods (i.e., B2B, B2C, B2B2C, P2P, etc.).
- Defining value proposition components, such as products, services, one-time versus recurring sales, warranty, after-sales services, and ongoing support.

- Solidifying proof of concept and go-to-market strategies.
- Determining sustainable and recurring revenue models and forecasting scenarios (i.e., pessimistic, realistic, and optimistic).
- Designing, developing, and executing scalable, replicable, and growth organization.
- Gaining additional knowledge and feedback through integrated platform approaches (i.e., CRM, ERP) to improve market reputation, trust, and legitimacy.

Value Extraction: *Outputs*

Value extraction outputs for market/demand-driven business models must also answer the same two fundamental questions: what is the value output and what's in it for the value beholder? Here, ***monetization*** is the key word for value extraction for the ESU and triple customers:

- Paying customers: value proposition benefits outweigh its incurred costs, direct or indirect, through smooth service, positive experiences, and gained knowledge.
- Financing customers: higher future valuation through discounted cash flow (DCF) leads to improved ROI potential and further investment into the ESU.
- Future trade sales customers: ESU monetization is a proof of concept that can create strategic (and financial) value through ESUs developed value proposition and markets.

Figure 5.8 below summarizes what fundamental questions market/demand-driven ESU business models must answer in simplified form:

Revenue Modeling

ESU's Revenue models follow the same value logic as their business model. Key to designing ESU's revenue model is understanding what paying customers get in return for what they are paying for, whether the revenue is derived from products, services, one-time purchases, subscriptions, monthly or annually recurring revenue (MRR/ARR). In other words, what's in it for the paying customer that would commit them to buy and continue buying? It is essential to know that revenue for the ESU is a cost to its paying customers. Henceforth, the ***pricing model*** must take into consideration the ***costs incurred*** by the paying customer.

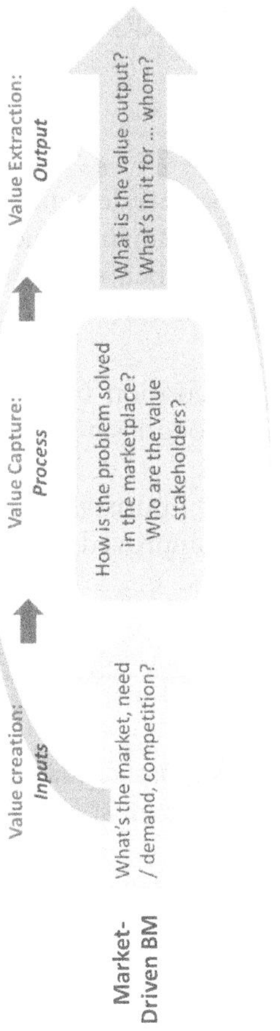

Fig. 5.8 Market/demand-driven business model development questions

Revenue for the ESU is a cost to its paying customers

First and foremost, however, is to identify who the ESU's paying customer is, versus users who could one day become paying customers or not (i.e., freemium vs. premium revenue models). It is not only defining the paying customers' needs, but also identifying and measuring the value proposition's cost benefit. In determining the real customer needs, ESU founders should ask the following questions: "how is a customer solving the identified problem currently, or purchasing and utilizing products and services?" "What are the current processes and market offerings to solve such problems?" What is costing time and money for a business or end customer to perform a task, or to utilize and benefit from a product or service?" "What is an acceptable cost for paying customers?" "What benefits and experiences would a customer desire and/or receive from such services?".

Business models are value driven, not product/service driven. Revenue models follow the same value logic

Answers to such questions should be relayed to paying customer in the ESU value proposition. For business customers, it's all about innovation and performance: doing something better, faster, less costly, efficiently, and effectively. This includes a cost–benefit value. For consumers or end users/customers, understanding the value they receive is essential—is it merely nice-to -have, or truly need-to -have? Let's recall that *business models are value driven, not product/service driven*. ESU teams need to understand and clearly and simply drive the message and narrative to their paying customers. To reach there, they first need to understand the market needs and paying customer pain points related to their offers. Value needs to be perceived from the paying customers' perspective, not ESUs. This will make or break the ESU from the earlier stages onwards. To convince customers of the value propositions, they must be *distinctive* from market competition; *measurable* in terms of tangible differentiation; and *sustainable* in the long run. Otherwise, customers may only look at the price they are paying rather than a sales pitch (Anderson et al., 2006).

Example—Dynamic Pricing
Pricing plays the role of mediator and moderator between the ESU's value proposition and the paying customer's cost benefit. In the mediator

role, pricing defines the relationship between the ESU offering and the customer's willingness to pay. To improve this relationship, ESUs need to conduct research on what resonates value for the customers. Whereas the moderating role reveals how the relationship between the ESU and paying customers is strengthened or weakened.

While there are several forms of pricing,[6] there are a couple of pricing methods based on the value that stand out supporting value-driven propositions. One quite variable pricing approach is *smart pricing* or *dynamic pricing* utilized by online retailers and web-based double-sided platforms. This method uses AI algorithms coupled with big data to adjust prices just-in-time or in real-time based on customer demand and behavior (sometimes personalized), supply availability, seasonality, market conditions, and other variables (Cheung et al., 2017; Den Boer, 2015; Den Boer & Keskin, 2022). Such dynamic pricing is coupled with demand learning (Lin, 2006). This pricing is often used for commoditized products (i.e., kitchen supplies and computer peripherals) and services (i.e., airline tickets).

Example—Value-Based Pricing
Value-based pricing (VBP) is another method that is based on a paying customer's perception of the ESU's value proposition. This pricing method is best used with highly perceived and unique value propositions and is least utilized by commoditized products and services. VBP is ideally used when value propositions are paying customer-focused, providing high-value problem-solutions that customers want, need, and are willing to pay for, and that can be differentiated from the competition. Hinterhuber (2004), for instance, suggests the use of specific tools in the VBP analysis that incorporates customer, competition, and company dimensions. These may Utilize:

- *Economic value analysis* to comprehend customer's perception of the value proposition.
- *Competitive analysis* to gain insights of market developments and the competitive landscape.

[6] For extensive review on pricing, see works by Nagle and Müller (2018) and Smith (2012).

- *Cost-volume-profit (CVP) analysis* to determine the company's internal dynamics of how volume and profit are affected by certain prices.

The greater the learning from customers, the stronger the value discovery. This requires higher learning capabilities to adapt, adjust, and replicate pricing (Raja et al., 2020). Such higher learning capabilities are associated with ESU's dynamic capabilities.

One simple tool or *source model* the ESUs can adopt for *pricing target models* is using a SMART goal approach where pricing can be Specific, Measurable, Achievable, Relevant, and Time bound:

- Specific: keep the pricing model Specific and clearly understood by everyone—seller and buyer. What would the price of the value proposition accomplish in the short to long run? What are specifically included? The latter is important to avoid any pricing perception gaps and unpleasant surprises. This is specifically relevant to intangible services, such as subscriptions.
- Measurable: what is the cost benefit for the paying customer in the short versus the long run? How is this compared to their existing situation and compared to existing solutions in the marketplace? For more complex high-tech value propositions, can the objective be quantified? What data to use to track and measure performance?
- Achievable: the pricing value proposition can be better understood if it is broken down to bite-size portions where achievements, such as customer cost savings, can be measured. By design, *achievability* would also need to correspond to the ESUs capabilities and capacities. The latter may render ESUs own SMART goals.
- Relevant: the value proposition, its pricing, and paying customer costs must be aligned to (a) the customer's own goals and objectives, and then (b) to the ESU's core business model.
- Time Bound: pricing has to be time bound, explicitly stating the time and timing of ESU value proposition execution periods.

5.7.3 *Exit-Driven Business Models*

Exits are a natural part of the ESU lifecycle. ESU founders exit either (1) by design, due to strategy, planning, and good performance; or (2) by default, due to bad performance, including financial distress.

There are multitude of reasons why startups fail. A much-quoted study conducted by CBinsights (2022; Hunt, 2024) suggests there are five dimensions of why startups fail: financial (i.e., running out of cash), value proposition (i.e., lack of market need or demand), human (i.e., founder or team related), strategic (i.e., lack of coherent business model), and execution (i.e., launch, sales, and growth). Exits as disengagement from the ESU by founders can be proactive, *intelligent*, informed, and planned (i.e., knowing when its time to shut down); or reactive, uninformed, and unplanned due to inexperience or blindness to reality (Yusuf, 2012). *Proactive* means that founders (along with financing customers) determine the ESUs value proposition may be attractive in the marketplace but may not be successful in the long run or may plateau early without an exit through an M&A into a larger organization. Therefore, they plan to exit proactively. Whereas *reactive* means that the ESU finds itself in dire straits due to its inability to comprehend ESU performance indicators or manage finances or solve problems or lack of experience, and has to shut down on short notice or exit with lower or little valuation, unplanned.

To mitigate the risk of failure and disengagement, this chapter (and this book as a whole) focuses on providing pathways that would avoid early *unnatural failures*. While these pathways are not the holy grail of success (which is relative), they can assist ESUs and founders in avoiding early unnatural failures by making exits strategic, planned, and proactive when its time. These founder attributes are either learnt early on or come with experience as part of their human capital (Kato & Honjo, 2015). They also have a positive influence on attracting financing customers as well as a higher exit value (Banal-Estañol et al., 2023; Wennberg & DeTienne, 2014).

DeTienne et al., (2015) have divided exit strategies into three categories: *financial harvest*, *stewardship*, and *voluntary cessation*, and concluded that "entrepreneurs who believe they have found or have developed a radically new innovation are more likely to employ a financial harvest exit" (p. 268), which has a more causal reasoning approach. Exit strategies may also be influenced by institutional investor pressures, such as VC requirements of firms to write business plans that include financial harvest scenarios in specific periods (DeTienne, 2010; DeTienne et al., 2015).

The exit-driven business model highlights and focuses on how experienced and serial ESU entrepreneur treat their ventures *as a product for eventual sale in the M&A trade sale markets* (Chammassian, 2016). As the third component of their business model portfolio (Chammassian & Sabatier, 2020), the inputs and planning begin from the early stages as the third business model dimension. Most research and entrepreneurial discussions are on technology-driven ESU exits, that tech startups are designed for exit through trade sales to a larger company. However, they are not exclusive to tech-driven ESUs. They can apply to all innovative ESUs. "Buying startups is one of the fastest ways for companies to grow, enter a new market, acquire new technology and embrace disruption and innovation" (Pisoni & Onetti, 2018, p. 26).

Entrepreneurs must treat their ventures as a product (by itself) for eventual sale in the M&A trade sale markets or for an IPO

Developing an Exit-Driven Mindset

Exit *imprinting* by design becomes part of the ESU founders' mindset and strategy from the early stages (Fauchart & Gruber, 2011; Kato & Honja, 2015; Montanaro et al., 2022). ESU exits are intentional, strategic, and planned (Wennberg & DeTienne, 2014). As long as there is external financing (customers) involved, it is inevitable that those external investors' main goal is to earn a high ROI on their investments through the ESU's financial harvest. Financing customers can only do so when they exit from their investment when the ESU has some kind of financially viable liquidation event, such as trade sale M&A (or IPOs in rare cases). In fact, VCs may already include exit scenarios with certain trade sales customers in mind during their due diligence process and assessment prior to investment. They can advise and nudge ESU founders to establish special relationships within certain industries to become more attractive. During late stages, financing customers may be particularly attracted to the venture when the possibility for an exit through trade sales, an initial public offering (IPO), or acqui-hiring could be better foreseen within a shorter horizon, even though late-stage investor ROI may be lower than earlier investors' ROI.

When ESUs resort to external financing, they must always think of an exit scenario for their financing customers

To do so, ESU founders, especially experienced ones and serial entrepreneurs, develop exit strategies as part of their business model from earlier stages (DeTienne et al., 2015). Based on my interviews with ESU founders (Chammassian, 2016), follows some direct quotes:

- "We always knew that we wanted to build a sustainable company with an appreciation value which would not be flipped in a year or a few months, and therefore we still needed to understand and articulate what our paths to acquisitions and liquidity [were] and [our] potential targets for being acquired."
- "Once you take in funding in a major amount of money as they had, you have to deliver on time something that's exit worthy for the investors. Otherwise, it's not going to be a success; they don't have infinite time."
- "[Our] exit strategy [was] basically [to] create the company then sell it... We always knew that we wanted to build a sustainable company with an appreciation value, which would not be flipped in a year or a few months, and therefore, we still needed to understand and articulate what our paths to liquidity were, acquisitions, and potential targets for being acquired."

ESU exits must be intentional, strategic, and planned throughout the entrepreneurial lifecycle

ESU exits are not only important for its founders, shareholders, and financing customers, but also for the industry the ESU is in and the economy in general (DeTienne, 2010; Pisoni & Onetti, 2018). Exits are also ***pathological*** where there is an actual process involved from a ESU's inception value creation input through to its value extraction output (DeTienne, 2010; Lemley & McCreary, 2021; Wennberg & DeTienne, 2014). Therefore, an exit through a liquidation event is the ultimate harvest scenario:

- ESUs, like any products, reach a lifecycle peak or determine to be exit ready. Exits are a natural evolution of the entrepreneurial lifecycle. However, it is not clear and it's difficult to determine when is a good time to exit. Ideally, exits should occur when ESUs are in their peak performance (i.e., high-growth stage) with a very high valuation, and not during early maturity. Exit timing also depends on financial customers' desires and market conditions (Ball et al., 2011).

- ESU founders, shareholders, and financing customers' wealth is extracted at exit as ROI. Exits are the ultimate value extraction of the venture capital industry's business model. Employees with stock options benefit from exits also.
- Since by design ESUs are growth oriented and require external financing, the only fundamental way investors can get a return on their investment is when they cash out from an exit, just like buying a company share in the stock market at a low price and selling it at its peak.
- Exits, like any problem–solution or product market fit, must be planned in advance. ESUs need to determine which industry, sector, or types of companies would be good potential trade sale (exit) customers. Treating the ESU as a product for a future trade sale changes strategic thinking, positioning, and potential exit routes.
- If not explicitly, exits must be implicitly included with the ESU founders' narrative. Entrepreneurial experience, especially one with an exit scenario, makes a difference in this mindset.

Exits effect not only ESUs' founders, shareholders, and financing customers, but also the industry and the economy as a whole. Industry is impacted when a larger company acquires an ESU with a strong IC and UVP. This effects the competitive landscape and balance, plus it may improve the valuation of the acquiring companys (DeTienne, 2010). Also, many existing industrialized companies struggle developing innovative value propositions through their existing R&D centers due to the general corporate culture of focusing on predictability. They acquire innovation and create value through acquisition of smaller ESUs. Hence, in theory at least, when one lifecycle ends during the exit, a new lifecycle starts for the ESU within a larger context.

From an economy and economic impact perspective, ESU exits create wealth for its founders and employees. This wealth is then redistributed through the economy with the launch of new startups by exit beneficiaries (such as ex-employees and ex-founders), by investing in local economy and other ESUs as business angels, and even by creating their own venture fund (DeTienne, 2010).

Value Creation, Capture, and Extraction with Exit-Driven Business Models

The Success or failure of an ESU is very much dependent on the founders' and later on the ESU teams' human capital and its dynamic capabilities. Founders' background with learnt or previous experiences and education has a positive effect on exit value (Montanaro et al., 2021). The approach and effects of a firm's founding also make a difference and could be a critical determinant of exit rates (Geroski, Mata, & Portugal, 2010).

If costs are perceived and treated as investment, then that investment must have returns for its investors, such as the ESU founders and financing customers. ROI is realized during a liquidation event or a financial harvest which is mainly through an exit—a trade sale or IPO. This intrinsic (mindset) value as an input can lead to extrinsic (financial) value as an output, especially when it comes to planning an exit strategy from the start. Follows some direct quotes from experienced entrepreneurs:

- "There's a history of what choices you've made, and it reflects culture and values." "Cost isn't usually 'I'm throwing money outside my window.' It usually means I'm spending something to build a better business."
- "You can speculate; you can use all the financial models in the world. But at the end of the day, there is only one value: its what people are ready to pay" for the value of the technology, product, or service it creates, and eventually for the ESU.

Figure 5.9 illustrates the value creation, capture, and extraction flow of exit-driven business models throughout the ESU lifecycle.

Value Creation *Inputs*:

Exit-driven business model inputs begin with the mindset and imprinting of the ESU founders, followed by the capacities and dynamic capabilities of the ESU team, especially management team human capital, which leads to IC development: organizational, social, and relational capital. In short, value creation *inputs* are mainly people or human capital-driven.

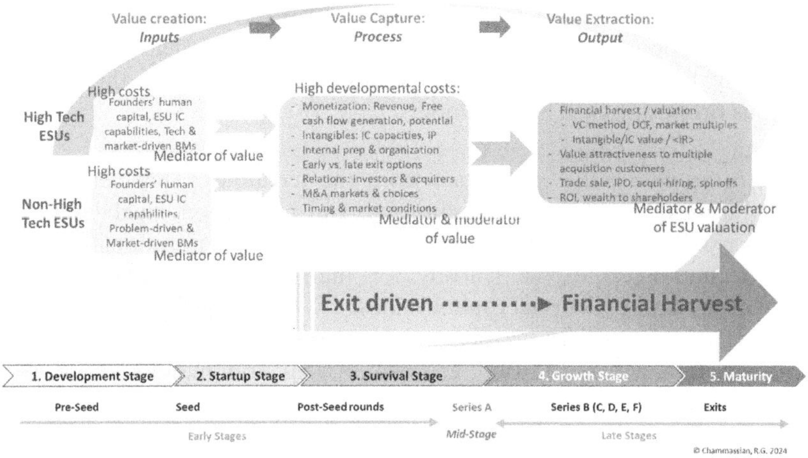

Fig. 5.9 Exit-driven business model components

This is followed by tech/problem-driven and market/demand-driven business model processes as further inputs and drivers for exit-driven business model value creation. The additional difference to the previous two business model components is that *the ESU is the main product* to be developed for a future sale in the trade sale markets. This means ESUs need to be strategically and operationally preparing for a future exit scenario. This preparation is internal and organizational.

As the exit-driven business model is an all-encompassing component of the 3D business model, it perceives costs as mainly investment and mediator of value inputs to develop the ESU for an eventual exit in the long run. When costs are treated as an investment, then there is a natural belief and desire that there will be a return on that investment in the long run. In general, preparations for actual exits are time-consuming. However, when they are planned and organized from earlier stages, it reduces time, ongoing preparation costs, and the opportunity cost of ill preparation or last-minute preparation, which is very stressful.

Value Capture Process:

The development period for exits very much depends on the ESUs' business survival, scaling, and growth. In fact, ESU survival may depend on this growth path (Coad et al., 2013). It also incorporates key performance components from the other two business model components, primarily how the ESU is capturing and extracting value through its various propositions. These include:

1. *Intangibles value generation* from the technology/problem-driven business model: any IP rights, IC, and innovation capabilities and capacities, including ESUs human capital, organizational capital, technological capital (mostly for high-tech-driven ESUs), social capital, and relational capital values.
2. *Monetization* from demand/market-driven business models: revenue generation and growth, margin and marginal cost gain through economies of scale, profitability with growth, and free (net) cash flow generation from operating activities.

Ongoing internal preparation and organization is a critical part of exit value capture process. It includes documenting and disclosure of financial policies and management practices, such as management control systems (MCS), audit trail, and original electronic documents that correspond to what would be presented, discussed, and agreed with potential trade sales customers. Examples include (but are not limited to):

- Financial Statements: how revenue is recognized, and expenses are incurred. What is the physical inventory counts and practices (if any products)? Any unusual events, material gaps, revenue restatements, large, incurred costs, and accruals that need to be explained. What is the state of the internal controls' environment?
- Major customer and supplier contracts, general terms and conditions, warranty, ongoing legal challenges or litigations.
- IP rights, designs, and processes; big data, ICT, and internal systems (i.e., CRM, ERP).
- Human capital capabilities and capacities.

The opportunity cost of not proactively preparing for an exit scenario during ESU's development, scaling, and growth period is very high. *Intentional preparations* include clearly defined processes and auditable documentation and systems, such as financial, operational, marketing, and technological.

During a trade sale event, there is an intermediate phase after the signed term sheet between the buyer (i.e., acquirer) and the seller (i.e., ESU) and the final contract. This phase is called ***due diligence*** which is conducted by the acquirer's team. The due diligence process is highly detailed, cumbersome, and time consuming for the ESU and its team. It is also a very stressful period especially if the ESU and its team are not prepared for it. It takes time away from day-to-day work to support the due diligence process, creating work backlogs.

During due diligence, larger companies assign key people from their teams of auditors, financial analysts, lawyers, HR professionals, supply chain, IT, R&D, and similar functions who descend on the ESU to validate what is said and agreed on the term sheet as value proposition vis-a-vis the reality. It is the ***caveat emptor*** (buyer be aware) process to ***audit, identify issues,*** and ***validate*** before the final agreement is signed. If material issues or undisclosed issues are identified, then the agreed price offer could be altered, usually reduced, and in worse-case scenarios, the trade sale agreement could be annulled by the buyer.

Value Extraction Output:

Exit-driven business models incorporate the combined value of tech/problem and demand/market-driven business model development process and output. The best way to understand the value extraction output for exit-driven business is to view it from the filters of the three customers and the ESU. One of the exercises for the ESU founders would be to comprehend these outputs well and reverse engineer them to design their 3D business models accordingly. This can be used as *a tool* and *a means* to design 3D business models, and not as an end.

Exit Value Extraction in the Eyes of Financial Stakeholders

Exits have benefits and consequences for the ESUs main financial stakeholders, who are the ESU (i.e., founders, employees, and other non-financing shareholders, such as advisors and family members), and the triple customers—paying, financing, and trade sales. Table 5.2 summarizes the value extraction goals of the three customers and ESU and highlights *what's in it for each one* of them in terms of their desired value.

For Paying Customers, exit-driven business model *output* ensures that ESU's value proposition has a higher value recognition in the industry. ESU exits can lead to:

Table 5.2 Exit-driven business model outputs: *What's in it for …?*

Value extraction Output	*Customers*			*ESU*
	Paying	*Financing*	*Trade sales*	
Tech/problem- driven BM	– Incorporated with larger company offerings – Improved efficiency, effectiveness and Cost savings – Add'l knowledge / exposure – Longevity & sustainability – Upgrades – Improved experiences	– Intangible value / IC – ESU Dynamic capabilities – Innovation – Improved ESU valuation – Potentially higher ROI – Sustainability orientation	– Strategic value / intangibles – Human capital/ acqui-hiring – Dynamic capabilities – Innovation / IC / new techs – Incorporation into existing & new products & services – Longevity & Sustainability	– Intangible assets / IC – Innovation capabilities – Long-term potential – Platform to scale & grow – Marketable products/services – Possible licensing & royalties – Higher ESU valuation – Attractive to all 3 customres

Value extraction Output	*Customers*			*ESU*
	Paying	*Financing*	*Trade sales*	
Market/demand- driven BM	– Improved value, cost/ benefit – Innovation exploitation – Sustainability orientation B2B: Improvement in: – Business processes – Cost, benefit, & optimization – Revenue, margin & EBIDTA	– Tangible value / financial – Revenue multiples for ROI – M&A Market value – Improved valuation / DCF – Market reputation / trust	– Proof of concept – New markets & networks – Big data / customer/ networks – Additional value proposition – Market reputation / trust – Future financial value – Scale & growth potential	– Monetization / market proof – Paying customer cost-benefit – Big data / CRM – Financial value: revenue, profits, & ESU valuation / DCF – Scalable & sustainable growth – UVP: multi-products/ services – Financing customers / growth – Strategic value: M&A markets

(continued)

Table 5.2 (continued)

Value extraction Output	*Customers*			*ESU*
	Paying	*Financing*	*Trade sales*	
Exit- driven BM	– Larger company benefits: – Longer term / sustainability – Extended services – Exposure to other offerings – Expanded availability	– Multi-exit options / scenarios – Higher ROI = intangible + DCF – Wealth creation / IRR	– Strategic value / fit – Human capital, IC, dynamic capabilities – Controlled environment – Innovation exploitation opportunities for development & growth – Long-term financial value	– Strategic value: M&A market – Financial value: founders, employees, shareholders, & financing customers (ROI) – Higher ROI = intangibles + DCF – Wealth creation – Larger scale innovation benefits to industry & economy

- Extended value proposition offerings through a larger organization.
- Improved efficiency and effectiveness of products and service offerings.
- Optimized cost–benefit with larger company economies of scale.
- Expanded knowledge and exposure to innovation.
- Longevity and sustainability of value propositions.
- B2B(2C) customers:
  - New or expanded experiences, processes, services, and offerings.
  - Improved revenue, higher margin, and profitability potential.

For Financing Customers, it is all about ROI through the ESU's value extraction from its tech-/problem-driven and market/demand-driven business models. This value extraction is through higher ROI from the ESU's combined intangibles (mainly IC) and DCF valuation that could lead to wealth creation and meeting its investments' internal rate of return (IRR).

For the Trade Sales Customer, as most acquisitions are strategic in nature, it is all about acquiring ESU's with IC capacities (mainly human capital), dynamic capabilities, innovation capabilities, new networks, and opportunities for growth and expansion. As a return on their investment, trade sales customer goals are:

- To acquire external knowledge and innovation from ESU's human capital, IC, and their dynamic capabilities;
- That could lead to new opportunities for development and growth;
- With long-term scaling and financial growth potential.

What is interesting from a lifecycle perspective, the value extraction *output* for the ESU becomes a value creation *input* for the acquiring company. Hence, the ESU's cycle of life continues and takes on a different form (incorporated and imbedded) into a larger company context. In a way, a successful exit through trade sales M&A is a complementary form of survival of the ESU in a larger context.

From a lifecycle perspective, the ESU's ultimate venture value extraction (output) through trade sales becomes a value-creating input for the acquiring company.

Financially, before an acquisition, the ESU value is calculated and speculated with little linkage to the ESUs book value. The first *real book value* of the ESU is recorded in the acquiring company's balance sheet on a *cost basis* per the *acquisition purchase price* for the first time, whether it is classified as an *acquisition*, *intangibles,* or *goodwill* or a combination thereof in the acquiring company's balance sheet.

For the ESU, the trade sale is the ultimate financial value extraction from its venture and a major wealth creation for its shareholders (i.e., founders, employees, and financing customers). This can only be done when the ESU creates strategic, market, intangible, and tangible value for trade sales customers. In return, the created wealth is then recycled by the ESU's ex-shareholders into the economy in various ways, such as launching and/or investing in other ESUs, creating a venture fund as a general partner, and/or participating in a venture fund as a limited partner. Ex-shareholders themselves may become future business angels (i.e., financing customers), advisors, and mentors for new and aspiring ESU founders. The vast majority of wealth extracted from an ESU is created at exit rather than from ongoing operating activities. Whereas ESU Founders' (financial) wealth is not a prerequisite prior to the creation of the ESU (Frid et al., 2016), wealth extraction from the ESU's exit is usually the founders' ultimate goal of value extraction.

Vast majority of wealth extraction from an ESU is during an exit event

To summarize and simplify, Fig. 5.10 exhibits the key questions that exit-driven business models must answer:

Intention and Timing to Exit (or not to Exit)

ESUs have the strategic option to exit early or exit later. The timing decision is based on ESU's internal conditions and external factors. Internally, ESUs with limited founder human capital capabilities, experience, and education may opt to exit earlier. Whereas founders with higher dynamic capabilities and experiences tend to be more patient to grow the business and exit later. Founder teams with intermediate capabilities are flexible and in between the two other capabilities (Arora et al., 2021). ESU's value proposition, its business model, organizational setup (i.e., limited social and relational versus a multi-sided platform), and technological and market developments impact exit decisions.

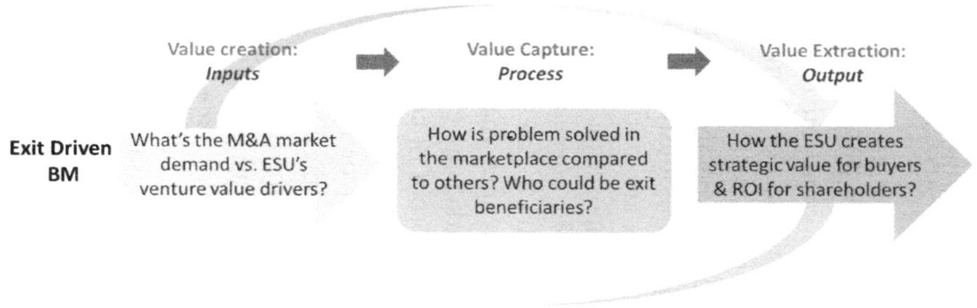

Fig. 5.10 Exit-driven business model development questions

External factors such as market and economic conditions may also affect the timing for exits. Market conditions are difficult to predict and determine. It may depend on the financing customers' goals and reactions to market conditions as well as on the trade sales customer's position and market opportunities. If the trade sales customer's own present and future opportunities are not attractive (i.e., its own markets are mature or declining), they may resort to acquisitions (Arora et al., 2021; Ball et al., 2011).

Timing exits may also be relative to general economic conditions (i.e., bull or bear markets), especially relative to ESU's industry, sector, technological advancements, and competitive landscape. Opportunities and challenges of market conditions for future exit scenarios can be mitigated if and when inputs for the previous two business model components (i.e., technology/problem-driven and market/demand-driven) are conducted appropriately and continuously. For instance, a significant number of high-tech-driven ESUs attempt to exit earlier through trade sales since they develop value propositions addressing three dimensions related to *potential synergies, credible alternatives, and uncertainty reduction* between the ESU and the trade sales customer (Mathisen et al., 2022). One of the biggest challenges that tech-driven ESUs have is finding markets or developing market-driven business models. Whereas, problem-driven ESUs must have proof of concept and market validation during mid-stage, before scaling and growing.

There are some exceptions to exit or not to exit strategies for ESUs from their inception or during later stages when they have survived and maintained a level of growth. One of the biggest exceptions is when ESUs intend to remain independent either as a small medium-sized enterprise (SME) or to become a corporation. *Intention* and *decision timing* are the two key words here. Intention could be from the earliest stages where the founders decide to remain independent from the start and not seek an exit. In this case, if founders would like to eventually seek external financing, they need to (a) be explicit about their strategy and (b) look for and attract the kind of financing customers who wish to remain with ESU and earn regular dividends as income. Consequences of this strategy are mainly related to finding and attracting such financing customers who would be difficult to find. The decision to remain independent could also be at later stages, where the M&A markets are not attractive enough due to market or economic conditions, or the ESU has a steady but lower growth potential or strategic intangible value. There are consequences, challenges, and opportunities for all cases.

Takeaways

- In the process of value creation, capture, and extraction, ESU founders develop their BMs in a portfolio of three sub-BMs that work together simultaneously.
- They are technology-/problem-driven, market/demand-driven, and exit-driven.
- High-tech ESUs develop tech-driven BMs and non-tech ESUs develop problem-driven BMs from the early stages of development through later stages, with the goal of IC value capture and firm value extraction (i.e., high valuation).
- Both types of ESUs begin developing demand/market-driven business models to identify diverse markets and paying customers for their value proposition.
- As BMs are value driven not product driven, revenue models follow that same value logic.
- Customer pricing models have to be customer centric, demand and value driven. Two examples include dynamic (smart) pricing and value-based pricing.
- ESU exit-driven business models are intentional, strategic, and planned throughout the ESU lifecycles.
- ESU founders treat their projects as ***products*** for sale in a future trade sale event.
- Financial harvests through exits are the main wealth (value) extraction for ESU founders, financing customers, and other shareholders. They are also important innovation sources for industry and the economy in general.
- Early active and ongoing preparation with documentation and disclosures is an essential part of an efficient and effective exit value capture process.
- Exit-driven BMs have different corresponding value extraction for ESU financial stakeholders, who are the three customers and other ESU shareholders.
- From a lifecycle perspective, ESU's ultimate venture value extraction (output) through trade sales becomes a value-creating input for the acquiring company.
- The vast majority of wealth extraction from an ESU is during an exit event.

- Intention and timing of exits depend on internal and external factors.

5.8 3D BMs Combined and Simplified: How Does It Work?

Combined, the three business models converge three-dimensionally, overlapping each other to form a pattern of checks and balances. The tech/problem-driven business model focuses on the actual problem that needs to be solved, whether technological, social, environmental, business, or a mix. This leads to the problem–solution fit where its people as human capital establishes the biggest intangible assets of an ESU. People (initially founders, later the ESU team) are the main drivers and mediators of value creation, capture, and extraction. The main value extraction is through intangible assets orchestration, mainly through intellectual capital: human, organizational (and technological), social, and relational.

Parallel to the above development, a new dimension arises when market/demand-driven business models emerge. In this case, after extensive studies and analysis, a true problem–solution-market fit must be aligned addressing a real need in the marketplace that customers are willing to pay. This market consists of three types of customers: paying, financing, and (eventually) trade sales. The market-driven business model itself must be viable as the second step of the ESU value creation process. When executed appropriately, this will lead to value capture through ESU's value proposition as proof of concept, go-to-market, scale, and growth strategies, where the ultimate value extraction is monetization. This includes revenue, margin, profitability (i.e., EBIDTA), and free cash flow generation from operating activities.

Yet, the ultimate goal of the ESU founders is to treat the ESU as a product for eventual sale in the M&A markets. To do this, they would need to add the third dimension which is the exit-driven business model. This BM dimension combines the other two BM dimensions to position the ESU in the M&A marketplace from the earlier mid stages. All exit-driven business model value creation, capture, and extraction elements are strategic and need to be planned as part of or parallel to the other two business model dimensions. The ultimate value extraction goal for this is to create ESU's venture value and valuation for all its financial

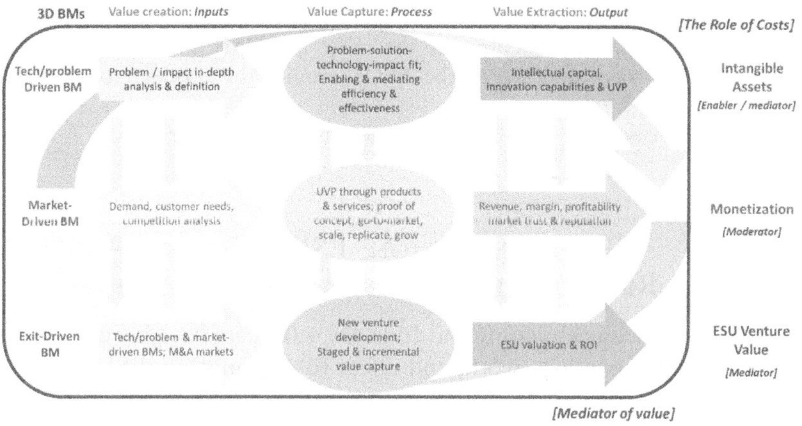

Fig. 5.11 3D business model iterative process

stakeholders. For the trade sales customer, it must create strategic value with a long-term horizon. Whereas for the ESU shareholders, it should create wealth for the founders and employees, and a substantial ROI for investors (i.e., financing customers). It is important to note that although the value creation, capture, and extraction follows an input, process, and output logic, the actual experimentation, trial and error, recalibration, and reconfiguration are iterative. The value logic may sound linear (input-process-output), but the process itself is iterative.

Figure 5.11 combines the three business models and illustrates how they work parallel to each other in a cohesive and comprehensive way:

Takeaways

- Combined, the three business models join three-dimensionally, overlapping each other to form a pattern of checks and balances.
- They complement each other in value creation, capture, and extraction.
- Tech/problem-driven BMs focus on IC capabilities and the main driver.
- Demand/market-driven BMs develop attractive value propositions for monetization purposes.

- Exit-driven BMs incorporate the other two BMs into an attractive value proposition where the ESU becomes the product for trade sales.
- In all cases, the 3D BM development is an iterative process.

5.9 Conclusion: ESU Luck is a Residue of Business Model Design

With the knowledge economy and Industry 4.0, there have been dramatic shifts in the way we live, work, and relate to one another. ESU business models have become a value proposition platform, a culmination of flexibility, interconnectedness, matchmaking, trust building, and a network of social contracts, with multiple offerings through a mix of products, services, information sharing, and blogs, that are designed to be scalable and growth oriented. This is a move away from pure and traditional new product development and marketing models. Along with the onset of the knowledge economy, many parallel economic models have emerged, such as the experience economy, platform economy, sharing economy, and circular economy to name a few.

Availability of information and knowledge, powered by the advancement of the internet, cloud computing and storage, AI, and algorithms have made the way we live, work, and relate seem easier and to some extent linear. If we want something, we can easily get it within minutes. With a couple of internet searches, we can locate an old friend, shop for products and services, and book our holidays from anywhere.

This *easiness*, however, is deceiving especially when it comes to developing ESUs with scalable and growth-oriented business models. In fact, Industry 4.0 integrated economic models have added multiple layers of *complexity* that all ESU founders must tackle in order to build successful businesses. Yet, I find that many ESU founders (especially novices) pursue their ideas in a linear fashion, thinking that by creating a website (for instance) they can easily convince people *to buy* what they are offering. Majority are either not prepared to take on the challenge or do not understand the task at hand and the hard work required to get things done.

Anecdotally people talk about the role luck plays in success or failure. This begs the question, what role does *luck* play in ESU development and success? What does luck have to do with success? Is it luck or hard work (or the lack of it in both cases) that leads to success (or failure)? Scientifically, luck is *an elusive theoretical concept* that leads to *unexpected performance* (Liechti, & Loderer, 2014; Ma, 2002). *Pure luck* is something that is external or exogenous to a company, that may give it a competitive advantage, versus *prepared luck* that a firm proactively defines its business model based on market and economic, trends, innovation and tech developments, and competitive environment (Ma, 2002). Serial entrepreneurs rank luck last in importance and VCs attribute it to skill (or the lack of it), which impacts success (or failure) (Gompers et al., 2006; Liechti, & Loderer, 2014; Zunino et al., 2022).

Luck, in other words, is an unexpected event. It could be a *good luck event* or a *bad luck event*. What matters is how well is the ESU prepared in case of a luck event, to take advantage of a good luck event, and to be ready for or deal with a bad luck event (Collins & Hansen, 2011). Therefore, preparedness is key to make one's own luck work.

ESU luck follows the same luck event-response logic. A well-designed and developed 3D business model addresses most of the essentials. This includes defining the problem extensively, understanding market demand and customer needs to build the problem–solution fit where technology plays a mediating role, and finally developing the ESU as a product for future sale in trade sales M&A markets. Contingent to this is being close to and fully understanding how its three main customers' (i.e., paying, financing, and trade sales) mindset is working. With this 3D business model design mindset ESUs can create their own luck where they are better attuned to gain competitive advantage with good luck events and can overcome undesirable bad luck events.

Takeaways

- The knowledge economy and Industry 4.0 have created many new business opportunities and dramatic shifts in the way we live, work, and relate.
- Although the advances of the internet and technology have made many things easier to achieve, buy and sell, and connect, it has also added multiple layers of complexity that ESU founders must tackle unlike in the past.
- Some anecdotes suggest that luck plays a key role in ESU success or failure.

- Research has shown that the exogeneous pure luck can be either advantageous or not advantageous for ESUs, depending on how ESUs are prepared for luck.
- Serial entrepreneurs rank luck last in importance and VCs attribute it to skill (or the lack of it), which impacts success (or failure).
- Luck as an unexpected event could be a good luck event or a bad luck event.
- How ESU founders respond to these events depends on how well-prepared they are by design.
- Therefore, ESU's lucky event responses very much depend on their 3D BM design.
- This is contingent to fully understanding and being close to its triple customers.

Bibliography

Amit, R., & Zott, C. (2012). Creating value through business model innovation. MIT Sloan management Review, 53(3), 40–50.

Amit R. & Zott C. (2021). Business Model Innovation Strategy. John Wiley & Sons.

Alvarez, S. A. & Barney, J. B. (2005). How do entrepreneurs organize firms under conditions of uncertainty? *Journal of Management*, *31*(5), 776–793.

Ancillai, C., Sabatini, A., Gatti, M., & Perna, A. (2023). Digital technology and business model innovation: A systematic literature review and future research agenda. *Technological Forecasting and Social Change*, *188*, 122307. https://doi.org/10.1016/j.techfore.2022.122307

Anderson, J. C., Narus, J. A., & van Rossum, W. (2006). Customer value propositions in business markets. *Harvard Business Review*.

Arora, A., Fosfuri, A., & Rønde, T. (2021). Waiting for the payday? The market for startups and the timing of entrepreneurial exit. *Management Science*, *67*(3), 1453–1467. https://doi.org/10.1287/mnsc.2020.3627

Bailetti, T. (2012). Technology entrepreneurship: Overview, definition, and distinctive aspects. Technology innovation management review. 5–12.

Ball, E., Chiu, H. H., & Smith, R. (2011). Can VCs time the market? An analysis of exit choice for venture-backed firms. *Review of Financial Studies*, *24*(9), 3105–3138. https://doi.org/10.1093/rfs/hhr042

Banal-Estañol, A., Macho-Stadler, I., Nieto-Postigo, J., & Pérez-Castrillo, D. (2023). Early individual stakeholders, first venture capital investment, and exit in the UK startup ecosystem. *Journal of Corporate Finance*, *80*, 102420. https://doi.org/10.1016/j.jcorpfin.2023.102420

Barney, J. B. (1991). Firm resources and sustained competitive advantage. *Journal of Management*, *17*(1), 99–120.

Battisti, S., Agarwal, N., & Brem, A. (2022). Creating new tech entrepreneurs with digital platforms: Meta-organizations for shared value in data-driven retail ecosystems. *Technological Forecasting and Social Change*, *175*, 121392. https://doi.org/10.1016/j.techfore.2021.121392

Beattie, V., & Smith, S. J. (2013). Value creation and business models: Refocusing the intellectual capital debate. *The British Accounting Review*, *45*(4), 243–254. https://doi.org/10.1016/j.bar.2013.06.001

Bock, A. J., & George, G. (2017). *The business model book*: Design, build and adapt business ideas that drive business growth. Pearson UK.

Bohan, S., Tippmann, E., Levie, J., Igoe, J., & Bowers, B. (2024). What is scaling? *Journal of Business Venturing*, *39*(1), 106355. https://doi.org/101016/j.jbusvent.2023.106355

Bojovic, N., Genet, C., & Sabatier, V. (2018). Learning, signaling, and convincing: The role of experimentation in the business modeling process. *Long Range Planning*, *51*(1), 141–157. https://doi.org/10.1016/j.lrp.2017.09.001

Burnell, D., Stevenson, R., & Fisher, G. (2023). Early-stage business model experimentation and pivoting. *Journal of Business Venturing*, *38*(4), 106314. https://doi.org/10.1016/j.jbusvent.2023.106314

Budde, L., Hänggi, R., Laglia, L., & Friedli, T. (2024). Leading the transition to multi-sided platforms (MSPs) in a B2B context—The case of a recycling SME. *Industrial Marketing Management*, *116*, 106–119. https://doi.org/10.1016/j.indmarman.2023.12.002

Burmaoglu, S., Sartenaer, O., & Porter, A. (2019). Conceptual definition of technology emergence: A long journey from philosophy of science to science policy. *Technology in Society*, *59*, 101126. https://doi.org/10.1016/j.techsoc.2019.04.002

Carroll, L. (2017). A Comprehensive Definition of technology from an ethological perspective. *Social Sciences*, *6*(4), 126. https://doi.org/10.3390/socsci6040126

Cavallo, A., Cosenz, F., & Noto, G. (2024). Business model scaling and growth hacking in digital entrepreneurship. *Journal of Small Business Management*, *62*(4), 2058–2085. https://doi.org/10.1080/00472778.2023.2195463

CBInsights. (2022, December 1). The top 12 reasons Startups fail. CBInsights Research. https://www.cbinsights.com/research/report/startup-failure-reasons-top/

Chammassian, R.G. (2016). *Towards a new cost paradigm for technology startup entrepreneurs* (Doctoral Dissertation). Grenoble Ecole de Management, Grenoble, France.

Chammassian, R. G., & Sabatier, V. (2020). The role of costs in business model design for early-stage technology startups. *Technological Forecasting and Social Change*, *157*, 120090. https://doi.org/10.1016/j.techfore.2020.120090
Chenhall, R. H. (2003). Management control systems design within its organizational context: Findings from contingency-based research and directions for the future. Accounting, *Organizations and Society*, 28(2–3), 127–168.
Chesbrough, H. (2007). Business model innovation: It's not just about technology anymore. *Strategy & Leadership*, *35*(6), 12–17. https://doi.org/10.1108/10878570710833714
Chesbrough, H. (2010). Business Model Innovation: Opportunities and Barriers. *Long Range Planning*, *43*(2–3), 354–363. https://doi.org/10.1016/j.lrp.2009.07.010
Cheung, W. C., Simchi-Levi, D., & Wang, H. (2017). Dynamic pricing and demand learning with limited price experimentation. *Operations Research*, *65*(6), 1722-1731. https://doi.org/10.1287/opre.2017.1629
Clausen, T. H., & Rasmussen, E. (2013). Parallel business models and the innovativeness of research-based spin-off ventures. *The Journal of Technology Transfer*, *38*(6), 836–849. Retrieved from https://doi.org/10.1007/s10961-012-9294-3
Coad, A., Frankish, J., Roberts, R. G., & Storey, D. J. (2013). Growth paths and survival chances: An application of Gambler's Ruin theory. *Journal of Business Venturing*, *28*(5), 615–632. https://doi.org/10.1016/j.jbusvent.2012.06.002
Coad, A., & Reid, A., (2012). *The role of technology and technology-based firms in economic development:* Rethinking innovation and enterprise policy in Scotland. Technopolis Group, Scotland.
Collins, J., & Hansen, M. T. (2011). Great by choice: Uncertainty, Chaos and Luck-Why some thrive despite them all. Random House.
Cooper, J. (2000). Turning knowledge into value. *CMA Management*, *74*(8), 22–26.
Conner, K. R. (1991). A historical comparison of resource-based theory and five schools of thought within industrial organization economics: Do we have a new theory of the firm? *Journal of Management*, *17*(1), 121–154.
DaSilva, C. M., & Trkman, P. (2014). Business model: What it is and what it is not. *Long Range Planning*, *47*(6), 379–389. https://doi.org/10.1016/j.lrp.2013.08.004
Datar, S.M., & Rajan, M.V. (2021). *Horngren's cost accounting: A managerial emphasis* (17th.ed. Global edition). New York: Pearson
Demil, B., & Lecocq, X. (2010). Business model evolution: In search of dynamic consistency. *Long Range Planning*, *43*(2–3), 227–246. https://doi.org/10.1016/j.lrp.2010.02.004

Den Boer, A. V. (2015). Dynamic pricing and learning: Historical origins, current research, and new directions. *Surveys in Operations Research and Management Science*, *20*(1), 1–18. https://doi.org/10.1016/j.sorms.2015.03.001

Den Boer, A. V., & Keskin, N. B. (2022). Dynamic pricing with demand learning and reference effects. *Management Science*, *68*(10), 7112–7130. https://doi.org/10.1287/mnsc.2021.4234

DeTienne, D. R. (2010). Entrepreneurial exit as a critical component of the entrepreneurial process: Theoretical development. *Journal of Business Venturing*, *25*(2), 203–215. https://doi.org/10.1016/j.jbusvent.2008.05.004

DeTienne, D. R., McKelvie, A., & Chandler, G. N. (2015). Making sense of entrepreneurial exit strategies: A typology and test. *Journal of Business Venturing*, *30*(2), 255–272. https://doi.org/10.1016/j.jbusvent.2014.07.007

Doganova, L., & Eyquem-Renault, M. (2009). What do business models do? *Research Policy*, *38*(10), 1559–1570. https://doi.org/10.1016/j.respol.2009.08.002

Drucker, P. (1969). The age of discontinuity: Guidelines to our changing society. New York: Harper and Row.

Duxbury, D. (2012). Sunk costs and sunk benefits: A re-examination of re-investment decisions. *The British Accounting Review*, *44*(3), 144–156. https://doi.org/10.1016/j.bar.2012.07.004

Eisenmann, T. R. (2020). Determinants of early-stage startup performance: Survey results. *Harvard Business School.* 21–057, 1–63. https://doi.org/10.2139/ssrn.3725023. Entrepreneurial management working paper.

Fauchart, E., & Gruber, M. (2011). Darwinians, communitarians, and missionaries: The role of founder identity in entrepreneurship. *Academy of Management Journal*, *54*(5), 935–957. https://doi.org/10.5465/amj.2009.0211

Fjeldstad, Ø. D., & Snow, C. C. (2018). Business models and organization design. *Long Range Planning*, *51*(1), 32–39. https://doi.org/10.1016/j.lrp.2017.07.008

Frid, C. J., Wyman, D. M., & Coffey, B. (2016). Effects of wealth inequality on entrepreneurship. *Small Business Economics*, *47*(4), 895–920. https://doi.org/10.1007/s11187-016-9742-9

Gawer, A., & Cusumano, M. A. (2008). How companies become platform leaders. *MIT Sloan Management Review*, *49*(2), 27–35.

Gawer, A., & Cusumano, M. A. (2014). Industry platforms and ecosystem innovation. *Journal of Product Innovation Management*, *31*(3), 417–433. https://doi.org/10.1111/jpim.12105

George, G., & Bock, A. J. (2011). The business model in practice and its implications for entrepreneurship research. *Entrepreneurship Theory and Practice*, *35*(1), 83–111. https://doi.org/10.1111/j.1540-6520.2010.00424.x

Geroski, P. A., Mata, J., & Portugal, P. (2009). Founding conditions and the survival of new firms. *Strategic Management Journal*, *31*(5), 510–529. https://doi.org/10.1002/smj.823

Ghezzi, A. (2020). How entrepreneurs make sense of lean startup approaches: Business models as cognitive lenses to generate fast and frugal heuristics. *Technological Forecasting and Social Change*, *161*, 120324. https://doi.org/10.1016/j.techfore.2020.120324

Giones, F., & Brem, A. (2017). Digital technology entrepreneurship: A definition and research agenda. *Technology innovation management review*, *7*(5), 44–51. http://timreview.ca/article/1076

Gompers, P., Kovner, A., Lerner, J., & Scharfstein, D. (2006). *Skill versus. Luck in entrepreneurship and venture capital: Evidence from serial entrepreneurs.* National Bureau of economic research. Working paper 12592. https://doi.org/10.3386/w12592

Gompers, P., Kovner, A., Lerner, J., & Scharfstein, D. (2006). *Skill vs. Luck in entrepreneurship and venture capital: Evidence from serial entrepreneurs.* National Bureau of economic research. Working paper 12592. https://doi.org/10.3386/w12592

Graña-Alvarez, R., Gomez-Conde, J., Lopez-Valeiras, E., & González-Loureiro, M. (2024). Management control systems, business financial literacy and financial leverage in business-incubated start-ups. *The British Accounting Review*, 101427. https://doi.org/10.1016/j.bar.2024.101427

Grewal, D., Roggeveen, A. L., Compeau, L. D., & Levy, M. (2012). Retail value-based pricing strategies: New times, new technologies, new consumers. *Journal of Retailing*, *88*(1), 1–6. https://doi.org/10.1016/j.jretai.2011.12.001

Gruber, M. (2010). Getting to plan B: Breaking through to a better business model. *The Academy of Management Perspectives*, *24*(3), 93–96.

Guo, H., Wang, C., Su, Z., & Wang, D. (2020). Technology push or market pull? Strategic orientation in business model design and digital start-up performance. *Journal of Product Innovation Management*, *37*(4), 352–372. https://doi.org/10.1111/jpim.12526

Habtay, S. R. (2012). A firm-level analysis on the relative difference between technology-driven and market-driven disruptive business model innovations. *Creativity and Innovation Management*, *21*(3), 290–303. https://doi.org/10.1111/j.1467-8691.2012.00628.x

Hahn, G. J. (2019). Industry 4.0: A supply chain innovation perspective. *International Journal of Production Research*, *58*(5) 1425–1441. https://doi.org/10.1080/00207543.2019.1641642

Hagiu, A., & Wright, J. (2015). Multi-sided platforms. *International Journal of Industrial Organization*, *43*, 162–174. https://doi.org/10.1016/j.ijindorg.2015.03.003

Haskel, J., & Westlake, S. (2018). *Capitalism without capital: The Rise of the Intangible Economy*. Princeton University Press.

He, J., & Ortiz, J. (2021). Sustainable business modeling: The need for innovative design thinking. *Journal of Cleaner Production*, *298*, 126751. https://doi.org/10.1016/j.jclepro.2021.126751

Hinterhuber, A. (2004). Towards value-based pricing—An integrative framework for decision making. *Industrial Marketing Management*, *33*(8), 765–778. https://doi.org/10.1016/j.indmarman.2003.10.006

Hunt, E. (2024). *483 startup failure post-mortems*. CB Insights Research. https://www.cbinsights.com/research/startup-failure-post-mortem/

Hunt, R. A., Townsend, D. M., Lerner, D. A., & Brownell, K. M. (2024). Pivot, persist or perish? Knowledge problems and the extraordinarily tight boundary conditions of entrepreneurs as scientists. *Journal of Business Venturing Insights*, *21*, e00459. https://doi.org/10.1016/j.jbvi.2024.e00459

Jansen, J. J. P., Heavey, C., Mom, T. J. M., Simsek, Z., & Zahra, S. A. (2023). Scaling-up: Building, leading and sustaining rapid growth over Time. *Journal of Management Studies*, *60*(3), 581–604. https://doi.org/10.1111/joms.12910

Jiang, H., & Murmann, J. P. (2023). Functional knowledge versus strategic knowledge: What type of knowledge matters most for the long-term performance of startups. *Management and Organization Review*, *19*(3), 417–461. https://doi.org/10.1017/mor.2021.77

Kalaignanam, K., Kushwaha, T., & Rajavi, K. (2018). How does web personalization create value for online retailers? Lower cash flow volatility or enhanced cash flows. *Journal of Retailing*, *94*(3), 265–279. https://doi.org/10.1016/j.jretai.2018.05.001

Karami, M., & Read, S. (2021). Co-creative entrepreneurship. *Journal of Business Venturing*, *36*(106125), 1–16. https://doi.org/10.1016/j.jbusvent.2021.106125

Kato, M., & Honjo, Y. (2015). Entrepreneurial human capital and the survival of new firms in high- and low-tech sectors. *Journal of Evolutionary Economics*, *25*(5), 925–957. https://doi.org/10.1007/s00191-015-0427-3

Kesting, P., & Günzel-Jensen, F. (2015). SMEs and new ventures need business model sophistication. *Business Horizons*, *58*(3), 285–293. https://doi.org/10.1016/j.bushor.2015.01.002

Konya-Baumbach, E., Schuhmacher, M. C., Kuester, S., & Kuharev, V. (2019). Making a first impression as a start-up: Strategies to overcome low initial trust perceptions in digital innovation adoption. *International Journal of Research in Marketing*, *36*(3), 385–399. https://doi.org/10.1016/j.ijresmar.2019.01.008

Kretschmer, T., Leiponen, A., Schilling, M., & Vasudeva, G. (2022). Platform ecosystems as meta-organizations: Implications for platform strategies. *Strategic Management Journal*, *43*(3), 405–424. https://doi.org/10.1002/smj.3250

Leach, C., & Melicher, R. (2021). *Entrepreneurial finance* (7th ed.). Cengage.

Lemley, M. A., & McCreary, A. (2021). Exit strategy. *Boston University Law Review*, *101*, 1.

Li, X., Nosheen, S., Haq, N. U., & Gao, X. (2021). Value creation during fourth industrial revolution: Use of intellectual capital by most innovative companies of the world. *Technological Forecasting and Social Change*, *163*, 120479. https://doi.org/10.1016/j.techfore.2020.120479

Liechti, D., & Loderer, C. (2014). Luck and entrepreneurial success. *Swiss Finance Institute*, *14–51*, 1–59. https://doi.org/10.2139/ssrn.2476839

Lin, K. Y. (2006). Dynamic pricing with real-time demand learning. *European Journal of Operational Research*, *174*(1), 522–538. https://doi.org/10.1016/j.ejor.2005.01.041

Lin, Y., & Wu, L.-Y. (2014). Exploring the role of dynamic capabilities in firm performance under the resource-based view framework. *Journal of Business Research*, *67*(3), 407–413. https://doi.org/10.1016/j.jbusres.2012.12.019

Ma, H. (2002). Competitive advantage: What's luck got to do with it? *Management Decision*, *40*(6), 525–536. https://doi.org/10.1108/00251740210433927

Magretta, J. (2002). Why business models matter. *Harvard Business Review*, *80*(5), 86–92.

Mañez, J. A., & Love, J. H. (2020). Quantifying sunk costs and learning effects in R&D persistence. *Research Policy*, *49*(7), 104004. https://doi.org/10.1016/j.respol.2020.104004

Mathisen, M. T., Shankar, R. K., Widding, Ø., Rasmussen, E., & McKelvie, A. (2022). Enablers of exit through trade sale: The case of early-stage research-based spin-offs. *Small Business Economics*, *59*(2), 521–535. https://doi.org/10.1007/s11187-021-00484-7

McDonald, R. M., & Eisenhardt, K. M. (2020). Parallel play: Startups, Nascent markets, and effective business-model design. *Administrative Science Quarterly*, *65*(2), 483–523. https://doi.org/10.1177/0001839219852349

McGrath, R. G. (2010). Business models: A discovery driven approach. *Long Range Planning*, *43*(2–3), 247–261. https://doi.org/10.1016/j.lrp.2009.07.005

McMullen, J. S., & Dimov, D. (2013). Time and the entrepreneurial Journey: The problems and promise of studying entrepreneurship as a Process. *Journal of Management Studies*, *50*(8), 1481–1512. https://doi.org/10.1111/joms.12049

Montanaro, B., Cavallo, A., Giudici, G., & Ghezzi, A. (2022). Determinants of the exit value in European venture capital-backed technology startups. *Competitiveness Review: An International Business Journal*, *32*(7), 62–84. https://doi.org/10.1108/CR-03-2021-0032

Muzellec, L., Ronteau, S., & Lambkin, M. (2015). Two-sided Internet platforms: A business model lifecycle perspective. *Industrial Marketing Management*, *45*, 139–150. https://doi.org/10.1016/j.indmarman.2015.02.012

Nagle, T. T., & Müller, G. (2018). *The strategy and tactics of pricing:* A guide to growing more profitably (6th ed.). Routledge.

Nigro, C. A., & Stahl, J. R. (2021). Venture capital-backed firms, unavoidable value-destroying trade sales, and fair value protections. *European Business Organization Law Review*, *22*(1), 39–86. https://doi.org/10.1007/s40804-020-00196-7

OECD. (1996). *The knowledge-based economy*. Paris: OECD.

Pisoni, A., & Onetti, A. (2018). When startups exit: Comparing strategies in Europe and the USA. *Journal of Business Strategy*, *39*(3), 26–33. https://doi.org/10.1108/JBS-02-2017-0022

Pavlou, P. A., & Sawy, O. a. E. (2011). Understanding the elusive black box of dynamic capabilities. *Decision Sciences*, *42*(1), 239–273. https://doi.org/10.1111/j.1540-5915.2010.00287.x

Phelps, R., Adams, R., & Bessant, J. (2007). Life cycles of growing organizations: A review with implications for knowledge and learning. *International Journal of Management Reviews*, *9*(1), 1–30. https://doi.org/10.1111/j.1468-2370.2007.00200.x

Rahman, K. S., & Thelen, K. (2019). The rise of the platform business model and the transformation of twenty-first-century capitalism. *Politics & Society*, *47*(2), 177–204. https://doi.org/10.1177/0032329219838932

Raja, J. Z., Frandsen, T., Kowalkowski, C., & Jarmatz, M. (2020). Learning to discover value: Value-based pricing and selling capabilities for services and solutions. *Journal of Business Research*, *114*, 142–159. https://doi.org/10.1016/j.jbusres.2020.03.026

Ries, E. (2011). The lean startup: How today's entrepreneurs use continuous innovation to create radically successful businesses. Crown Publishing, New York.

Ritter, M., & Schanz, H. (2019). The sharing economy: A comprehensive business model framework. *Journal of Cleaner Production*, *213*, 320–331. https://doi.org/10.1016/j.jclepro.2018.12.154

Rohn, D., Bican, P. M., Brem, A., Kraus, S., & Clauss, T. (2021). Digital platform-based business models—An exploration of critical success factors. *Journal of Engineering and Technology Management*, *60*, 101625. https://doi.org/10.1016/j.jengtecman.2021.101625

Sarasvathy, S. D. (2001). Causation and effectuation: Toward a theoretical shift from economic inevitability to entrepreneurial contingency. *Academy of Management Review*, *26*(2), 243–263.
Sarasvathy, S. D. (2004). Making it happen: Beyond theories of the firm to theories of firm design. *Entrepreneurship Theory and Practice*, *28*(6), 519–531.
Schwab, K. (2016). *The fourth industrial revolution*: What it means, how to respond. *The World Economic Forum*. https://www.weforum.org/agenda/2016/01/the-fourth-industrial-revolution-what-it-means-and-how-to-respond/
Smith, T. (2012). *Pricing strategy*: Setting price levels, managing price discounts, & establishing price structures. South-Western Cengage Learning
Stewart, T. A. (1997, 2010). *Intellectual capital*: The new wealth of organization. Crown Currency.
Sutherland, W., & Jarrahi, M. H. (2018). The sharing economy and digital platforms: A review and research agenda. *International Journal of Information Management*, *43*, 328–341. https://doi.org/10.1016/j.ijinfomgt.2018.07.004
Teece, D. J. (2009). Dynamic capabilities and strategic management: Organizing for innovation and growth. New York, NY: Oxford University Press.
Teece, D. J. (2011). Dynamic capabilities: A framework for profitability. *Ivey Business Journal*, *18*(7), 509–533.
Teece, D. J. (2012). Dynamic capabilities: Routines versus entrepreneurial action. *Journal of Management Studies*, *49*(8), 1395–1401. https://doi.org/10.1111/j.1467-6486.2012.01080.x
Teece, D. J. (2014). The foundations of enterprise performance: Dynamic and ordinary capabilities in an (economic) theory of firms. *Academy of Management Perspectives*, *28*(4), 328–352. https://doi.org/10.5465/amp.2013.0116
Tzabbar, D., & Margolis, J. (2017). Beyond the startup stage: The founding team's human capital, new venture's stage of life, founder–CEO duality, and breakthrough innovation. *Organization Science*, *28*(5), 857–872. https://doi.org/10.1287/orsc.2017.1152
Van Alstyne, M., & Parker, G. (2017). Platform business: From resources to relationships. *NIM Marketing Intelligence Review*, *9*(1), 24–29. https://doi.org/10.1515/gfkmir-2017-0004
Van Alstyne, M. W. V., Parker, G. G., & Choudary, S. P. (2016). Pipelines, platforms, and the new rules of strategy. *Harvard Business Review*, 1–9.
Van de Ven, A. H., Ganco, M., & Hinings, C. R. (Bob). (2013). Returning to the frontier of contingency theory of organizational and institutional designs. *The Academy of Management Annals*, *7*(1), 393–440. https://doi.org/10.1080/19416520.2013.774981

Van Le, H., & Suh, M. (2019). Changing trends in internet startup value propositions, from the perspective of the customer. *Technological Forecasting and Social Change*, *146*, 853–864. https://doi.org/10.1016/j.techfore.2018.06.021

Van Meeteren, M., Trincado-Munoz, F., Rubin, T. H., & Vorley, T. (2022). Rethinking the digital transformation in knowledge-intensive services: A technology space analysis. *Technological Forecasting and Social Change*, *179*, 121631. https://doi.org/10.1016/j.techfore.2022.121631

Velu, C. (2015). Business model innovation and third-party alliance on the survival of new firms. *Technovation*, *35*, 1–11. https://doi.org/10.1016/j.technovation.2014.09.007

Wernerfelt, B. (1984). A resource-based view of the firm. *Strategic Management Journal*, *5*(2), 171–180.

Waßenhoven, A., Rennings, M., Laibach, N., & Bröring, S. (2023). What constitutes a "Key Enabling Technology" for transition processes: Insights from the bioeconomy's technological landscape. *Technological Forecasting and Social Change*, *197*, 122873. https://doi.org/10.1016/j.techfore.2023.122873

Wennberg, K., & DeTienne, D. R. (2014). What do we really mean when we talk about 'exit'? A critical review of research on entrepreneurial exit. *International Small Business Journal: Researching Entrepreneurship*, *32*(1), 4–16. https://doi.org/10.1177/0266242613517126

You, X. (2022). Applying design thinking for business model innovation. *Journal of Innovation and Entrepreneurship*, *11*(1), 59. https://doi.org/10.1186/s13731-022-00251-2

Yusuf, J.-E. (2012). A tale of two exits: Nascent entrepreneur learning activities and disengagement from start-up. *Small Business Economics*, *39*(3), 783–799. https://doi.org/10.1007/s11187-011-9361-4

Zaheer, H., Breyer, Y., Dumay, J., & Enjeti, M. (2022). The entrepreneurial journeys of digsital start-up founders. *Technological Forecasting & Social Change*, *179*(121638), 1–27. https://doi.org/10.1016/j.techfore.2022.121638

Zott, C., & Amit, R. (2010). Business model design: An activity system perspective. *Long Range Planning*, *43*(2–3), 216–226. https://doi.org/10.1016/j.lrp.2009.07.004

Zunino, D., Dushnitsky, G., & Van Praag, M. (2022). How do investors evaluate past entrepreneurial failure? unpacking failure due to lack of skill versus bad luck. *Academy of Management Journal*, *65*(4), 1083–1109. https://doi.org/10.5465/amj.2018.0579

Index

0–9
2-20 model, 158
24–48-hour crisis, 65
80-20 rule, 58, 141, 234

A
abilities, 120
ability to exploit, 242
absorptive capacity, 232
academic researcher(s), 199
acceleration, 14
acceleration program, 130
accelerator program, 130
accelerators, 63, 66, 97, 128, 135, 157, 165, 249
access to networks, 128
accountability, 38, 64, 96
accountable, 204
accounted value, 3, 41
accounting, 2
achievements, 26
acqui hiring, 226
acqui-hiring talent, 176
acquire, 41
acquiring company, 200
acquisition(s), 178, 326
acquisition strategies, 287
active investors, 254
active users, 214
activity-based costing, 6
adaptability, 26, 70
adaptations, 22
adaptive platform, 283
advancements in technologies, 152
advice, 31, 125
advise, 63
advisors, 31, 95
advisory board(s), 31, 95
Advisory Services Agreement, 96
advisory shares, 31
afford, 3
affordability, 122
affordable, 196
affordable loss, 58
agile, 63

R. G. Chammassian, *Costs, Value, and the Entrepreneurial Venture Journey*, Palgrave Studies in Accounting and Finance Practice,
https://doi.org/10.1007/978-3-031-86216-8

agile performance management, 237
agility, 65
agricultural products, 57
agricultural terms, 59
alleviating risks, 283
allowances, 83
Alphabet Series B, C, D, E, 59, 173
alternative funding mechanism, 40
amortize, 42
annual recurring revenue (ARR), 122, 274
antenarrative, 29
Anthony, R.N., 6
app-based, 153
application domains, 13, 70, 198, 279
arbitration, 106
artificial intelligence (AI), 2, 12, 70, 130, 214, 278
asset
  long-term, 2
assign, 40
assigned value, 41
assumptions, 22, 107
attitude, 225
attracting investors, 22
attract knowledgeable people, 31
audience(s), 63, 131
audit, 321
audit trail, 320
authenticity, 20, 214
automated processes, 58, 141
available, 196
avoid, 101

B

B2B2B2C, 144
background, 199
background diversity, 224
bad luck event, 333
balanced scorecard, 237
balance sheet, 2, 82, 204
bank, 44
barter, 285
bear market, 328
becoming an entrepreneur, 71
behavioral dimension, 6
beneficiaries, 305
benefit(s), 137, 204
big data, 20, 42, 196, 203, 214
big data analytics, 279
biotech, 156
blindness to reality, 314
blind trust, 239
blockchain, 12, 70, 196, 214, 274, 279
blogs, 13
book value, 39, 41
Bootstrapping, 63, 77
brand recognition, 203
brand reputation, 203
breakdown, 216
breakeven, 6
breaking even (BE), 128
build, 67, 173
build consensus, 128
building relationships, 63
building(s), 41, 63
bull market, 328
bundling, 106
burden, 136
  conversion, 136
  debt, 136
business angels (BA), 56, 58, 109, 120, 128, 150, 157
Business Development Officer (BDO), 172
business failure, 224
business model, 129
business model design, 199
business models (BMs), 13, 119, 282, 283
  exit-driven, 273
  market/demand-driven, 273

product-driven, 273
technology/problem-driven, 273
value driven, 273
business model scaling, 286
business plans, 162
business problem, 119
business setup costs, 100
initial inventory, 101
marketing related costs, 101
office space, 100
people costs, 101
technology infrastructure setup, 101
business-to-business (B2B), 74, 122, 144, 273
business to consumer (B2C), 74, 144, 273
buyer be aware, 321
buying trigger point, 93

C

cancellations, 106
capacity, 125
capacity to build networks, 242
capital, 42
capital asset, 2, 203
capital expenditures (CapEx), 143, 144
capitalization, 82
capitalization (cap) tables, 135
Capitalization Table. *See* cap tables
cap tables, 82, 90, 157
capture, 120, 197, 201
captured value, 2
carried interest, 158
cash, 1, 22, 44
financing, 44
investing, 44
operating, 44
cash breakeven, 119
Cash budgeting, 291
cash budgeting, 41, 56, 83
cash build, 45, 155
cash burn, 45
cash burn rate, 23
cash financing intermediaries, 130
cash inflow, 44
cash outflow, 45, 66
cash reduction, 8
cash reserves, 120
catastrophic error, 91
causal reasoning, 314
caveat emptor, 321
CBinsights, 77
cessation, 178
channel development, 59
channel(s), 25, 75, 273
characteristics, 119
Chief Digital Information Officer (CDIO), 171
Chief Executive Officer (CEO), 171
Chief Financial Officer (CFO), 172
Chief Information Office (CIO), 171
Chief Marketing Officer (CMO), 172
Chief Operating Officer (COO), 171
Chief Technology Officer (CTO), 171
choices, 201
circular economy, 17, 152, 196, 252
circular knowledge economy, 240
circular value chain, 137
civil society, 199
cloud computing, 12, 70, 279
cloud storage, 285
coachability, 97, 131, 134, 225
coaching, 34
coaching services, 95
coalition, 252
cognitive diversity, 223
collaboration, 240, 252
commissions, 83
commitment, 130, 133
commitment blueprint, 237
common shares, 90
communicative, 70

communities of interest, 201
community building, 148
company's registry, 90
compensation, 96
competition, 6
competition analysis, 13, 63, 68
competitive advantage, 9, 119, 169, 203, 211, 275
competitive analysis, 312
competitive environment, 307
competitive landscape, 19
complementary, 15
complementary backgrounds, 225
complementary skills, 62
complexity, 74, 199, 332
complimentary technologies, 288
composition, 227
comprehensive, 199
Comprehensive IC Management model, 209
computer software, 203
conflict, 153
conflict of business interest, 161
connectiveness, 132
consequences, 106
consumables, 143
consumption, 43
contingency, 6
contingency planning, 6, 283
contracts, 104, 320
  product contracts, 105
  services contracts, 105
contractual rights, 203
controlled experimentation, 26
controlling correlation, 29
convenience, 194
conventional, 41
convertible, 130
convertible loans, 82, 136, 138, 158
coordination, 211
copyrights, 42, 203
core technological problems, 197
core technology, 12, 13, 70, 278
core values, 235
Corporate Venture Capital (CVC), 120, 128
  financial, 160
  hybrid, 160
  in-transition, 160
  strategic, 160
corporations and corporate VC (CVC), 157
cost, 71
  efficient, 71
cost accounting, 6
cost basis, 2, 41, 179
cost challenges, 56
cost efficiency, 175
cost leadership, 9
cost literacy, 64, 278
costly surprises, 86
cost models, 78
cost of capital, 132, 158
cost of change, 4
cost of goods sold (COGS), 2, 83, 146
cost of human capital, 58
cost of revenue, 83
cost of services, 83
costs, 1, 38, 39, 56, 59, 69, 83, 273
  controlling, 1
  defining costs
    affordability, 3
    perception, 3
    predictability, 3
  enabling, 26, 273
  estimated, 73
  fixed, 2, 78
  incurred, 2
  managing, 1
  manufacturing cost, 2
    labor cost, 2
    material cost, 2
    overhead cost, 2

meaning, 3
mediating, 273
moderating, 273
optimizing, 1
saving, 1
cost structures, 142
cost-value returns, 120
cost-volume-profit (CVP), 6
cost-volume-profit (CVP) analysis, 313
created value, 2, 58
creative conceptualization, 211
credibility, 96, 106
credible alternatives, 328
credit, 105
credit card fees, 83
crisis, 65
crowdfunding, 65, 109, 129, 135, 157
crowdlending, 109, 129, 136
cues consensus, 92, 93
cultural diversity, 62
cultural norms, 206
current asset, 2, 82
custom-built, 254
customer acquisition, 25, 57, 63
customer acquisition costs (CAC), 25, 42, 73
customer capital, 210
customer-centric mindset, 93
customer engagement, 73
customer lifetime value (CLV), 75
customer lists, 42, 203
customer needs, 119, 305
customer needs analysis, 18, 63, 68
customer needs-centric, 55
customer pain points, 68
customer price, 104
customer relationship management (CRM), 286
customer(s), 55, 127, 149, 202, 273, 311
access, 138
empowerment, 138
experiences, 138
financing, 201, 273
freemium, 153
paying, 201, 273
premium, 154
trade sales, 273
customer satisfaction, 43
customer segment identification, 148
customer segments, 75
customers gain, 137
customer value, 10
customer's KPI, 93
customr engagement, 63
customs duties, 145

D

dashboard, 13
data-driven solutions, 126
data to prove, 68
deadlock, 62
deal conditions, 132
debt based, 129
debt burden, 136
debt financing, 158
debt-to-equity conversions, 136
deceptive, 122
decision-making, 56
decision timing, 328
deconstruct, 28
deductibility, 8
deeptech, 164
degrees, 225
demand, 284, 307
demand learning, 312
democratized, 240
democratizing availability, 194
denial, 78
depreciated, 41
design thinking, 288

desired outcome, 181
destination, 26
developing economies, 191
developing value proposition, 119
development(s), 45, 194
development stage, 56
develop relationships, 56
diagnostic controls, 235
differentiation, 311
digital, 153
digital enabling technologies, 70, 198
digitalization, 70, 152, 169
digital marketing, 169
digital platforms, 279, 285
digital startups, 286
dilution of equity, 135
dimension, 237
direct costs, 103
direct material, 83
disclosures, 120
discount, 35
discounted cash flow (DCF), 133, 154, 200, 273
discount future cash flows, 133
discounting, 103
discount rate, 132
discounts, 83
discovery-driven business models, 284
disruptive value propositions, 247
distinctive, 246, 311
diversity, 15, 31, 55, 62, 134, 225, 278
diversity of thinking, 62
dividends, 174
donations, 109
double-sided platform, 201
drive, 131
Drucker, Peter, 191
due diligence, 162, 321
dynamic capabilities, 15, 55, 171, 211, 277, 298
dynamic pricing, 312
dynamics, 27
dysfunction, 62

E

eagerness, 131
early adopter, 69
early adopting customers, 73
early-to-mid stage, 140
easiness, 332
EBIDTA (Earnings Before Interest Depreciation, Taxes, and Amortization), 122, 154, 200
ecological impact, 17
economic characteristics, 204
economic conditions, 177, 328
economic downturn, 35
economic impact, 17, 69, 281
economic life, 2, 42
economic value, 41, 200
economic value analysis, 312
economies, 152, 201
economies of scale, 126, 155, 192, 275
ecosystem facilitators, 66
ecosystem platform, 287
ecosystem(s), 15, 281, 286
educated confidence, 87
education, 225, 278
effective, 32, 254, 278
effectiveness, 43, 93, 122
effectual logic, 12, 58
effectuation, 22
effectuation process, 22, 210
efficiency, 43, 93
efficient, 32, 254
efficiently, 278
elusive, 333
emerging technologies, 74
employee costs, 2
empowering, 175
enabler, 24, 278

enabling cost, 65
enabling role, 57
enabling technology, 12, 13, 279
enabling value creation, 12
energy, 120
engagement, 137
enterprise value, 194, 202
entrepreneur, 71
entrepreneur characteristics, 132
entrepreneurial ecosystem, 153
entrepreneurial ecosystem players, 165
entrepreneurial finance, 59
entrepreneurial journey, 55, 273, 277
entrepreneurial mindset, 59, 92
entrepreneurial narrative, 12
entrepreneurial passion, 29
entrepreneurial pedigree, 131
entrepreneurial startups (ESUs), 3, 55, 119, 197, 201, 276
entrepreneurial tasks, 212
entrepreneurial ventures, 11
entrepreneurship, 59, 278
environment, 163, 201
environmental impact, 17, 69, 281
environmental problem, 119
equipment, 41
equity, 17, 157
equity based, 129
equity dilution, 97, 130
equity stake, 130
erroneous evaluation, 29
ESU accountability, 170
ESU lifecycles, 276
ESU market value, 210
ESU's shares, 82
exaggeration, 29
exclusion, 210
executing value proposition, 119
executional costs, 234
(ex)employee, 199
existential implication, 44
exit challenges, 136
exit early, 326
exit event, 277
Exit *imprinting*, 315
exit later, 326
exit mindset, 287
exit potential, 159
exits, 58, 163, 197
  strategic planning, 163
exit scenario, 56, 181
exit strategy, 163, 314
exit value, 150
expenses, 1, 200
expensive, 90
expensive race, 138
expensive sunk cost, 130
experienced entrepreneurial startup, 273
experience economy, 43
experience(s), 43, 62, 71, 128, 137, 152, 194, 201, 225, 278
experiences, 210
experience value propositions, 43
experiment, 291
experimental, 63
experimentation, 58, 148, 283
expertise, 62, 153
experts, 95
explicit, 12
exploitation, 243
exploration, 72
  limited, 72
exploratory process, 22
exponential growth, 169
exposure, 129
extensive network, 249
external, 126, 333
external capital, 214
external financing, 11, 56
external financing sources, 20, 279
externally-acquired, 42
external marketplace, 210
external sources, 73, 127

external value, 91
extracted value, 2
extraction, 120, 197, 201
Extrinsic, 318

F

facilities, 146
fail, 134
failure, 77
family offices, 157
features, 137
feedback loop, 93, 137
fiction, 26
films, 203
filtering, 134, 135
financial accounting, 58, 200
financial acquisitions, 164, 179
financial capital, 125
financial certainty, 22
financial control, 163
financial forecasting, 56, 291
financial forecasts, 2
financial harvesting, 178, 318
financial literacy, 15, 22, 56, 64, 78, 214, 278
financially independent, 149
financial reporting, 7
financial resources, 73, 132
financial rewards, 178
financial statements, 2, 78
financial test, 13, 276
financial transactions, 64
Financial value, 287
financing, 79, 124, 126
financing buyer, 134
financing customers, 127, 157, 274, 279
financing requirements, 56, 59, 291
financing rounds, 128
financing sources, 126
finished goods, 145
fintech, 130, 274
firm characteristics, 132
firm size, 224
First impressions, 287
first in first out (FIFO), 146
fixed costs, 99, 119
flexibility, 26, 58, 65, 251
flexible, 63
forecasting, 102
forecasts, 120
foundations, 157
founder based, 62
founder(s), 15, 21, 71, 97, 171, 199, 273
  experienced, 74
  novice, 71
founders' beliefs, 235
Founders' knowledge, 298
founding team, 13, 278
Fourth Industrial Revolution, 199, 273, 275
free cash flow, 157
freemium, 76, 154, 201
freight-in, 83
friendly, 90
friends, family and fools (FFF), 56
frugality, 26, 63
frugally, 125
full costing, 6
functional capacities, 56, 227, 278
functional expertise, 229
functionality, 106, 225
funding commitments, 120
funding sources, 120
fundraising, 76, 225
fundraising options, 63
fundraising series, 173
funnel of choices, 61
future conflicts, 133
future economic benefits, 204
Future exit scenario, 319
future liability, 133

future trade sales, 201

G
gap, 207
gender diversity, 62
general human capital, 223
generalists, 95
general ledger, 80
General Partners (GP), 158
general-purpose technologies, 13, 70, 198, 279
generating, 204
goal harmony, 153
goals, 102, 134
going public, 164
good luck event, 333
goodwill, 43, 239, 326
governance, 96, 201
governing laws, 106
grant(s), 24, 40, 66, 251
greenwashing, 17
gross margin, 59, 122, 154
gross operating profit, 122, 154
gross profit, 6
gross sales, 83
groupthink, 64
grow, 56
growing, 120
growth, 56, 58, 120, 155, 201
growth hacking, 149, 169, 229
growth-oriented, 12, 58, 119, 124, 169
growth-oriented business, 277
guarantees, 56, 106
gut feeling, 132

H
harvesting, 161
harvesting mindset, 162
health and safety, 17
hidden cost(s), 39, 104, 163
higher margins, 3
high-growth, 4
high net worth individuals (HNWI), 131
high-risk ventures, 274
high-skilled labor, 191
high switching cost, 288
high-tech ESUs, 56
high technology driven, 278
high-tech startups, 197
high-trust countries, 238
hiring people, 125
historical data, 59
historical precedent, 280
holistic, 201
human behavior, 6
human capital, 15, 20, 55, 58, 74, 126, 206, 214, 277
human component, 6
humbling feedback, 92, 130
humility, 72
hybrid(s), 70, 168
hydrogen fuel cell, 278

I
IC model, 209
idea incubation, 60
ideation, 56
identifiable, 203
identifiable when separable, 203
imitable, 211, 298
impact, 13, 16, 138, 153, 196
  definition, 57, 63
  economic, 138
  environmental, 138, 196
  social, 138, 196
Impact investors, 165
impact-oriented, 153
implicit, 12
import quotas, 203
impression management approach, 29

improved company valuation, 102
improved predictability, 59
improving efficiency, 122
in-bound, 145
in-bound freight, 145
inclusion, 210
inclusion, 239
income statement, 82, 200
incorporate, 86
incremental costs, 39
incremental development, 63, 67
incremental growth, 149
incremental investment, 4, 26
incrementality, 25, 45, 71
incrementalize, 125, 138, 143
incubation, 4, 14
incubators, 63, 65, 66, 97, 165, 249
incurred cost, 39
industrialized, 210
industrialized companies, 2, 234
industry, 278
industry 4.0, 70, 299
industry benchmarks, 75
industry contacts, 224
industry experience, 229
ineffective, 69
inefficient, 69
inexperience, 72
inexperienced founders, 11
influencers, 201, 214
information, 132, 201
informational signalling, 97, 132, 279
information and communication technologies (ICT), 285
infrastructure, 125, 279
inimitability, 42
inimitable, 212
initial public offerings (IPO), 162, 164, 276
in-kind services, 130
innovation capabilities, 230
innovation fund, 40
innovation(s), 4, 58, 127, 152, 177, 278
  knowledge-driven, 4
innovative, 119
innovative business models, 2, 61
  value-driven, 2
innovative companies, 199
innovative value propositions, 55
in-person, 153
input controls, 7
input oriented, 6
inputs, 274, 304
insufficient research, 63
intangible asset(s), 41, 194, 203, 204, 275
intangible capital, 210
intangible-intensive, 4
intangible investments, 205
intangible(s), 2, 39, 122, 142, 191, 326
intangible value, 2
intangible value creation, 201
Integrated Reporting (IR) framework, 215
integration, 199, 211, 252
intellectual capital (IC), 15, 125, 155, 173, 197, 199, 206, 273, 297
  externally focused, 215
  materially valued, 215
  voluntarily disclosed, 215
intellectual capital capabilities, 19, 201
intellectual capital capacities, 19
intellectual capital development, 58
intellectual property (IP), 20, 42, 82, 162, 203
intelligent, 314
Intention, 328
intentional preparations, 320
interactive, 70
interconnected, 138
interconnected process, 152
intermediary, 127, 153

internal capital, 213
internal knowledge, 209
internally generated, 42
internally generated cash, 120
internal rate of return (IRR), 133, 159
internal sources, 127
international, 225
International Accounting Standards (IAS), 203
international business, 191
international expansion, 59
International Financial Reporting Standards (IFRS) foundation, 215
internet, 240
interns, 74
interorganizational collaboration, 246
interpersonal, 132
interrelated, 216
intimidation, 252
intrinsic, 318
inventory, 2, 77, 83, 146
inventory carrying costs, 66
investability, 16, 33, 109, 159
investable, 71
investible, 127, 131
investing, 79
investing cash, 45
investment milestones, 291
investment needs, 127
investment(s), 56, 73, 206, 207
investments in intangibles, 207
investor characteristics, 132
investor(s), 57, 58, 90, 127, 150, 273
irrational decisions, 24
iteration, 61
iterative planning, 65
iterative process, 27

J
joint ventures, 214
journey, 26, 153
judgement calls, 246
jurisdiction, 106

K
key characteristics, 149
key customers, 149
  financing, 149
  future trade sales, 149
  paying, 149
key performance indicators, 72
know-how, 209, 225, 278, 282, 298
knowledge, 152, 199, 225, 278
knowledge acquisition, 212
knowledge-based equity, 209
knowledge-based view, 209
knowledge economy, 2, 191, 197, 275
KPI, 72

L
labor costs, 83
last in, first out (LIFO), 146
lead angel investor, 133
lead investor, 133
lead users, 247
lean, 67
lean startup, 63
lean startup methodology, 237
learn, 67
learning, 22, 26, 63, 211
learning capacity, 226
legal company, 86
legal entity, 87
legal formation fees, 100
legal rights, 203
legitimacy, 20, 131, 194, 251, 283
less expensive, 138
liability, 82, 130
licences/licenses, 100, 106, 162, 203
licensed, 203

licensing agreement(s), 105, 156
licensing income, 156
licensing partnerships, 214
Lifecycle peak, 316
life cycles, 168, 200
lifecycle stages, 11
lifespan, 76
lifestyle, 11
limitations, 26
Limited Liability Company (LLC), 87
Limited Partners (LP), 158
limited resources, 63, 64
liquid, 44
liquid assets, 44
liquidate, 77
liquidation, 274, 276
liquid funds, 82
listening, 127
litigation, 106
longer-term development, 119
longer-term value, 214
long-term relationships, 122
lower costs, 3
loyalty, 43
luck, 332

M

M&A, 162, 276
M&A exits, 273
maintenance, 83
make an impact, 122
management accounting, 2
management advice, 128
management controls, 7
management control systems (MCS), 320
management fees, 158
management reporting, 78
managing expectations, 27
mandatory reporting requirements, 90
manufacturing overhead, 83
margin, 6
market, 75, 177
marketability, 163
marketable products, 210
marketable value propositions, 120
market-assigned value, 41
market conditions, 132
market definition, 25
market demand, 63
market driven, 278, 307
marketing, 20, 42, 214, 278
  digital, 74
marketing channels, 94
marketing skills, 56
market penetration pricing, 103
marketplace, 121, 128, 305
market position, 200
market share, 203
market validation, 148
mass education, 191
matchmaking, 285
matchmaking process, 134
matchmaking technology platforms, 205
material impact, 163
maturity, 56
measurable, 25, 311
measure, 67
measure intangible, 207
measuring, 63
me-centric, 93
mediating role, 58, 59, 120, 333
mediating value capture, 122
mediating value creation, 12
mediation, 12, 119, 274
mediator, 278
medical devices, 278
medtech, 156
mentors, 95
mentorship, 63
messaging, 128
meta-organization, 281

metrics, 63
micro investors, 129
mid and low-tech startups, 198
mid-stage, 124, 140
milestone(s), 26, 56, 73
  investment, 73
mindfulness, 225
mindset, 27, 30, 120, 281
minimize recurring (cash) fixed costs, 101
moderating effect, 122
moderating role, 59, 200
moderating value creation, 12
moderator of margin, 44
moderator of profitability, 44
modern management accounting, 6
  manufacturing, 6
  production environment, 6
monetary value, 8
monetization, 25, 43, 309
money, 35
monthly recurring revenue (MRR), 274
motivational drivers, 235
multi-customer base, 137
multidimension, 119
multidimensionality, 71
multidimensional platform, 142, 153
multi-dimensional solutions, 19
multi-founder, 220
multi-founder teams, 15, 62
multiple locations, 191
multiple offerings, 25, 201
multiple purposes, 191
multi-sided, 119, 142
multi-sided platforms, 13, 281, 285
multi-year horizon, 201

N

nanotech, 164
nanotechnology, 278
narration, 97
narrative(s), 12, 28, 273, 276
narrative test, 13, 276
national culture, 77
need-based, 68
needs assessment, 137
needs driven, 284
need-want-pay, 122
negative signal, 63
net basis, 83
net cash burn, 57
net cash flows, 200
net revenue, 83
net sales, 83
network, 17, 285
networked, 152
networked world economy, 191
network effect(s), 201, 275, 288
networking, 63, 76, 96
network model, 137
networks, 13, 96, 133, 214
network utilization, 242
neutrality, 153
new market, 59
new money, 138, 157
new product development (NPD), 4, 197, 199, 276
new shares, 157, 166
new technologies, 191
new trends, 177
new ventures, 120, 199
new venture development (NVD), 4, 59, 91, 197, 201, 276
niche markets, 224
non-current asset, 82, 204
non-high-tech, 198, 278
non-imitable, 119, 211
non-linear, 152, 153
non-physical resource, 142
non-predictive control, 22, 210
non-sequential, 153
non-substitutable, 119, 212

non-trivial changes, 304
notary, 100
novice entrepreneurs, 30
novice founders, 15

O
objective, 22, 95, 132, 227
obligations, 106
off-financial statement, 120
office space, 65
one-off costs, 99
one-time, 153
one-year horizon, 200
online platforms, 70
open innovation, 160
inbound, 160
openness, 26, 72
open-source, 77
operating, 79
operating asset, 82
operating cash, 45
operating expense, 2
fixed, 2
mixed, 2
operating expenses (OpEx), 143, 144, 207
operating liabilities, 82
operating models, 141
operating profitability, 59
operating profits, 6
operational control, 163
operational planning, 56, 291
opportunity cost-benefit, 42
opportunity cost impact, 19
opportunity cost of capital, 35
opportunity cost of time, 27
opportunity cost(s), 2, 17, 39, 133, 206, 290, 320
optimal pivoting, 67
optimism, 29, 30
optimistic forecasting, 78
optimistic overconfidence, 29, 91
options, 61
ordinary capabilities, 171, 298
organizational capital, 20, 58, 126, 206, 214, 282
organizational design, 208
organizational dynamic capabilities, 218, 230
organizational model, 142
organizational processes, 125
organized, 211
out-bound logistics, 145
out-of-pocket expenses, 74
output controls, 7
outputs, 274, 306
outside-in, 253
overconfident, 120
overestimate, 92
overestimation, 29
over-exposed, 77
over-optimism, 29, 64, 120
overspending, 72, 78
owner's equity, 82
ownership transfer, 105

P
P2P, 144
pain points, 93, 311
parallel business models, 283, 307
paralysis by analysis, 62
partners, 153
partnerships, 20
passion, 131
passive investors, 254
patentable, 278
patents, 42, 203
Pathology, 316
patriarchal cultures, 226
paying customers, 25, 122, 127, 154
pedigree, 130
peer-to-peer lending, 109

people, 125
perceived value, 39
perception, 11, 21
perception of value, 34
perceptive, 3
perceptive capacity, 21, 227
permits, 100
perseverance, 91, 222
personal, 132
personal development, 95
personal experiences, 132
personality clashes, 134
personal loans, 24
personal opportunity cost(s), 77
persuasion, 252
pessimistic, 8, 30
pharma, 156
pharmaceutical patent, 42
pharma-tech, 164
physical infrastructure, 285
physically identifiable, 204
physical products, 191
physical resources, 142
physical substance, 203
pilot projects, 73
pioneering mindset, 247
pitch, 13, 130
pitching, 63, 76
pitch narratives, 279
pivotal mid-stages, 280
pivoting, 32, 92, 120, 134
pivots, 56, 130, 134
Plan B, 283
planning, 119
plan to exit, 314
platform, 196
platform-as-a-Service (PaaS), 285
platform business models, 285
platform economy, 281
platforms, 71, 109, 128, 274, 286
  digital, 196
  ecosystem, 196
  multi-sided, 196
pooled, 133
Porter, M.E., 9
portfolio, 130, 300
positive experiences, 122
positive impact, 119
positive perception, 87, 91
positive reputation, 43
positive signal, 63
post-money value, 157
post-seed, 128
potential synergies, 328
pre-company, 61
predictability, 2, 57
preferred shares, 90
premium, 153
premium pricing, 103
pre-money, 150
pre-money value, 157
prepared luck, 333
price per earnings (P/E), 207
price x quantity, 83
pricing, 22, 59, 83
  achievable, 313
  measurable, 313
  relevant, 313
  specific, 313
  time bound, 313
pricing model, 309
pricing target models, 313
prioritization, 25, 45, 71, 102, 125, 148
prioritized assumptions, 94
privacy, 138, 194
private equity, 56
private equity financing, 136
proactive, 314
proactive innovation, 127, 128
problem, 13, 57
  definition, 63
problem analytics, 18, 68, 69

problem-solution fit, 13, 57, 63, 69, 94, 196
pro bono, 40, 65
processes, 274
process oriented, 6
product driven, 2, 153, 199
productive resource, 209
product life cycle, 4, 6, 197, 201
product(s), 200, 201
professional fees, 100
professional liability insurance, 100
profitability, 3, 194, 200
profitability-driven valuation, 210
profitability margin, 74
profitable, 120
pro forma, 120
project pitching, 131
Proof of concept, 63
proof of concept, 24, 25, 57, 75, 128, 140, 208
propensity, 223
proprietary, 153, 246, 253
proprietary manufacturing, 20, 42, 214, 253
proprietary marketing, 254
prototype, 24, 248
public financing, 251
purchase costs, 83
pure luck, 333

Q

qualitative, 4
qualitative measures, 132
quantifiable, 204
quantitatively, 132

R

R&D centers, 214
R&D costs, 200
raise money, 120
Rare, 298
rareness, 42, 119, 211
rareness-performance, 119, 211
raw material(s), 83, 145
reactive innovation, 127, 314
real need, 121
real problem, 16, 60
reasonability, 124
recalibrate, 26, 134
reconfiguring, 171
re-crafting, 171
recurring, 153, 202
recurring cash, 99
recurring monthly (MRR), 122
recurring revenue, 2
re-defining, 171
reflective trust, 239
refund, 105
regulatory, 169
relational capital, 20, 42, 58, 76, 122, 126, 194, 206, 214
relationship(s), 119, 122, 203
remembered, 99
repairs, 83
repeat, 202
repeat entrepreneurs, 30
replicable, 58, 119, 124, 155, 277
replicable operations, 58
replicable processes, 59
reporting, 200
reputable data, 17
reputation, 2, 20, 122, 214
reputational risk, 63, 77, 136
research and development (R&D), 7
research orientation, 92
re-shaping, 171
resource, 130
resource acquisition, 240
resource-based view (RBV), 210, 297
resource capabilities, 211
resource considerations, 142
resource planning, 63, 74
resourcing needs, 208

responsibilities, 106
retention rates, 75
return on cost investment, 120
return on costs, 4
returns, 83
returns on investment (ROI), 4, 173, 274
revenue, 83, 120, 122, 141, 200
revenue channels, 43
revenue-generating model, 127, 156
revenue generation, 120, 202, 273
revenue income, 65
revenue model(s), 13, 32, 58, 106, 274, 309
revenue receipts, 45
revenue recognition, 106, 163
reverse-engineer, 127
reward-based, 109, 129
rewards, 35
rhetorical signals, 98
right crowd, 129
risk factors, 76
risk of failure, 57
risk premium, 133
risks, 35
risk taking, 12
risk tolerance, 159
robotics, 278
ROI expectation, 57
roles, 171
rolling basis, 120
royalties, 156
running out of cash, 45
run rates, 2, 59

S
S/N, 146
sacrifice, 8
safety, 194
salary-replacement, 11
sales cycle, 76
sales prospects, 120
satisfaction, 122
saving money, 31
scalability, 16, 169, 192, 201
scalable, 12, 58, 119, 124, 169, 205, 275, 277
scalable business, 128
scalable business model, 4, 142, 149
scale, 56, 120, 148, 199
scaling, 59, 120, 155, 171
scenario, 274
scenario planning, 41
scope, 199
scoreboard, 78
seedling, 124
seed rounds, 57
seed stage, 59
segmentation, 25
seizing, 212, 298
self-doubt, 26
self-finance, 73
self-financing, 108
self-fund, 120
selling costs, 74
Selling, General and Administrative Expenses (SG&A), 83
sense-giving strategy, 98
sensemaking, 23
sensing, 211, 298
separable assets, 203
serial, 24
serial entrepreneurs, 30, 128, 333
Series A, 58, 128
  post-, 58
  pre-, 58, 128
Series B, 173
Service Level Agreement (SLA), 105
services, 201
share corporation, 87
Shareholder Register, 90
shareholders, 201
shareholdings, 82

sharing, 152, 252
sharing economy, 239, 285
sharing experiences, 240
shorter-term survival, 119
short-sightedness, 136
short-to-medium term, 126
signalling, 128, 132
signals, 33, 57, 68
  false-positive, 68
  negative, 68
  positive, 68
simple, 99
simulated cap tables, 136
simultaneous experimentation, 58
single founder, 62, 220
skeptical audiences, 98
skill, 333
SKU, 146
SMART goal, 313
social, 201
social capital, 20, 58, 76, 122, 126, 194, 206, 214
social capital dimensions
  cognitive, 239
  relational, 239
  structural, 239
social capital value, 43
social competence, 242
social contracts, 285
social impact, 69, 214, 281
social media, 70, 279
social metrics, 17
social networks, 20, 76, 148, 203, 214, 242
social platforms, 241
social relationship(s), 240, 278
social resource(s), 97, 132
social trust, 20, 240, 241
social value creation strategy, 17
societal problem, 119
socio-relational trust capital, 241
software, 42
software-as-a-service (SaaS), 130
software development, 169
sold, 203
solidifying proof of concept, 137
solutions, 69
  alternative, 69
  incremental, 69
  multidimensional, 69
  potential, 69
source models, 125, 313
sources, 45
sourcing talent, 175
specialists, 95
specific human capital, 224, 242
spending, 102
spillover(s), 201, 205
spinoffs, 101, 278
sponsors, 214
sponsorship(s), 20, 252
staged, 25, 58
staged financing, 159
stakeholder approach, 18
stakeholder impact, 25
stakeholder relationships, 214
stakeholder(s), 55, 153, 199, 201, 273
standard financial statements, 120
standard industrial economy, 199
standard industrial model, 197
standardization, 170
startup-supplier, 253
statement of cash flows, 83
stewardship, 178
storage costs, 83
strategic accounting, 38
strategic acquisitions, 164, 178
strategic compatibility, 247
strategic cost, 38
Strategic Cost Management (SCM), 9, 234
strategic CVCs, 160
strategic fit, 200

Strategic goal, 287
strategic guidance, 96
Strategic Management Accounting (SMA), 9
strategic option(s), 211, 297, 326
strategic partnerships, 20, 146, 214
strategic planning, 9
strategic role, 58
strategic significance, 209
strategic thinking, 56, 227
Strategic value, 287
strategy, 2, 3, 126
structural costs, 234
structure, 56
structured thematic programs, 130
stubbornness, 91
subjective, 21, 95, 132
subjective bias, 24
subjective component, 227
subjectivity, 21
subscription model, 274
substantive signals, 98
substitutable, 211
success, 56
sunk benefit, 24
sunk cost benefit, 58
sunk cost(s), 24, 200, 204
sunken unrecoverable, 8
supplier collaboration, 247
suppliers, 153
supplies, 83
supply chain, 74, 145, 278
survival, 32, 45, 56
survival stage, 149
sustainability, 2, 237
sustainability orientation, 152, 153
Sustainability transparency, 170
sustainability washing, 170
sustainable, 311
sustainable business model, 141, 166
sustainable growth, 58, 141
sustainable growth strategy, 138
sustainable project, 137
sustainable value, 194
sustainable value propositions, 170
sustainably, 278
sweat equity, 74
syndicate, 133, 158
synergies, 205
systemic liquidation, 178

T

tangible assets, 41
tangible(s), 2, 39, 122, 126, 142, 201
tangible value, 2
target personas, 75
team(s), 131, 220, 227
tech capital, 214
tech disruptions, 177
tech innovation, 125
technological discoveries, 255
technological infrastructure, 194
technological median, 13
technological medium, 240
technological problem, 119
technological revolution, 199
technology, 70, 273, 303
technology-driven, 70
technology-driven ESU, 57
technology entrepreneurship, 303
technology-mediated, 70
technology-oriented, 4
tech requirement(s), 63
Teece, D.J., 282
termination, 106
terminology, 59
term sheets, 158, 162
three-dimensional (3D) business models (BMs), 273
time, 27, 120, 130, 191
  underestimating, 78
time and money, 138
timeframe, 74

time is money, 76, 139
time value, 35
timing, 27, 72, 73
  estimated, 73
top line, 122
traction, 120
trademarks, 42, 203
trade sales, 276
trade sales M&A customers, 127
transaction, 95
transaction management, 285
transactions, 79
  business, 79
  financial, 79
transfer of knowledge, 212
transferred, 203
transformation, 197, 199, 212, 298
transformative, 124
transparency, 136
transportation, 83
travel expenses, 83
triple, 202
Triple bottom line (3BL), 17
triple-bottom line impact, 60, 165, 201
  economic, 60
  environmental, 60
  social, 60
triple customers, 305
trust, 2, 122, 134, 194
  legitimacy, 138
  relational, 134
  social, 134
trust building, 285
trust cultural attributes, 239
trust legitimacy, 214
trust perception, 98, 287
type of investors, 12

U
unaligned visions, 134
uncertain futures, 21
uncertainty reducers, 164
uncertainty reduction, 328
underestimate, 92, 125, 134
understood, 99
undisclosed liabilities, 163
unexpected performance, 333
unique, 153, 298
unique characteristics, 56
unique dynamic capabilities, 214
uniqueness, 288
unique processes, 203
unique relationships, 246
unique selling propositions, 73
unique value proposition (UVP), 13, 19, 60, 140, 210, 218
universities, 20, 66
unnatural failures, 314
unpredictable, 63, 65
unpredictable environments, 21
unrecoverable, 24
upgrades, 106
useful economic life, 204
user experiences, 25
user(s), 55, 199
uses, 45
USP, 73
utility, 42, 83

V
vague contracts, 163
validate, 67
validation, 63
valuable, 253, 298
valuation, 41, 207
valuation methods, 41
valuation multiples, 200
valuation process, 38
value, 273
  capture, 122, 200, 276
  captured, 273

create, 276
created, 273
extract, 276
extracted, 273
intangible, 138
tangible, 138
value alignment, 273
value-based pricing (VBP), 312
value beholder, 273
value capture, 58
value capture process, 305
value-chain model, 10
value chains, 275
value configuration, 208
value-creating activities, 10
value creation, 58, 120, 121, 197, 199, 304
Value discovery, 287, 313
value driven, 153
value-driven, 9
value-driven cycles, 200
value enabling, 12
value extraction, 58, 306
value logic, 32, 149, 309
value narrative in action, 231
value proposition, 23, 69, 201, 273, 305
multidimensional, 69
value proposition logic narrative, 140
value proposition narrative, 14
value proposition product, 150
value-relevance, 7
value(s) driven, 199
VAT, 83, 104
venture capital (VC), 56, 58, 109, 120, 128, 157
venture development, 58
venture funds, 128
venture's journey, 273
venture value, 200
video game, 56
vinted, 196, 206
visibility, 129
vision alignment, 133
voluntary associations, 240
voucher, 105

W
want to buy, 121
warehouse, 65
warehousing, 145
Warrantee(s), 105
warranty, 106, 320
wealth, 277
wealth creation, 60, 178
wealth extracted, 326
web-based, 153
web-based platforms, 71
weighted average cost (WAC), 146
white label, 70
work ethics, 62
working capital, 66, 82, 120, 145
work-in-progress, 83
workshop, 65

The manufacturer's authorised representative in the EU is Springer Nature Customer Service Centre GmbH, Europaplatz 3, 69115 Heidelberg, Germany. If you have any concerns regarding our products, please contact ProductSafety@springernature.com

Printed and bound by CPI Group (UK) Ltd, Croydon, CR0 4YY
30/09/2026
02225565-0017